W9-CEB-765

Your opinion matters. It matters to us. It matters to your fellow Fodor's travelers, too. And we'd like to hear it. In fact, we need to hear it.

When you share your experiences and opinions, you become an active member of the Fodor's community. That means we'll not only use your feedback to make our books better, but we'll publish your names and comments whenever possible. Throughout our guides, look for "Word of Mouth," excerpts of your unvarnished feedback.

Here's how you can help improve Fodor's for all of us.

Tell us when we're right. We rely on local writers to give you an insider's perspective. But our writers and staff editors—who are the best in the business—depend on you. Your positive feedback is a vote to renew our recommendations for the next edition.

Tell us when we're wrong. We're proud that we update most of our guides every year. But we're not perfect. Things change. Hotels cut services. Museums change hours. Charming cafés lose charm. If our writer didn't quite capture the essence of a place, tell us how you'd do it differently. If any of our descriptions are inaccurate or inadequate, we'll incorporate your changes in the next edition and will correct factual errors at fodors.com immediately.

Tell us what to include. You probably have had fantastic travel experiences that aren't yet in Fodor's. Why not share them with a community of like-minded travelers? Maybe you chanced upon a beach or bistro or B&B that you don't want to keep to yourself. Tell us why we should include it. And share your discoveries and experiences with everyone directly at fodors.com. Your input may lead us to add a new listing or highlight a place we cover with a "Highly Recommended" star or with our highest rating, "Fodor's Choice."

Give us your opinion instantly at our feedback center at www.fodors.com/feedback. You may also e-mail editors@fodors.com with the subject line "Alaska Ports of Call Editor." Or send your nominations, comments, and complaints by mail to Alaska Ports of Call Editor, Fodor's, 1745 Broadway, New York, NY 10019.

You and travelers like you are the heart of the Fodor's community. Make our community richer by sharing your experiences. Be a Fodor's correspondent.

Happy traveling!

Tim Jarrell, Publisher

CONTENTS

ALASKA PORTS OF CALL IN FOCUS

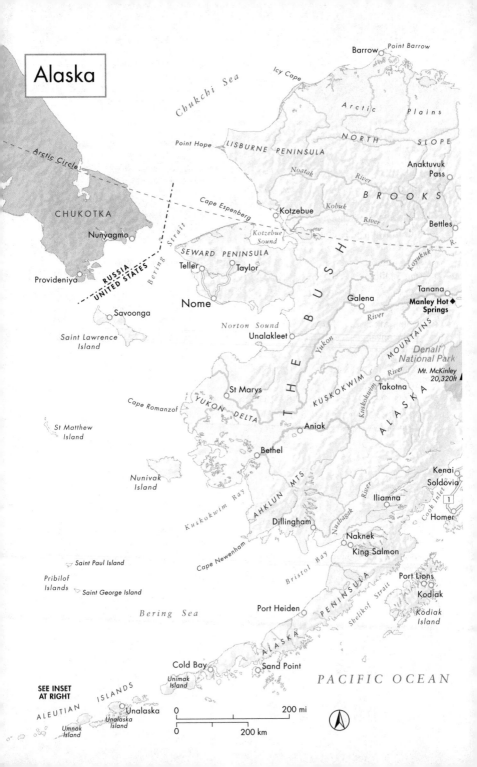

ABOUT THIS BOOK

Up front you'll find a **Cruise Primer,** with some basic information about cruising and what to expect.

Choosing Your Cruise gives you the lowdown on the cruise lines and cruise ships that regularly ply the waters of Alaska. This section will help you sort through the various lines, ships, and itineraries available.

Ports of Embarkation gives you background on the most important ports for joining a cruise, including suggestions on where to stay and eat, and what you might want to do if you spend an extra day or two there before or after.

Ports of Call gives you our best advice on what to do in each major Alaska cruise port if you want to go your own way, as well as a run-down of our favorite shore excursions offered by most ships if you don't.

Disagree with any of our choices? Care to nominate a place or suggest that we rate one more highly? Visit our feedback center at www.fodors.com/feedback.

Budget Well

Hotel price categories from ¢ to $$$$ are defined in the opening pages of Chapter 2, restaurant price categories in the opening pages of chapters 2 and 3. For attractions, we always give standard adult admission fees; reductions are usually available for children, students, and senior citizens. Want to pay with plastic? **AE, D, DC, MC, V** following restaurant and hotel listings indicate whether American Express, Discover, Diners Club, MasterCard, and Visa are accepted.

Restaurants

Unless we state otherwise, restaurants are open for lunch and dinner daily. We mention dress only when there's a specific requirement and reservations only when they're essential or not accepted—it's always best to book ahead.

Hotels

Hotels have private bath, phone, TV, and air-conditioning and operate on the European Plan (aka EP, meaning without meals), unless we specify that they use the Continental Plan (CP, with a Continental breakfast), Breakfast Plan (BP, with a full breakfast), or Modified American Plan (MAP, with breakfast and dinner), or are all-inclusive (AI, including all meals and most activities). We always list facilities but not whether you'll be charged an extra fee to use them, so when pricing accommodations, find out what's included.

Many Listings

☆	Fodor's Choice
★	Highly recommended
⊠	Physical address
✛	Directions or Map coordinates
⌖	Mailing address
☎	Telephone
🖷	Fax
⊕	On the Web
✉	E-mail
🎫	Admission fee
☉	Open/closed times
Ⓜ	Metro stations
🖃	Credit cards

Hotels & Restaurants

🏨	Hotel
🛏	Number of rooms
⚒	Facilities
⑩	Meal plans
✗	Restaurant
✍	Reservations
⟍	Smoking
🍸	BYOB

Outdoors

⛳	Golf
⛺	Camping

Other

ℭ	Family-friendly
⇨	See also
⊠	Branch address
☞	Take note

Choosing Your Cruise

WORD OF MOUTH

"I think that of any of the popular cruise destinations, Alaska would be the one to splurge and get a balcony for. Imagine this—sitting with your mom on your private balcony, sipping a glass of wine while you enjoy the passing scenery or perhaps a beautiful sunset vs. sitting in one of the public areas of the ship with another 100 or so people."

—chepar

"Well is [a balcony] a must? No. However it sure is nice. Ultimately it depends on your budget. I would advise to budget the excursions first. If you can after then get a balcony by all means."

—jacketwatch

By Linda
Coffman

ALASKA IS ONE OF CRUISING'S showcase destinations. Itineraries give passengers more choices than ever before—from traditional loop cruises of the Inside Passage, round-trips from Vancouver or Seattle, to one-way Inside Passage–Gulf of Alaska cruises.

Though Alaska cruises have generally attracted an older-passenger demographic, more young people and families are setting sail for the 49th state and children are a common sight aboard ship. Cruise lines have responded with youth programs and some discounted shore excursions for youngsters under 12. Shore excursions have become more active, too, often incorporating activities families can enjoy together, such as bicycling, kayaking, and hiking. Many lines also offer pre- or post-cruise land tours as an optional package trip, and onboard entertainment and learning programs are extensive. Most also hire native speakers, naturalists, or local personalities to lead discussions stimulated by the local environment.

Cruise ships may seem like floating resorts, but you can't check out and go elsewhere if you don't like your ship. The one you choose will be your home—it determines the type of accommodations you have, what kind of food you eat, what style of entertainment you see, and even the destinations you visit. If you don't enjoy your ship, you probably won't enjoy your cruise. That is why the most important choice you'll make when booking a cruise is the combined selection of cruise line and cruise ship.

CRUISING IN ALASKA

Which cruise is right for you depends on numerous factors, notably your budget, the size and style of ship you choose, and the itinerary.

ITINERARIES

Cruise ships typically follow one of two itineraries in Alaska: round-trip Inside Passage loops and one-way Inside Passage–Gulf of Alaska cruises. Itineraries are usually seven days, though some lines offer longer trips.

The most popular Alaskan ports of call are Haines, Juneau, Skagway, Ketchikan, and Sitka. Lesser-known ports in British Columbia, such as Victoria and the charming fishing port of Prince Rupert, have begun to see more cruise traffic.

Small ships typically sail within Alaska, setting sail from Juneau or other Alaskan ports, stopping at the popular ports as well as smaller, less visited villages. Some expedition vessels focus on remote beaches and fjords, with few, if any, port calls.

ROUND-TRIP INSIDE PASSAGE LOOPS

A seven-day cruise typically starts and finishes in Vancouver, British Columbia, or Seattle, Washington. The first and last days are spent at sea, traveling to and from Alaska along the mountainous coast of British Columbia. Once in Alaska, most ships call at a different port on each of four days, and reserve one day for cruising in or near Glacier Bay National Park or another glacier-rich fjord.

ONE-WAY INSIDE PASSAGE–GULF OF ALASKA ITINERARIES

These cruises depart from Vancouver, Seattle or, occasionally, San Francisco or Los Angeles, and finish at Seward or Whittier, the seaports for Anchorage (or vice versa). They're a good choice if you want to explore Alaska by land, either before or after your cruise. For this itinerary, you'll need to fly into and out of different cities (into Vancouver and out of Anchorage, for

TIMING TIP

Keep in mind that the landscape along the Inside Passage changes dramatically over the course of the summer. You'll see snowcapped mountains and dramatic waterfalls that are made by the melting process cascading down the cliff faces in May and June, but by July and August most of the snow and waterfalls will be gone.

example), which can be pricier than round-trip airfare to and from the same city.

SMALL-SHIP ALASKA-ONLY ITINERARIES

Most small ships and yachts home port in Juneau or other Alaskan ports and offer a variety of one-way and round-trip cruises entirely within Alaska. A typical small-ship cruise is a seven-day, one-way or round-trip from Juneau, stopping at several Inside Passage ports—including smaller ports skipped by large cruise ships.

SMALL-SHIP INSIDE PASSAGE REPOSITIONING CRUISES

Alaska's small cruise ships and yachts are based in Juneau throughout the summer. In September they sail back to their winter homes in the Pacific Northwest; in May they return to Alaska via the Inside Passage. These trips are usually about 11 days and are often heavily discounted, because they take place during the shoulder season.

OTHER ITINERARIES

Although mainstream lines stick to the popular seven-day Alaskan itineraries, some smaller excursion lines add more exotic options. Cruise West, for example, offers voyages across the Bering Sea to Japan and Asia. You can also create your own itinerary by taking an Alaska Marine Highway System ferry to ports of your choosing.

FERRY TRAVEL

The cruise-ship season is over by October, but for independent, off-season ferry travel November is the best month. After the stormy month of October, it's still relatively warm on the Inside Passage (temperatures will average about 40°F), and it's a good month for wildlife-watching. In particular, humpback whales are abundant off Sitka, and bald eagles congregate by the thousands near Haines.

CRUISE TOURS

Most cruise lines offer the option of independent, hosted, or fully escorted land tours before or after your cruise. Independent tours give you a preplanned itinerary with confirmed hotel and transportation arrangements, but you're free to follow your interests in each town. Hosted tours are similar, but tour-company representatives are available along the route for assistance. On fully escorted tours you travel with a group, led by a tour director. Activities are preplanned (and typically prepaid), so you have a good idea of how much your trip will cost (not counting incidentals) before departure. Most lines offer cruise tour itineraries that include a ride aboard the Alaska Railroad.

Running between Anchorage, Denali National Park, and Fairbanks are Holland America Line's McKinley Explorer, Princess Tours' Denali Express and McKinley Express, and Royal Caribbean's Wilderness Express, which offer unobstructed views of the passing terrain and wildlife from private glass-domed railcars. Princess Cruises and Holland America Line have the most extensive Alaska cruise tours, owning and operating their own coaches, railcars, and lodges.

> **TIP**
>
> Although most other kinds of travel are booked over the Internet nowadays, cruises are a different story. Your best bet is still to work with a travel agent who specializes in cruises. Agents with strong relationships with the lines have a much better chance of getting you the cabin you want, and possibly even extras.

In addition to rail trips to Denali, Holland America offers tours into the Yukon, as well as river cruises on the Yukon River. Princess's cruise tours include trips to the Yukon and the Kenai Peninsula. Both lines offer land excursions across the Arctic Circle to Prudhoe Bay. Several cruise lines also offer pre- and post-cruise tours of the Canadian Rockies. Of the traditional cruise-ship fleets, only Norwegian Cruise Line does not currently offer cruise tour packages in Alaska. Many cruise lines also offer pre- or post-cruise hotel and sightseeing packages in Vancouver, Seattle, or Anchorage lasting one to three days.

SMALL SHIP LINES

Most small-ship lines offer hotel add-ons, but not land tours. The exception is Cruise West, which offers fully escorted tours by rail and bus from Anchorage to Denali and Fairbanks.

DO-IT-YOURSELF LAND SEGMENTS

Independent travel by rental car or RV before or after a cruise is another option. Passengers generally begin or end their cruise in Anchorage, the most practical port city to use as a base for exploring Alaska. Almost any type of car or recreational vehicle can be rented here.

WHEN TO GO

Cruise season runs from mid-May to late September. The most popular sailing dates are from late June through August, when warm days are apt to be most plentiful. In spring, wildflowers are abundant, and you'll likely see more wildlife along the shore because the animals haven't yet migrated to higher elevations. May and June are traditionally drier than July and August. Alaska's early fall brings the splendor of autumn hues and the first snowfalls in the mountains. Animals return to low ground, and shorter days bring the possibility of seeing the northern lights. Daytime temperatures in May, June, and September are in the 50s and 60s. July and August averages are in the 60s and 70s, with occasional days in the 80s. Cruising in the low and shoulder seasons provides other

Cabin Cruising

1

INSIDE CABINS

An inside cabin is just that: a stateroom that's inside the ship with no window. These are always the least expensive cabins and are ideal for passengers who would rather spend on excursions than on upgraded accommodations. Inside cabins are generally as spacious as outside cabins, and decor and amenities are similar. Many ships locate cabins accommodating three or more passengers on the inside. ■TIP➔**For passengers who want a very dark room for sleeping, an inside cabin is ideal.**

OUTSIDE CABINS

Outside cabins have either a picture window or porthole. To give the illusion of more space, these cabins might rely on the generous use of mirrors. Outside cabins are the better choice for those prone to motion sickness. ■TIP➔**Check to make sure your view of the sea is not** obstructed by a lifeboat. The ship's deck plan will help you figure it out.

BALCONY CABINS

A balcony—or veranda—cabin is an outside cabin with floor-to-ceiling glass doors that open onto a private deck. Balconies are sometimes cut out of the cabin's square footage (depending on the ship). ■TIP➔ **If you have small children, a veranda cabin isn't the best choice. Accidents can happen, even on balconies with solid barriers beneath the railing.**

SUITES

Suites are the most lavish accommodations. Although they're always larger than regular cabins, they don't always have separate rooms for sleeping. The most expansive (and expensive) have large living rooms and separate bedrooms and may also have huge private outdoor sundecks with hot tubs and dining areas.

advantages besides discounted fares: availability of ships and particular cabins is greater, and ports are almost completely free of tourists.

BOOKING YOUR CRUISE

As a rule, the majority of cruisers plan their trips four to six months ahead of time. It follows then, that a four- to six-month window should give you the pick of sailing dates, ships, itineraries, cabins, and flights to the port city. If you're looking for a standard itinerary and aren't choosy about the vessel or dates, you could wait for a last-minute discount, but they are harder to find than in the past.

If particular shore excursions are important to you, consider booking them when you book your cruise to avoid disappointment later.

CRUISE COSTS

Average fares for Alaskan itineraries vary dramatically depending on when you sail, which ship and grade of cabin you choose, and when you book. Published rates are highest during July and August; you'll

Before You Book

If you've decided to use a travel agent, ask yourself these 10 simple questions, and you'll be better prepared to help the agent do his or her job:

1. Who will be going on the cruise?

2. What can you afford to spend for the entire trip?

3. Where would you like to go?

4. How much vacation time do you have?

5. When can you get away?

6. What are your interests?

7. Do you prefer a casual or structured vacation?

8. What kind of accommodations do you want?

9. What are your dining preferences?

10. How will you get to the embarkation port?

pay less, and have more space on ship and ashore, if you sail in May, June, or September.

Whenever you choose to sail, remember that the brochure price is the highest fare the line can charge for a given cruise. Most lines offer early-booking discounts. Although these vary tremendously, many lines will offer at least 10% off if you book several months ahead of time, usually by the end of January for a summer cruise; this may require early payment as well. Sometimes you can book a discounted last-minute cruise if the ship hasn't filled all its cabins, but you won't get your pick of ships, cabins, or sailing dates. However, since most cruise lines will, if asked, refund the difference in fare if it drops after you've paid your deposit and before you make your final payment, there's little advantage in last-minute booking. Some other deals to watch for are "kids sail free" deals, where children under 12 sail free in the same cabin as their parents; free upgrades rather than discounts; or special deals for home port residents. Frequent cruisers also get discounts from their preferred cruise lines.

SOLO TRAVELERS
Single cabins for solo travelers are nonexistent on most ships; taking a double cabin can cost as much as twice the advertised per-person rates (which are based on two people sharing a room). Some cruise lines will find roommates of the same sex for singles so that each can travel at the regular per-person rate.

EXTRAS
Cruise fares typically include accommodation, onboard meals and snacks, and most onboard activities. Not normally included are airfare, shore excursions, tips, soft drinks, alcoholic drinks, or spa treatments. Port fees, fuel surcharges, and sales taxes are generally added to your fare at booking.

OTHER CONSIDERATIONS

Children's programs: Virtually every line has children's programs, but some only offer them during school holidays. Small ships are less likely to offer kids' programs. Check whether the available shore excursions include activities that will appeal to kids.

> **TIP**
>
> Notify the cruise line of any dietary restrictions when booking your cruise, and follow up on the arrangements a couple of months before embarking.

Dining: Some cruise lines offer traditional assigned dining, meaning you will dine each evening at the same table with the same companions. Others offer open seating, allowing you to dine whenever and with whomever you like; still others offer a choice between the two systems. Most cruise ships have at least one restaurant in addition to the main dining room; some have more. Most ships offer vegetarian and heart-healthy or low-carb options.

Ports of call: You'll want to know where and when you will be stopping. Will there be enough time in port to do what you want to do there? Will it be the right time of day for your chosen activity? Will you tender to shore by boat or moor up at the dock? This is important, as tendering can take some time away from your port visit.

Onboard activities: Your cruise will likely include one or two full days at sea. Think about how you'd like to fill the time. Do you want great workout facilities or a spa? What about educational opportunities or shopping? If seeing Alaska itself is your priority, choose a ship with lots of outdoor *and* indoor viewing space.

ABOUT THE SHIPS

CRUISE SHIPS

Large cruise lines account for the majority of passengers sailing to Alaska. These typically have large cruise ships in their fleets with plentiful deck space and, often, a promenade deck that allows you to stroll the ship's perimeter. In the newest vessels, traditional meets trendy with resort-style innovations; however, they still feature cruise-ship classics, like afternoon tea and complimentary room service. The smallest cruise ships carry as few as 400 passengers, while the biggest can accommodate between 1,500 and 3,000 passengers—enough people to outnumber the residents of many Alaskan port towns. Large ships are a good choice if you're looking for nonstop activity and lots of options; they're especially appealing for groups and families with older kids. If you prefer a gentler pace and a chance to get to know your shipmates, try a smaller ship.

SMALL SHIPS

Compact expedition-type vessels bring you right up to the shoreline to skirt the face of a glacier and pull through narrow channels where big ships don't fit. These cruises focus on Alaska, and you'll see more wildlife and call into smaller ports, as well as some of the better-known towns. Talks—conducted by naturalists, native Alaskans, and other

WHAT TO PACK

■ Eye covers for sleeping: the 24-hour light may disrupt your sleep patterns.

■ Bug spray: mosquitoes in Alaska can be huge!

■ Film or digital media: bring twice as much film or digital storage cards as you think you'll need.

■ Sunscreen: you can still get burned, even in Alaska.

■ Clothes for all temperatures: you can go from boiling to freezing within hours.

■ Supply of $1 bills: they'll come in handy for tipping shore-excursion guides and porters at the pier.

■ Germicidal hand cleaner: a must-have for adventure excursions or for where soap and water might be hard to find.

■ Short extension cord: since most cabins have only one or two electrical outlets, an extension cord will allow you to use more than one appliance at a time, and give you more flexibility to move around.

■ Travel alarm clock: if you don't want to rely on shipboard wake-up calls, bring your own alarm, as most staterooms don't have them.

experts in the state's natural history and native cultures—are the norm. Cabins on expedition ships can be tiny, usually with no phone or TV, and bathrooms are often no bigger than cubbyholes. The dining room and lounge are usually the only public areas on these vessels; however, some are luxurious with cushy cabins, comfy lounges and libraries, and hot tubs. You won't find much nightlife aboard, but what you trade for space and onboard diversions is a unique and unforgettable glimpse of Alaska.

Many small ships are based in Juneau or another Alaska port and sail entirely within Alaska. Twice annually, some offer an Inside Passage cruise as the ships reposition to and from their winter homes elsewhere.

Small-ship cruising can be pricey, as fares tend to be inclusive (except for airfare), with few onboard charges, and, given the size of ship and style of cruise, fewer opportunities to spend on board.

ABOUT THESE REVIEWS

For each cruise line described, ships that regularly cruise in Alaska are grouped by class or similar configuration. Some ships owned by the cruise lines listed do not include regularly scheduled Alaska cruises on their published itineraries as of this writing and are not reviewed in this book. *For a complete listing of the ships and the itineraries they are scheduled to follow in the 2010 cruising season, see the chart ⇨ Ships by Itinerary and Home Port, below.*

Many ships are designed with an eye to less than perfect weather. For that reason, you're likely to find indoor swimming pools featured on their deck plans. Except in rare cases, these are usually dual-purpose pools that can be covered when necessary by a sliding roof or magro-dome to create an indoor swimming environment. Our reviews indicate the total number of swimming pools found on each ship, with such permanently and/or temporarily covered pools included in the total and also noted as "# indoors" in parentheses.

When ships belong to the same class—or are basically similar—they're listed together in the subhead under the name of the class; the year each was introduced is also given in the same order in the statistics section. Capacity figures are based on double occupancy, but when maximum capacity numbers are available (the number of passengers a ship holds when all possible berths are filled), those are listed in parentheses. Many larger ships have three- and four-berth cabins that can substantially increase the total number of passengers on board when all berths are booked.

Unlike other cruise guides, we describe not only the features but also list the cabin dimensions for each accommodation category available on the ships reviewed. Dimensions should be considered approximate and used for comparison purposes, since they sometimes vary depending on the actual location of the cabin. For instance, while staterooms are largely prefabricated and consistent in size and configuration, those at the front of some ships may be oddly curved to conform to the shape of the bow.

Demand is high, and cruise ships are sailing at full capacity these days, so someone is satisfied by every ship. When you're armed with all the right information, we're sure you'll be able to find one that not only fits your style but that offers you the service and value you expect.

LARGE CRUISE LINES

Ship	Embarkation Port	Cruise Length	Itinerary and Ports of Call
CARNIVAL CRUISE LINES			
Carnival Spirit	Seattle	7	Round-trip: Juneau, Skagway, Ketchikan, Victoria, BC, Sawyer Glacier
	Vancouver	6	One-way: Ketchikan, Juneau, Skagway, disembark Seattle
	Seattle	7	One-way: Ketchikan, Juneau, Skagway, Glacier Bay, disembark Vancouver
CELEBRITY CRUISES			
Celebrity Infinity	Seattle	7	Round-trip: Ketchikan, Juneau, Skagway, Victoria, BC, Sawyer Glacier
Celebrity Mercury	Vancouver	7	Round-trip: Ketchikan, Juneau, Icy Strait Point, Hubbard Glacier
Celebrity Millennium	Vancouver	7	North-bound: Skagway, Ketchikan, Icy Strait Point, Hubbard Glacier
	Seward	7	South-bound: Skagway, Ketchikan, Icy Strait Point, Hubbard Glacier
HOLLAND AMERICA LINE			
Amsterdam	Seattle	14	Round-trip: Ketchikan, Skagway, Sitka, Anchorage, Homer, Kodiak, Juneau, Victoria, BC, Hubbard Glacier, Sawyer Glacier
Oosterdam	Seattle	7	Round-trip: Juneau, Sitka, Ketchikan, Victoria, BC, Glacier Bay
Rotterdam	Seattle	7	Round-trip: Juneau, Ketchikan, Sitka, Victoria, BC, Hubbard Glacier
Ryndam	Vancouver	7	North-bound: Ketchikan, Skagway Juneau, College Fjord, Glacier Bay
	Seward	7	South-bound: Ketchikan, Haines, Juneau, College Fjord, Glacier Bay
Statendam	Vancouver	7	North-bound: Skagway, Juneau, Ketchikan, College Fjord, Glacier Bay
	Seward	7	South-bound: Haines, Juneau, Ketchikan, College Fjord, Glacier Bay
Volendam	Vancouver	7	Round-trip: Skagway, Juneau, Ketchikan, Sawyer Glacier, Glacier Bay
Zaandam	Seattle	7	Round-trip: Juneau, Sitka, Ketchikan, Victoria, BC, Hubbard Glacier
Zuiderdam	Vancouver	7	Round-trip: Skagway, Juneau, Ketchikan, Sawyer Glacier, Glacier Bay
NORWEGIAN CRUISE LINE			
Norwegian Pearl	Seattle	7	Round-trip: Juneau, Skagway, Ketchikan, Victoria, BC, Glacier Bay
Norwegian Star	Seattle	7	Round-trip: Juneau, Skagway, Ketchikan, Prince Rupert, BC, Sawyer Glacier

LARGE CRUISE LINES

Ship	Embarkation Port	Cruise Length	Itinerary and Ports of Call
Norwegian Sun	Vancouver	7	North-bound: Ketchikan, Juneau, Skagway, Icy Strait Point, Hubbard Glacier
	Whittier	7	South-bound: Sitka, Juneau, Skagway, Ketchikan, College Fjord
PRINCESS CRUISES			
Coral Princess	Vancouver	7	North-bound: Ketchikan, Juneau, Skagway, Glacier Bay, College Fjord
	Whittier	7	South-bond: Ketchikan, Juneau, Skagway, Glacier Bay, Hubbard Glacier
Diamond Princess	Vancouver	7	North-bound: Ketchikan, Juneau, Skagway, Glacier Bay, College Fjord
	Whittier	7	South-bond: Ketchikan, Juneau, Skagway, Glacier Bay, Hubbard Glacier
Golden Princess	Seattle	7	Juneau, Skagway, Ketchikan, Victoria, BC, Sawyer Glacier or Glacier Bay
Island Princess	Vancouver	7	North-bound: Ketchikan, Juneau, Skagway, Glacier Bay, College Fjord
	Whittier	7	South-bond: Ketchikan, Juneau, Skagway, Glacier Bay, Hubbard Glacier
Royal Princess	Seattle	14	Round-trip: Ketchikan, Skagway, Seward, Kodiak, Juneau, Icy Strait Point, Victoria, BC, Sawyer Glacier, Glacier Bay
Sapphire Princess	Seattle	7	Juneau, Skagway, Ketchikan, Victoria, BC, Sawyer Glacier or Glacier Bay
Sea Princess	San Francisco	10	Round-trip: Juneau, Ketchikan, Victoria, BC, either Icy Strait Point, Haines, or Skagway, either Sawyer Glacier or Glacier Bay
REGENT SEVEN SEAS CRUISES			
Seven Seas Navigator	Vancouver	7	North-bound: Sitka, Juneau, Skagway, Ketchikan, Hubbard Glacier, Sawyer Glacier
	Seward	7	South-bound: Sitka, Juneau, Skagway, Ketchikan, Hubbard Glacier, Sawyer Glacier
ROYAL CARIBBEAN INTERNATIONAL			
Radiance of the Seas	Vancouver	7	North-bound: Ketchikan, Juneau, Skagway, Icy Strait Point, Hubbard Glacier
	Seward	7	South-bound: Ketchikan, Juneau, Skagway, Icy Strait Point, Hubbard Glacier
Rhapsody of the Seas	Seattle	7	Round-trip: Juneau, Skagway, Victoria, BC, Sawyer Glacier
SILVERSEA CRUISES			
Silver Shadow	San Francisco	10 or 12	Port calls vary by sailing and include Ketchikan, Juneau, Skagway,
	Vancouver	7 or 9	Wrangell, Sitka, Haines, Valdez, Prince Rupert, BC, or Victoria, BC, and
	Seward	7	College Fjord, Hubbard Glacier, or Sawyer Glacier

SMALL CRUISE SHIP LINES

Ship	Embarkation Port	Cruise Length	Itinerary and Ports of Call
AMERICAN SAFARI LINE			
Safari Explorer	Juneau	7	Round-trip: Elfin Cove, Glacier Bay
	Seattle	14	North-bound: Friday Harbor, WA, Misty Fiords, Ketchikan, Meyer's Chuck, Wrangell, Petersburg, Warm Springs Bay, Tenakee Springs, Glacier Bay
	Juneau	14	South-bound: Glacier Bay, Tenakee Springs, Warm Springs Bay, Petersburg, Wrangell, Meyer's Chuck, Ketchikan, Misty Fiords, Friday Harbor, WA
Safari Quest	Juneau	7	Round-trip: Elfin Cove, Glacier Bay, Sitka
	Sitka	7	Round-trip: Elfin Cove, Glacier Bay, Juneau
	Seattle	14	North-bound: Prince Rupert, BC, Ketchikan, Meyer's Chuck, Petersburg, Glacier Bay
	Juneau	14	South-bound: Glacier Bay, Petersburg, Meyer's Chuck, Ketchikan, Prince Rupert, BC
Safari Spirit	Juneau	7	North-bound: Glacier kayaking, Tenakee Springs, Petersburg
	Petersburg	7	South-bound: Tenakee Springs, Glacier kayaking, Juneau
	Seattle	14	North-bound: Friday Harbor, WA, Prince Rupert, BC, Ketchikan, Meyer's Chuck, Petersburg, Glacier Bay, Juneau
	Juneau	14	South-bound: Glacier Bay, Petersburg, Meyer's Chuck, Ketchikan, Prince Rupert, BC, Seattle
CRUISE WEST			
Spirit of Columbia	Seattle	10	North-bound: Ketchikan, Petersburg, Sitka, Skagway, Haines, Sawyer Glacier, Glacier Bay, Juneau
	Juneau	10	South-bound: Ketchikan, Petersburg, Sitka, Skagway, Haines, Sawyer Glacier, Glacier Bay, Seattle
	Whittier	4	Round-trip: College Fjord, Knight Island, Chenega Glacier
Spirit of Discovery	Seattle	10	North-bound: Ketchikan, Petersburg, Sitka, Skagway, Haines, Sawyer Glacier, Glacier Bay, Juneau
	Juneau	10	South-bound: Ketchikan, Petersburg, Sitka, Skagway, Haines, Sawyer Glacier, Glacier Bay, Seattle
	Juneau	4	Round-trip: Glacier Bay (2 days)

SMALL CRUISE SHIP LINES

Ship	Embarkation Port	Cruise Length	Itinerary and Ports of Call
Spirit of Endeavour	Seattle	10	North-bound: Ketchikan, Petersburg, Sitka, Skagway, Haines, Sawyer Glacier, Glacier Bay, Juneau
	Juneau	10	South-bound: Ketchikan, Petersburg, Sitka, Skagway, Haines, Sawyer Glacier, Glacier Bay, Seattle
	Juneau	7	Round-trip: Petersburg, Sitka, Skagway, Haines, Ketchikan, Sawyer Glacier, Glacier Bay
Spirit of Yorktown	Seattle	10	North-bound: Ketchikan, Petersburg, Sitka, Skagway, Haines, Sawyer Glacier, Glacier Bay, Juneau
	Juneau	10	South-bound: Ketchikan, Petersburg, Sitka, Skagway, Haines, Sawyer Glacier, Glacier Bay, Seattle
	Juneau	7	Round-trip: Petersburg, Sitka, Skagway, Haines, Ketchikan, Sawyer Glacier, Glacier Bay
LINDBLAD EXPEDITIONS			
National Geographic Sea Bird & Sea Lion	Sitka	7	North-bound: Point Adolphus, Glacier Bay, Petersburg, Sawyer Glacier, Juneau
	Juneau	7	South-bound: Sawyer Glacier, Petersburg, Glacier Bay, Point Adolphus, Sitka
	Seattle	11	North-bound: Alert Bay, Misty Fiords, Sitka, Baranof Island, Glacier Bay, Point Adolphus, Juneau
	Juneau	11	South-bound: Point Adolphus, Glacier Bay, Baranof Island, Sitka, Misty Fiords, Alert Bay, Seattle

CARNIVAL CRUISE LINES

The world's largest cruise line originated the Fun Ship concept in 1972 with the relaunch of an aging ocean liner, which got stuck on a sandbar during its maiden voyage. In true entrepreneurial spirit, founder Ted Arison shrugged off an inauspicious beginning to

Lobby Bar on board *Carnival Fantasy*

introduce superliners only a decade later. Sporting red-white-and-blue flared funnels, which are easily recognized from afar, new ships are continuously added to the fleet and rarely deviate from a successful pattern. If you find something you like on one vessel, you're likely to find something similar on another.

✉ *3655 N.W. 87 Ave., Miami, FL*
☎ *305/599–2600 or 800/227–6482*
⊕ *www.carnival.com*

☞ *Cruise Style: Mainstream.*

Each vessel features themed public rooms, ranging from ancient Egypt to futuristic motifs. More high-energy than cerebral, the entertainment consists of lavish Las Vegas–style revues presented in main show lounges by a company of singers and dancers. Other performers might include comedians, magicians, jugglers, acrobats, and even passengers taking part in the talent show or stepping up to the karaoke microphone. Live bands play a wide range of musical styles for dancing and listening in smaller lounges, and each ship has a disco.

Arrive early to get a seat for bingo and art auctions. Adult activities, particularly the competitive ones, tend to be silly and hilarious and play to full houses. Relaxing poolside can be difficult when bands crank up the volume or the cruise director selects volunteers for pool games; fortunately, it's always in fun and mostly entertaining. There's generally a quieter second pool to retreat to.

Carnival is so sure passengers will be satisfied with their cruise experience that they are the only cruise line to offer a Vacation Guarantee. Just notify them before arriving at the first port of call if you're unhappy for any reason. Should you choose to disembark at the ship's first non-U.S. port, Carnival will refund the unused portion of your cruise fare and pay for your flight back to your embarkation port. It's a generous offer for which they get very few takers.

Food
Carnival ships have both flexible dining options and casual alternative restaurants. While the tradition of two set mealtimes for dinner still prevails, the line is experimenting with an open seating concept, which could be implemented fleetwide.

Choices are numerous, and the addition of Georges Blanc Signature Selections have elevated Carnival's menus to an unexpected level. While the waiters still sing and dance, the good-to-excellent dining room food appeals to American tastes. Upscale supper clubs on certain ships serve cuisine comparable to the best mid-range steak houses ashore.

Carnival serves the best food of the mainstream cruise lines. In addition to the regular menu, vegetarian, low-calorie, low-carbohydrate, low-salt, and no-sugar selections are available. A children's menu includes such favorites as macaroni and cheese, chicken fingers, and peanut butter-and-jelly sandwiches. If you don't feel like dressing up for dinner, the Lido buffet serves full meals, including sandwiches, a salad bar, rotisserie chicken, Asian stir-fry, and excellent pizza.

Fitness and Recreation
Manned by staff members trained to keep passengers in shipshape form, Carnival's trademark spas and fitness centers are some of the largest and best equipped at sea. Spas and salons are operated by Steiner Leisure, and treatments include a variety of massages, body wraps, and facials; salons offer hair and nail services. Tooth whitening is a recent addition. Fitness centers have state-of-the-art cardio and strength-training equipment, a jogging track, and basic exercise classes at no charge. There's a fee for personal training, body composition analysis, and specialized classes such as yoga and Pilates.

Your Shipmates
Carnival's passengers are predominantly active Americans, mostly couples in their mid-30s to mid-50s. Many families enjoy Carnival cruises in the Caribbean year-round. Holidays and school vacation periods are very popular with families, and you'll see a lot of kids in summer. More than 600,000 children sailed on Carnival ships in 2008—a sixfold increase in slightly over a decade.

Top: *Carnival Victory* dining room
Bottom: *Carnival Legend* waterslide

1

CARNIVAL CRUISE LINES

Top: *Carnival Triumph* walking and jogging track
Middle: *Carnival Elation* at sea
Bottom: *Carnival Destiny* penthouse suite.

Dress Code

Two "cruise elegant" nights are standard on seven-night cruises; one is the norm on shorter sailings. Although men should feel free to wear tuxedos, dark suits (or sport coats) and ties are more prevalent. All other evenings are "cruise casual," with jeans and dress shorts permitted in the dining rooms. All ships request that no short-shorts or cutoffs after 6 PM, but that policy is often ignored.

Junior Cruisers

Camp Carnival, run year-round by professionals, earns high marks for keeping young cruisers busy and content. Dedicated children's areas include great playrooms with separate splash pools. Toddlers from two to five years are treated to puppet shows, sponge painting, face painting, coloring, drawing, and crafts. As long as diapers and supplies are provided, staff will change toddlers. Activities for ages six to eight include arts and crafts, pizza parties, computer time, T-shirt painting, a talent show, and fitness programs. Nine- to 11-year-olds can play Ping-Pong, take dance lessons, play video games, and participate in swim parties, scavenger hunts, and sports. Tweens aged 12 to 14 appreciate the social events, parties, contests, and sports in Circle C. Every night they have access to the ships' discos, followed by late-night movies, karaoke, or pizza.

Club O2 is geared toward teens from 15 to 17. Program directors play host at the spacious teen clubs, where kicking back is the order of the day between scheduled activities. The fleetwide Y-Spa program for older teens offers a high level of pampering. Staff members also accompany teens on shore excursions designed just for them.

Daytime group babysitting for infants two and under allows parents the freedom to explore ports of call without the kids until noon. Parents can also pursue leisurely adults-only evenings from 10 PM to 3 AM, when slumber party–style group babysitting is available for children from ages 4 months to 11 years. Babysitting fees are $6 an hour for one child and $4 an hour for each additional child.

CHOOSE THIS LINE IF . . .

You want an action-packed casino with a choice of table games and rows upon rows of clanging slot machines.

You don't mind standing in line—these are big ships with a lot of passengers, and lines are not uncommon.

You don't mind hearing announcements over the public-address system reminding you of what's next on the schedule.

Service

Service on Carnival ships is friendly but not polished. Stateroom attendants are not only recognized for their attention to cleanliness but also for their expertise in creating towel animals—cute critters fashioned from bath towels that appear during nightly turndown service. They've become so popular that Carnival publishes an instruction book on how to create them yourself.

Tipping

A gratuity of $10 per passenger, per day is automatically added to passenger accounts, and gratuities are distributed to stewards and waitstaff. Passengers may adjust the amount based on the level of service experienced. All beverage tabs at bars get an automatic 15% addition.

Past Passengers

After sailing on one Carnival cruise, you'll receive a complimentary two-year subscription to *Currents,* the company magazine, and access to your past sailing history on the Carnival Web site. You are recognized on subsequent cruises with color-coded key cards—Gold (starting you're your 2nd cruise) or Platinum (starting with your 10th cruise)—which serve as your entrée to a by-invitation-only cocktail reception. You're also eligible for exclusive discounts on future cruises on all the cruise lines owned by Carnival Corporation.

Platinum members are eligible for Concierge Club benefits, including priority embarkation and debarkation, guaranteed dining assignments, supper club and spa reservations, logo items, and complimentary laundry service.

GOOD TO KNOW

If you've never sailed on a Carnival ship, or haven't sailed on one in recent years, you may not understand how Carnival cruises have evolved. The shipboard atmosphere is still bright, noisy, and fun, but the beer-drinking contests and bawdy, anything-goes image are history. Unfortunately, much like Casual Friday has evolved from no tie in the office to jeans and a polo shirt, it isn't unusual to see Carnival passengers dressed very casually after dinner, even on "cruise elegant" nights. You may be surprised at how quickly some passengers can swap their fancy duds for T-shirts and shorts between the dining room and show lounge. The fun of a Carnival cruise can begin before you leave home if you log on to the Carnival Web site (⊕ *www. carnivalconnections.com*), where you will find planning tips, cruise reviews, and a message board.

DON'T CHOOSE THIS LINE IF . . .

You want an intimate, sedate atmosphere. Carnival's ships are big and bold.

You want elaborate accommodations. Carnival suites are spacious but not as feature-filled as the term *suite* may suggest.

You're turned off by men in tank tops. Casual on these ships means casual indeed.

SPIRIT CLASS
Carnival Spirit

	CREW MEMBERS
	930
	ENTERED SERVICE
	2001
700 ft.	**GROSS TONS**
	88,500
	LENGTH
	960 feet
500 ft.	**NUMBER OF CABINS**
	1,062
	PASSENGER CAPACITY
	2,124 (2,667 max)
300 ft.	**WIDTH**
	105.7 feet

Top: *Carnival Legend* at sea
Bottom: Spirit-class balcony
stateroom

Public Areas and Facilities

Spirit-class vessels may seem to be a throwback in size, but these sleek ships have the advantage of fitting through the Panama Canal and, with their additional length, include all the trademark characteristics of their larger fleet mates. They're also racehorses with the speed to reach far-flung destinations.

A rosy red skylight in the front bulkhead of the funnel—which houses the reservations-only upscale Supper Club—caps a soaring, 11-deck atrium. Lovely chapels are available for weddings, either upon embarkation or while in a port of call, and are also used for shipboard religious services.

The upper and lower interior promenade decks are unhampered by a midship restaurant or galley, which means that passenger flow throughout the ships is much improved over earlier, and even subsequent, designs.

Restaurants

One formal restaurant serves open seating breakfast and lunch; while it also serves dinner in two traditional assigned evening seatings, the line is experimenting with an open seating concept, which, if successful, will be implemented fleetwide. The casual Lido buffet with stations offers a variety of food choices (including a deli, salad bar, dessert station, and different daily regional cuisines); at night it becomes the Seaview Bistro for casual dinners. There's also an upscale supper club that requires reservations and an additional charge, a pizzeria, poolside outdoor grills for burgers, hot dogs, and the trimmings, a specialty coffee bar and patisserie, a complimentary sushi bar, and 24-hour room service with a limited menu of breakfast selections, sandwiches, and snacks.

Accommodations

Cabins: Cabins on Carnival ships are generally more spacious than industry standard, and these are no exception. Nearly 80% have an ocean view and, of those, more than 80% have balconies. Suites and some ocean-view cabins have private balconies outfitted with chairs and tables; some cabins have balconies at least 50% larger than average. Every cabin has adequate closet and drawer–shelf storage, as well as bathroom shelves. High-thread-count linens and plush pillows and duvets are a luxurious touch in all accommodations. Suites also have a whirlpool tub and walk-in closet.

Decor: Light-wood cabinetry, soft pastels, mirrored accents, a small refrigerator, a personal safe, a hair dryer, and a sitting area with sofa, chair, and table are typical for ocean-view cabins and suites. Inside cabins have ample room but no sitting area.

Bathrooms: Extras include shampoo and bath gel provided in shower-mounted dispensers and an array of sample toiletries, as well as fluffy towels and a wall-mounted magnifying mirror. Bathrobes for use during the cruise are provided for all.

Other Features: Decks 5, 6, and 7 each have a pair of balcony staterooms that connect to adjoining interior staterooms that are ideal for families because of their close proximity to children and teen areas. Sixteen staterooms are designed for wheelchair accessibility.

In the Know

Take a walk on the wild side. The gently curving staircase to the Supper Club is clear Plexiglas and definitely a challenge to descend if heights make you dizzy. Try it anyway—it's quite a heady experience. Wimps can use the elevator.

Pros and Cons

Pros: A quieter choice for reading than the library, which also houses the Internet center, is the delightful enclosed winter garden space located forward on the exterior promenade deck. For relaxation, a soothing therapy pool sits under a skylight in the fitness center, and his-and-hers saunas and steam rooms have glass walls and sea views. Complimentary self-serve ice cream dispensers are on the Lido Deck.

Cons: These are long ships—really long ships—and you may want to consider any mobility issues and select a cabin near one of the three banks of well-placed elevators. Connecting staterooms are relatively scarce throughout the ships, but balcony dividers can be unlocked between some higher-category cabins. Avid gamers may have difficulty locating the video arcade, which is tucked away at the forward end of the ship in front of the main show lounge and accessible from the interior promenade.

Cabin Type	Size (sq. ft.)
Penthouse Suites	370 (average)
Suite	275
Ocean View	185
Interior	185

FAST FACTS

- 12 passenger decks
- Specialty restaurant, dining room, buffet, ice cream parlor, pizzeria
- Wi-Fi, safe, refrigerator
- 3 pools (1 indoor), children's pool
- Fitness classes, gym, hair salon, 4 hot tubs, sauna, spa, steam room
- 7 bars, casino, 2 dance clubs, library, showroom, video game room
- Children's programs (ages 2–17)
- Laundry facilities, laundry service
- Internet terminal

Carnival Miracle Gatsby's Garden

CELEBRITY CRUISES

The Chandris Group, owners of budget Fantasy Cruises, founded Celebrity in 1989. Initially utilizing an unlovely, refurbished former ocean liner from the Fantasy fleet, Celebrity gained a reputation for professional service and fine food despite the shabby-chic vessel

Celebrity Century at anchor

where it was elegantly served. The cruise line eventually built premium sophisticated cruise ships. Signature amenities followed, including large standard staterooms with generous storage, fully equipped spas, and butler service. Valuable art collections grace the fleet.

✉ *1050 Caribbean Way, Miami, FL*
☎ *800/647–2251*
⊕ *www.celebrity cruises.com*
☞ *Cruise Style: Premium.*

Entertainment has never been a primary focus of Celebrity Cruises, although a lineup of lavish revues is presented in the main show lounges. In addition to shows featuring comedians, magicians, and jugglers, bands play a wide range of musical styles for dancing and listening in smaller lounges. You'll find guest lecturers on every Celebrity cruise. Presentations may range from financial strategies, astronomy, wine appreciation, photography tips, and politics to the food, history, and culture of ports of call. Culinary demonstrations, bingo, and art auctions are additional diversions throughout the fleet. There are plenty of activities, all outlined in the daily program of events. There are no public address announcements for bingo or hawking of gold-by-the-inch sales. You can still play and buy, but you won't be reminded repeatedly.

While spacious accommodations in every category are a Celebrity standard, ConciergeClass, an upscale element on all ships, makes certain premium ocean-view and balcony staterooms almost the equivalent of suites in terms of service. A ConciergeClass stateroom includes numerous extras such as chilled champagne, fresh fruit, and flowers upon arrival, exclusive room-service menus, evening canapés, luxury bedding, pillows, and linens, upgraded balcony furnishings, priority boarding and luggage service, and other VIP perks. At the touch of a single telephone button, a ConciergeClass desk representative is at hand to offer assistance. Suites are still the ultimate, though, and include the services of a butler to assist with unpacking, booking spa services and dining reservations, shining shoes, and even replacing a popped button.

Food

Aside from the sophisticated ambience of its restaurants, the cuisine has always been a highlight of a Celebrity cruise. However, in early 2007, Celebrity and longtime chef Michael Roux ended their affiliation. His hands-on involvement—personally creating menus and overseeing all aspects of dining operations—was integral in helping the line achieve the reputation it enjoys today. Happily, every ship in the fleet has a highly experienced team headed by executive chefs and food and beverage managers who have developed their skills in some of the world's finest restaurants and hotels.

Alternative restaurants on the Solstice-class ships, Millennium-class ships, and *Celebrity Century* offer fine dining and tableside food preparation amid classic ocean liner and Venetian splendor. A less formal evening alternative is offered fleetwide in Lido restaurants, where you'll find a sushi bar, pizza and baked pasta, healthy spa items, and desserts. The AquaSpa Café on Solstice-class and Millennium-class ships serves light and healthy cuisine from breakfast until evening. Cafés serve a variety of coffees, teas, and pastries; some offerings carry an additional charge. Gourmet Bites, the late-night treats served by white-gloved waiters in public rooms throughout the ships, can include mini–beef Wellingtons and crispy tempura.

To further complement the food, in 2004 Celebrity introduced a proprietary Cellarmaster Selection of wines, formulated specifically for Celebrity passengers.

Fitness and Recreation

Celebrity's AquaSpa by Elemis and fitness centers are some of the most tranquil and nicely equipped at sea with thalassotherapy pools on all but Solstice-class ships and *Century* (complimentary on Millennium-class ships; a fee is assessed on *Celebrity Mercury*). Spa services are operated by Steiner Leisure, and treatments include a variety of massages, body wraps, and facials. Trendy and traditional hair and nail services are offered in the salons.

Top: The *Millennium* AquaSpa
Bottom: Millennium-class cinema and conference center

CELEBRITY CRUISES

State-of-the-art exercise equipment, a jogging track, and basic fitness classes are available at no charge. There's a fee for personal training, body composition analysis, and specialized classes such as yoga and Pilates. Golf pros offer hands-on instruction, and game simulators allow passengers to play world-famous courses. Each ship also has an Acupuncture at Sea treatment area staffed by licensed practitioners of Oriental Medicine.

Your Shipmates

Celebrity caters to American cruise passengers, primarily couples from their mid-30s to mid-50s. Many families enjoy cruising on Celebrity's fleet during summer months and holiday periods, particularly in the Caribbean. Lengthier cruises and exotic itineraries attract passengers in the over-60 age group.

Dress Code

Two formal nights are standard on seven-night cruises. Men are encouraged to wear tuxedos, but dark suits or sport coats and ties are more prevalent. Other evenings are designated "smart casual and above." Although jeans are discouraged in formal restaurants, they are appropriate for casual dining venues after 6 PM. The line requests that no shorts be worn in public areas after 6 PM, and most people observe the dress code of the evening, unlike on some other cruise lines.

Junior Cruisers

Each Celebrity vessel has a dedicated playroom and offers a four-tier program of age-appropriate games and activities designed for children ages 3 to 5, 6 to 8, and 9 to 11. Younger children must be toilet trained to participate in the programs and use the facilities; however, families are welcome to borrow toys for their non–toilet-trained kids. A fee may be assessed for participation in children's dinner parties, the Late-Night Slumber Party, and Afternoon Get-Togethers while parents are ashore in ports of call. Evening in-cabin babysitting can be arranged for a fee. All ships have teen centers, where tweens (12 to 14) and teenagers (15 to 17) can hang out and attend mock-tail and pizza parties.

Top: *Century* Rendezvous Lounge
Middle: Lunch on deck
Bottom: Lounging on deck

CHOOSE THIS LINE IF . . .

You want an upscale atmosphere at a really reasonable fare.

You want piping-hot late-night pizza delivered to your cabin in pizzeria fashion.

You want to dine amid elegant surroundings in some of the best restaurants at sea.

Service

Service on Celebrity ships is unobtrusive and polished. ConciergeClass adds an unexpected level of service and amenities that are usually reserved for luxury ships or passengers in top-category suites on other premium cruise lines.

Tipping

Gratuities (in cash) are personally distributed by passengers on the last night of the cruise. Suggested guidelines are per person per day: waiter $3.65; assistant waiter $2.10; assistant maitre d' $1; cabin steward $3.50; cabin attendant in ConciergeClass $4; other service personnel $1.25; and, for suite occupants only, butler $3.50. Passengers may adjust the amount based on the level of service experienced. An automatic gratuity of 15% is added to all beverage tabs.

Past Passengers

Once you've sailed with Celebrity, you become a member of the Captain's Club and receive benefits commensurate with the number of cruises you've taken, including free upgrades, the chance to make dining reservations before sailing, and other benefits. Classic members have been on at least one Celebrity cruise. Select members have sailed least six cruises and get more perks, including an invitation to a senior officer's cocktail party. After 10 cruises, you become an Elite member and can take advantage of a private departure lounge. Royal Caribbean International, the parent company of Celebrity Cruises, also extends the corresponding levels of their Crown & Anchor program to Celebrity Captain's Club members.

GOOD TO KNOW

Small refinements add touches of luxury to a Celebrity cruise. White-gloved stewards are present at the gangway upon embarkation to greet weary passengers with the offer of assistance.

Waiters will happily carry your trays from the buffet line to your table in the casual restaurant. Just ask the bartender for the recipe if a specialty martini or other cocktail appeals to you so you can re-create it at home.

DON'T CHOOSE THIS LINE IF . . .

You need to be reminded of when activities are scheduled. Announcements are kept to a minimum.

You look forward to boisterous pool games and wacky contests. These cruises are fairly quiet and adult-centered.

You think funky avant-garde art is weird. Abstract modernism abounds in the art collections.

MILLENNIUM CLASS
Millennium, Infinity

CREW MEMBERS	999
ENTERED SERVICE	2000, 2001
GROSS TONS	91,000
LENGTH	965 feet
NUMBER OF CABINS	975
PASSENGER CAPACITY	1,950 (2,450)
WIDTH	105 feet

700 ft.

500 ft.

300 ft.

Top: *Millennium* Cova Café
Bottom: *Millennium* Ocean Grill

Public Areas and Facilities
Millennium-class ships are among the largest and most feature-filled in the Celebrity fleet. Innovations include the Conservatory, a unique botanical environment, show lounges reminiscent of splendid opera houses, and an alternative restaurant where diners find themselves in the midst of authentic ocean liner decor and memorabilia. The spas simply have to be seen to be believed—they occupy nearly as much space inside as is devoted to the adjacent outdoor Lido Deck pool area. Although the spas offer just about any treatment you can think of—and some you probably haven't—they also house a complimentary hydrotherapy pool and café. These ships have a lot to offer for families, with some of the most expansive children's facilities in the Celebrity fleet.

Rich fabrics in jewel tones mix elegantly with the abundant use of marble and wood accents throughout public areas. The atmosphere is not unlike a luxurious European hotel filled with grand spaces that flow nicely from one to the other.

Restaurants
The formal two-deck restaurant serves open seating breakfast and lunch; evening meals are served in two traditional assigned seatings. The casual Lido buffet offers breakfast and lunch. By night, the Lido restaurant is transformed into a sit-down restaurant with limited table service and a sushi café. Each ship features a poolside grill for burgers and other fast-food favorites, the spa café serves lighter fare, and Cova Café has specialty coffees, teas, and pastries for an extra charge. Each ship has an upscale alternative restaurant that specializes in tableside food preparation and houses a demonstration kitchen and wine cellar (and also requires reservations and a per-person cover charge). Pizza delivery and 24-hour room service augment dining choices.

Accommodations
Cabins: As on all Celebrity ships, cabins are thoughtfully designed with ample closet and drawer/shelf storage, as well as bathroom shelves in all standard inside and outside categories. Some ocean-view cabins and suites have private balconies. Penthouse suites have guest powder rooms.

Amenities: Wood cabinetry, mirrored accents, a small refrigerator, a personal safe, a hair dryer, and a sitting area with sofa, chair, and table are typical standard amenities. Extras include bathroom toiletries (shampoo, soaps, and lotion) and bathrobes for use during the cruise. Suite luxuries vary, but most include a whirlpool tub, a DVD or VCR, an Internet-connected computer, and a walk-in closet, while all have butler service, personalized stationery, and a logo tote bag. For pure pleasure, Penthouse and Royal suites have outdoor whirlpool tubs on the balconies.

Worth Noting: Most staterooms and suites have convertible sofa beds, and many categories are capable of accommodating third and fourth occupants. Connecting staterooms are available in numerous categories, including Celebrity suites. Family staterooms feature huge balconies and some have not one but two sofa beds. Twenty-six staterooms are designed for wheelchair accessibility.

In the Know

Enhance your personal outdoor space by booking cabins 6035, 6030, or any of the seven cabins forward of those two on deck 6. You can't tell from the deck plan, but your balcony will be extra deep, and you won't be looking down into a lifeboat.

Pros and Cons

Pros: In lieu of atriums, Grand Foyers on these ships are stylishly appointed, multideck lobbies, with sweeping staircases crying out for grand entrances. There's no charge for use of the thalassotherapy pool in the huge AquaSpa, a facility that rivals the fanciest ashore. The AquaSpa Café serves light and healthy selections for breakfast, lunch, and dinner, as well as fresh fruit smoothies.

Cons: Crew members try extremely hard to make everyone feel special, but there are just too many passengers to expect that your every wish will be granted on a ship this size. Although you'd expect to pay far more ashore for a comparable meal in one of the extra-charge specialty restaurants, the suggested wines are overpriced. Self-service laundries are not a feature of Celebrity ships, so you'll have to pack more or use the priced-per-item laundry option.

Cabin Type	Size (sq. ft.)
Penthouse Suite	1,432
Royal Suite	538
Celebrity Suite	467
Sky Suite	251
Family Ocean View	271
ConciergeClass	191
Ocean View/ Interior	170

FAST FACTS

- 11 passenger decks
- Specialty restaurant, dining room, buffet, ice cream parlor, pizzeria
- Internet (*Constellation*), Wi-Fi, safe, refrigerator, DVD (some), VCR (some)
- 3 pools (1 indoor), children's pool
- Fitness classes, gym, hair salon, 6 hot tubs, sauna, spa, steam room
- 7 bars, casino, cinema, dance club, library, showroom, video game room
- Children's programs (ages 3–17)
- Dry cleaning, laundry service
- Internet terminal
- No-smoking cabins

Millennium-class conservatory

CENTURY CLASS
Mercury

CREW MEMBERS	909
ENTERED SERVICE	1997
GROSS TONS	77,713
LENGTH	866 feet
NUMBER OF CABINS	943
PASSENGER CAPACITY	1,886 (2,681)
WIDTH	105 feet

700 ft.

500 ft.

300 ft.

Top: Formal dining on *Century*
Bottom: *Century* Shipmates
Fun Factory

Public Areas and Facilities

While the Century Class sister ships have essentially the same layout, they differ dramatically in decor. *Mercury* is traditional in design and quietly elegant displaying fine collections of modern and classical art. *Mercury* has room for a children's pool as well as a third swimming pool with a sliding roof for cover in inclement weather.

Each vessel has facilities for children and teens, but on *Mercury* they seem almost an afterthought. Adults fare better with spectacular spas and sophisticated lounges dedicated to a variety of tastes. The dining rooms are nothing short of gorgeous. Overall, the first impression is that these are fine resort hotels that just happen to float.

Restaurants

The formal two-deck restaurant serves open seating breakfast and lunch and evening meals in two assigned seatings. Formal dining is supplemented by a casual Lido restaurant offering buffet-style breakfast and lunch. By night, the Lido restaurant is transformed into a sit-down restaurant with table service and a sushi bar. Each ship features two poolside grills for burgers and other fast-food favorites and Cova Café, where specialty coffees, teas, and pastries are available for an additional charge. *Mercury*'s restaurant features windows that stretch from floor to ceiling, key for not missing a second of the scenery outside. Room service is available 24 hours and includes pizza delivered to your door.

Accommodations

Cabins: As on all Celebrity ships, cabins are thoughtfully designed with ample closet and drawer/shelf storage and bathroom shelves. Some ocean-view cabins and suites have balconies with chairs and tables. Penthouse and Royal suites have a whirlpool bathtub and separate shower as well as a walk-in closet; Penthouse suites have a guest powder room.

Amenities: Light-wood cabinetry, mirrored accents, a refrigerator, a personal safe, a hair dryer, and a sitting area with sofa, chair, and table are typical standard amenities. Extras include bathroom toiletries (shampoo, soaps, and lotion) and bathrobes for use during the cruise. Penthouse and Royal suites have an elaborate entertainment center with a large TV, while all suites include butler service, personalized stationery, VCR or DVD, and a tote bag.

Worth Noting: Spacious family ocean-view staterooms have a double bed, sofa bed, and upper berth. Eight staterooms are designed for wheelchair accessibility.

In the Know

While the rest of the industry was rushing to add affordable balconies to a high percentage of staterooms, Celebrity was somewhat slower to get on the bandwagon. While Celebrity has remedied this situation in recent years with other ships, *Mercury* is still slightly behind the curve; if you want a balcony, book early to be safe.

Pros and Cons

Pros: The stogie craze has all but died, and the air has cleared in Michael's Clubs, the lounges formerly devoted to cigar smoking and now billed as piano bars. While there's a charge for the specialty coffee and Cova Café treats, complimentary croissants and pastries are available in the morning and late afternoon. Descending to dine was the tradition of great ocean liners, and these ships have stunning, descent-worthy staircases flanked by soaring columns in double-height dining rooms.

Cons: Unless you're occupying a suite or have booked a massage or other treatment from the spa menu, plan to pay a fee for relaxing in the huge saltwater therapy pool on *Mercury*. *Mercury* is the only ship in the Celebrity fleet that lacks a specialty restaurant.

Cabin Type	Size (sq. ft.)
Penthouse Suite	1,101
Royal Suite	537
Sky Suite	246
Sunset Veranda	224
Century Suite	190
Family Stateroom	192–218
Concierge, Veranda	170–175
Ocean View	172–175
Interior	171–174

FAST FACTS

- 10 passenger decks
- Dining room, buffet, ice cream parlor, pizzeria
- Wi-Fi, safe, refrigerator, DVD (some), VCR (some)
- 3 pools (1 indoor), children's pool
- Fitness classes, gym, hair salon, 5 hot tubs, sauna, spa, steam room (*Mercury*)
- 8 bars, casino, cinema, dance club, library, showroom, video game room
- Children's programs (ages 3–17)
- Dry cleaning, laundry service
- Internet terminal
- No-smoking cabins

1

CELEBRITY CRUISES

HOLLAND AMERICA

Holland America Line has enjoyed a distinguished record of traditional cruises, world exploration, and transatlantic crossings since 1873—all facets of its history that are reflected in the fleet's multi-million dollar shipboard art and antiques collections. Even the

A day on the Lido Deck

ships' names follow a pattern set long ago: all end in the suffix *dam* and are either derived from the names of various dams that cross Holland's rivers, important Dutch landmarks, or points of the compass. The names are even recycled when vessels are retired, and some are in their fifth and sixth generation of use.

✉ *300 Elliott Ave. W, Seattle, WA* ☎ *206/281–3535 or 800/577–1728* ⊕ *www. hollandamerica.com*

☞ *Cruise Style: Premium Deluxe.*

Noted for focusing on passenger comfort, Holland America Line cruises are classic in design and style, and with an infusion of younger adults and families on board, they remain refined without being stuffy or stodgy. Following a basic design theme, returning passengers feel as at home on the newest Holland America vessels as they do on older ones.

Entertainment tends to be more Broadway-stylish than Las Vegas–brash. Colorful revues are presented in main show lounges by the ships' companies of singers and dancers. Other performances might include a range of cabaret acts: comedians, magicians, jugglers, and acrobats. Live bands play a wide range of musical styles for dancing and listening in smaller lounges and piano bars. Movies are shown daily in cinemas that double as the Culinary Arts Centers.

Holland America Line may never be considered cutting edge, but the Signature of Excellence concept introduced in 2003 sets it apart from other premium cruise lines. An interactive Culinary Arts Center offers cooking demonstrations and wine-tasting sessions; Explorations Café (powered by the *New York Times*) is a coffeehouse-style library and Internet center; and the Explorations Guest Speakers Series is supported by in-cabin televised programming on flat-screen TVs in all cabins; the traditional Crow's Nest observation lounge has a new nightclub-disco layout, video wall, and sound-and-light systems; and facilities for children and teens have been greatly expanded. Signature of Excellence upgrades were completed on the entire Holland America fleet in 2006.

Food

Holland America Line chefs, led by Master Chef Rudi Sodamin, utilize more than 500 different food items on a typical weeklong cruise to create the modern Continental cuisine and traditional favorites served to their passengers. Vegetarian options as well as health-conscious cuisine are available, and special dietary requests can be handled with advance notice. Holland America's passengers used to skew older than they do now, so the sometimes bland dishes were no surprise. But the food quality, taste, and selection have greatly improved in recent years. A case in point is the reservations-required Pinnacle Grill alternative restaurants, where fresh seafood and premium cuts of Sterling Silver beef are used to prepare creative specialty dishes. The $20 per person charge for dinner would be worth it for the Dungeness crab cakes starter and dessert alone. Other delicious traditions are afternoon tea, a Dutch Chocolate Extravaganza, and Holland America Line's signature bread pudding.

Flexible scheduling allows for early or late seatings in the two-deck, formal restaurants. Open seating from 5:15 to 9 has been introduced fleetwide.

Fitness and Recreation

Well-equipped and fully staffed fitness facilities contain state-of-the-art exercise equipment; basic fitness classes are available at no charge. There's a fee for personal training, body composition analysis, and specialized classes such as yoga and Pilates.

Treatments in the Greenhouse Spa include a variety of massages, body wraps, and facials. Hair styling and nail services are offered in the salons. All ships have a jogging track, multiple swimming pools, and sports courts; some have hydrotherapy pools and soothing thermal suites.

Your Shipmates

No longer just your grandparents' cruise line, today's Holland America Caribbean sailings attract families and discerning couples, mostly from their late-30s on up. Holidays and summer months are peak periods when

Top: Casino action
Bottom: Stay fit or stay loose

you'll find more children in the mix. Comfortable retirees are often still in the majority, particularly on longer cruises. Families cruising together who book five or more cabins receive perks such as a fountain-soda package for each family member, a family photo for each stateroom, and complimentary water toys at Half Moon Cay (for Caribbean itineraries that call at the private island). If the group is larger than 10 cabins or more, the Head-of-Family is recognized with an upgrade from outside stateroom to a veranda cabin. It's the best family deal at sea, and there's no extra charge.

Dress Code

Evenings on Holland America Line cruises fall into two categories: smart casual and formal. For the two formal nights standard on seven-night cruises, men are encouraged to wear tuxedos, but dark suits or sport coats and ties are acceptable, and you'll certainly see them. On smart–casual nights—expect the type of attire you'd see at a country club or upscale resort. It's requested that no T-shirts, jeans, swimsuits, tank tops, or shorts be worn in public areas after 6 PM.

Junior Cruisers

Club HAL is Holland America Line's professionally staffed youth and teen program. Age-appropriate activities planned for children ages 3 to 7 include storytelling, arts and crafts, ice cream or pizza parties, and games; for children ages 8 to 12 there are arcade games, Sony PlayStations, theme parties, on-deck sports events, and scavenger hunts. Club HAL After Hours offers late-night activities from 10 PM until midnight for an hourly fee. Baby food, diapers, cribs, high chairs, and booster seats may be requested in advance of boarding. Private in-cabin babysitting is sometimes available if a staff member is willing.

Teens aged 13 to 17 have their own lounge with activities including dance contests, arcade games, sports tournaments, movies, and an exclusive sundeck on some ships. Select itineraries offer water park–type facilities and kid-friendly shore excursions to Half Moon Cay, Holland America Line's private island in the Bahamas.

Top: Wine tasting
Middle: Production showtime
Bottom: Spa relaxation

CHOOSE THIS LINE IF . . .

You crave relaxation. Grab a padded steamer chair on the teak promenade deck and watch the sea pass by.

You like to go to the movies, especially when the popcorn is free.

You want to bring the kids. Areas designed exclusively for children and teens are hot new features on all ships.

Service

Professional, unobtrusive service by the Indonesian and Filipino staff is a fleetwide standard on Holland America Line. It isn't uncommon for a steward or server to remember the names of returning passengers from a cruise taken years before. Crew members are trained in Indonesia at a custom-built facility called the MS *Nieuw Jakarta,* where employees polish their English-language skills and learn housekeeping in mock cabins.

Tipping

Eleven dollars per passenger per day is automatically added to shipboard accounts, and gratuities are distributed to stewards and waitstaff. Passengers may adjust the amount based on the level of service experienced. Room-service tips are usually given in cash (it's at the passenger's discretion here). An automatic 15% gratuity is added to bar-service tabs.

Past Passengers

All passengers who sail with Holland America Line are automatically enrolled in the Mariner Society and receive special offers on upcoming cruises, as well as insider information concerning new ships and product enhancements. Mariner Society benefits also include preferred pricing on many cruises; Mariner baggage tags and buttons that identify you as a member during embarkation; an invitation to the Mariner Society champagne reception and awards party hosted by the captain; lapel pins and medallions acknowledging your history of Holland America sailings; a special collectible gift delivered to your cabin; and a subscription to *Mariner,* the full-color magazine featuring news and Mariner Society savings. Once you complete your first cruise, your Mariner identification number will be assigned and available for lookup online.

GOOD TO KNOW

The sound of delicate chimes still alerts Holland America Line passengers that it's mealtime. Artful flower arrangements never seem to wilt. A bowl of candied ginger is near the dining room entrance if you need a little something to settle your stomach. These simple, but nonetheless meaningful, touches are what make Holland America Line stand out from the crowd.

DON'T CHOOSE THIS LINE IF...

You want to party hard. Most of the action on these ships ends relatively early.

Dressing for dinner isn't your thing. Passengers tend to ramp up the dress code most evenings.

You have an aversion to extending tips. The line's "tipping not required" policy has been amended.

ROTTERDAM, AMSTERDAM

CREW MEMBERS	644, 647
ENTERED SERVICE	1997, 2000
GROSS TONS	59,652, 61,000
LENGTH	780 feet
NUMBER OF CABINS	700, 690
PASSENGER CAPACITY	1,400, 1,380 (1,792 max)
WIDTH	106 feet

700 ft.

500 ft.

300 ft.

Public Areas and Facilities

Amsterdam and *Rotterdam* are sister ships, which sail on world cruises and extended voyages. The most traditional ships in the fleet, their interiors display abundant wood appointments in the public areas on promenade and lower promenade decks and priceless works of art throughout.

The Ocean Bar, Explorer's Lounge, Wajang Theater, and Crow's Nest are familiar lounges to longtime Holland American passengers. Newer additions include the spa's thermal suite, a culinary-arts demonstration center in the theater, Explorations Café, and expansive areas for children and teens. Multimillion-dollar collections of art and artifacts are showcased throughout both vessels. In addition to works commissioned specifically for each ship, Holland America Line celebrates its heritage by featuring antiques and artworks that reflect the theme of worldwide Dutch seafaring history.

Restaurants

The formal dining room offers open seating breakfast and lunch and a choice between two traditional assigned dinner seatings or open seating. The upscale Pinnacle Grill alternative restaurant serves lunch and dinner, requires reservations, and has a cover charge. A casual Lido restaurant serves buffet breakfast and lunch; at dinner, the Lido offers waiter service. Poolside lunch at the Terrace Grill features a variety of items ranging from nachos, grilled hamburgers, and hot dogs with all the trimmings to sandwiches and gourmet sausages. The extra-charge Explorations Café offers specialty coffees and pastries. Daily afternoon tea service is elevated to Royal Dutch High Tea once per cruise. Complimentary hors d'oeuvres are served by waiters during cocktail hour, hand-dipped chocolates are offered after dinner in the Explorer's Lounge, and a late-night buffet and chocolate extravaganza is served in the Lido Restaurant during every cruise. Room service is available 24 hours.

Accommodations

Cabins: Staterooms are spacious and comfortable, although fewer have private balconies than newer fleet mates. Every cabin has adequate closet and drawer/shelf storage, as well as bathroom shelves. Some suites

Top: Pinnacle Grill dining
Bottom: *Rotterdam* at sea

also have a whirlpool tub, powder room, and walk-in closet.

Suites: Extras include duvets on beds, a fully stocked minibar, and personalized stationery. Penthouse Verandah and Deluxe Verandah suites have exclusive use of the private Neptune Lounge, personal concierge service, canapés before dinner on request, binoculars and umbrellas for use during the cruise, an invitation to a VIP party with the captain, and complimentary laundry, pressing, and dry-cleaning services.

Amenities: All staterooms and suites are appointed with pillow-top mattresses, 250-thread-count cotton bed linens, magnifying halo-lighted mirrors, hair dryers, a fruit basket, flat-panel TVs, and DVD players. Bathrooms have Egyptian cotton towels, shampoo, body lotion, and bath gel, plus deluxe bathrobes to use during the cruise.

Worth Noting: Connecting cabins are available in a range of categories. Although there are a number of triple cabins to choose from, there are not as many that accommodate four. Twenty-one staterooms are designed for wheelchair accessibility on *Amsterdam*, 22 on *Rotterdam*.

In the Know

The creation of the expansive floral stained-glass ceiling that provides a focal point for *Amsterdam*'s formal dining room required the use of some state-of-the-art technology that was developed especially for the ship.

Pros and Cons

Pros: More balcony cabins, spa staterooms, and a new category of Lanai staterooms with direct access to the promenade deck, and The Retreat (a resort-style pool on the aft Lido Deck) was added to *Rotterdam* in 2009. Servers circulate throughout lounges before and after dinner with canapés and other treats. Realistic landscapes with surreal touches accent dining alcoves in the Pinnacle Grill.

Cons: Although outside cabins on the lower promenade deck are ideally situated for easy access to fresh air, occupants should heed the warning that the one-way window glass does not offer complete privacy when interior lights on. Lounges are lively before and after dinner, but many passengers tend to call it a night early. While you'll find excellent facilities designed for kids and teens, suitable accommodations for families are sparse.

Cabin Type	Size (sq. ft.)
Penthouse Suite	973
Deluxe Verandah Suite	374
Verandah Suite	225
Ocean View	197
Inside	182

FAST FACTS

- 9 passenger decks
- Specialty restaurant, dining room, buffet
- Wi-Fi, safe, refrigerator, minibar (some), DVD
- 2 pools (1 indoor), 2 children's pools
- Fitness classes, gym, hair salon, 2 hot tubs, sauna, spa
- 6 bars, casino, cinema, dance club, library, showroom, video game room
- Children's programs (ages 3–17)
- Dry cleaning, laundry facilities, laundry service
- Internet terminal
- No-smoking cabins (some)

A brisk walk starts the day

VISTA CLASS
Zuiderdam, Oosterdam

CREW MEMBERS	817, 817
ENTERED SERVICE	2002, 2003
GROSS TONS	82,000
LENGTH	936 feet
NUMBER OF CABINS	958, 958
PASSENGER CAPACITY	1,916; 1,916
WIDTH	106 feet

700 ft.

500 ft.

300 ft.

Public Areas and Facilities

Ships for the 21st century, Vista-class vessels successfully integrate new, youthful and family-friendly elements into Holland America Line's classic fleet. Exquisite Waterford crystal sculptures adorn triple-deck atriums and reflect vivid, almost daring color schemes throughout. Although all the public rooms carry the traditional Holland America names (Ocean Bar, Explorer's Lounge, Crow's Nest) and aren't much different in atmosphere, their louder decor (toned down a bit since the introduction of the *Zuiderdam*) may make them unfamiliar to returning passengers.

Only two decks are termed *promenade*, and the exterior teak promenade encircles public rooms, not cabins. As a result, numerous outside accommodations have views of the sea restricted by lifeboats on the upper promenade deck. Veterans of cruises on older Holland America ships will find the layout of public spaces somewhat different; still, everyone's favorite Crow's Nest lounges still offer those commanding views.

Restaurants

The formal dining room offers open seating breakfast and lunch and a choice between two traditional assigned dinner seatings or open seating. The upscale Pinnacle Grill alternative restaurant serves lunch and dinner, requires reservations, and has a cover charge A casual Lido restaurant serves buffet breakfast and lunch; at dinner the Lido offers waiter service featuring entrées from both the Lido and main dining room menus. Poolside lunch at the Terrace Grill features a variety of items ranging from nachos, grilled hamburgers, and hot dogs with all the trimmings to sandwiches and gourmet sausages. The extra-charge Explorations Café offers specialty coffees and pastries. Daily afternoon tea service is elevated to Royal Dutch High Tea once per cruise. Complimentary hors d'oeuvres are served by waiters during cocktail hour, hand-dipped chocolates are offered after dinner in the Explorer's Lounge, and a late-night buffet and chocolate extravaganza is served in the Lido Restaurant during every cruise. Room service is available 24 hours.

Top: *Oosterdam* hydro pool
Bottom: Vista-class ocean-view stateroom

Accommodations

Cabins: Comfortable and roomy, 85% of all Vista-class accommodations have an ocean view, and almost 80% of those also have the luxury of a private balcony furnished with chairs, loungers, and tables. Every cabin has adequate closet and drawer/shelf storage, as well as bathroom shelves. Some suites have a whirlpool tub, powder room, and walk-in closet.

Suites: Suite luxuries include duvets on beds and a fully stocked minibar; some also have a whirlpool tub, powder room, and walk-in closet. Penthouse Verandah and Deluxe Verandah suites have exclusive use of the private Neptune Lounge, personal concierge service, canapés before dinner, and complimentary laundry, pressing, and dry-cleaning services.

Amenities: All staterooms and suites are appointed with pillow-top mattresses, 250-thread-count cotton bed linens, magnifying halogen-lighted makeup mirrors, hair dryers, a fruit basket, flat-panel TVs, and DVD players. Bathroom extras include Egyptian cotton towels, shampoo, body lotion, and bath gel, plus deluxe bathrobes to use during the cruise.

Worth Noting: Twenty-eight staterooms are wheelchair accessible.

In the Know

If you want complete privacy on your balcony, choose your location carefully. Take a close look at the deck plans for the ones alongside the exterior panoramic elevators. Riders have views of adjacent balconies as well as the seascape.

Pros and Cons

Pros: Adjacent to the Crow's Nest, outdoor seating areas covered in canvas are wonderful, quiet hideaways during the day as well as when the interior is transformed into a dance club at night. Exterior panoramic elevators offer an elevated view of the seascape. Half-hour shipboard art tours are available on board the ship, loaded on iPods that you may borrow.

Cons: Missing from the Vista-class ships are self-service laundry rooms, a serious omission for families with youngsters and anyone sailing on back-to-back Caribbean itineraries or cruises of more than a week. Murals in Pinnacle Grill restaurants are strangely chintzy looking, especially considering the priceless art throughout the rest of the ships' interiors. Traditional appointments stop at the table top in the Pinnacle Grill—some chairs are silvery cast aluminum and so heavy that they don't budge without a great deal of effort.

Cabin Type	Size (sq. ft.)
Penthouse Suites	1,000
Deluxe Verandah Suite	380
Superior Verandah Suite	298
Deluxe Ocean View	200
Standard Ocean View	194
Inside	185

FAST FACTS

- 11 passenger decks
- Specialty restaurant, dining room, buffet, pizzeria
- Internet, Wi-Fi, safe, refrigerator, DVD
- 2 pools (1 indoor)
- Fitness classes, gym, hair salon, 5 hot tubs, sauna, spa, steam room
- 9 bars, casino, cinema, 2 dance clubs, library, showroom, video game room
- Children's programs (ages 3–17)
- Dry cleaning, laundry service
- Internet terminal

Westerdam at sea

VOLENDAM, ZAANDAM

CREW MEMBERS	647
ENTERED SERVICE	1999, 2000
GROSS TONS	60,906
LENGTH	781 feet
NUMBER OF CABINS	716
PASSENGER CAPACITY	1,432 (1,850 max)
WIDTH	106 feet

Public Areas and Facilities

Similar in layout to Statendam-class vessels, these slightly larger sister ships introduced playful art and interior design theme elements to Holland America Line's classic vessels. Triple- deck atriums are distinguished by a fiber-optic-lighted Murano-glass sculpture on Volendam and an almost scary towering pipe organ on Zaandam. These ships' atriums open onto three promenade decks.

The interior decor and much of the artwork found in each vessel has a predominant theme—Volendam centers around flowers and Zaandam around music. Look for Zaandam's collection of guitars autographed by famous musicians such as the Rolling Stones and a saxophone signed by former President Bill Clinton. Since the ships are larger than the original Statendam-class ships, the extra space allows for a larger specialty restaurant and a roomier feel throughout.

Restaurants

The formal dining room offers open seating breakfast and lunch and a choice between two traditional assigned dinner seatings or open seating. The upscale Pinnacle Grill alternative restaurant serves lunch and dinner, requires reservations, and has a cover charge A casual Lido restaurant serves buffet breakfast and lunch; at dinner the Lido offers waiter service featuring entrées from both the Lido and main dining room menus. Poolside lunch at the Terrace Grill features a variety of items ranging from nachos, grilled hamburgers, and hot dogs with all the trimmings to sandwiches and gourmet sausages. The extra-charge Explorations Café offers specialty coffees and pastries. Daily afternoon tea service is elevated to Royal Dutch High Tea once per cruise. Complimentary hors d'oeuvres are served by waiters during cocktail hour, hand-dipped chocolates are offered after dinner in the Explorer's Lounge, and a late-night buffet and chocolate extravaganza is served in the Lido Restaurant during every cruise. Room service is available 24 hours.

Accommodations

Cabins: Staterooms are spacious and comfortable with a few more balconies than Statendam-class but still fewer than newer fleet mates. Every cabin has adequate closet

Top: Celebrate a special occasion
Bottom: Deluxe veranda suite

and drawer/shelf storage, as well as bathroom shelves. Some suites have a whirlpool tub, powder room, and 5 walk-in closet.

Suites: Suite amenities include duvets on beds, a fully stocked minibar, and personalized stationery. Penthouse Verandah and Deluxe Verandah suites have exclusive use of the private Neptune Lounge, personal concierge service, canapés before dinner on request, binoculars and umbrellas for use during the cruise, an invitation to a VIP party with the captain, and complimentary laundry, pressing, and dry-cleaning services.

Amenities: All staterooms and suites are appointed with pillow-top mattresses, 250-thread-count cotton bed linens, magnifying halo-lighted mirrors, hair dryers, a fruit basket, flat-panel TVs, and DVD players. Bathrooms have Egyptian cotton towels, shampoo, body lotion, and bath gel, plus deluxe bathrobes to use during the cruise.

Worth Noting: As a nod to families, connecting cabins are featured in a range of categories. However, although the number of triple cabins is generous, there are not many that accommodate four. Twenty-two staterooms are designed for wheelchair accessibility.

In the Know

Don't be surprised if you suddenly feel you're in a ticker-tape parade during one of the high-energy production shows. Not only are the show lounges outfitted with revolving stages and hydraulic lifts, but they also feature a moving light system and confetti cannons.

Pros and Cons

Pros: The home of Holland America's new Culinary Arts Institute cooking demonstrations, the ship's theaters also continue to function as cinemas, and moviegoers still relish the complimentary freshly popped popcorn. Waiters serve made-to-order entrées in the Lido restaurant at dinner, and an evening poolside barbecue buffet is usually scheduled during each cruise. If you love cooking classes but just can't face anyone during a bad hair day, you can watch the culinary-arts demonstration on your cabin television.

Cons: Expanded spa facilities make the gym area somewhat tight. The same spa expansion also eliminated individual men's and women's steam rooms to make room for an extra-charge thermal suite. Sandwiched between the Lido pool and Lido bar, the children's wading pool area can become quite boisterous when there are a lot of families with young children on board.

Cabin Type	Size (sq. ft.)
Penthouse Suite	973
Deluxe Verandah Suite	390
Verandah Suite	230
Ocean View	197
Inside	182

FAST FACTS

- 10 passenger decks
- Specialty restaurant, dining room, buffet
- Wi-Fi, safe, minibar (some), refrigerator, DVD
- 2 pools (1 indoor), 2 children's pools
- Fitness classes, gym, hair salon, 2 hot tubs, sauna, spa
- 6 bars, casino, cinema, dance club, library, showroom, video game room
- Children's programs (ages 3–17)
- Dry cleaning, laundry facilities, laundry service
- Internet terminal

Zaandam atrium organ

STATENDAM CLASS
Statendam, Ryndam

CREW MEMBERS	602
ENTERED SERVICE	1993, 1994
GROSS TONS	55,451
LENGTH	720 feet
NUMBER OF CABINS	675
PASSENGER CAPACITY	1,350
WIDTH	101 feet

700 ft.
500 ft.
300 ft.

Public Areas and Facilities

The sister ships included in the S- or Statendam-class retain the most classic and traditional characteristics of Holland America Line vessels. Routinely updated with innovative features, including Signature of Excellence upgrades, they combine all the advantages of intimate, midsize vessels with high-tech and stylish details.

At the heart of the ships, triple-deck atriums graced by suspended glass sculptures open onto three so-called promenade decks; the lowest contains staterooms encircled by a wide, teak outdoor deck furnished with padded steamer chairs, while interior, art-filled passageways flow past lounges and public rooms on the two decks above. It's easy to find just about any area on board, with the possible exception of the main level of the dining room. Either reach the lower dining room floor via the aft elevator, or enter one deck above and make a grand entrance down the sweeping staircase.

Restaurants

The formal dining room offers open seating breakfast and lunch and a choice between two traditional assigned dinner seatings or open seating. The upscale Pinnacle Grill alternative restaurant serves lunch and dinner, requires reservations, and has a cover charge A casual Lido restaurant serves buffet breakfast and lunch; at dinner the Lido offers waiter service featuring entrées from both the Lido and main dining room menus. Poolside lunch at the Terrace Grill features a variety of items ranging from nachos, grilled hamburgers, and hot dogs with all the trimmings to sandwiches and gourmet sausages. The extra-charge Explorations Café offers specialty coffees and pastries. Daily afternoon tea service is elevated to Royal Dutch High Tea once per cruise. Complimentary hors d'oeuvres are served by waiters during cocktail hour, hand-dipped chocolates are offered after dinner in the Explorer's Lounge, and a late-night buffet and chocolate extravaganza is served in the Lido Restaurant during every cruise. Room service is available 24 hours.

Accommodations

Cabins: Staterooms are spacious and comfortable, although fewer of them have private balconies than on newer fleet mates. Every cabin has adequate closet and

Top: Select from an extensive wine list
Bottom: Deluxe veranda suite

drawer/shelf storage, as well as bathroom shelves. Some suites have a whirlpool tub, powder room, and walk-in closet.

Suites: Suites have duvets on beds, a fully stocked minibar, and personalized stationery. Penthouse Verandah and Deluxe Verandah suites have exclusive use of the private Neptune Lounge, personal concierge service, canapés before dinner on request, binoculars and umbrellas for use during the cruise, an invitation to a VIP party with the captain, and complimentary laundry, pressing, and dry-cleaning services.

Amenities: Gone are the flowery chintz curtains and bedspreads of yesteryear—all staterooms and suites are now appointed with pillow-top mattresses, 250-thread-count cotton bed linens, magnifying lighted mirrors, hair dryers, a fruit basket, flat-panel TVs, and DVD players. Bathroom extras include Egyptian cotton towels, shampoo, body lotion, and bath gel, plus deluxe bathrobes to use during the cruise.

Worth Noting: Connecting cabins are featured in a range of categories. Six staterooms are wheelchair accessible; nine are modified with ramps although doors are standard width.

In the Know

Do you recognize the portraits etched into the glass doors to the main show lounges? They are the likenesses of great Dutch artists for whom the spaces are named.

Pros and Cons

Pros: When the Statendam-class ships emerge from extensive dry docks scheduled over the next two years, they will feature more accommodations with balconies, Spa staterooms, a new Lanai stateroom category with direct access to the walk-around promenade deck, and The Retreat, a resort-style pool area on the aft Lido Deck. Ask for the recipe for Holland America Line's signature bread-and-butter pudding with a creamy sauce, which just might be the best in the world. Popular with the after-dinner crowd, yet quiet enough for conversation, the Ocean Bar hits just the right balance for late-night socializing.

Cons: Try to make it to the production shows in time to grab seats on the lower level of the main show lounges—railings on the balcony level obstruct the view. Club HAL may not be too kid-friendly if your cruise is primarily booked by older passengers. With the addition of an extra-charge Explorations Café, the popular—and free—Java coffee bars have been eliminated.

Cabin Type	Size (sq. ft.)
Penthouse Suite	946
Deluxe Verandah Suite	385
Verandah Suite	230
Ocean View	196
Inside	186

FAST FACTS

- 10 passenger decks
- Specialty restaurant, dining room, buffet
- Wi-Fi, safe, minibar, refrigerator, DVD
- 2 pools (1 indoor), 2 children's pools
- Fitness classes, gym, hair salon, 2 hot tubs, sauna, spa, steam room
- 9 bars, casino, cinema, dance club, library, showroom, video game room
- Children's programs (ages 3–17)
- Dry cleaning, laundry facilities, laundry service
- Internet terminal
- No-smoking cabins (some)

Share a sunset

HOLLAND AMERICA

1

NORWEGIAN CRUISE LINE

Norwegian Cruise Line (NCL) set sail in 1966 with an entirely new concept: regularly scheduled Caribbean cruises from the then obscure port of Miami. Good food and friendly service combined with value fares established NCL as a winner for active adults

Le Cirque–style extravaganza on Norwegian Cruise Line

and families. With the introduction of the now-retired SS *Norway* in 1979, NCL ushered in the era of cruises on megasize ships. Innovative and forward-looking, NCL has been a cruise-industry leader for four decades and is as much at home in Europe as it is in the Caribbean.

✉ *7665 Corporate Center Dr., Miami, FL* ☎ *305/436–4000 or 800/327–7030* ⊕ *www.ncl.com*

☞ *Cruise Style: Mainstream.*

Noted for top-quality, high-energy entertainment and emphasis on fitness facilities and programs, NCL combines action, activities, and a variety of dining options in a casual, free-flowing atmosphere. Freestyle cruising has meant an end to rigid dining schedules and dress codes. NCL ships now offer a host of flexible dining options that allow passengers to eat in the main dining rooms or any of a number of à la carte and specialty restaurants at any time and with whom they please. Now co-owned by Star Cruises and Apollo Management, a private equity company, NCL continues to be an industry innovator.

More high jinks than high-brow, entertainment after dark features extravagant Las Vegas–style revues presented in main show lounges by lavishly costumed singers and dancers. Other performers might include comedians, magicians, jugglers, and acrobats. Passengers can get into the act by taking part in talent shows or step up to the karaoke microphone. Live bands play for dancing and listening passengers in smaller lounges, and each ship has a lively disco. Some ships include shows by Chicago's world-famous Second City improvisational comedy company. With the launch of

Norwegian Epic in 2010, the Blue Man Group and Cirque Productions (a U.S.-based company somewhat similar in style to Cirque du Soleil) join NCL's talent line-up.

Casinos, bingo sessions, and art auctions are well attended. Adult games, particularly the competitive ones, are fun to participate in and provide laughs for audience members. Goofy pool games are an NCL staple, and the ships' bands crank up the volume during afternoon and evening deck parties.

From a distance, most cruise ships look so similar that it's often difficult to tell them apart, but NCL's largest, modern ships stand out with their distinctive use of hull art. Each new ship is distinguished by murals extending from bow to midship.

When others scoffed at winter cruises to the Caribbean, Bahamas, and Florida from New York City, NCL recognized the demand and has sailed with such success that others have followed in its wake. A Winter Weather Guarantee is offered should foul weather threaten to spoil your vacation plans. If departure from New York is delayed for more than 12 hours due to weather, you will receive an onboard credit of $100 per person on your current departure, or, if you decide to cancel your cruise, you will receive a cruise credit equal to the amount you paid to use on a future NCL cruise within one year and any reasonable incidental expenses you incur in rearranging your travel plans.

Food

Main dining rooms serve what is traditionally deemed Continental fare, although it's about what you would expect at a really good hotel banquet. Health-conscious menu selections are nicely prepared, and vegetarian choices are always available. Where NCL really shines is the specialty restaurants, especially the French-Mediterranean Le Bistro (on all ships), the pan-Asian restaurants, and steak houses (on the newer ships). As a rule of thumb, the newer the ship, the wider the variety, because new ships were purpose-built with as many as 10 or more places to eat. You may find Spanish tapas, an Italian trattoria, a steak house, and a pan-Asian restaurant complete with a sushi and sashimi bar and teppanyaki room. Almost all carry a cover charge or are priced à la carte and require reservations. An NCL staple, the late-night Chocoholic Buffet continues to be a favorite event.

NOTEWORTHY

■ Numerous connecting staterooms and suites can be combined to create multicabin family accommodations.

■ Freestyle cruising offers the flexibility of dining with anyone you choose and when you actually wish to eat.

■ The ships in the NCL fleet sport hull art—huge murals that make them easily recognizable from afar.

Top: Casual Freestyle dining
Bottom: *Norwegian Jewel* spa relaxation suite

Fitness and Recreation

Mandara Spa offers unique and exotic spa treatments fleetwide on NCL, although facilities vary widely. Spa treatments include a long menu of massages, body wraps, and facials, and current trends in hair and nail services are offered in the salons. The latest addition on board is a medi-spa physician, who can create individualized treatment plans using nonsurgical treatments such as Botox Cosmetic. State-of-the-art exercise equipment, jogging tracks, and basic fitness classes are available at no charge. There's a fee for personal training, body composition analysis, and specialized classes such as yoga and Pilates.

Your Shipmates

NCL's mostly American cruise passengers are active couples ranging from their mid-30s to mid-50s. Many families enjoy cruising on NCL ships during holidays and summer months. Longer cruises and more exotic itineraries attract passengers in the over-55 age group.

Dress Code

Resort casual attire is appropriate at all times; the option of one formal evening is available on all cruises of seven nights and longer. Most passengers actually raise the casual dress code a notch to what could be called casual chic attire.

Junior Cruisers

For children and teens, each NCL vessel offers a Kid's Crew program of supervised entertainment for young cruisers ages 2 to 17. Younger children are split into three groups, ages 2 to 5, 6 to 9, and 10 to 12; activities range from storytelling, games, and arts and crafts to dinner with counselors, pajama parties, and treasure hunts.

Group Port Play is available in the children's area to accommodate parents booked on shore excursions. Evening babysitting services are available for a fee. Parents whose children are not toilet trained are issued a beeper to alert them when diaper changing is necessary. Children under two cruise at a reduced fare, and certain itineraries offer specials on third and fourth guests

Top: Casino play
Middle: Stay connected to the Internet
Bottom: *Norwegian Dream* superior Ocean View stateroom

CHOOSE THIS LINE IF . . .

Doing your own thing is your idea of a real vacation. You could almost remove your watch and just go with the flow.

You want to leave your formal dress-up wardrobe at home.

You're competitive. There's always a pickup game in progress on the sports courts.

in the same stateroom. Infants under six months of age cannot travel on NCL ships.

For teens ages 13 to 17, options include sports, pool parties, teen disco, movies, and video games. Some ships have their own cool clubs where teens hang out in adult-free zones.

Service

Somewhat inconsistent, service is nonetheless congenial. Although crew members tended to be outgoing Caribbean islanders in the past; they have largely been replaced by Asians and Eastern Europeans who are well trained yet are inclined to be more reserved.

Tipping

A fixed service charge of $12 per person per day is added to shipboard accounts. An automatic 15% gratuity is added to bar tabs. Staff members may also accept cash gratuities. Passengers in suites who have access to concierge and butler services are asked to offer a cash gratuity at their own discretion.

Past Passengers

Upon completion of your first NCL cruise you're automatically enrolled in Latitudes, the club for repeat passengers. Membership benefits accrue based on the number of cruises completed: Bronze (1 through 4), Silver (5 through 8), Gold (9 through 13), and Platinum (14 or more). Everyone receives *Latitudes*, NCL's quarterly magazine, Latitudes pricing, Latitudes check-in at the pier, a ship pin, access to a special customer service desk and liaison on board, and a members-only cocktail party hosted by the captain. Higher tiers receive a welcome basket, an invitation to the captain's cocktail party, and dinner in Le Bistro, and priority for check-in, tender tickets, and disembarkation.

GOOD TO KNOW

When considering an NCL cruise, keep in mind that the ships weren't cut from a cookie-cutter mold and they differ widely in size and detail. Although all are brightly appointed and attempt to offer a comparable experience, the older ships just don't have the panache or as many Freestyle dining venues found on the newer, purpose-built ships. On the plus side, the newest vessels have many options for families, including large numbers of interconnecting staterooms that make them ideal for even supersize clans. NCL has one of the newest fleets at sea, following the introduction of two large, new vessels and retirement of some older, smaller ships.

1

NORWEGIAN CRUISE LINE

DON'T CHOOSE THIS LINE IF . . .

You don't like to pay extra for food on a ship. All the best specialty restaurants have extra charges.

You don't want to stand in line. There are lines for nearly everything.

You don't want to hear announcements. They're frequent on these ships—and loud.

JEWEL CLASS
Norwegian Pearl

CREW MEMBERS	
1,124	
ENTERED SERVICE	
2006	
700 ft. **GROSS TONS**	
93,530	
LENGTH	
965 feet	
500 ft. **NUMBER OF CABINS**	
1,197	
PASSENGER CAPACITY	
2,394	
300 ft. **WIDTH**	
105 feet	

Public Areas and Facilities

Jewel-class ships are the next step in the continuing evolution of Freestyle ship design: the interior location of some public rooms and restaurants has been tweaked since the introduction of Freestyle cruising vessels, and new categories of deluxe accommodations have been added.

These ships have more than a dozen dining alternatives, a variety of entertainment options, enormous spas with thermal suites (for which there is a charge), and expansive areas reserved for children and teens. Pools have waterslides and a plethora of lounge chairs, although when your ship is full it can be difficult to find one in a prime location. *Norwegian Pearl* (along with *Norwegian Gem*) introduced the line's first rock-climbing walls as well as Bliss Lounge, which has trendy South Beach decor and the first full-size 10-pin bowling alleys on modern cruise ships.

Restaurants

Two main complimentary dining rooms serve open seating breakfast, lunch, and dinner. Specialty restaurants, including NCL's signature French restaurant Le Bistro, Cagney's Steakhouse, an Asian restaurant, sushi bar, teppanyaki room, tapas and salsa eatery, and an Italian trattoria–style restaurant carry varying cover charges and require reservations. Screens located throughout the ship illustrate the status (full, moderately busy, empty) and waiting time you can expect for each restaurant on board. Casual choices are the Lido Buffet for breakfast, lunch, and dinner; Blue Lagoon for soup, sandwiches, and snacks around the clock; and the poolside grill for lunch. Java Café serves specialty coffees and pastries for an additional charge. While the 24-hour room service menu is somewhat limited, suite occupants may order from any restaurant on the ship.

Accommodations

Cabins: NCL ships are not noted for large staterooms, but all have a small sitting area with sofa, chair, and table. Every cabin has adequate closet and drawer/shelf storage, as well as limited bathroom storage. Suites have walk-in closets.

Garden and Courtyard Villas: Garden Villas, with three bedrooms, a living-dining room, and private deck

Top: *Norwegian Jewel's* Azura restaurant
Bottom: Hydropool in the spa

garden with a spa tub, are among the largest suites at sea. Courtyard Villas—not as large as Garden Villas—nevertheless have an exclusive concierge lounge and a shared private courtyard with pool, hot tub, sundeck, and small gym.

Amenities: A small refrigerator, tea/coffeemaker, personal safe, broadband Internet connection, duvets on beds, a wall-mounted hair dryer, and bathrobes are standard. Bathrooms have a shampoo/bath-gel dispenser on the shower wall and a magnifying mirror. Suites have a whirlpool tub, an entertainment center with a CD/DVD player, and concierge and butler service.

Worth Noting: Some staterooms interconnect in most categories. Twenty-seven staterooms are wheelchair-accessible.

In the Know

You may feel you've slipped into wonderland when you first encounter some of the fanciful furniture in the lounges aboard each ship and in Bliss Ultra Lounge on *Norwegian Pearl* (and *Norwegian Gem*). Some are covered in wildly colorful velvets and are designed as thrones and even lounging beds.

Pros and Cons

Pros: Performances by Second City, Chicago's famous improvisation artists, are scheduled in the theater as well as in more intimate nightclub settings. Escape the crowds in the ship's tranquil library, which is also a good spot to gaze at the sea if your book proves to be less than compelling. With access to a private courtyard pool, hot tub, steam room, exercise area, and sundeck, Courtyard Villa accommodations are like a ship within a ship.

Cons: The thermal suites in the spa have large whirlpools, saunas, steam rooms, and a relaxation area with loungers facing the sea, but there is an additional charge to use the facility. "Freestyle" dining doesn't mean you can get a table in the main dining rooms at precisely the moment you want, but waiting times can be reduced if you time your arrival at nonpeak periods. For such a large ship, the Internet center is tiny.

Cabin Type	Size (sq. ft.)
Garden Villa	4,390
Courtyard Villa	574
Owner's Suites	823
Deluxe Owners Suites	928
Penthouse Suite	575
Minisuite	284
Ocean View with Balcony	205–243
Ocean View	161
Inside	143

FAST FACTS

- 15 passenger decks
- 7 restaurants, 2 dining rooms, buffet, ice cream parlor, pizzeria
- Internet, Wi-Fi, safe, refrigerator, DVD (some)
- 2 pools, children's pool
- Fitness classes, gym, hair salon, 6 hot tubs, spa, steam room
- 9 bars, casino, cinema, dance club, library, showroom, video game room
- Children's programs (ages 2–17)
- Dry cleaning, laundry facilities, laundry service
- Internet terminal

The sports deck

DAWN CLASS
Norwegian Star

CREW MEMBERS	1,095
ENTERED SERVICE	2001
GROSS TONS	91,740
LENGTH	935 feet
NUMBER OF CABINS	1,120
PASSENGER CAPACITY	2,240
WIDTH	105 feet

700 ft.
500 ft.
300 ft.

Public Areas and Facilities

Purpose-built for NCL's Freestyle cruising concept, Dawn class ships each have more than a dozen dining options, a variety of entertainment selections, expansive facilities for children and teens, and enormous spas with indoor lap pools. In what might be termed a supersize "thermal suite" on other ships, the spa areas feature indoor lap pools surrounded by lounge chairs, large whirlpools, saunas, and steam rooms, and—best of all—there's no additional charge to use any of it, unlike on other NCL ships.

Dawn class ships unveiled NCL's superdeluxe Garden Villa accommodations, English pubs, and 24-hour dining in the Blue Lagoon Restaurant. Interior spaces are bright and cheerful, especially the atrium area adjacent to the outdoor promenade, which is flooded with sunlight through expansive windows. A second smaller garden atrium with a prominent waterfall leads the way to the spa lobby. Located near the children's splash pool is a hot tub for parents' enjoyment.

Restaurants

Two complimentary dining rooms serve open seating meals for breakfast, lunch, or dinner. Specialty restaurants, including NCL's signature French restaurant Le Bistro, Cagney's Steakhouse, an Asian restaurant, sushi bar, teppanyaki room, Tex-Mex eatery, and Italian restaurant carry varying cover charges and require reservations. Screens located throughout the ship illustrate the status (full, moderately busy, empty) and waiting time you can expect for each restaurant on board. Casual choices are the Lido Buffet for breakfast, lunch, and dinner; Blue Lagoon for soup, sandwiches, and snacks around the clock; and the poolside grill for lunch. Java Café serves specialty coffees and pastries for an extra charge. While the 24-hour room service menu is somewhat limited, suite occupants may order from any restaurant on the ship.

Accommodations

Cabins: NCL ships are not noted for large staterooms, but all have a small sitting area with sofa, chair, and table. Most bathrooms are compartmentalized with a sink area, shower, and toilet separated by sliding glass doors. Every cabin has adequate closet and drawer/

Top: Cagney's Steakhouse on *Norwegian Dawn*
Bottom: Minisuite

shelf storage, as well as limited bathroom storage. Suites have walk-in closets.

Amenities: Cherrywood cabinetry, tropical decor, mirrored accents, a small refrigerator, tea/coffeemaker, personal safe, broadband Internet connection, duvets on beds, a wall-mounted hair dryer over the dressing table, and bathrobes for use during the cruise are standard. Bathrooms have a shampoo/bath-gel dispenser mounted on the shower wall as well as a magnifying mirror. Suites have a whirlpool tub, an entertainment center with a CD/DVD player, and concierge and butler service.

Worth Noting: Family-friendly staterooms interconnect in most categories, enabling families of nearly any size to find suitable accommodations. Nearly every stateroom has a third or fourth berth, and some can sleep as many as five and six. Twenty staterooms on *Norwegian Star* are designed for wheelchair accessibility.

In the Know

The *Norwegian Star* was built without a casino because it was originally going to sail Hawaiian itineraries, and gambling isn't allowed in that state's waters. The nightclub has since been seamlessly retrofitted into the spacious Star Club Casino.

Pros and Cons

Pros: Reminiscent of European opera houses, the showrooms are grand settings for the lavish production shows and have full proscenium stages. Other ships might have comedy shows, but on these you can look forward to performances by Second City, Chicago's incomparable improvisation artists, with shows in the theater as well as in more intimate nightclub settings. Three-bedroom Garden Villas are among the largest suites at sea, with private whirlpools and outdoor patios for alfresco dining.

Cons: Freestyle dining doesn't mean you can get a table in the main dining rooms at precisely the moment you want, but waiting time can be lessened by timing your arrival at nonpeak periods. Don't stop to smell the banks of flowers in the lobby—they are unabashedly fake, Overcrowding can be a problem in the buffet, popular bars, and around the Lido pools when the ships are booked to their maximum capacity.

Cabin Type	Size (sq. ft.)
Garden Villa	5,350
Owner's Suite	750
Penthouse Suite	366
Romance Suite	288
Minisuite	229
Ocean View with Balcony	166
Ocean View	158
Inside	142

FAST FACTS

■ 11 passenger decks

■ 7 restaurants, 2 dining rooms, buffet, ice cream parlor, pizzeria

■ Internet, Wi-Fi, safe, refrigerator, DVD (some)

■ 2 pools (1 indoor), children's pool

■ Fitness classes, gym, hair salon, 6 hot tubs, sauna, spa, steam room

■ 9 bars, casino, cinema, 2 dance clubs, library, showroom, video game room

■ Children's programs (ages 2–17)

■ Dry cleaning, laundry service

■ Internet terminal

Norwegian Dawn at sea

NORWEGIAN SUN

CREW MEMBERS	946
ENTERED SERVICE	2001
GROSS TONS	78,309
LENGTH	853 feet
NUMBER OF CABINS	968
PASSENGER CAPACITY	1,936
WIDTH	105 feet

700 ft.

500 ft.

300 ft.

Public Areas and Facilities

Norwegian Cruise Line hadn't introduced many new ships in awhile at the time *Norwegian Sun* was on the drawing board, but it didn't take long before they got the hang of it. With Freestyle cruising growing in popularity, the vessel moved into the forefront of the fleet with multiple restaurant choices, expansive casino, trendy spa, and more family- and kid-friendly facilities.

Rich wood tones and fabric colors prevail throughout. The Observation Lounge is a subdued spot for afternoon tea in a light, tropical setting with nothing to distract attention from the expansive views beyond the floor-to-ceiling windows.

The Internet café is large, and the nearby coffee bar is a delight. Sunshine pours into the atrium through an overhead skylight by day, while at night it's the ship's glamorous hub of activity.

Restaurants

Two complimentary dining rooms serve open seating breakfast, lunch, and dinner. Specialty restaurants that carry varying cover charges and require reservations include NCL's signature French restaurant Le Bistro, steak houses, and Italian eateries; Norwegian Sun also has an extra-charge Japanese restaurant, sushi bar, and teppanyaki room, and complimentary tapas bar. Screens located throughout the ship illustrate the status (full to empty) and waiting time you can expect for each restaurant. Casual choices are the Lido Buffet for breakfast, lunch, and dinner; the poolside grill for lunch; a pizzeria; and an ice cream bar. A coffee bar serves specialty coffees and pastries priced by item. Room service is available 24 hours from a somewhat limited menu.

Accommodations

Cabins: Staterooms are a bit more generous in size than on the older vessels in the NCL fleet and contain adequate closet and drawer space for a one-week cruise. More than two-thirds have an ocean view, and nearly two-thirds of those have a private balcony. All have a sitting area with sofa, chair, and table. Clever use of primary colors and strategically placed mirrors achieves an open feeling.

Top: Las Ramblas Tapas Bar & Restaurant
Bottom: *Norwegian Sun* at sea

Suites: Suites have walk-in closets as well as whirlpool tubs and entertainment centers. Butlers and a concierge are at the service of suite occupants.

Amenities: Light-wood cabinetry, mirrored accents, a small refrigerator, a tea/coffeemaker, a personal safe, broadband Internet connections, duvets on beds, a wall-mounted hair dryer over the dressing table, and bathrobes for use during the cruise are typical standard amenities. Bathrooms have shampoo and bath gel in shower-mounted dispensers, as well as limited storage.

Worth Noting: Connecting staterooms are available in several categories, including those with balconies. Oddly sandwiched in between decks 6 and 7 forward is deck 6A, which has no direct elevator access. Sixteen cabins are wheelchair accessible.

In the Know

For newlyweds and couples celebrating a second honeymoon, an elegant honeymoon/anniversary romance suite is a luxurious hideaway for two.

Pros and Cons

Pros: While not the newest ship in the NCL fleet, *Norwegian Sun* has been renovated to add many of the elements found in Dawn- and Jewel-class vessels. For live broadcasts of sporting events and meals and snacks from the nearby buffet, head to the Sports Bar. *Norwegian Sun* has steam rooms and saunas for men and women.

Cons: Plot your course carefully if you plan to dine in the aft main restaurant—a huge galley separates it from the midship restaurant, and you can't get there on a direct route from the atrium. These are sister ships but not twins, and dining facilities vary widely. Standard accommodations are somewhat tight for more than two people on these ships, as is storage space.

Cabin Type	Size (sq. ft.)
Owner's Suite	828
Penthouse and Romance Suite	504
Minisuite	332
Ocean View Balcony	221
Ocean View	145
Deluxe Interior	172
Interior	145

FAST FACTS

- 11 passenger decks
- 4 specialty restaurants, 2 dining rooms, buffet, ice cream parlor, pizzeria
- Wi-Fi, safe, refrigerator (some), DVD (some)
- 2 pools , children's pool
- Fitness classes, gym, hair salon, 5 hot tubs, spa, sauna and steam room
- 8 bars, casino, dance club, library, showroom, video game room
- Children's programs (ages 2–17)
- Dry cleaning, laundry service
- Internet terminal

Balcony stateroom

PRINCESS CRUISES

Princess Cruises may be best known for introducing cruise travel to millions of viewers, when its flagship became the setting for *The Love Boat* television series in 1977. Since that heady time of small-screen stardom, the Princess fleet has grown both in the num-

Splash around in the family pool

ber and size of ships. Although most are large in scale, Princess vessels manage to create the illusion of intimacy through the use of color and decor in understated yet lovely public rooms graced by multimillion-dollar art collections.

✉ *24305 Town Center Dr., Santa Clarita, CA* ☎ *661/753–0000 or 800/774–6237* ⊕ *www.princess.com*
☞ *Cruise Style: Premium.*

Princess has also become more flexible; Personal Choice Cruising offers alternatives for open seating dining (when you wish and with whom you please) and entertainment options as diverse as those found in resorts ashore.

The roster of adult activities still includes standbys like bingo and art auctions, but also enrichment programs featuring guest lecturers, cooking classes, wine-tasting seminars, pottery workshops, and computer and digital photography classes. Nighttime production shows tend toward Broadway-style revues presented in the main show lounge, and performers might include comedians, magicians, jugglers, and acrobats. Live bands play a wide range of musical styles for dancing and listening, and each ship has a disco.

On Pub Night the cruise director's staff leads a rollicking evening of fun with passenger participation. At the conclusion of the second formal night, champagne trickles down over a champagne waterfall, painstakingly created by the arrangement of champagne glasses in a pyramid shape. Ladies are invited to join the maître d' to assist in the pouring for a great photo op.

Lovely chapels or the wide-open decks are equally romantic settings for weddings at sea. However, the captain can officiate only on some Princess ships.

Food

Personal choices regarding where and what to eat abound, but because of the number of passengers, unless you opt for traditional assigned seating, you might have to wait for a table in one of the open seating dining rooms. Menus are varied and extensive in the main dining rooms, and the results are good to excellent considering how much work is going on in the galleys. Vegetarian and healthy lifestyle options are always on the menu, as well as steak, fish, or chicken. A special menu is designed especially for children.

Alternative restaurants are a staple throughout the fleet but vary by ship class. Grand-class ships have upscale steak houses and Sabatini's, an Italian restaurant; both require reservations and carry an extra cover charge. Sun-class ships offer complimentary sit-down dining in the pizzeria and a similar steak-house option, although it's in a sectioned-off area of the buffet restaurant. On *Caribbean, Crown, Emerald, and Ruby Princess,* a casual evening alternative to the dining rooms and usual buffet is Café Caribe—adjacent to the Lido buffet restaurant, it serves cuisine with a Caribbean flair. With a few breaks in service, Lido buffets on all ships are almost always open, and a pizzeria and grill offer casual daytime snack choices. The fleet's patisseries and ice cream bars charge for specialty coffee, some pastries, and premium ice cream. A daily British-style pub lunch served in the ships' Wheelhouse Bar is being introduced fleetwide.

Ultimate Balcony Dining—either a champagne breakfast or full-course dinner—is a full-service meal served on your cabin's balcony. The Chef's Table allows guests (for a fee) to dine on a special menu with wine pairings. After a meeting with the executive chef in the galley (and some champagne and appetizers), guests sit at a special table in the dining room. The chef joins them for dessert.

Fitness and Recreation

Spa rituals include a variety of massages, body wraps, and facials; numerous hair and nail services are offered in the salons. Both the salons and spa are operated by Steiner Leisure, and the menu of spa services includes special pampering treatments designed specifically for men and teens as well as couples. For a half-day fee, escape to The Sanctuary, which offers a relaxing

Top: Place a bet in the casino
Bottom: Disco into the night

Top: Sunset at sea
Middle: Morning stretch
Bottom: Freshwater Jacuzzi

outdoor spa-inspired setting with signature beverages, light meals, massages, attentive service, and relaxing personal entertainment. All ships will feature this adults-only haven by 2010.

Modern exercise equipment, a jogging track, and basic fitness classes are available at no charge. There's a fee for personal training, body composition analysis, and specialized classes such as yoga and Pilates. Grand-class ships have a resistance pool so you can get your laps in effortlessly.

Your Shipmates

Princess Cruises attract mostly American passengers, ranging from their mid-30s to mid-50s. Families enjoy cruising together on the Princess fleet, particularly during holiday seasons and summer months, when many children are on board. Longer cruises appeal to well-traveled retirees and couples who have the time.

Dress Code

Two formal nights are standard on seven-night cruises; an additional formal night may be scheduled on longer sailings. Men are encouraged to wear tuxedos, but dark suits are appropriate. All other evenings are casual, although jeans are discouraged, and it's requested that no shorts be worn in public areas after 6 PM.

Junior Cruisers

For young passengers ages 3 to 17, each Princess vessel (except *Ocean, Royal,* and *Pacific Princess*) has a playroom, teen center, and programs of supervised activities designed for different age groups: ages 3 to 7, 8 to 12, and 13 to 17. Activities to engage youngsters include arts and crafts, pool games, scavenger hunts, deck parties, backstage and galley tours, games, and videos. Events such as dance parties in their own disco, theme parties, athletic contests, karaoke, pizza parties, and movie fests occupy teenage passengers. With a nod toward science and educational entertainment, children also participate in learning programs focused on the environment and wildlife in areas where the ships sail.

CHOOSE THIS LINE IF . . .

You're a traveler with a disability. Princess ships are some of the most accessible at sea.

You like to gamble but hate a smoke-filled casino. Princess casinos are well ventilated and spacious.

You want a balcony. Princess ships feature them in abundance at affordable rates.

To allow parents independent time ashore, youth centers operate as usual during port days, including lunch with counselors. For an additional charge, group babysitting is available nightly from 10 PM until 1 AM. Family-friendly conveniences include self-service laundry facilities and two-way family radios that are available for rent at the Purser's Desk. Infants under six months are not permitted; private in-cabin babysitting is not available on any Princess vessel. Children under age three are welcome in the playrooms if supervised by a parent.

Service

Professional service by an international staff is efficient and friendly. It's not uncommon to be greeted in passageways by smiling stewards who know your name.

Tipping

A gratuity of $10.50 per person per day ($11 for passengers in suites and minisuites) is added to shipboard accounts for distribution to stewards and waitstaff. Passengers may adjust the amount based on the level of service experienced. An automatic 15% is added to all bar tabs for bartenders and drink servers; gratuities to other staff members may be extended at passengers' discretion.

Past Passengers

Membership in the Captain's Circle is automatic following your first Princess cruise. All members receive a free subscription to *Captain's Circle News,* a quarterly newsletter, as well as discounts on selected cruises.

Perks are determined by the number of cruises completed: Gold (2 through 5), Platinum (6 through 15), and Elite (16 and above). While Gold members receive only the magazine, an invitation to an onboard event, and the services of the Circle Host on the ship, benefits really begin to accrue once you've completed five cruises. Platinum members receive upgraded insurance (when purchasing the standard policy), expedited check-in, a debarkation lounge to wait in on the ship, and, best of all, limited free Internet access during the cruise. Elite benefits are even more lavish, with many complimentary services.

GOOD TO KNOW

Some people like the time-honored tradition of assigned seating for dinner, so they can get to know their table companions and their servers; others prefer to choose with whom they dine as well as when. Princess lets you have things your way or both ways. If you're unsure whether Personal Choice is for you, select Traditional dining when you reserve your cruise. You can easily make the switch to anytime dining once on board; however, it can be impossible to change from Personal Choice to Traditional.

DON'T CHOOSE THIS LINE IF . . .

You have a poor sense of direction. Most ships, especially the Grand-class ships, are very large.

You want to meet *The Love Boat* cast. That was just a TV show, and it was more than three decades ago.

You're too impatient to stand in line or wait. Debarkation from the large ships can be lengthy.

CORAL CLASS
Coral Princess, Island Princess

CREW MEMBERS	900
ENTERED SERVICE	2003, 2003
GROSS TONS	92,000
LENGTH	964
NUMBER OF CABINS	987
PASSENGER CAPACITY	1,970
WIDTH	106 feet

700 ft.

500 ft.

300 ft.

Public Areas and Facilities

Princess includes *Coral Princess* and *Island Princess* in their Sun-class category; however, they are larger ships (albeit with a similar capacity to *Sun Princess* and her two sisters), which means much more space per passenger; we feel this necessitates a separate category. All the Personal Choice features attributed to the larger Grand-class ships were incorporated into this design as well as a few unique additions, such as a demonstration kitchen and ceramics lab complete with kiln where ScholarShip@Sea programs are presented. The four-story atrium is similar to that on Sun-class ships, but public rooms are mainly spread fore and aft on two lower decks.

While signature rooms such as the Wheelhouse Bar are more traditional, the casinos have subtle London- or Paris-like atmospheres with themed slot machines; Crooner's Bar is a retro 1960s Vegas-style martini and piano bar. In addition to the stately Princess Theater showroom, the Universe Lounge has three stages for shows and flexible seating on two levels, making it a multipurpose space.

Restaurants

Passengers may choose between traditional dinner seating times in one assigned dining room or open seating in the other formal dining room; breakfast and lunch are open seating. Alternative dinner options include reservations-only Sabatini's Italian trattoria and Bayou Café & Steakhouse (both with an extra charge). With a few breaks in service, Lido buffets on all ships are almost always open. A pub lunch is served in the Wheelhouse Bar, and a pizzeria and grill offer casual daytime snack choices. The patisseries and ice cream bars charge for specialty coffee, some pastries, and premium ice cream. Ultimate Balcony Dining and Chef's Table options are available, as is afternoon tea, and 24-hour room service.

Accommodations

Cabins: Stepped out in wedding-cake fashion, over 83% of ocean-view staterooms include Princess Cruises' trademark private balconies. Even the least expensive inside categories have plentiful storage and a small sitting area with a chair and table. Suites have two TVs,

Top: Fast-paced shows
Bottom: Aqua biking

a sitting area, a wet bar, a large walk-in closet, and a separate bathtub and shower. Minisuites have a separate sitting area, two televisions, a walk-in closet, and a combination bathtub/shower.

Suites: Occupants of 16 suites receive complimentary Internet access, dry cleaning, and shoe polishing, afternoon tea and evening canapés delivered to their suites, and priority embarkation, disembarkation, and tendering privileges. An extended room service menu is also available for them, as are priority reservations for dining and shore excursions.

Amenities: Decorated in pastels and light-wood tones, typical staterooms have a personal safe, hair dryer, refrigerator, and bathrobes for use during the cruise. Bathrooms have shampoo, lotion, and bath gel.

Worth Noting: Twenty staterooms are designed for wheelchair accessibility and range in size from 217 to 374 square feet, depending upon category.

In the Know

Most midship ocean-view cabins on Emerald Deck are designated as obstructed view, and even some balcony staterooms on Emerald and Dolphin decks are considered partially obstructed. And when balconies are arranged in a stepped-out design, the lower ones aren't totally private.

Pros and Cons

Pros: As many as 20 courses in the ScholarShip@Sea Program are offered on each cruise, and you can select from ceramics, cooking fundamentals, computer, and photography classes or attend lectures on a wide range of topics. Cabins that sleep third and fourth passengers are numerous, and the best bet for families are interconnecting balcony staterooms adjacent to facilities dedicated to children and teens on Aloha Deck. The Fine Art Gallery is a dedicated spot for art-auction stock, meaning that displays don't clutter the passageways and distract from the art pieces selected to complement the decor.

Cons: Oddly, the library and card room are situated so they are often used as passageways, which results in a bit more noise than usual in areas that should be quiet. There are only 16 suites on each ship, and none are aft-facing with a view of the wake; engine pods on the funnel give the ships a futuristic space-age appearance of jet speed but function mainly as decoration—they can easily make 24 knots, but they don't fly.

Cabin Type	Size (sq. ft.)
Suite	470
Minisuite	285–302
Ocean-view Balcony	217–232
Ocean-view Stand	162
Deluxe	212
Inside	156–166

All dimensions include the square footage for balconies.

FAST FACTS

- 11 passenger decks
- 2 specialty restaurants, 2 dining rooms, buffet, ice cream parlor, pizzeria
- Wi-Fi, safe, refrigerator, DVD (some)
- 3 pools (1 indoor), children's pool
- Fitness classes, gym, hair salon, 5 hot tubs, sauna, spa
- 7 bars, casino, 2 dance clubs, library, 2 showrooms, video game room
- Children's programs (ages 3–17)
- Dry cleaning, laundry facilities, laundry service
- Internet terminal
- No kids under 6 months

Lavish buffets in Horizon Court

GRAND CLASS
Golden Princess

CREW MEMBERS	1,100
ENTERED SERVICE	2001
GROSS TONS	109,000
LENGTH	951 feet
NUMBER OF CABINS	1,300
PASSENGER CAPACITY	2,600
WIDTH	118 feet

700 ft.

500 ft.

300 ft.

Top: *Star Princess* at sea
Bottom: *Golden Princess*
grand plaza atrium

Public Areas and Facilities

When *Grand Princess* (the first Grand Class ship) was introduced as the world's largest cruise ship in 1998, she also boasted one of the most distinctive profiles. Not only did the Skywalker's Disco appear futuristic, hovering approximately 150 feet above the waterline, but Grand-class vessels also advanced the idea of floating resort to an entirely new level with more than 700 staterooms that included private balconies.

Like their predecessors, the interiors of Grand-class ships feature soothing pastel tones with splashy glamour in the sweeping staircases and marble-floor atriums. Surprisingly intimate for such large ships, human scale in public lounges is achieved by judicious placement of furniture as unobtrusive room dividers.

The 300-square-foot Times Square–style LED screens that hover over the pools show up to seven movies or events daily.

Restaurants

Passengers may choose between two traditional dinner seating times in an assigned dining room or open seating in the ships' other two formal dining rooms; breakfast and lunch are open seating. Alternative dinner options include the reservations-only Italian and steak-house restaurants (both with an extra charge). With a few breaks in service, Lido buffets on all ships are open around the clock. A pub lunch is served in the Wheelhouse Bar, and a pizzeria and grill offer casual daytime snack choices. The patisseries and ice cream bars charge for specialty coffee, some pastries, and premium ice cream. Ships have been outfitted with a wine bar that serves extra-charge evening snacks and artisan cheeses. Ultimate Balcony Dining and Chef's Table options are available, as is afternoon tea and 24-hour room service.

Accommodations

Cabins: On these ships, 80% of the outside staterooms have balconies. The typical stateroom has a sitting area with a chair and table; even the cheapest categories have ample storage. Minisuites have a separate sitting area, a walk-in closet, a combination shower-tub, and a balcony, as well as two TVs. Grand Suites have a separate sitting room and dining room, as well as a walk-in closet. Owner's, Penthouse, Premium, and Vista suites have a separate sitting room with a sofa bed and desk, as well as a walk-in closet.

Amenities: Decorated in attractive pastel hues, all cabins have a refrigerator, hair dryer, personal safe, and bathrobes to use during the cruise. Bathrooms have shampoo, lotion, and bath gel.

Worth Noting: Two family suites are interconnecting staterooms with a balcony that can sleep up to eight people (D105/D101 and D106/D102). Staterooms in a variety of categories will accommodate three and four people, and some adjacent cabins can be interconnected through interior doors or by unlocking doors in the balcony dividers. Twenty-eight staterooms are wheelchair accessible.

In the Know

Port and starboard balconies are stepped out from the ships' hulls in wedding-cake fashion. That means, depending on location, yours will likely be exposed a bit—or a lot—to passengers on higher decks. Exceptions are balconies on Emerald Deck, which are covered.

Pros and Cons

Pros: Skywalker's Disco has comfy semiprivate alcoves facing port and starboard and is virtually deserted during the day, when it's the ideal spot to read or just watch the sea. The convenient self-service passenger laundry rooms have ironing stations to touch up garments wrinkled from packing, and you can wash and dry a load of dirty clothing for only a few dollars. The Wheelhouse Bar, with soft lighting, comfortable leather chairs, shining brass accents, ship paintings, and nautical memorabilia, has become a Princess tradition for pre- and postdinner cocktails and dancing.

Cons: Sports bars get jam-packed and lively when important games are televised, but that also means they can become stuffy and close. Staterooms and suites located aft and above the Vista lounge can be noisy when bands crank up the volume.

Cabin Type	Size (sq. ft.)
Grand Suite	1,314
Other Suites	468–591
Family Suite	607
Minisuite	323
Ocean View Balcony	232–274
Standard	168
Inside	160

All dimensions include the square footage for balconies.

FAST FACTS

- 14 passenger decks
- 2 specialty restaurants, 3 dining rooms, buffet, ice cream parlor, pizzeria
- Wi-Fi, safe, refrigerator
- 4 pools (1 indoor), children's pool
- Fitness classes, gym, hair salon, 9 hot tubs, sauna, spa, steam room
- 9 bars, casino, outdoor cinema, 2 dance clubs, library, 2 showrooms, video game room
- Children's programs (ages 3–17)
- Dry cleaning, laundry facilities, laundry service
- Internet terminal
- No kids under 6 months

Grand-class balcony stateroom

DIAMOND PRINCESS, SAPPHIRE PRINCESS

CREW MEMBERS	1,100
ENTERED SERVICE	2004, 2004
GROSS TONS	116,000
LENGTH	952 feet
NUMBER OF CABINS	1,337
PASSENGER CAPACITY	2,670
WIDTH	123 feet

700 ft.

500 ft.

300 ft.

Public Areas and Facilities

Launched in the same year, these sister ships include all the features traditionally enjoyed on Princess's Grand-class vessels, but with a twist. They're larger than their Grand-class fleetmates, yet carry fewer passengers relative to their size. As a result, they have sleeker profiles, a higher ratio of space per person, and feel much roomier.

Inside, the arrangement of public rooms is a bit different, with the signature Wheelhouse Bar moved forward of its position on Grand-class ships and, in its place, an expanded Internet Café, where beverages and snacks are served. An Asian-themed full-service spa offers a relaxing thermal suite, for a fee. All the elements of a Princess ship are included, particularly the small-ship atmosphere and sparkling, yet understated, interior decoration.

Restaurants

In addition to a dining room with two traditional assigned dinner seatings, these ships have four additional dining rooms for open-seating Personal Choice cruisers. Each is smaller than those on other large Princess ships, but all offer the same menus with a few additional selections that reflect the "theme" of each dining room. Alternative dining options are the two specialty restaurants, Sabatini's and Sterling Steakhouse, which have a surcharge and require reservations. The pizzeria, grill, patisserie, and ice-cream bar offer casual daytime dining and snack options. The Lido buffet and complimentary room service are available 24 hours. Ultimate Balcony Dining is offered to passengers with balcony accommodations.

Accommodations

Layout: More than 70% of accommodations feature an ocean view, and of those 78% include private balconies. Even the least expensive inside categories have ample storage and a small sitting area with chair and table. Cabins that sleep third and fourth passengers are numerous. The best for families are Family Suites on Dolphin Deck, which sleep up to six in two self-contained staterooms that connect through a living room.

Top: *Sapphire Princess* at sea
Bottom: *Diamond Princess*
Grand Plaza

Amenities: Typical stateroom features are personal safes, refrigerators, hair dryers, and bathrobes for use during the cruise. Bathroom toiletries include shampoo, lotion, and bath gel.

Suites: Suites have two televisions, a sitting area, dining area, wet bar, large walk-in closet, and separate whirlpool bathtub and shower. Minisuites have a separate sitting area, two televisions, walk-in closet, and a combination bathtub–shower.

Worth Noting: Twenty-seven staterooms are designed for wheelchair accessibility.

In the Know

Princess's trademark Skywalkers disco/lounge concept moved a step ahead on these ships with a 125-foot-wide balcony that provides commanding views over the aft end of the ship, where passengers can enjoy stargazing or a view of the wake.

Pros and Cons

Pros: With fewer passengers on board than other ships of the same size, these Princess ships feel very spacious; the swim-against-the-current pool is ideal for getting in your laps at sea; linked with Club Fusion by a spiral staircase, the tiny Wake View Bar is a romantic spot for a nightcap.

Cons: The four intimate open-seating dining rooms are smaller than on other large Princess ships and can fill up fast, so keep an alternate to your first choice in mind; there is a charge for specialty coffee drinks and premium ice cream; to walk all around the ship on Promenade Deck you'll have to negotiate a flight of stairs.

Cabin Type	Size (sq. ft.)
Suites	535–1,329
Family Suites/ Minisuites	522–354
Oceanview with Balcony	237–277
Deluxe Oceanview	197–200
Oceanview	183–194
Inside	168–182
Wheelchair Accessible	249–412

All dimensions include the square footage for balconies.

FAST FACTS

- 13 passenger decks
- 2 specialty restaurants, 5 dining rooms, buffet, ice-cream parlor, pizzeria
- Wi-Fi, in-cabin safes, in-cabin refrigerators
- 5 pools
- Fitness classes, gym, hair salon, 8 hot tubs, sauna, spa, steam room
- 11 bars, casino, 2 dance clubs, library, 2 showrooms, video game room
- Children's programs (ages 3–17)
- Dry cleaning, laundry facilities, laundry service
- Computer room
- No kids under 6 months

Grand Casino on the *Diamond Princess*

ROYAL PRINCESS

CREW MEMBERS	373
ENTERED SERVICE	2001
GROSS TONS	30,277
LENGTH	592 feet
NUMBER OF CABINS	355
PASSENGER CAPACITY	710
WIDTH	84 feet

700 ft.

500 ft.

300 ft.

Public Areas and Facilities

At 30,277 tons, *Royal Princess* appears positively tiny beside her megaship fleetmates. In reality, she is a medium-size ship that entered service for the now-defunct Renaissance Cruises. With her entry into the Princess line-up, real choice is available to Princess passengers—a true alternative for passengers who prefer the clubby atmosphere of a smaller "boutique"-style ship, yet one that has big-ship features galore.

Royal Princess has cozy public spaces, a stunning observation lounge—where the view is visible through floor-to-ceiling windows on three sides— and the loveliest libraries at sea, with their domed trompe l'oeil–painted ceilings, faux fireplaces, comfortable seating areas, and (most importantly) well-stocked bookshelves. Although the main showroom isn't particularly suited for glitzy production-company performances, it is ideal for cabaret shows.

Restaurants

The only disappointment is the lack of a Personal Choice dining room; while breakfast and lunch are served open seating in the main dining room, the only dinner option available is in one of two assigned seatings. Sabatini's Italian Trattoria and Sterling Steakhouse specialty restaurants are reservations-required and extra-charge dinner alternatives. With a few breaks in service, Lido buffets are almost always open. A pizzeria window in the buffet area and a separate poolside grill serve casual lunches and snacks. Ultimate Balcony Dining is available, as are afternoon tea and 24-hour room service.

Accommodations

Layout: Designed for longer cruises, all staterooms have ample closet and storage space, although bathrooms in lower-priced categories are somewhat tight. Dark-wood cabinetry adds warmth to the decor. In keeping with the rest of the fleet, 73% of all outside cabins and suites have a balcony, and interiors are similar in size to those you'll find on other Princess ships.

Top: relaxing in the library
Bottom: owner's suite

Amenities: Amenities in standard cabins are a bit spartan compared to other Princess ships, yet all have at least a small sitting area. Bath toiletries, a hair dryer, a personal safe, and robes for use during the cruise are all included, but you must move up to a suite to have a real bathtub.

Suites: Full suites are particularly nice, with living/dining rooms, entertainment centers, separate bedrooms, whirlpool bathtubs, a guest powder room, and large balconies overlooking the bow or stern.

Worth Noting: Three staterooms are wheelchair accessible.

In the Know

The view from forward-facing suites is stupendous, but if you are a late sleeper you might want to check the itinerary for the number of ports where the ship will anchor instead of docking. A wake-up call is unnecessary when the anchor is lowered.

Pros and Cons

Pros: Decks 6 and 7 each have two aft-facing standard balcony cabins sandwiched between suites that have terrific views of the wake, and the balconies are larger than other similar cabins; cozy antique-style chairs are located near the faux fireplace in the Casino Bar, where the piano drowns out the clanging of slot machines; this ship offers many of Princess Cruises' trademark big-ship features, despite the fact it is smaller and was built to another cruise line's specifications.

Cons: Showrooms are all on one level with a low ceiling that precludes the presentation of spectacular production shows, which are a staple on larger ships; there are no dedicated children's facilities, but when the numbers warrant it, counselors conduct a limited kid's program in a variety of public rooms; Personal Choice dining is limited, and the solitary main dining room offers only assigned seating for dinner.

Cabin Type	Size (sq. ft.)
Suites	786–962
Ocean-View Balcony	216
Ocean View	165
Inside	158

All dimensions include the square footage for balconies.

FAST FACTS

- 9 passenger decks
- 2 specialty restaurants, dining room, buffet, pizzeria
- Wi-Fi, in-cabin safes, some in-cabin minibars, some in-cabin refrigerators, some in-cabin DVDs
- 1 pool
- Fitness classes, gym, hair salon, 3 hot tubs, spa, steam room
- 8 bars, casino, dance club, library, showroom
- Children's programs (ages 3–17)
- Dry cleaning, laundry facilities, laundry service
- Computer room
- No kids under 6 months

Atrium, *Royal Princess*

REGENT SEVEN SEAS

The December 1994 merger of Radisson Diamond Cruises and Seven Seas Cruise Line launched Radisson Seven Seas Cruises with an eclectic fleet of vessels that offered a nearly all-inclusive cruise experience in sumptuous, contemporary surroundings. The

The end of a perfect day

line was rebranded as Regent Seven Seas Cruises in 2006, and ownership passed to Prestige Cruise Holdings (which also owns Oceania Cruises) in 2008.

✉ *1000 Corporate Dr., Suite 500, Fort Lauderdale, FL* ☎ *954/776–6123 or 877/505–5370* ⊕ *www.rssc.com*
☞ *Cruise Style: Luxury.*

Even more inclusive than in the past, the line has maintained its traditional tried-and-true formula—delightful ships offering exquisite service, generous staterooms with abundant amenities, a variety of dining options, and superior lecture and enrichment programs. Guests are greeted with champagne upon boarding and find an all-inclusive beverage policy that offers not only soft drinks and bottled water, but also cocktails and select wines at all bars and restaurants throughout the ships.

The cruises are destination focused, and most sailings host guest lecturers—historians, anthropologists, naturalists, and diplomats. Spotlight cruises center around popular pastimes and themes, such as food and wine, photography, history, archaeology, literature, performing arts, design and cultures, active exploration and wellness, antiques, jewelry and shopping, the environment, and marine life. Passengers need no urging to participate in discussions and workshops led by celebrated experts. All passengers have access to these unique experiences on board and on shore.

Activities and entertainment are tailored for each of the line's distinctive ships with the tastes of sophisticated passengers in mind. Don't expect napkin-folding demonstrations or nonstop action. Production revues, cabaret acts, concert-style piano performances, solo performers, and comedians may be featured in show lounges, with combos playing for listening and dancing in lounges and bars throughout the ships. Casinos are more akin to Monaco than Las Vegas. All ships display tasteful and varied art collections, including pieces that are for sale.

Food

Menus may appear to include the usual beef Wellington and Maine lobster, but in the hands of Regent Seven Seas chefs, the results are some of the most outstanding meals at sea. Specialty dining varies within the fleet, but the newest ships, *Seven Seas Voyager* and *Seven Seas Mariner,* have the edge with the sophisticated Signatures, featuring the cuisine of Le Cordon Bleu of Paris, and Prime 7, a contemporary adaptation of the classic American steak house offering a fresh, distinctive decor and an innovative menu of the finest prime-aged steak and chops, along with fresh seafood and poultry specialties. In addition, Mediterranean-influenced bistro dinners that need no reservations are served in La Veranda, the venue that is the daytime casual Lido buffet restaurant.

Evening alternative dining in *Seven Seas Navigator*'s Portofino focuses on food and wines from four major regions of Italy and requires reservations.

Held in a tranquil setting, Wine Connoisseurs Dinners are offered occasionally on longer cruises to bring together people with an interest in wine and food. Each course on the degustation menu is complemented by a wine pairing. The cost varies according to the special vintage wines that are included.

Room service menus are fairly extensive, and you can also order directly from the restaurant menus during regular serving hours.

Although special dietary requirements should be relayed to the cruise line before sailing, general considerations such as vegetarian, low-salt, or low-cholesterol food requests can be satisfied on board the ships simply by speaking with the dining room staff. Wines chosen to complement dinner menus are freely poured each evening.

Fitness and Recreation

Although gyms and exercise areas are well equipped, these are not large ships, so the facilities tend to be on

Top: Sunrise jog
Bottom: *Seven Seas Navigator*

the small size. Each ship has a jogging track, and the larger ones feature a variety of sports courts.

Exclusive to Regent Seven Seas, the spa and salon are operated by high-end Carita of Paris. The extensive range of beauty treatments offered follow the Carita approach of tailoring services to the unique needs of the individual

Your Shipmates

Regent Seven Seas Cruises are inviting to active, affluent, well-traveled couples ranging from their late-30s to retirees who enjoy the ships' chic ambience and destination-rich itineraries. Longer cruises attract veteran passengers in the over-60 age group.

Dress Code

Formal attire is required on designated evenings. Men are encouraged to wear tuxedos, and many do so; dark suits are acceptable. Cruises of 7 to 10 nights usually have one or two formal nights; longer cruises may have three. Other evenings are informal or resort casual; the number of each is based on the number of sea days. It's requested that dress codes be observed in public areas after 6 PM.

Junior Cruisers

Regent Seven Seas' vessels are adult-oriented and do not have dedicated children's facilities. However, a Club Mariner youth program for children ages 5 to 8, 9 to 12, and 13 to 17 is offered on selected sailings, both during summer months and during school holiday periods. Supervised by counselors, the organized, educational activities focus on nature and the heritage of destinations the ship will visit. Activities, including games, craft projects, movies, and food fun, are organized to ensure that every child has a memorable experience. Teens are encouraged to help counselors select the activities they prefer.

Service

The efforts of a polished, unobtrusive staff go almost unnoticed, yet special requests are handled with ease. Butlers provide an additional layer of personal service to guests in the top-category suites.

Top: Fitness center
Middle: Pool decks are never crowded
Bottom: Pampering in the Carita of Paris spa

CHOOSE THIS LINE IF. . . .

You want to learn the secrets of cooking like a Cordon Bleu chef (for a charge, of course).

You want to stay connected. Regent Seven Seas Internet packages are reasonably priced by the hour.

A really high-end spa experience is on your agenda.

Tipping

Gratuities are included in the fare, and none are expected. To show their appreciation, passengers may elect to make a contribution to a crew welfare fund that benefits the ship's staff.

Past Passengers

Membership in the Seven Seas Society is automatic upon completion of a Regent Seven Seas cruise. Members receive 5% to 10% cruise fare savings on select sailings, exclusive shipboard and shoreside special events on select sailings, a Seven Seas Society recognition cocktail party on every sailing, and *Inspirations* newsletter highlighting special events, sailings, and destination- and travel-related information. The tiered program offers rewards based on the number of nights you have sailed with RSSC. The more you sail, the more you accrue. Bronze benefits are offered to members with 4 to 20 nights. From 21 through 74 nights, Silver members also receive complimentary Internet access on board, free pressing, and an hour of free phone time. From 75 through 199 nights, Gold members are awarded priority disembarkation at some ports, another hour of complimentary phone time, more complimentary pressing, an exclusive Gold & Platinum activity aboard or ashore on every sailing, and priority reservations at restaurants and spas. From 200 through 399, Platinum members can add complimentary air deviation services (one time per sailing), six hours of complimentary phone use, and unlimited free pressing and laundry services; Titanium members who have sailed 400 or more nights get free dry cleaning and free transfers.

GOOD TO KNOW

So why did former owners Carlson Hospitality change the name from Radisson to Regent Seven Seas back in 2006? It probably seemed logical at the time to give their new cruise line a recognizable name—Radisson. However, the name wasn't recognizable for the right reasons. Radisson Seven Seas Cruises aspired to be recognized as upscale cruise line (which it was), while the Radisson hotel chain is decidedly middle-of-the-road. The hotel name turned off some potential passengers, who didn't perceive the cruise line as being luxurious or exclusive. It just so happened that Carlson Hospitality's small, but growing, Regent chain of hotels is more in tune with today's definition of luxury and a better fit to co-brand with a top-of-the-line cruising experience. *Voilà!* A "fleet christening" accomplished the renaming and, best of all, the cruise line's initials didn't change and neither did its Web site address.

DON'T CHOOSE THIS LINE IF...

Connecting cabins are a must. Very few are available, and only the priciest cabins connect.

You can't imagine a Caribbean cruise without the hoopla of pool games and steel bands.

You think dressing up for dinner is too much trouble. Most passengers look forward to the ritual.

SEVEN SEAS NAVIGATOR

CREW MEMBERS	340
ENTERED SERVICE	1999
GROSS TONS	33,000
LENGTH	560 feet
NUMBER OF CABINS	245
PASSENGER CAPACITY	490
WIDTH	81 feet

700 ft.

500 ft.

300 ft.

Public Areas and Facilities

The first ship outfitted uniquely to Regent Seven Seas' specifications, the *Seven Seas Navigator* is a particular favorite of returning passengers for its small-ship intimacy, big-ship features, and comfortable, well-designed accommodations.

The generous use of wood and the addition of deep-tone accents to the predominantly blue color palette give even the larger lounges an inviting feel. Artwork and elaborate flower arrangements add a bit of sparkle and interest to the somewhat angular modern decor.

Due to the aft location of the two-deck-high main showroom, the only lounges that afford sweeping seascapes are Galileo's—typically the most popular public space—and the Vista Lounge. Although views from the Vista Lounge are spectacular, there's no permanent bar, and it's primarily a quiet spot for reading when there are no lectures or activities scheduled there.

Restaurants

Compass Rose restaurant, the main dining room, functions on an open seating basis for breakfast, lunch, and dinner, so there are no set dining assignments. Portofino Grill, the daytime buffet, serves breakfast and lunch and is converted to a reservations-only evening trattoria serving regional Italian specialties. Wines are chosen to complement each luncheon and dinner menu. At least once during each cruise, dinner is served alfresco on the pool deck. In addition to the buffet, a choice for casual lunch and snacks is the poolside grill. Afternoon tea is served daily, and room service is available 24 hours a day. Dinner can be ordered from the main dining room menu during restaurant hours and served en suite, course by course.

Accommodations

Cabins: Attractive textured fabrics and honeyed wood finishes add a touch of coziness to the larger-than-usual suites in all categories, 90% of which have balconies. All have a vanity-desk, walk-in closet, and sitting area with a sofa, chairs, and table. Marble bathrooms have a separate tub and shower. Master Suites have a separate sitting/dining room, a separate bedroom, and a powder room; only Grand Suites also have a powder room. Master Suites have a second TV in the bedroom,

Top: Casino
Bottom: *Navigator* suite

butler service, and whirlpool tub in the master bathroom. Grand and Navigator suites are similarly outfitted. The top three suite categories feature Bose music systems. Penthouse Suites, which include butler service, are only distinguished from Deluxe Suites by location and do not have a whirlpool bathtub.

Amenities: Every suite has an entertainment center with CD/DVD player, stocked refrigerator, stocked bar, personal safe, hair dryer, and beds dressed with fine linens and duvets. Bath toiletries include shampoo, lotion, and bath gel.

Worth Noting: Very few suites have the capacity to accommodate three people, and only 10 far-forward suites adjoin with those adjacent to them. Four suites are wheelchair accessible.

In the Know

From Russia, With Love: Regent Seven Seas took over an unfinished hull that was originally destined to be a Soviet spy ship and redesigned it to create the *Seven Seas Navigator*. They did such a good job completing the interiors that even James Bond would feel at home.

Pros and Cons

Pros: The library contains hundreds of novels, best sellers, and travel books, as well as newspapers, movies for in-suite viewing, and even a selection of board games. Fellow passengers might be as wealthy as Midas, but most are unpretentious. When nothing on the menu appeals to you, don't hesitate to ask for what you'd really like to have for dinner.

Cons: Internet use can be heavy on sea days, and the lines that form in the computer area can add a bit of congestion—and inevitable noise—to the adjacent library, a space that should be a quiet haven. If you book a suite in the far-aft section of the ship, be prepared for an annoying vibration. Unless you prebook a table in Portofino online before your cruise, you could be disappointed to find it unavailable once you board.

Cabin Type	Size (sq. ft.)
Master Suite	1,067
Grand Suite	539
Navigator Suite	448
Penthouse/Balcony Suite	301
Window Suite	301*

*Except for Suite 600, which measures 516

FAST FACTS

- 8 passenger decks
- Specialty restaurant, dining room, buffet
- Wi-Fi, safe, refrigerator, DVD
- Pool
- Fitness classes, gym, hair salon, hot tub, sauna, spa, steam room
- 4 bars, casino, dance club, showroom
- Children's programs (ages 5–17)
- Dry cleaning, laundry facilities, laundry service
- Internet terminal
- No-smoking cabins

Casual poolside dining

ROYAL CARIBBEAN

Big, bigger, biggest! More than a decade ago, Royal Caribbean launched Sovereign-class ships, the first of the modern megacruise liners, which continue to be an all-around favorite of passengers who enjoy traditional cruising ambience with a touch of daring

Adventure of the Seas solarium

and whimsy tossed in. Plunging into the 21st century, each ship in the current fleet carries more passengers than the entire Royal Caribbean fleet of the 1970s and has features—such as new surfing pools—that were unheard of in the past.

✉ *1050 Royal Caribbean Way, Miami, FL* ☎ *305/539–6000 or 800/327–6700* ⊕ *www. royalcaribbean.com*

☞ *Cruise Style: Mainstream.*

All Royal Caribbean ships are topped by the company's distinctive signature Viking Crown Lounge, a place to watch the seascape by day and dance away at night. Expansive multideck atriums and the generous use of brass and floor-to-ceiling glass windows give each vessel a sense of spaciousness and style. The action is nonstop in casinos and dance clubs after dark, while daytime hours are filled with poolside games and traditional cruise activities. Port talks tend to lean heavily on shopping recommendations and the sale of shore excursions.

A variety of lounges and high-energy stage shows draws passengers of all ages out to mingle and dance the night away. Production extravaganzas showcase singers and dancers in lavish costumes. Comedians, acrobats, magicians, jugglers, and solo entertainers fill show lounges on nights when the ships' companies aren't performing. Professional ice shows are a highlight of cruises on Voyager-, Freedom-, and Oasis-class ships—the only ships at sea with ice-skating rinks.

Food

Dining is an international experience with nightly changing themes and cuisines from around the world.

Passenger preference for casual attire and a resort-like atmosphere has prompted the cruise line to add laid-back alternatives to the formal dining rooms in the Windjammer Café and, on certain ships, Johnny Rockets Diner; Seaview Café evokes the ambience of an island beachside stand. Royal Caribbean offers you the choice of early or late dinner seating and is introducing an open seating program fleet-wide.

Room service is available 24 hours, but for orders between midnight and 5 AM there is a $3.95 service charge. There's a limited menu.

Royal Caribbean doesn't place emphasis on celebrity chefs or specialty alternative restaurants, although they have introduced a more upscale and intimate dinner experience in the form of an Italian specialty restaurant and/or a steak house on all but the Vision-class ships.

Fitness and Recreation

Royal Caribbean has pioneered such new and previously unheard of features as rock-climbing walls, ice-skating rinks, bungee trampolines, and even the first self-leveling pool tables on a cruise ship. Interactive water parks, boxing rings, surfing simulators, and cantilevered whirlpools suspended 112 feet above the ocean made their debuts on the Freedom-class ships.

Facilities vary by ship class, but all Royal Caribbean ships have state-of-the-art exercise equipment, jogging tracks, and rock-climbing walls; passengers can work out independently or in classes guaranteed to sweat off extra calories. Most exercise classes are included in the fare, but there's a fee for specialized spin, yoga, and Pilates classes, as well as the services of a personal trainer. Spas and salons are top-notch, with full menus of day spa–style treatments and services for pampering and relaxation for adults and teens.

Your Shipmates

Royal Caribbean cruises have a broad appeal for active couples and singles, mostly in their 30s to 50s. Families are partial to the newer vessels that have larger staterooms, huge facilities for children and teens, and seemingly endless choices of activities and dining options.

Dress Code

Two formal nights are standard on seven-night cruises; one formal night is the norm on shorter sailings. Men are encouraged to wear tuxedos, but dark suits or sport coats and ties are more prevalent. All other evenings are casual, although jeans are discouraged in restaurants. It's requested that no shorts be worn in public

NOTEWORTHY

■ Each ship's Schooner Bar features nautically inspired decor right down to a unique scent.

■ The signature Viking Crown Lounge found on every RCI ship was originally inspired by the Seattle World's Fair Space Needle.

■ Hot tubs and certain swimming pools are designated for adults only on Royal Caribbean ships.

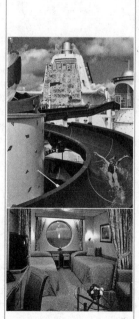

Top: Adventure Beach for kids
Bottom: Voyager-class interior stateroom

Top: Miniature golf
Middle: *Adventure of the Seas*
Bottom: *Serenade of the Seas*
rock-climbing wall

areas after 6 PM, although there are passengers who can't wait to change into them after dinner.

Junior Cruisers

Supervised age-appropriate activities are designed for children ages 3 through 17; babysitting services are available as well (either group or in-stateroom babysitting, but sitters will not change diapers). Children are assigned to the Adventure Ocean youth program by age. They must be at least three years old and toilet trained to participate (children who are in diapers and pull-ups or who are not toilet trained are not allowed in swimming pools or whirlpools). Youngsters who wish to join a different age group must participate in one daytime and one night activity session with their proper age group first; the manager will then make the decision based on their maturity level.

In partnership with toy maker Fisher-Price, Royal Caribbean offers interactive 45-minute Aqua Babies and Aqua Tots play sessions for children ages 6 months to 36 months. The playgroup classes, which are hosted by youth staff members, were designed by early childhood development experts for parents and their babies and toddlers, and teach life skills through playtime activities.

A teen center with a disco is an adult-free gathering spot that will satisfy even the pickiest teenagers.

Service

Service on Royal Caribbean ships is friendly but inconsistent. Assigned meal seatings assure that most passengers get to know the waiters and their assistants, who in turn get to know the passengers' likes and dislikes; however, that can lead to a level of familiarity that is uncomfortable to some people. Some ships have a concierge lounge for the use of suite occupants and top-level past passengers.

Tipping

Tips can be prepaid when the cruise is booked, added on to shipboard accounts, or given in cash on the last night of the cruise. Suggested gratuities per passenger per day are $3.50 for the cabin steward ($5.75 for

---

CHOOSE THIS LINE IF . . .

You want to see the sea from atop a rock wall—it's one of the few activities on these ships that's free.

You're active and adventurous. Even if your traveling companion isn't, there's an energetic staff on board to cheer you on.

You want your space. There's plenty of room to roam; quiet nooks and crannies are there if you look.

suites), $3.50 for the waiter, $2 for the assistant waiter, and $0.75 for the headwaiter. An 15% gratuity is automatically added to all bar tabs.

Past Passengers

After one cruise, you can enroll in the Crown & Anchor Society. All members receive the *Crown & Anchor* magazine and have access to the member section on the Royal Caribbean Web site. All members receive an Ultimate Value Booklet and an invitation to a welcome-back party. Platinum members (after five cruises) also have the use of a private departure lounge and receive priority check-in (where available), the onboard use of robes during the cruise, an invitation to an exclusive onboard event, and complimentary custom air arrangements.

Diamond members (after 10 cruises) also receive consideration on a priority wait list for sold-out shore excursions and spa services, concierge service on select ships, priority departure from the ship, complimentary custom air fee, and special rates on balcony and suite accommodations. When members achieve Diamond Plus status (after 24 cruises), they're offered behind-the-scenes tours and preferred seating in main dining rooms.

Royal Caribbean ships are truly resorts afloat with an emphasis on recreation and family enjoyment. You could spend a week on board the huge Oasis-class, Voyager-class, and Freedom-class ships and never leave. You would also be hard-pressed to try to do everything at hand, so it's important to pace yourself by setting priorities and budgeting your time. A good idea is to try new things that you may not be able to do at home—climb a rock wall and learn to snorkel, for example.

If you're a Crown & Anchor member, your status level is the same whenever you sail on Royal Caribbean's sister cruise line, Celebrity Cruises.

DON'T CHOOSE THIS LINE IF . . .

Patience is not one of your virtues. Lines are not uncommon.

You want to do your own laundry. There are no self-service facilities on any Royal Caribbean ships.

You don't want to hear announcements, especially in your cabin. There are a lot on RCI cruises.

RADIANCE CLASS
Radiance of the Seas

CREW MEMBERS	857
ENTERED SERVICE	2001
GROSS TONS	90,090
LENGTH	962 feet
NUMBER OF CABINS	1,056
PASSENGER CAPACITY	2,112 (2,501 max)
WIDTH	106 feet

700 ft.

500 ft.

300 ft.

Public Areas and Facilities

Considered by many people to be the most beautiful vessels in the Royal Caribbean fleet, Radiance-class ships are large but sleek and swift, with sun-filled interiors and panoramic elevators that span 10 decks along the ships' exteriors.

High-energy and glamorous spaces are abundant throughout these sister ships. From the rock-climbing wall, children's pool with waterslide, and golf area to the columned dining room, sweeping staircases, and the tropical garden of the solarium, these ships hold appeal for a wide cross section of interests and tastes.

The ships are packed with multiple dining venues, including the casual Windjammer, with its indoor and outdoor seating, and the Latte-Tudes patisserie, offering specialty coffees, pastries, and ice cream treats.

Restaurants

The double-deck-high formal dining room serves open seating breakfast and lunch; dinner is served in two assigned seatings or open seating My Timing Dining. For a more upscale dinner, each ship has two specialty restaurants—Portofino, serving Italian fare, and Chops Grille, a steak house. Both charge a supplement and require reservations. The casual Lido buffet offers service nearly around the clock for breakfast, lunch, dinner, and snacks. Seaview Café is open for quick lunches and dinners in a laid-back setting. A pizzeria in the Solarium serves pizza by the slice. The coffee bar features specialty coffees and pastries, for which there is a charge. Room service is available 24 hours.

Accommodations

Cabins: With the line's highest percentage of outside cabins, standard staterooms are bright and cheery as well as roomy. Nearly three-quarters of the outside cabins have private balconies. Every cabin has adequate closet and drawer/shelf storage, as well as bathroom shelves.

Suites: All full suites and family suites have private balconies and include concierge service. Top-category suites have wet bars, separate living/dining areas, multiple bathrooms, entertainment centers with flat-screen TVs, DVD players, and stereos. Some bathrooms have twin sinks, steam showers, and whirlpool tubs. Junior

Top: pool deck
Bottom: Shared moments on your personal balcony

suites have a sitting area, vanity area, and bathroom with a tub.

Amenities: Light-wood cabinetry, a small refrigerator-minibar, broadband Internet connection, a vanity-desk, a TV, a personal safe, a hair dryer, and a sitting area with sofa, chair, and table are typical Radiance-class features in all categories. Bathroom extras include shampoo and bath gel.

Worth Noting: Fifteen staterooms are wheelchair accessible on Radiance and Brilliance; 19 on Serenade and Jewel.

In the Know

Other cruise ships may have rollicking sports bars (and these do as well), but only on the Radiance-class Royal Caribbean vessels will you find self-leveling pool tables.

Pros and Cons

Pros: Aft on deck 6, four distinct lounges and a billiard room with self-leveling pool tables form a clubby adult entertainment center furnished in rich colors and accented by warm woods. Not everyone discovers the out-of-the-way Seaview Café, making it a favored casual dining spot for those passengers who take the time to locate it. Spacious family ocean-view cabins sleep up to six people and can accommodate a roll-away bed and/or a crib; the suites also come with two twin beds (convertible into one queen size), additional bunk beds in a separate area, and a separate sitting area with a sofa bed.

Cons: With the traditional and nautical-leaning decor on these otherwise classy ships, the weird free-form atrium sculptures are a jarring throwback to earlier design elements. The location of the pizzeria in the Solarium adds a layer of confusion to an otherwise tranquil retreat. The libraries are tiny and poorly stocked for ships this size.

Cabin Type	Size (sq. ft.)
Royal Suite	1,001
Owner's Suite	512
Grand Suite	358–384
Royal Family Suite	533–586
Junior Suites	293
Superior Ocean View	204
Deluxe Ocean View	179
Large Ocean View	170
Family Ocean View	319
Interior	165

FAST FACTS

- 12 passenger decks
- 2 specialty restaurants, dining room, buffet, pizzeria
- Internet, Wi-Fi, safe, refrigerator, DVD (some)
- 2 pools (1 indoor), children's pool
- Fitness classes, gym, hair salon, 3 hot tubs, sauna, spa, steam room
- 11 bars, casino, cinema, dance club, library, showroom, video game room
- Children's programs (ages 3–17)
- Dry cleaning, laundry service
- Internet terminal
- No-smoking cabins

Sports courts

VISION CLASS
Rhapsody of the Seas

CREW MEMBERS	765
ENTERED SERVICE	1997
GROSS TONS	78,491
LENGTH	915 feet
NUMBER OF CABINS	1,000
PASSENGER CAPACITY	1,800–2,000 (2,076–2,435 max)
WIDTH	106 feet

700 ft.
500 ft.
300 ft.

Top: Vision-class Owner's Suite
Bottom: *Splendour of the Seas*

Public Areas and Facilities

The first Royal Caribbean ships to offer private balconies in a number of categories, these Vision-class vessels, named for sister ship *Vision of the Seas*, have acres of glass skylights that allow sunlight to flood in and windows that offer wide sea vistas. The soaring central atrium at the heart of each ship is anchored by champagne bars and fills with music after dark.

Built in pairs, the ships follow the same general layout but are different in overall size and the total number of passengers on board. Cabin sizes also vary somewhat; as the total size of the ships increased from *Legend* and *Splendour* at 69,130 tons (1,800 passengers) to *Grandeur* at 74,140 tons (1,950 passengers), and finally, *Rhapsody* and *Vision* at 78,491 tons (2,000 passengers), so did the size of the accommodations. In some categories, it's only a matter of a few feet, so don't look for huge—or even noticeable—differences.

Restaurants

As was the norm when these ships were built, dining selections on board are pretty basic. The double-deck-high formal dining room serves evening meals in two assigned evening seatings or open seating My Timing Dining, while breakfast and lunch in the dining room are always open seating. Windjammer, the casual Lido buffet, serves three meals a day, including a laid-back dinner. Evening meals in the formal dining room and buffet are often regionally themed and feature menus that focus on Italian, French, and American dishes. Room service is available 24 hours a day, and a poolside grill serves burgers and snacks in the solarium. A coffee bar offers specialty coffees and pastries for an additional fee. Sadly, there are no specialty restaurants on these ships.

Accommodations

Cabins: Cabins are airy and comfortable, but the smaller categories are a tight squeeze for more than two adults. Every cabin has adequate closet and drawer/shelf storage.

Suites: All full suites and family suites have private balconies and a small minibar; full suites also include concierge service. Royal Suites have a living room; wet bar; separate dining area; entertainment center with TV, stereo, and DVD player; separate bedroom; bathroom (twin sinks, whirlpool tub, separate steam shower, bidet); and separate powder room. Owner's Suites have a separate living area; minibar; entertainment center with TV, stereo, and DVD player; dinette area; and one bathroom (twin sinks, bathtub, separate shower, bidet). Grand Suites have similar amenities on a smaller scale.

Amenities: Light woods, pastel colors, a vanity-desk, a TV, a personal safe, a hair dryer, and a sitting area with sofa, chair, and table are typical Vision-class features in all categories. Bathrooms have shampoo and bath gel.

Worth Noting: On *Grandeur*, *Vision*, and *Rhapsody*, 14 cabins are wheelchair accessible.

In the Know

Not all suites on Vision-class ships are created equal. A Royal Family Suite is a roomy choice for parents with younger children, but goodies that other suites receive—including bathrobes to use on board, welcome-aboard champagne, evening canapés, and concierge service—aren't included.

Pros and Cons

Pros: Open, light-filled public areas offer sea views from almost every angle on these ships. Each vessel features a double-deck-high dining room with sweeping staircases that are a huge improvement over previous ship designs. Tucked into an atrium nook, the Champagne Bar on each ship is not only an elegant spot for predinner cocktails and dancing but also for quiet after-dinner or after-the-show drinks and conversation.

Cons: Some lounges, particularly the popular Schooner Bars, serve as a thoroughfare and suffer from continuous traffic flow before and after performances in the ships' main show lounges. Accommodations lean toward the small side, unless you are willing to pay a premium for a suite. There are no specialty restaurants, and dining options are severely limited as a result.

Cabin Type	Size (sq. ft.)
Royal Suite	1,074
Owner's Suite	523
Grand Suite	355
Royal Family Suite	512
Junior Suite	240
Family Ocean View	237
Superior Ocean View	193
Large Ocean View*	154
Interior	135–174

All cabin sizes are averages of the five ships since cabins vary somewhat in size among the Vision-class ships

FAST FACTS

■ 11 passenger decks

■ Dining room, buffet, ice cream parlor, pizzeria

■ Wi-Fi, safe, refrigerator (some), DVD (some)

■ 2 pools (1 indoor)

■ Fitness classes, gym, hair salon, 4–6 hot tubs, sauna, spa

■ 6 bars, casino, dance club, library, showroom, video game room

■ Children's programs (ages 3–17)

■ Dry cleaning, laundry service

■ Internet terminal

■ No-smoking cabins

Viking Crown lounge overlooks the pool deck

SILVERSEA CRUISES

Silversea Cruises was launched in 1994 by the former owners of Sitmar Cruises, the Lefebvre family of Rome, whose concept for the new cruise line was to build and sail the highest-quality luxury ships at sea. Intimate ships, paired with exclusive amenities and unparal-

The most captivating view on board

leled hospitality are the hallmarks of Silversea cruises. All-inclusive air-and-sea fares can be customized to include not just round-trip airfare but all transfers, porterage, and deluxe precruise accommodations as well.

✉ *110 E. Broward Blvd., Fort Lauderdale, FL* ☎ *954/522–4477 or 800/722–9955* ⊕ *www.silversea.com* ☞ *Cruise Style: Luxury.*

Personalization is a Silversea maxim. Their ships offer more activities than other comparably sized luxury vessels. Take part in those that interest you, or opt instead for a good book and any number of quiet spots to read or snooze in the shade. Silversea's third generation of ships will introduce even more luxurious features when the 36,000-ton Silver Spirit launches late in 2009.

Guest lecturers are featured on nearly every cruise; language, dance, and culinary lessons and excellent wine appreciation sessions are always on the schedule of events. Silversea also schedules culinary arts cruises and a series of wine-focused voyages that feature award-winning authors, international wine experts, winemakers, and acclaimed chefs from the world's top restaurants. During afternoon tea, ladies gather for conversation over needlepoint, and the ranks of highly competitive trivia teams increase every successive afternoon.

After dark, the Bar is a predinner gathering spot and the late-night place for dancing to a live band. A multitiered show lounge is the setting for talented singers and musicians, classical concerts, magic shows, big-screen movies, and folkloric entertainers from ashore. A small casino offers slot machines and gaming tables.

Food

Dishes from the galleys of Silversea's master chefs are complemented by those of La Collection du Monde, created by Silversea's culinary partner, the world-class chefs of Relais & Châteaux. Menus include hot and cold appetizers, at least four entrée selections, a vegetarian alternative, and Cruiselite cuisine (low in cholesterol, sodium, and fat). Special off-menu orders are prepared whenever possible, provided that the ingredients are available on board. In the event that they aren't, you may find after a day in port that a trip to the market was made in order to fulfill your request.

Chef Marco Betti, the owner of Antica Pasta restaurants in Florence, Italy, and Atlanta, Georgia, has designed a new menu for La Terrazza that focuses on one of the most luxurious food trends, the "slow food" movement. The goal of the movement is to preserve the gastronomic traditions of Italy through the use of fresh, traditional foods, and it has spread throughout the world. At La Terrazza (by day, a casual buffet) the menu showcases the finest in Italian cooking, from classic favorites to Tuscan fare. The restaurant carries no surcharge. Seating is limited, so reservations are a must to ensure a table—it's one reservation you'll be glad you took the time to book.

An intimate dining experience aboard each vessel is the Wine Restaurant by Relais & Châteaux—Le Champagne. Adding a dimension to dining, the exquisite cuisine is designed to celebrate the wines served—a different celebrated vintage is served with each course. Menus and wines are chosen by Relais & Chateaux sommeliers to reflect regions of the world noted for their rich wine heritage.

An evening poolside barbecue is a weekly dinner event, weather permitting. A highlight of every cruise is the Galley Brunch, when passengers are invited into the galley to select from a feast decorated with imaginative ice and vegetable sculptures. Even when meals are served buffet-style in La Terrazza, you will seldom have to carry your own plate as waiters are at hand to assist you to your table. Wines are chosen to complement each day's luncheon and dinner menus.

Grilled foods, sandwiches, and an array of fruits and salads are served daily for lunch at the poolside Grill. Always available are extensive selections from the room-service menu. The full restaurant menu may be

Top: Stylish entertainment
Bottom: Terrace Café alfresco dining

ordered from room service and can be served course by course in your suite during regular dining hours.

Fitness and Recreation

The rather small gyms are equipped with cardiovascular and weight-training equipment, and fitness classes on *Silver Whisper* and *Silver Shadow* are held in the mirror-lined, but somewhat confining, exercise room.

South Pacific–inspired Mandara Spa offers numerous treatments including exotic-sounding massages, facials, and body wraps. Hair and nail services are available in the busy salon. A plus is that appointments for spa and beauty salon treatments can be made online from 60 days until 48 hours prior to sailing.

Golfers can sign up with the pro on board for individual lessons utilizing a high-tech swing analyzer and attend complimentary golf clinics or participate in a putting contest.

Your Shipmates

Silversea Cruises appeal to sophisticated, affluent couples who enjoy the country-club-like atmosphere, exquisite cuisine, and polished service on board, not to mention the exotic ports and unique experiences ashore.

Dress Code

Two formal nights are standard on seven-night cruises and three to four nights, depending on the itinerary, on longer sailings. Men are required to wear tuxedos or dark suits after 6 PM. All other evenings are either informal, when a jacket is called for (a tie is optional, but most men wear them), or casual, when slacks with a jacket over an open-collar shirt for men and sporty dresses or skirts or pants with a sweater or blouse for women are suggested.

Junior Cruisers

Silversea Cruises is adult-oriented, does not accommodate children less than six months of age, and the cruise line limits the number of children under the age of three on board. The availability of suites for a third passenger is capacity controlled. A youth program staffed by counselors is available on holiday and select sailings. No dedicated children's facilities are available, so

Top: Table tennis
Middle: Caring personal service
Bottom: Veranda Suite

Your taste leans toward learning and exploration.

You enjoy socializing as well as the option of live entertainment, just not too much of it.

You like to plan ahead. You can reserve shore tours, salon services, and spa treatments online.

parents are responsible for the behavior and entertainment of their children.

Service
Personalized service is exacting and hospitable yet discreet. The staff strive for perfection and often achieve it. The attitude is decidedly European and begins with a welcome-aboard flute of champagne, then continues throughout as personal preferences are remembered and satisfied. The word *no* doesn't seem to be in the staff vocabulary in any language. Guests in all suites are pampered by butlers.

Tipping
Tipping is neither required nor expected.

Past Passengers
Membership in the Venetian Society is automatic upon completion of one Silversea cruise, and members begin accruing benefits: Venetian Society cruise days and eligibility for discounts on select voyages, onboard recognition and private parties, milestone rewards; exclusive gifts, the *Venetian Society Newsletter*, ship visitation privileges, complimentary early embarkation or late debarkation at certain milestones, members-only benefits at select Leading Hotels of the World and Relais & Châteaux hotels and resorts, and select offers through Silversea's preferred partners.

Through the Friends of Society programs, members can double their accumulated cruise days and receive a shipboard spending credit by inviting friends or family members to sail on select Venetian Society sailings. Friends or family will enjoy the same Venetian Society savings as members for those cruises, a really nice perk.

SILVER SHADOW

CREW MEMBERS	295
ENTERED SERVICE	2000
GROSS TONS	28,258
LENGTH	610 feet
NUMBER OF CABINS	191
PASSENGER CAPACITY	382
WIDTH	82 feet

700 ft.

500 ft.

300 ft.

Top: The casino
Bottom: *Silver Shadow* at sea

Public Areas and Facilities

The logical layout of this ship (and its sister ship, *Silver Whisper*), with suites located in the forward two-thirds of the ship and public rooms aft, makes orientation simple. The clean, modern decor that defines public areas and lounges might seem almost stark, but it places the main emphasis on large expanses of glass for sunshine and sea views as well as passenger comfort.

Silversea ships boast unbeatable libraries stocked with best sellers, travel books, classics, and movies for in-suite viewing. Extremely wide passageways in public areas are lined with glass-front display cabinets full of interesting and unusual artifacts from the places the ships visit.

The Humidor by Davidoff is a clubby cigar smoking room with overstuffed leather seating and a ventilation system that even nonsmokers can appreciate.

Restaurants

The Restaurant, formal yet simply named, offers open seating breakfast, lunch, and dinner during scheduled hours. Specialty dining is offered by reservation in Le Champagne, where an extra charge applies for the gourmet meal and wine pairings, and La Terrazza, which is complimentary and serves Italian cuisines. For casual meals, La Terrazza has indoor and outdoor seating for buffet-style breakfast and lunch. The outdoor Grill offers a laid-back lunch option with poolside table service. Elaborate afternoon tea is served daily. An evening poolside barbecue is a weekly dinner event as is the Galley Brunch, when passengers are invited into the galley to make their selections. Room service arrives with crystal, china, and a linen tablecloth for a complete dining room–style setup en suite. You may order at any time from the extensive room service menu or the full restaurant menu, which can be served course by course in your suite during regular dining hours.

Accommodations

Cabins: Every suite is outside with an ocean view, and more than 80% have a private teak-floor balcony. Standard suites have a sitting area that can be curtained off from the bed for more privacy. Marble bathrooms have double sinks and a separate glass-enclosed shower as well as a tub. All suites have generous walk-in closets.

Top Suites: In addition to much more space, top-category suites have all the standard amenities plus dining areas, separate bedrooms, and CD players. Silver Suites and above have whirlpool tubs. The top three categories have espresso makers and separate powder rooms.

Amenities: Standard suites have an entertainment center with a TV and DVD, personalized stationery, cocktail cabinet, personal safe, and refrigerator stocked with complimentary beer, soft drinks, and bottled water. A hair dryer is provided at a vanity table, and you can request a magnifying mirror. Beds are dressed with high-quality linens, duvets, or blankets, and your choice of synthetic or down pillows. Bathrooms have huge towels and terry bathrobes for use during the cruise as well as designer shampoo, soaps, and lotion.

Worth Noting: Two suites are designed for wheelchair accessibility. All suites are served by butlers.

In the Know

Nine Terrace Suites on deck 5 have doors to the outside that access a common, semiprivate veranda area. Even though the area is not furnished, it's like having a balcony without paying a higher fare.

Pros and Cons

Pros: Champagne on ice welcomes you to your suite and continues to flow freely throughout your cruise. Sailing on a Silversea ship is like spending time as a pampered guest at a home in the Hamptons where everything is at your fingertips, and if it isn't, all you have to do is ask. Silversea is so all-inclusive that you'll find your room key–charge card is seldom used for anything but opening your suite door.

Cons: Just about the only line you're likely to encounter on a Silversea ship is the one to use a washing machine in the smallish, yet totally free laundry rooms. In an odd contrast to the contents of display cases and lovely flower arrangements, artwork on the walls is fairly ho-hum and not at all memorable. Although small, the spa's complimentary saunas and steam rooms are adequate and seldom occupied.

Cabin Type	Size (sq. ft.)
Grand Suite	1,286–1,435
Royal Suite	1,312–1,352
Owner's Suite	1,208
Silver Suite	701
Medallion Suite	521
Verandah Suite	345
Terrace Suite	287
Vista Suite	287

FAST FACTS

- 7 passenger decks
- 2 specialty restaurants, dining room, buffet
- Wi-Fi, safe, refrigerator, DVD
- Pool
- Fitness classes, gym, hair salon, 2 hot tubs, sauna, spa, steam room
- 3 bars, casino, dance club, library, showroom
- Dry cleaning, laundry facilities, laundry service
- Internet terminal

The Poolside Grille serves lunch and light snacks

1

SILVERSEA CRUISES

AMERICAN SAFARI

"Luxury in pursuit of adventure" is the tagline for American Safari Cruises, the high-end yacht-cruise line, which operates some of the smallest vessels in Alaska. Founded in 1997 to provide up-scale, luxurious yacht cruising in Alaska's Inside Passage, American Safari Cruises' assets were acquired in February 2009 by Inner-Sea Discoveries LLC. The company continues to operate under the same well-established executive leadership and professional onboard crew, providing a seamless inclusive yacht cruise adventure. All shore excursions and activities are included in the price.

🖂 *American Safari Cruises, 3826 18th Ave. W, Seattle, WA 98119* 📞*206/284–0300 or 888/862–8881* ⊕*www.amsafari.com.*

With just 12 to 21 passengers and such decadent amenities as ocean-view hot tubs, American Safari's yachts are among the most comfortable small ships cruising Alaska. Shallow drafts mean these little ships and their landing craft can reach hidden inlets and remote beaches and slip in for close-up looks at glaciers and wildlife. Itineraries are usually flexible; there's no rush to move on if the group spots a pod of whales or a family of bears. All sailing is in daylight, with nights spent at anchor in secluded coves, and the yachts stop daily to let you kayak, hike, or beachcomb. An onboard naturalist offers informal lectures and guides you on expeditions ashore. Guests on all ships have access to the bridge, so you can sip coffee and chat with the captain during the day. All three ships carry binoculars, exercise equipment, kayaks, mountain bikes, Zodiac landing crafts, and insulated suits for Zodiac excursions. There's even fishing gear, but you'll have to purchase a license to fish.

Unlike most other yachts, which have to be chartered, American Safari's vessels sail on a regular schedule and sell tickets to individuals. There's no need to charter the entire ship, although that is an option many people choose for family reunions and other group events.

Food
Chefs serve a choice of nicely presented dinner entrées, featuring fresh local ingredients and plenty of seafood. All cruises are offered as all-inclusive, so premium wines and liquors are available at every meal, and guests are welcome to help themselves to the well-provisioned bar as well as snack options set up between meals.

Fitness and Recreation
Exercise equipment and hot tubs are featured on board. Kayaks are available for a more adventurous workout.

Your Shipmates
Typical passengers tend to be discerning and well-to-do couples from mid-40s to retirees. Children are welcome, but there are no facilities designed for them.

Dress Code
Dress is always comfortably casual, and tends to be more upscale casual than jeans and a flannel shirt in the evening.

Service
Crew members tend to passenger needs discreetly, yet in a personal way—they know your name and preferences, and will even go ashore to find a particular beverage if it isn't stocked on board.

Tipping
Tips are discretionary, but a hefty 5% to 10% of the fare is suggested. A lump sum is pooled among the crew at the end of the cruise.

Choose This Line If . . .
You are curious about new places and appreciate roads less traveled.

You want to come so close to pristine waterfalls that you feel the invigorating spray.

Your plans include chartering an entire yacht for a group of friends or family to travel together.

Don't Choose This Line If . . .
You have to ask the price; these are very expensive cruises.

You can't take care of yourself and make your own good times without a rigid schedule of activities.

You have a high-maintenance wardrobe; there is an iron, but no laundry service onboard.

NOTEWORTHY

■ Umbrellas, rain slickers and pants, and mud boots are provided for your use.

■ Ports of call are close enough that ships usually anchor overnight.

■ When ships spend two full days sailing in Glacier Bay, you will not merely cruise past the scenery, but stop to go ashore or kayak with an expedition leader or park ranger.

Top: the bar on *Safari Quest*
Bottom: kayaking, *Safari Explorer*

SAFARI SPIRIT, SAFARI QUEST, SAFARI EXPLORER

CREW MEMBERS	6, 9, 16
ENTERED SERVICE	1999, 1998, 2008
GROSS TONS	231, 345, 698
LENGTH	105, 120, 145 feet
NUMBER OF CABINS	6, 11, 18
PASSENGER CAPACITY	12, 22, 36
WIDTH	25, 28, 36 feet

700 ft.

500 ft.

300 ft.

Public Areas and Facilities

Safari Spirit is one of Alaska's most luxurious yachts. A forward-facing library with a 180-degree view, covered outside deck space, an on-deck hot tub, and even a sauna–steam bath are part of the pampering.

Safari Quest has warm wood trim throughout and plenty of outer deck space for spotting wildlife and taking in the passing scenery. A lounge on the top deck is a pleasant hideaway from which to enjoy the views in a relaxing setting.

American Safari's largest vessel, *Safari Explorer*, offers comfort amid casually elegant appointments. The library and cozy salons for dining and socializing are nicely balanced, with a large open viewing deck highlighted by a hot tub and nearby sauna.

Restaurants

Each ship has a dining room spacious enough to seat all passengers at once. An early-risers Continental breakfast is followed by a full breakfast, lunch, pre-dinner appetizers, and a single-seating dinner where meals are served family-style. After dinner you can retire to the Salon for cordials and chocolate truffles. Coffee, tea, and hot chocolate are available day and night, although there is no room service.

Accommodations

Layout: *Safari Spirit*'s bright, cheerful cabins—all with plush bedding, televisions and DVDs, Jacuzzi bathtubs, separate showers, and heated bathroom floors—are among the roomiest in the American Safari fleet. Three have king-size beds, and two of those feature small balconies. The other three staterooms have queen- or twin-size beds.

The four higher-end Admiral Staterooms on *Safari Quest* have sliding glass doors leading to a small balcony. Five rooms have elevated portlights rather than picture windows. One stateroom is reserved for single travelers, but also has a Pullman upper; the rest have king or queen beds. All feature televisions and DVD players; bathrooms have showers only.

Staterooms on *Safari Explorer,* the newest entry in American Safari's yachting fleet, all feature a television with DVD player, and most open directly to an outside deck. Two Admiral Staterooms have private balconies

Top: Admiral Stateroom, *Safari Spirit*
Bottom: *Safari Quest* at sea

and bathrooms with whirlpool tubs and showers. Bedding configurations range from fixed king-size to twins that can be joined to form a single larger bed. Two suites and two staterooms offer triple accommodations, and there is even one stateroom with a twin bed and Pullman upper that is available for single occupancy—a rarity afloat these days.

Amenities: Accommodations on all ships feature hair dryers, terry bathrobe for use on board, slippers, and alarm clocks. Shampoo, conditioner, soap, and lotion are provided.

Worth Noting: None of American Safari's ships have wheelchair-accessible accommodations.

In the Know

With the onboard naturalist as "teacher," American Safari's Kids in Nature program is offered during popular summer vacation time in Alaska's Inside Passage for children age 12 and under.

Pros and Cons

Pros: A large flat-screen TV/DVD in each ship's salon is equipped with a Hydrophone and underwater camera; in addition to fiction and non-fiction titles, educational materials highlighting destination information are available in the libraries; with the casual ambience on board and so much included—even insect repellant—you can pack light.

Cons: None of American Safari's ships has an elevator, making them a poor choice for mobility-impaired passengers; while there is exercise equipment on board, there is no fitness center or spa facility; there is no Internet access onboard, and cell-phone service is only available when the ships are near shore and within range of a cell tower.

Cabin Type	Size (sq. ft.)
Safari Spirit Staterooms	172–266
Safari Quest Staterooms	125–168
Safari Explorer Staterooms	124–263
Safari Explorer Suites	255–275

Note: American Safari literature includes specific square footage for each stateroom and suite.

FAST FACTS

- 4/4/3 passenger decks
- Dining room
- In-cabin DVD
- 1 hot tub, sauna (*Safari Spirit* and *Safari Explore*r only)
- 1 bar, library
- No-smoking cabins

Wine Library on *Safari Explorer*

CRUISE WEST

A big player in small ships, Seattle-based Cruise West is family-owned, which is reflected in the ships' homey atmosphere. After returning to Alaska from flying in World War II, founder Chuck West went to work as a bush pilot and dreamt of sharing Alaska's

unspoiled frontier with the rest of the world. After launching and subsequently selling a tour company, he and his family founded West Travel, now known as Cruise West. Initially the company operated sightseeing tours, then expanded into cruises in the mid-1980s.

🛥 *Cruise West, 2301 5th Ave., Suite 401, Seattle, WA 98121* ☎ *206/441–8687 or 888/851–8133* 🌐 *www. cruisewest.com.*

Alaskan wilderness, wildlife, and culture take precedence over shipboard diversions on Cruise West ships. Ports of call include small fishing villages and native settlements as well as major towns. An exploration leader, who is both a naturalist and cruise coordinator, offers evening lectures and joins passengers on many of the shore activities—at least one of which is included at each port of call. At some stops local guides come on board to add their insights; schedules are flexible to make the most of wildlife sightings. Binoculars in every cabin, a library stocked with books of local interest (as well as movies on some ships), and crew members as keen to explore Alaska as the passengers all enhance the experience.

Cruise West has partnered with **PENTAX Imaging Company**, a leader in digital photography, to offer a series of Photographers' Cruises on select Alaska itineraries. There is no additional cost for the sailings co-hosted by a professional PENTAX photographer who conducts special field events and onboard workshops throughout the cruise.

1

CRUISE WEST

Food

Wholesome meals focus on the freshest ingredients available, including an abundance of Alaska seafood. Bread is freshly baked on board every day.

Fitness and Recreation

Passengers are limited to one or two pieces of fitness equipment on board; however, the shore excursions that are included in the fare are often walking tours.

Your Shipmates

The passengers, who inevitably get to know one another during the cruise, are typically active, well-traveled over-fifties. They come from all regions of the United States, as well as from Australia, Canada, and the United Kingdom. While children are certainly welcome, there are no facilities or programs designed for them.

Dress Code

Attire is always casual on board and ashore, and jeans are as formal as it gets.

Service

Provided by an all-American crew, service is friendly and personal, if not overly polished.

Tipping

Tips are included in most Cruise West fares, but gratuities for exceptional service by crew members are warmly appreciated. For shore excursions and land extension, $2 to $3 for drivers and $5 per day for shore exploration leaders is suggested.

Choose This Line If . . .

You consider yourself more of a traveler than a tourist.

Your idea of a fun evening includes board games and quiet conversation.

You want to get up close to whales and other wildlife.

Don't Choose This Line If . . .

You can't entertain yourself.

Room service is a requirement—you won't find it on these ships.

You would rather play a slot machine than attend an evening lecture.

NOTEWORTHY

■ All ships prohibit smoking indoors, and have limited smoking space outdoors.

■ The ships' shallow draft, small size, and skilled crews provide access to areas passengers on big ships can only dream about.

■ Exploration leaders share entertaining and fascinating stories from history, folklore, identification and information on the flora and fauna, and the cultural diversity of areas you will visit.

SPIRIT OF COLUMBIA, SPIRIT OF DISCOVERY

CREW MEMBERS	21, 21
ENTERED SERVICE	1979, 1976
GROSS TONS	97, 94
LENGTH	143, 166 feet
NUMBER OF CABINS	39, 43
PASSENGER CAPACITY	78, 84
WIDTH	28, 37 feet

700 ft.

500 ft.

300 ft.

Spirit of Discovery at sea

Public Areas and Facilities

Smaller and older than their fleetmates, these two ships bear more resemblance to coastal packets than traditional cruise ships or megayachts. While they have been extensively refurbished through the years, they haven't lost their cozy charm. Activities on board center around the wood-trimmed dining rooms and comfortable, if compact, lounges, each of which features a bar, some library shelving with books, and a coffee station.

The list of what you won't find aboard is longer than what you will; however, these two vessels are ideal for slipping into tight spaces and getting up close to what most passengers have come to Alaska to see—wildlife and the state's natural wonders. There's plenty of room on each ship's sun deck, and the *Spirit of Discovery*'s bow viewing area to enjoy the sights. It's worth noting that neither ship has an elevator.

Restaurants

Each ship has a single dining room with one seating for breakfast, lunch, and dinner. You may sit where and with whom you please, but should arrive at the beginning of the scheduled mealtime to avoid disappointment. Promptness is encouraged, and those who straggle in late will have no choice of table selection or companions. Early risers will find a Continental breakfast set up in the lounge, and substantial snacks are served there in the late afternoon. A serve-yourself coffee stand is located in the lounge and you might find freshly-baked cookies as well. There is no room service offered.

Accommodations

Layout: Compact is a generous description of accommodations on both vessels. The largest staterooms barely compare to an average standard cabin on modern cruise ships. Don't be surprised to find your sink located on a vanity in the sleeping area, even in the top categories. In the lowest categories the entire bathroom might be your shower. Note that "bed sizes vary from standard." What that means is that they are somewhat shorter than usual.

Amenities: *Spirit of Columbia* has deluxe and AAA categories that feature several different bedding configurations and TVs with VCR players. Deluxe cabins also have a small refrigerator. Upper Deck and Bridge Deck accommodations all open onto outside passageways. Lower Deck cabins are located "outside," but have no windows. All categories on *Spirit of Discovery* have windows for a view, but only the Deluxe accommodations have TVs with VCR players; lower categories have no TV. Neither of these Cruise West ships is equipped with hair dryers, so you should bring your own.

Worth Noting: There are no accessible accommodations for passengers who require wheelchairs or scooters for mobility. *Spirit of Discovery* has two single cabins.

In the Know

Tall people—those over six feet—may find the headroom on board both ships a bit too low for comfort. Ceilings are only about 6½ feet high, and can feel claustrophobic for even average-height passengers.

Pros and Cons

Pros: *Spirit of Columbia* is equipped for bow landing, which allows passengers to go ashore almost anywhere the ship can be beached; both ships can navigate in snug areas that larger vessels can't reach; captains of these small vessels have the authority to deviate from the scheduled itinerary if something comes up that is of more interest.

Cons: Closet and storage space in accommodations can be very tight for even two people; nightlife is virtually non-existent, unless you are fond of games; shelving that houses books in the lounges is limited, so you will want to bring your own reading material.

Cabin Type	Size (sq. ft.)
Spirit of Columbia	80–121
Spirit of Discovery	64–126

FAST FACTS

- 4/3 passenger decks
- Dining room
- In-cabin refrigerators (some), VCRs (some), no TV in some cabins
- 1 bar
- No-smoking cabins

SPIRIT OF ENDEAVOUR, SPIRIT OF YORKTOWN

CREW MEMBERS	25, 40
ENTERED SERVICE	1980, 1988
GROSS TONS	1,425; 2,354
LENGTH	217, 257 feet
NUMBER OF CABINS	51, 69
PASSENGER CAPACITY	102, 138
WIDTH	28, 43 feet

700 ft.

500 ft.

300 ft.

Public Areas and Facilities

One of Cruise West's largest and fastest ships, *Spirit of Endeavour* has a roomy lounge with large picture windows for superb views. There's ample deck space on the stern, where everyone gathers to observe wildlife, as well as on upper decks, which are good for watching sunsets.

The *Spirit of Yorktown*'s profile is dominated by picture windows that ensure bright interior spaces. In keeping with its size, there are only two public rooms, and deck space is limited. The glass-walled observation lounge does multi-purpose duty as the ship's bar, lecture room, and movie "theater."

Restaurants

Each ship has a single dining room with one seating for breakfast, lunch, and dinner. You may sit where and with whom you please, but should arrive at the beginning of the scheduled mealtime to avoid disappointment. Early risers will find a Continental breakfast set up in the lounge, and substantial snacks are served there in the late afternoon. A serve-yourself coffee stand is located in the lounge and you might find freshly baked cookies as well. There is no room service offered.

Accommodations

Layout: Most cabins aboard *Spirit of Endeavour* have picture windows, and some have connecting doors, which make them convenient for families traveling together. Most have twin beds, although a couple of cabins have queens, and all have a writing desk and TV with VCR. Bathrooms are small, but comfortable. You might want to bring your own hair dryer, as they are provided only upon request.

Amenities: Aboard *Spirit of Yorktown* most cabins have a picture window, but a few have portholes; none has a television, but all have a hair dryer. Toilets are wedged between sinks and showers, and might pose a tight squeeze for larger passengers. Although the largest staterooms are quite spacious, there are only eight of them, and only four of those have balconies. Cabins underwent refurbishment in 2007.

Worth Noting: No accommodations are designated accessible.

Spirit of Endeavor at sea

In the Know

As with all Cruise West ships, itineraries are flexible: the captain can linger to let passengers watch a group of whales and still make the next port stop on time.

Pros and Cons

Pros: Fleets of inflatable landing craft take passengers ashore for independent exploration; conversation and friendships with fellow passengers come easy on these small ships with their casual vibe; with a sun deck and bow viewing area, *Spirit of Endeavour* has plenty of outdoor space to watch for wildlife or glacier calving.

Cons: With the highest passenger concentration of Cruise West's larger ships, the *Spirit of Yorktown* can feel crowded when all passengers are inside; oddly, while the *Spirit of Endeavour* has Wi-Fi hot spots for Internet connections, none of the accommodations aboard *Spirit of Yorktown* has a TV; there are no laundry services, so pack accordingly.

Cabin Type	Size (sq. ft.)
Spirit of Endeavour	80–128
Spirit of Yorktown	121–138

FAST FACTS

- 4/4 passenger decks
- Dining room
- Wi-Fi (only *Spirit of Endeavour*), in-cabin safes (some), in-cabin refrigerators (some), VCRs (some, only *Spirit of Endeavour*), no TV in cabins (only *Spirit of Yorktown*)
- 1 bar
- No-smoking cabins

1

CRUISE WEST

LINDBLAD EXPEDITIONS

Founded in 1979 as Special Expeditions by Sven-Olof Lindblad, the son of Lars-Eric Lindblad, the company changed its name in 1984 to Lindblad Expeditions. Every cruise is educational, focusing on soft adventure and environmentally conscientious travel through ecologically sensitive regions of Alaska. Since 2004 the line has partnered with *National Geographic* to enhance the experience by including *National Geographic* experts and photographers on board; forums to discuss current events and world issues; and participation by fellowship-funded teachers of geography and other subjects.

Lindblad Expeditions, 96 Morton St., New York, NY 10014 ☎212/765–7740 or 800/397–3348 ⊕www.expeditions.com.

The ships of Lindblad Expeditions spend time looking for wildlife, exploring out-of-the-way inlets, and making Zodiac landings at isolated beaches. Each ship has a fleet of kayaks as well as a video-microphone: a hydrophone (underwater microphone) is combined with an underwater camera so passengers can listen to whale songs and watch live video of what's going on beneath the waves. In the evening the ships' naturalists recap the day's sights and adventures over cocktails in the lounge. A video chronicler makes a DVD of the entire cruise that you may purchase.

Food
Lindblad prides itself on serving fresh Alaska seafood, including Dungeness crab, halibut, and Alaska king salmon, but there are also plenty of meat and vegetarian options. Breakfast is buffet-style, and lunch is served family-style. The recently launched "Seafood for Thought" program is meant to ensure that sustainable seafood is being served.

Fitness and Recreation
Both ships carry exercise equipment on deck and have a Wellness Program, with fundamentals ranging from

kayaking and hiking to yoga and Pilates, massage therapy, and body treatments.

Your Shipmates

Lindblad attracts active, adventurous, well-traveled over-forties, and quite a few singles, as the line charges one of the industry's lowest single supplements. They are making a push, however, to be more family-friendly, and staff members have undergone extensive training to tailor activities toward children. In July and August some family expeditions are offered, which follow the same itinerary as Lindblad's other trips but include a crew member dedicated to running educational programs for school-age kids. All Lindblad cruises offer substantial discounts for young people up to 21 traveling with their parents. Smoking is not permitted on board.

Dress Code

Casual and comfortable attire is always appropriate.

Service

Service is friendly and helpful, if not overly polished.

Tipping

While gratuities are at your discretion, tips of $12–$15 per person per day are suggested; these are pooled among the crew at journey's end. Tip the massage therapist individually following a treatment.

Choose This Line If . . .

You want to be an ecologically responsible traveler.

You consider travel a learning experience.

What you see from the ship is more important than the vessel itself.

Don't Choose This Line If . . .

You are mobility impaired; the ships are not accessible, and Zodiacs are used to reach shore for certain explorations.

Your happiness depends on being entertained; other than enrichment programs, there is no formal entertainment.

You consider television essential; there are none in the staterooms.

NOTEWORTHY

■ While wine and cocktails are not included in the fare, non-alcoholic beverages are.

■ All shore excursions except flightseeing are included, as are transfers to and from airports.

■ Pre-trip information, including recommended reading, photography guidelines, what to pack, and other tips for your particular voyage, will arrive with your documents.

Top: Informal yet elegant dining
Bottom: kayaking

NATIONAL GEOGRAPHIC SEA BIRD/ NATIONAL GEOGRAPHIC SEA LION

CREW MEMBERS	22
ENTERED SERVICE	1982/1981
GROSS TONS	100
LENGTH	152 feet
NUMBER OF CABINS	31
PASSENGER CAPACITY	62
WIDTH	31 feet

700 ft.

500 ft.

300 ft.

Top: *Sea Lion* at sea
Bottom: comfortable
accomodations

Public Areas and Facilities

These small, shallow-draft sister ships can tuck into nooks and crannies that bigger ships can't reach. Artwork on both includes a collection of photographs by expedition staff naturalists as well as whale and dolphin sculptures. An open-top sundeck, a forward observation lounge, and a viewing deck at the bow offer plenty of room to take in the scenery. The ships are also equipped with bowcams (underwater cameras that monitor activity), and you can navigate the camera using a joystick to observe sea life. Additional expedition equipment includes a hydrophone for eavesdropping on marine mammals, an underwater video "splash" camera to record the passing undersea scenery, and a video microscope for use during naturalists' lectures. The ship's Internet kiosk provides e-mail access. Fitness equipment is set up on the bridge deck, and the LEXspa Wellness room offers massages, body treatments, and a morning stretching program on deck.

Restaurants

All meals are served open seating during scheduled times in a single dining room. Breakfast is a buffet with a wide selection; lunch if often served family-style. Dinner is equally informal. There is no room service.

Accommodations

Layout: These ships are comfortable, but cabins are proportionately small. All staterooms are outside, and upper-category cabins have picture windows that open; the lowest-category cabins on main deck have portholes that admit light, but do not open or afford much of a view. Most cabins have single beds that can convert to a double, and a few on the upper deck have pull-out beds to accommodate a third person.

Amenities: There are no TVs in accommodations. A functional in-cabin sink has good lighting over a square mirror and vanity that contains a hair dryer. A curtain separates the toilet and shower compartment in the "head"-style bathroom, where 100% natural, biodegradable conditioning shampoo, body wash, and body lotion are provided. It is recommended that you bring biodegradable products if you choose to use your own. There is just enough storage space to stow your belongings.

Worth Noting: No accommodations are designated accessible.

In the Know

An "open bridge" policy provides passengers the opportunity to meet the captain and his officers and learn the intricacies of navigation or simply observe.

Pros and Cons

Pros: A fleet of Zodiacs and kayaks can take you closer to the water and wildlife; a wellness specialist is onboard to lead classes in yoga and Pilates; itineraries are flexible, so as to take maximum advantage of reported wildlife sightings and weather conditions.

Cons: These ships have no elevators or accessible features for the mobility impaired; alcoholic beverages are not included in the fare, which tends to be rather steep; accommodations are basic in decor and spartan in size, with really tiny bathrooms.

Cabin Type	Size (sq. ft.)
Sea Bird and Sea Lion	73–202

FAST FACTS

- 3 passenger decks
- Dining room
- 1 bar, library
- Wi-Fi, no TV in cabins
- Computer room
- No-smoking cabins

LINDBLAD EXPEDITIONS

Taking in the view aboard the *Sea Bird*.

Ports of Embarkation

MANY NORTHBOUND CRUISES BEGIN IN VANCOUVER, British Columbia, but Seattle has become an important port as well, with some cruise lines even setting up their own facilities at SeaTac airport. A few ships sail out of San Francisco or Los Angeles. Anchorage is the primary starting point for cruise passengers heading south, but ships don't actually dock there. Instead, travelers fly into and may overnight in Anchorage before being transported by bus or train to the ports of Seward or Whittier for southbound departures.

Cruise travelers frequently opt for combination packages that include an Inside Passage cruise plus a tour by bus or train through interior Alaska (and sometimes the Yukon). Denali National Park, located too far inland to be included on Inside Passage cruises, is a particular focus of these trips. Before or after the cruise, travelers with a more independent streak may want to rent a car and strike out on their own to places not often visited by cruise ships, such as Homer or Valdez.

PORT ESSENTIALS

RESTAURANTS AND CUISINE

Given the seaside location of the embarkation towns, it's no surprise that fresh fish and other seafood are especially popular. Fresh halibut and salmon are available throughout summer, along with specialties such as shrimp, oysters, and crab. Seafood meals can be simply prepared fast food, like beer-battered fish-and-chips, or more elaborate dinners of halibut baked in a macadamia-nut crust with fresh mango chutney. If seafood isn't your first choice, rest assured that all the staples—including restaurants serving steaks, burgers, pizza, Mexican, or Chinese food—can also be found.

WHAT IT COSTS					
	¢	$	$$	$$$	$$$$
Anchorage	under $10	$10–$15	$15–$20	$20–$25	over $25
Seattle	under $8	$8–$16	$16–$24	$24–$32	over $32
Vancouver	under C$8	C$8–12	C$12–20	C$20–30	over C$30

Restaurant prices are for a main course at dinner, excluding tip, taxes, service charges, and liquor charges.

ABOUT THE HOTELS

Whether you're driving or flying into your port of embarkation, it's often more convenient to arrive the day before or to stay for a day (or longer) after your cruise. Cruise travelers typically stay in one of the larger downtown hotels booked by the cruise lines in order to be closer to the ports, but you might like to make your own arrangements for a pre- or post-cruise sojourn. Therefore, we offer lodging suggestions for each port.

The hotels we list are convenient to the cruise port and the cream of the crop in each price category. Properties are assigned price categories based on the range between their least and most expensive standard double room at high season (excluding holidays).

Assume that all hotel rooms have air-conditioning and cable TV unless otherwise noted, and that hotels operate on the **European Plan** (EP, with no meals) unless we specify that they use either the **Continental Plan** (CP, with a Continental breakfast), **Breakfast Plan** (BP, with a full breakfast), or the **Modified American Plan** (MAP, with breakfast and dinner). The following price categories are used in this book.

WHAT IT COSTS					
	¢	$	$$	$$$	$$$$
Anchorage	under $100	$100–$150	$150–$200	$200–$250	over $250
Seattle	under $100	$100–$150	$150–$200	$200–$250	over $250
Vancouver	under C$100	C$100–150	C$150–200	C$200–250	over C$250

Prices are for two people in a standard double room in high season, excluding tax and service.

ANCHORAGE

Updated by Tom Reale

By far Alaska's largest and most sophisticated city, Anchorage is situated in a truly spectacular location. The permanently snow-covered peaks and volcanoes of the Alaska Range lie to the west of the city, part of the craggy Chugach Range is actually within the eastern edge of the municipality, and the Talkeetna and Kenai Ranges are visible to the north and south. On clear days Mt. McKinley looms on the northern horizon, and two arms of Cook Inlet embrace the town's western and southern borders.

Anchorage is Alaska's medical, financial, and banking center, and home to the executive offices of most of the Native corporations. The city has a population of roughly 290,000, approximately 40%, of the people in the state. The relative affluence of this white-collar city—with a sprinkling of olive drab from nearby military bases—fosters fine restaurants and pricey shops, first-rate entertainment, and sporting events.

Boom and bust periods followed major events: an influx of military bases during World War II; a massive buildup of Arctic missile-warning stations during the Cold War; reconstruction following the devastating Good Friday earthquake of 1964; and in the late 1960s the biggest jackpot of all—the discovery of oil at Prudhoe Bay and the construction of the Trans-Alaska Pipeline. Not surprisingly, Anchorage positioned itself as the perfect home for the pipeline administrators and support industries, and it continues to attract a large share of the state's oil-tax dollars.

VISITOR INFORMATION

Anchorage Convention and Visitors Bureau (*ACVB* ⊠*524 W. 4th Ave., Downtown* ☎*907/276–4118, 800/478–1255 to order visitor guides* 🖷*907/278–5559* ⊕*www.anchorage.net*). **Log Cabin and Visitor Information Centers** (⊠*4th Ave. and F St., Downtown* ☎*907/274–3531* ⊕*www.anchorage.net*).

ON THE MOVE

GETTING TO THE PORT

Anchorage is the starting (or ending) point for many Alaskan cruises, but most passengers actually board or disembark in Seward (125 mi south on Resurrection Bay). Seward is a three-hour bus ride or four-hour train ride from Anchorage. The train station is a few blocks from downtown Anchorage. Another frequent embarkation port is Whittier (59 mi southeast of Anchorage), on the western shore of Prince William Sound. Access between Anchorage and these ports is by bus or train, and is generally included as part of your cruise. You'll spend virtually no shore time there before you

> ### SEWARD OR WHITTIER?
>
> Here's a rundown of which large cruise lines use Seward, Whittier, or both:
>
> ■ Carnival: Whittier
>
> ■ Celebrity: Seward
>
> ■ Holland America: Seward
>
> ■ Norwegian: neither
>
> ■ Princess: Whittier
>
> ■ Regent: Seward
>
> ■ Royal Caribbean: Seward

embark or after disembarkation—buses and the train also offer dock-to-airport service in both places. The few ships that do dock at Anchorage proper dock just north of downtown. There's an information booth on the pier. It's only a 15- or 20-minute walk from the town to the dock, but this is through an industrial area with heavy traffic, so it's best to take a taxi.

ARRIVING BY AIR

Ted Stevens Anchorage International Airport is 6 mi from downtown. Alaska Railroad trains have a stop both here and downtown, in addition to direct service for cruise-ship companies transporting their passengers to Seward or Whittier. Taxis queue up outside baggage-claim. A ride downtown runs about $20, not including tip. Alaska Shuttle offers transport from the airport to downtown for $30 for one to three people; they also offer standard, taxi-type service around town.

Contacts Ted Stevens Anchorage International Airport (☏ *907/266–2529* ⊕ *www.anchorageairport.com*). **Alaska Shuttle** (☏ *907/338–8888*). **Checker Cab** (☏ *907/276–1234*).

ARRIVING BY CAR

The Glenn Highway enters Anchorage from the north and becomes 5th Avenue near Merrill Field; this route leads directly into downtown. Gambell Street leads out of town to the south, becoming New Seward Highway at about 20th Avenue. South of town, it becomes the Seward Highway.

RENTAL CARS

Anchorage is the ideal place to rent a car for exploring sites farther afield before or after your cruise. National Car Rental has a downtown office. All the major companies (and several local operators) have airport desks and free shuttle service to the airport to pick up cars.

Contacts **Arctic Rent-a-Car** (☎907/561–2990). **Budget** (☎907/243–0150). **Denali Car Rental** (☎907/276–1230). **National Car Rental** (✉1300 E. 5th Ave., Downtown ☎907/265–7553 ✉Ted Stevens International Airport ☎907/243–3406).

TAXIS

Downtown Anchorage is easy to navigate on foot. If you want to see some of the outlying attractions, such as Lake Hood, you'll need to hire a taxi. Taxis are on a meter system; rates start at $2 to $3 for pickup and $2.50 for each mile. Most people call for a cab, although it's possible to hail one.

Contacts **Alaska Yellow Cab** (☎907/222–2222).

EXPLORING ANCHORAGE

❹ Alaska Center for the Performing Arts. The distinctive stone-and-glass building overlooks an expansive park filled with brilliant flowers all summer. Look inside for upcoming events, or relax amid the blossoms on a sunny afternoon. ✉621 W. 6th Ave., at G St., Downtown ☎907/263–2900, 800/478–7328 tickets ⊕www.alaskapac.org ⛟Tours by appointment only.

❶ Alaska Public Lands Information Center. Stop here for information on all
★ of Alaska's public lands, including national and state parks, national
☾ forests, and wildlife refuges. You can plan a hiking, sea-kayaking, bear-viewing, or fishing trip; find out about public-use cabins; learn about Alaska's plants and animals; or head to the theater for films highlighting different parts of the state. The bookstore sells maps and nature books. Guided walks to historic downtown sights depart daily. ✉605 W. 4th Ave., No. 105, at F St., Downtown ☎907/271–2737 ⊕www.nps.gov/aplic ⊙Memorial Day–Labor Day, daily 9–5; Labor Day–Memorial Day, weekdays 10–5.

❺ Anchorage Museum of History and Art. An impressive collection of historic
☾ and contemporary Alaskan art is exhibited along with dioramas and
Fodor'sChoice displays on Alaskan history and village life. You can join an informa-
★ tive 45-minute tour (given several times daily) or step into the theater to watch a film on Alaska. In July the first-floor atrium is the site of free daily presentations by local artists and authors. A café spills out into the atrium, serving delicious lunches from the Marx Bros. Cafe, and the gift shop sells Alaska Native art and souvenirs. After an extensive renovation in 2008–09, the Imaginarium, formerly at a separate site, was incorporated into the museum, along with other new attractions and upgrades. ✉121 W. 7th Ave., Downtown ☎907/343–4326, 907/343–6173 recorded information ⊕www.anchoragemuseum.org ⛟$8 ⊙Mid-May–mid-Sept., Fri.–Wed. 9–6, Thurs. 9–9; mid-Sept.–mid-May, Tues.–Sat. 10–6, Sun. noon–5.

❷ Resolution Park. This tiny park has a cantilevered viewing platform dominated by a monument to Captain Cook, whose explorations in 1778 led to the naming of Cook Inlet and many other geographic features in Alaska. Mt. Susitna, known as the Sleeping Lady, is the prominent low mountain to the northwest, and Mts. Spurr and Redoubt, active

2

volcanoes, are just south of Mt. Susitna. Mt. McKinley, Mt. Foraker, and other peaks of the Alaska Range are often visible from more than 100 mi away. ⊠*3rd Ave. at L St., Downtown.*

❸ Oscar Anderson House Museum. City butcher Oscar Anderson built Anchorage's first permanent frame house in 1915, at a time when most of Anchorage consisted of tents. Swedish Christmas tours are held the first two weekends of December. Guided 45-minute tours are available whenever the museum is open. ⊠*420 M St., Downtown ⊹In Elderberry Park* ☎*907/274–2336* ⊠*$3* ☉*June–mid-Sept., weekdays noon–5; group tours (maximum 10 participants per group) must be arranged in advance.*

OUTSIDE DOWNTOWN

❼ Alaska Aviation Heritage Museum. The state's unique aviation history is presented with 25 vintage aircraft—seven have been completely restored—three theaters, an observation deck along **Lake Hood,** the world's busiest seaplane base, a flight simulator, and a gift shop. Highlights include a Stearman C2B, the first plane to land on Mt. McKinley, back in the early 1930s. Volunteers are working to restore a 1931 Fairchild Pilgrim aircraft and make it flyable, and are eager to talk shop. ⊠*4721 Aircraft Dr., West Anchorage* ☎*907/248–5325* ⊕*www.alaskaairmuseum.org* ⊠*$10* ☉*May 15–Sept. 15, daily 9–5; Sept. 15–May 14, Wed.–Sun. 9–5.*

❻ Alaska Native Heritage Center. On a 26-acre site facing the Chugach Mountains, this facility provides an introduction to Alaska's native peoples. The spacious Welcome House has interpretive displays, artifacts, photographs, demonstrations, native dances, storytelling, and films, along with a café and an upgraded gift shop selling museum-quality crafts and artwork. Step outside for a stroll around the adjacent lake, where you will pass seven village exhibits representing the 11 native cultural groups through traditional structures and exhibitions. As you enter the homes, you can visit with the culture hosts, hear their stories, and experiment with some of the tools, games, and utensils used in the past. ■TIP➔ **The Heritage Center provides a free shuttle from the downtown Log Cabin and Visitor Information Centers several times a day in summer.** You can also hop a bus at the downtown transit center; Route 4 (Glenn Highway) will take you to the Heritage Center's front door. ⊠*8800 Heritage Center Dr. (Glenn Hwy. at Muldoon Rd.), East Anchorage* ☎*907/330–8000 or 800/315–6608* ⊕*www.alaskanative. net* ⊠*$24.95, $10 Alaska residents* ☉*Mid-May (Mother's Day)–Sept., daily 9–5; Oct.–mid-May, Sat. 10–5.*

Fodor'sChoice
★

WHERE TO EAT

Smoking is banned in all Anchorage restaurants. Most local restaurants are open daily in summer, with reduced hours in winter. Only a few places require reservations, but it's always best to call ahead, especially for dinner. *(For price categories, see About the Restaurants, above.)*

$$$$ ✕**Club Paris.** Alaska's oldest steak house has barely changed since open-
STEAK ing in 1957. The restaurant has dark wood and an old-fashioned feel, and serves tender, flavorful steaks of all kinds, including a 4-inch-thick

filet mignon. If you have to wait for a table, have a martini at the bar and order the hors-d'oeuvres platter ($30)—a sampler of top sirloin steak, cheese, and prawns that could be a meal for two. For dessert, try a tart key lime pie or a chocolate sweet-potato pie. Dinner reservations are advised. ⊠*417 W. 5th Ave., Downtown* ☎*907/277–6332* ⊕*www.clubparisrestaurant. com* ▤*AE, D, DC, MC, V* ⊗*No lunch Sun.*

> **"THE PLANE! THE PLANE!"**
>
> If you have the time, take a taxi to the **Lake Hood floatplane base**, where colorful aircraft come and go almost constantly in summer.
>
> The best vantage point is from the patio of the lounge at the **Millennium Anchorage Hotel** (⊠*4800 Spenard Rd., Lake Spenard* ☎*907/243–2300* or *800/544–0553*) .

$$ AMERICAN ✕**Downtown Deli.** A longtime favorite, this café is across the street from the Log Cabin and Visitor Information Centers. Although you can choose from familiar sandwiches like the French dip or the chicken teriyaki, this deli also has Alaskan favorites, like grilled halibut and reindeer stew. The dark, rich chicken soup comes with either noodles or homemade matzo balls, and breakfasts range from omelets and homemade granola to cheese blintzes. You can sit in one of the wooden booths for some privacy or out front at the sidewalk tables for some summertime people-watching. ⊠*525 W. 4th Ave., Downtown* ☎*907/276–7116* ⚠*Reservations not accepted* ▤*AE, D, DC, MC, V* ⊗*No dinner Oct.–May.*

$$$ AMERICAN Fodor'sChoice ★ ✕**Glacier BrewHouse.** The scent of hops permeates the cavernous, wood-beam BrewHouse, where a dozen or so ales, stouts, lagers, and pilsners are brewed on the premises. Locals mingle with visitors in this noisy, always-busy heart-of-town restaurant, where dinner selections range from thin-crust 10-inch pizzas to chipotle shrimp cocktail, and from barbecue pork ribs to fettuccine jambalaya and fresh seafood (in season). For dessert, don't miss the wood-oven-roasted apple-and-currant bread pudding. You can watch the hardworking chefs in the open kitchen. The brewery sits behind a glass wall, and the same owners operate the equally popular Orso, next door. ⊠*737 W. 5th Ave., Downtown* ☎*907/274–2739* ⊕*www.glacierbrewhouse.com* ▤*AE, D, MC, V.*

$$$$ JAPANESE ✕**Kumagoro.** A favorite of the suit-and-tie lunch crowd, Kumagoro has traditional Japanese lunches and a take-out deli with such specialties as herring roe on kelp, and a sleek sushi bar (dinner only). The best choices on the dinner menu are the sizzling salmon or beef teriyaki, both served with miso soup and a salad. With the shabu-shabu dinner ($39 for two people), you cook your own meats and vegetables in a stockpot of boiling broth. Inexpensive homemade ramen soups are also available. All entrée prices include a 10% gratuity. ⊠*533 W. 4th Ave., Downtown* ☎*907/272–9905* ▤*AE, D, DC, MC, V.*

$$$$ CONTINENTAL Fodor'sChoice ★ ✕**Marx Bros. Cafe.** Inside a little frame house built in 1916, this nationally recognized 46-seat café opened in 1979 and is still going strong. The menu changes every week, and the wine list encompasses more than 700 international choices. For an appetizer, try the black-bean-and-

duck soup or fresh Kachemak Bay oysters. The outstanding made-at-your-table Caesar salad is a superb opener for the baked halibut with a macadamia-nut crust served with coconut-curry sauce and fresh mango chutney. And if the sweet potato–and-pecan pie is on the menu, get it! ✉627 W. 3rd Ave., Downtown ☎907/278–2133 ⊕www.marxcafe. com ♠Reservations essential ▤AE, MC, V ⊘Closed Sun. and Mon. No lunch. Memorial Day–Labor Day, Tues.–Sat. 5:30–10; Labor Day–Memorial Day, Tues., Wed., Thurs. 6–9:30, Fri.–Sat. 5:30–10.

¢–$ ╳**New Sagaya's City Market.** Stop here for quick lunches and Kaladi
ECLECTIC Brothers espresso. The in-house bakery, L'Aroma, cranks out specialty breads and pastries of all types, and the international deli and grocery serves California-style pizzas, Chinese food, lasagna, rotisserie chicken, salads, and even stuffed cabbage. You can eat inside on the sheltered patio or grab an outside table on a summer afternoon. New Sagaya's has one of the best seafood counters in town, and will even box and ship your fish. The grocery stores carry an extensive selection of Asian foodstuffs, and the produce and meat selections are excellent. ✉900 W. 13th Ave., Downtown ☎907/274–6173, 907/274–9797, or 800/764–1001 ✉3700 Old Seward Hwy., Midtown ☎907/562–9797 ⊕www. newsagaya.com ▤AE, D, DC, MC, V.

$$$$ ╳**Orso.** One of Anchorage's culinary stars, Orso ("bear" in Italian)
ITALIAN evokes the earthiness of a Tuscan villa. Alaskan touches flavor rustic Mediterranean dishes that include traditional pastas, fresh seafood, and locally famous desserts—most notably a delicious molten chocolate cake. Be sure to ask about the daily specials. If you can't get a table at dinner (reservations are advised), you can select from the same menu at the large bar. Upstairs you'll find a cozier, quieter space. ✉737 W. 5th Ave., at G St., Downtown ☎907/222–3232 ⊕www.orsoalaska. com ▤AE, D, MC, V.

$$$–$$$$ ╳**Sacks Café.** This colorful restaurant serves light American cuisine such
AMERICAN as chicken and scallops over udon noodles, and local produce when available. It also features monthly wine flights, normally with three different selections of 3-ounce pours with information sheets on each wine. Be sure to ask about the daily specials, particularly the fresh king salmon and halibut. Flowers adorn the tables, and singles congregate along a small bar, sampling wines from California, Australia, and France. The café is especially crowded during lunch, served from 11 to 2:30, and dinner begins at 5. The weekend brunch menu includes eggs Benedict, a Mexican scrambled egg dish called migas, and various salads and sandwiches. ✉328 G St., Downtown ☎907/276–3546 or 907/274–4022 ⊕www.sackscafe.com ♠Reservations essential ▤AE, MC, V.

$$$$ ╳**Simon & Seafort's Saloon & Grill.** Windows overlooking Cook Inlet vis-
SEAFOOD tas, along with the high ceilings and a classic brass-and-wood interior, have long made this an Anchorage favorite. The menu includes prime rib (aged 28 days), pasta, and sesame chicken salad, but the main attraction is seafood: fish is blackened, grilled, fried, or prepared any other way you like it. Try the king crab legs or the grilled ahi tuna with ginger-and-mango salsa, and for dessert the Brandy Ice: vanilla ice cream whipped with brandy, Kahlúa, and crème de cacao. The bar is a great spot for microbrews, single-malt scotch, and martinis; the

2

best tables are adjacent to tall windows facing the water. ⊠*420 L St., Downtown* ☎*907/274–3502* ⊕*www.r-u-i.com/sim* ♨*Reservations essential* ☰*AE, DC, MC, V* ⊗*No lunch weekends.*

¢–$ ✕**Snow City Cafe.** At this unassuming café along "Lawyer Row" you'll
ECLECTIC find dependably good and reasonably priced breakfasts and lunches. Service is fast, and the setting, formerly a funky mix of mismatched chairs and Formica tables, has been upgraded, enlarged, and remodeled, but there's still a great mix of families and singles enjoying some of the best breakfasts in Anchorage. Snow City is consistently voted the best breakfast in a local poll. Breakfast is served all day, but arrive early on the weekend or be prepared to wait. Snow City's lunch menu consists of hot or cold sandwiches, fresh soups, and salads, and has lots of vegetarian options. The kitchen closes at 3 PM weekdays and 4 PM weekends. ⊠*4th Ave. at L St., Downtown* ☎*907/272–2489* ⊕*www. snowcitycafe.com* ☰*AE, D, DC, MC, V* ⊗*No dinner.*

$ ✕**Snow Goose Restaurant and Sleeping Lady Brewing Company.** Although
AMERICAN you can dine indoors at this comfortable edge-of-downtown eatery, the real attraction in summer is alfresco dining on the back deck and on the rooftop. On clear days you can see Mt. McKinley on the northern horizon and the Chugach Mountains to the east. The menu emphasizes Alaskan fare, but the beer and the view are the best reasons to visit. To sample the specialty beers, gather around oak tables in the upstairs bar for a brewed-on-the-premises ale, India Pale Ale, stout, barley wine, or porter. ⊠*717 W. 3rd Ave., Downtown* ☎*907/277–7727* ⊕*www. alaskabeers.com* ☰*AE, D, DC, MC, V.*

WHERE TO STAY

Lodging for most cruise-ship travelers is typically included in package tours set up through a travel agency, an online site, or directly from the cruise line. If you prefer to pick your own hotel or bed-and-breakfast, make your reservations well ahead of time, since many central hotels fill up months in advance for the peak summer season. Rooms are generally available, though you may be staying in midtown, 2 mi from downtown.

$$$$ 🏨**Anchorage Marriott Downtown.** One of Anchorage's biggest lodgings, the brightly decorated Marriott appeals to business travelers, tourists, and corporate clients. The hotel's Cafe Promenade serves American cuisine with an Alaskan flair. All guest rooms have huge windows; views are breathtaking from the top floors. If you stay on one of the top three levels of this 20-story hotel, you have access to a concierge lounge and are served a light breakfast as well as evening hors d'oeuvres and desserts. **Pros:** one of the newest hotels in town; modern, up-to-date facilities. **Cons:** no free Wi-Fi; cruise-ship crowds at times in summer. ⊠*820 W. 7th Ave., Downtown* ☎*907/279–8000 or 800/228–9290* ⊕*www.marriott.com* ⤂*392 rooms, 3 suites* ♿*In-room: Wi-Fi. In-hotel: restaurant, room service, bar, pool, gym, spa, bicycles, laundry service, parking (paid)* ☰*AE, D, DC, MC, V.*

$$–$$$ 🏨**Comfort Inn Ship Creek.** The namesake Ship Creek gurgles past this popular family hotel a short walk northeast of the Alaska Railroad

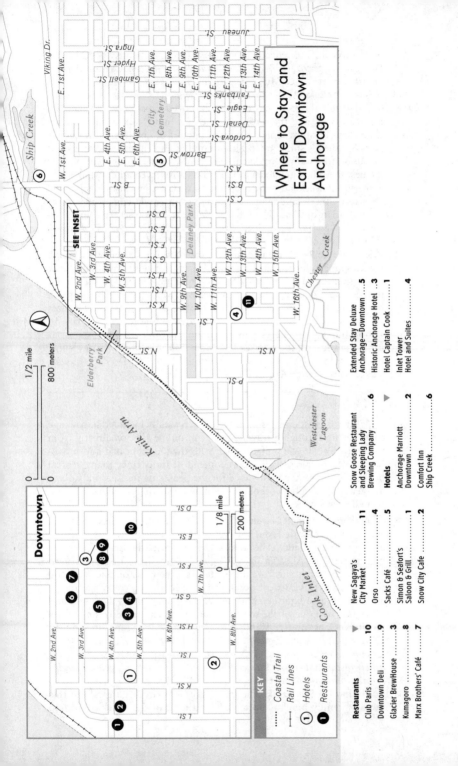

Where to Stay and Eat in Downtown Anchorage

KEY
···· Coastal Trail
✝ Rail Lines
① Hotels
❶ Restaurants

Restaurants
Club Paris 10
Downtown Deli 9
Glacier BrewHouse 3
Kumagoro 8
Marx Brothers' Café 7
New Sagaya's
City Market 11
Orso 4
Sacks Café 5
Simon & Seafort's
Saloon & Grill 1
Snow City Cafe 2
Snow Goose Restaurant
and Sleeping Lady
Brewing Company 6

Hotels
Anchorage Marriott
Downtown 2
Comfort Inn
Ship Creek 6
Extended Stay Deluxe
Anchorage–Downtown 5
Historic Anchorage Hotel .. 3
Hotel Captain Cook 1
Inlet Tower
Hotel and Suites 4

Historic Depot. Rooms come in a variety of configurations, including with kitchenette and two-room suites. A substantial Continental breakfast is served each morning, and the lobby has an enormous stuffed brown bear. The hotel stocks a limited number of fishing rods for those who want to try their luck catching salmon in Ship Creek. **Pros:** pet-friendly; pool; good location for fishing or watching the fisherfolk. **Cons:** if you're not into the fishing opportunity at Ship Creek, the location is a problem; the walk into the downtown area is an uphill climb; rooms are a bit noisy at times. ✉ *111 Ship Creek Ave., Downtown* ☎ *907/277–6887 or 800/424–6423* ✆ *www.comfortinn.com* ✎ *88 rooms, 12 suites* ♿ *In-room: kitchen (some), refrigerator, Wi-Fi. In-hotel: pool, gym, some pets allowed* ▤ *AE, D, DC, MC, V* ⎮◎⎮ *CP.*

$$$ ░ **Extended Stay Deluxe Anchorage—Downtown.** Formerly the Aspen Hotel, this is one of Anchorage's newest downtown hotels. Rooms are large and comfortably furnished with a single king or two queen beds, a writing table, 27-inch TV, DVD player, mini-refrigerator, and microwave. Two-room suites include a larger refrigerator, stovetop, and pullout sofa; some also have hot tubs. The hotel is a block from the Anchorage Museum of History and Art and Delaney Park Strip, and has limited off-street parking plus a pool and hot tub downstairs. Nightly, weekly, and monthly rates are available. **Pros:** very good rates available online; nice facilities for long stays; airport shuttle available. **Cons:** fee for Internet and laundry use; parking can be a hassle. ✉ *108 E. 8th Ave., Downtown* ☎ *907/868–1605* ✆ *www.extendedstay.com* ✎ *75 rooms, 14 suites* ♿ *In-room: kitchen, refrigerator, DVD, Wi-Fi. In-hotel: pool, gym, laundry service, Internet terminal* ▤ *AE, D, MC, V* ⎮◎⎮ *CP.*

$$$–$$$$ ░ **Historic Anchorage Hotel.** The little building has been around since
★ 1916. Experienced travelers call it the only hotel in Anchorage with charm: the original sinks and tubs have been restored, and upstairs hallways are lined with Old Anchorage photos. The rooms are nicely updated, with dark cherrywood furnishings and HD flat-screen TVs. The small lobby, its fireplace crackling in chilly weather, has a quaint European feel, and the staff is adept at meeting your needs. Request a corner room if possible; rooms facing the street may have traffic noise. The junior suites include sitting areas. **Pros:** excellent staff; new TVs; very convenient downtown location; kids under 12 are free. **Cons:** rooms are small; no airport shuttle; Wi-Fi can be spotty. ✉ *330 E St., Downtown* ☎ *907/272–4553 or 800/544–0988* ✆ *www.historican-choragehotel.com* ✎ *16 rooms, 10 junior suites* ♿ *In-room: no a/c, refrigerator, Wi-Fi. In-hotel: bar, gym, bicycles, laundry service, some pets allowed, no-smoking rooms* ▤ *AE, D, DC, MC, V* ⎮◎⎮ *CP.*

$$–$$$ ░ **Hotel Captain Cook.** Recalling Captain Cook's voyages to Alaska and
★ the South Pacific, dark teak paneling lines the hotel's interior, and a nautical theme continues into the guest rooms. All rooms have ceiling fans, and guests can use the separate men's and women's athletic clubs with shared indoor heated pool, the business center, and other facilities, including three restaurants and a coffee, wine, and martini bar. The hotel occupies an entire city block with three towers, the tallest of which is capped by the **Crow's Nest Restaurant.** The most luxurious accommodation is found on the 19th floor of Tower III—a sprawling,

1,600-square-foot two-bedroom suite, which costs a mere $1,500 per night. **Pros:** staff very well trained and accommodating; generally considered the nicest hotel in town. **Cons:** fixtures and furnishings a bit dated; hallways can be dark. ⊠*4th Ave. and K St., Downtown* ☎*907/276–6000 or 800/843–1950* ⊕*www.captaincook.com* ⇆*457 rooms, including 96 suites* ♿*In-room: Wi-Fi. In-hotel: 3 restaurants, room service, pool, gym* ⊟*AE, D, DC, MC, V.*

$$$–$$$$ 🏠**Inlet Tower Hotel and Suites.** Windows overlook either the Chugach
★   Mountains, the Cook Inlet, or downtown Anchorage. Built in 1952 in a residential area a few blocks south of downtown, this 14-story building was Alaska's first high-rise. A major remodeling brought spacious rooms and suites, uniquely Alaskan wallpaper, high-end linens, large televisions, high-speed Internet lines and wireless Internet in the lobby, kitchenettes, and blackout curtains for summer mornings when the sun comes up at 3 AM. The Mixx Grill Restaurant & Bar serves fresh seafood, steaks, vegetables, and other local favorites. **Pros:** excellent restaurant on-site; the New Sagaya store and restaurant is but a stone's throw away; airport shuttle available. **Cons:** downtown attractions are a bit of a hike; hallways narrow and can be dark. ⊠*1200 L St., Downtown* ☎*907/276–0110 or 800/544–0786* ⊕*www.inlettower. com* ⇆*156 rooms, 24 suites* ♿*In-room: kitchen (some), refrigerator, Wi-Fi. In-hotel: restaurant, gym, laundry facilities, Internet terminal, parking (free), no-smoking rooms* ⊟*AE, D, DC, MC, V.*

NIGHTLIFE

BARS AND NIGHTCLUBS

Anchorage does not shut down when it gets dark. Bars here—and throughout Alaska—open early (in the morning) and close as late as 3 AM on weekends. There's a ban on smoking in bars and bingo parlors, as well as restaurants. The listings in the *Anchorage Daily News* entertainment section, published on Friday, and in the free weekly *Anchorage Press* (⊕*www.anchoragepress.com*) range from concerts and theaters to movies and a roundup of nightspots featuring live music. You can also find concert and performance listings in the "Play" section in Friday editions of the *Anchorage Daily News* (or online at ⊕*www.adn.com*).

Fodor'sChoice   **Chilkoot Charlie's** (⊠*2435 Spenard Rd., Spenard* ☎*907/272–1010*
★   ⊕*www.koots.com*), a rambling timber building with sawdust floors, 11 bars (including one made of ice), 3 dance floors, loud music (rock or swing bands and DJs) nightly, two DJs every Thursday, Friday, and Saturday, and rowdy customers, is where young Alaskans go to get crazy. This legendary bar has many unusual nooks and crannies, including a room filled with Russian artifacts and serving the finest vodka drinks, plus a reconstructed version of Alaska's infamous Birdhouse Bar.

Lots of old-timers favor the dark bar of **Club Paris** (⊠*417 W. 5th Ave., Downtown* ☎*907/277–6332* ⊕*www.clubparisrestaurant.com*). The Paris mural and French street lamps hanging behind the bar have lost some luster, but there's still a faithful clientele. The jukebox favors swing. A trendy place for the dressy "in" crowd, the bar at **Simon & Seafort's Saloon & Grill** (⊠*420 L St., Downtown* ☎*907/274–3502* ⊕*www.r-u-i.*

com/sim) has stunning views of Cook Inlet, a special single-malt scotch menu, and a wide selection of imported beers. **Snow Goose Restaurant** (⊠*717 W. 3rd Ave., Downtown* ☎*907/277–7727* ⊕*www.alaskabeers. com*) is a good place to unwind with a beer inside or on the airy outside deck overlooking Cook Inlet. There's decent food, too.

SHOPPING

BOOKS

Easily the largest independent bookstore in Alaska, **Title Wave Books** (⊠*1360 W. Northern Lights Blvd., Midtown* ☎*907/278–9283 or 888/598–9283* ⊕*www.wavebooks.com*) fills a sprawling store at the other end of the REI strip mall. The shelves are filled with new and used titles and a large section of Alaska stuff, and the staff is very knowledgeable. Also here is **Kaladi Brothers Coffee Shop,** with Wi-Fi access for Web surfers.

MARKETS

In summer Anchorage's **Saturday and Sunday Markets** (☎*907/272–5634* ⊕*www.anchoragemarkets.com*) are open in the parking lot at 3rd Avenue and E Street. More than 300 vendors offer Alaskan-made crafts, ethnic imports, and deliciously fattening food. The open-air markets run from mid-May to mid-September, weekends 10–6. A smaller market sells local produce and crafts July through August, on Wednesday from 11 to 5, at Northway Mall in East Anchorage.

NATIVE CRAFTS

Several downtown shops sell quality Native Alaskan artwork, but the best buys can be found in the gift shop at the **Alaska Native Medical Center** (⊠*4315 Diplomacy Dr., at Tudor and Bragaw Rds., East Anchorage* ☎*907/563–2662*), which is open weekdays 10–2 and 11–2 on the first and third Saturday of the month. It doesn't take credit cards. **Oomingmak** (⊠*6th Ave. and H St., Downtown* ☎*907/272–9225 or 888/360–9665* ⊕*www.qiviut.com*), a Native-owned cooperative, sells items made of qiviut, the warm undercoat of the musk ox. **Artic Rose Gallery** (⊠*420 L St., Downtown* ☎*907/279–3911* ⊕*www.articrosegallery.com*) is in the same building as Simon and Seafort's restaurant. Alaska's oldest gallery, **Artique** (⊠*314 G St., Downtown* ☎*907/277–1663* ⊕*www. artiqueltd.com*), sells paintings, prints, and jewelry by prominent Alaskan artists.

SEAFOOD

Get smoked reindeer meat and salmon products at **Alaska Sausage and Seafood Company** (⊠*2914 Arctic Blvd., Midtown* ☎*907/562–3636 or 800/798–3636* ⊕*www.alaskasausage.com*). **New Sagaya's City Market** (⊠*900 W. 13th Ave., Downtown* ☎*907/274–6173*) sells an excellent selection of fresh seafood. If you don't want to carry the fish with you, the market will pack and ship it.

SEATTLE

Updated
by Heidi
Johansen

Seattle has much to offer: a beautiful setting, sparkling arts and enter-tainment, innovative restaurants, friendly residents, green spaces galore, and Pike Place Market, which provides a wonderfully earthy focal point for downtown Seattle, with views of the ferries crossing Elliott Bay. Visitors to the city will almost certainly wish they had set aside more time to take in Seattle's charms.

Seattle, like Rome, is said to be built on seven hills. As a visitor, you're likely to spend much of your time on only two of them (Capitol Hill and Queen Anne Hill), but the city's hills are indeed the most definitive element of the city's natural and spiritual landscape. Years of largely thoughtful building practices have kept tall buildings from obscuring the lines of sight, maintaining vistas in most directions and around almost every turn. The hills are lofty, privileged perches from which residents are constantly reminded of the beauty of the forests, moun-tains, and waters surrounding the city—that is, when it stops raining long enough for you to enjoy those gorgeous views.

VISITOR INFORMATION

In the heart of downtown Seattle's bustling retail core, the **Seattle Con-vention and Visitors Bureau** (⊠*7th and Pike, main floor, Washington State Convention and Trade Center* ☎*206/461–5888* ⊕*www.visitseattle. org*) offers ticket sales, reservation and concierge services, dining sug-gestions, and a handy visitor information packet and coupon book that can be e-mailed to you.

ON THE MOVE

GETTING TO THE PORT

Ships from Norwegian Cruise Line and Celebrity Cruises dock at the Bell Street Pier Cruise Terminal (Pier 66). Pier 66 is within walking distance of downtown attractions, and a city bus wrapped up in the Waterfront Streetcar logo (the real 1927 Waterfront Streetcars are out of commission until they can be upgraded) provides trolley service along the shoreline to the cruise terminal.

Holland America Line, Princess Cruises, and Royal Caribbean dock at the new Smith Cove Cruise Terminal at Terminal 91, located at the north end of the downtown waterfront Magnolia Bridge and best accessed by cruise-line motorcoach transfer, taxi, or shuttle service. Opened in spring 2009, the much-anticipated Terminal 91 replaces the old Pier 30.

New for 2010, Carnival Cruise Lines will also homeport in Seattle for the Alaska cruise season. As of this writing, the pier assignment for their ship has not been announced.

ARRIVING BY AIR

The major gateway is Seattle–Tacoma International Airport (Sea-Tac).

Contacts Seattle–Tacoma International Airport (Sea-Tac) (☎*206/433–5388* ⊕ *www.portseattle.org/seatac*).

AIRPORT TRANSFERS

Sea-Tac is about 15 mi south of downtown on I–5. It usually takes 25–40 minutes to ride between the airport and downtown. Metered cabs make the trip for about $30. Downtown Airporter has the only 24-hour door-to-door service, a flat $25 ($40 round-trip) from the airport to downtown (including cruise-ship pier No. 91). You can make arrangements at the Downtown Airporter counter upon arrival or online. Gray Line Downtown Airporter provides service to downtown hotels, as well, for $11–$20, depending on your destination.

Contacts Grayline of Seattle Downtown Airporter (☎ 206/624–5077 or 800/426–7532 ⊕ www.graylineofseattle.com).

ARRIVING BY TRAIN

Amtrak provides train service north to Vancouver; south to Portland, Oakland, and Los Angeles; and east to Spokane, Chicago, and other cities. Amtrak's King Street Station is just south of downtown at 3rd Avenue South and South King Street.

Contacts Amtrak (☎ 800/872–7245 ⊕ www.amtrak.com).

PUBLIC TRANSPORTATION

Between 6 AM and 7 PM, rides on the Metro bus are free within Downtown Seattle's Ride Free Zone. Outside downtown, rides cost $1.75 during the non-peak hours and $2 during the peak hours of 6 AM–9 AM and 3 PM–6 PM. The Seattle Monorail quickly and conveniently links downtown and the Seattle Center. The 1-mi journey takes 2 minutes and departs every 10 minutes daily 9 AM–11 PM. The round-trip fare is $4.

Contacts Metro Bus (☎ 206/553–3000, 206/287–8463 for automated schedule line ⊕ transit.metrokc.gov). **Seattle Monorail** (☎ 206/905–2620 ⊕ www.seattlemonorail.com).

TAXIS

Rides are about $2.50 per mile, and it's always easier to call for a taxi (no fee) than to hail one on the street. This is not a major means for transportation in Seattle, aside from late-night partying and airport trips. There are no surcharges for late-night pickups. Taxis are readily available at most hotels.

Contacts Orange Cab (☎ 206/522–8800). **Red Top Cab** (☎ 206/789–4949). **Yellow Cab** (☎ 206/622–6500).

EXPLORING SEATTLE

The Elliott Bay waterfront is Seattle's crown jewel. Pike Place Market, the Seattle Aquarium, and the Maritime Discovery Center stretch along its densely packed shore. Just south of downtown is the historic Pioneer Square area, and a short distance north of Pike Place Market lies the Olympic Sculpture Park, a magnificent urban playground filled with gigantic works of art overlooking the ocean. North of the sculpture park is Seattle Center, a civic gathering place that's home to the Space Needle, Experience Music Project, the Science Fiction Museum, the Children's Museum, and the Pacific Science Center.

DOWNTOWN AND PIONEER SQUARE

④ Pike Place Market. At this vibrant market, vendors purvey handmade crafts, homemade goodies, flowers, and fresh food—from fresh-caught salmon and shellfish to fruits and veggies—and waterside restaurants serve meals reflecting the Northwest's bounty. The market dates to 1907, when the city issued permits allowing farmers to sell produce from wagons parked at Pike Place. Urban renewal almost killed the market, but residents rallied and voted it a historical asset in 1973, and it remains a point of pride among Seattleites. In the fall of 2008, voters passed a measure to increase property taxes in order to support upgrades to Pike Place Market; renovations to the landmark began in the spring of 2009. *Pike Pl. at Pike St., west of 1st Ave., Downtown* ☎206/682–7453 ⊕*www.pikeplacemarket.org* ☉*Stall hours vary. First-level shops Mon.–Sat. 10–6, Sun. 11–5; underground shops, daily 11–5.*

FodorsChoice ★

⑥ Pioneer Square District. On the southern edge of downtown, Seattle's oldest neighborhood is a round-the-clock hub of activity. Cafés, galleries, and boutiques fill elegantly renovated turn-of-the-20th-century Victorian-style redbrick buildings, and leafy trees line the narrow streets surrounding the central square. Pioneer Square can be accessed from downtown via Metro bus or taxi, or on foot. The district's most notable structure, the 42-story **Smith Tower** on 2nd Avenue and Yesler Way, was the tallest building west of the Mississippi when it was completed in 1914. The ornate iron-and-glass **pergola** on 1st Avenue and Yesler Way marks the site where the pier and sawmill owned by Henry Yesler, one of Seattle's first businessmen, once operated. Today's Yesler Way was the original "Skid Row," where in the 1880s timber was sent to the sawmill on a skid of small logs laid crossways and greased so that the cut trees would slide down to the mill. The area later grew into Seattle's first commercial center. Be sure to check for upcoming events and festivals and Art in the Park and the First Thursday gallery walks on the first Thursday of every month (⊕*www.pioneersquare.org* or *www.firstthursdayseattle.com*). The newly open **Last Resort Fire Department Museum** (⊕*www.lastresortfd.org/museum.htm*) is at 301 2nd Avenue South, at Main. Also be sure to check out the small, enchanting **Waterfall Garden** on 2nd Avenue South and South Washington.

⑦ Klondike Gold Rush National Historical Park. A redbrick building with wooden floors and soaring ceilings contains a small museum illustrating Seattle's role in the 1897–98 gold rush in northwestern Canada's Klondike region. Antique equipment is on display, and the walls are lined with photos of gold miners, explorers, and the hopeful families who followed them. Film presentations, gold-panning demonstrations (daily in summer at 10 and 3), and rotating exhibits are scheduled throughout the year. Other sectors of this park are in southeast Alaska. ✉*319 2nd Ave. S, Pioneer Square* ☎206/220–4240 ⊕*www.nps.gov/klse/index.htm* 🎟*Free* ☉*Daily 9–5.*

③ Seattle Aquarium. In the Puget Sound Great Hall, "Window on Washington Waters," a slice of Neah Bay life, is presented in a 20-foot-tall tank holding 120,000 gallons of water. The aquarium's darkened rooms and large, lighted tanks brilliantly display Pacific Northwest marine life. The "Life on the Edge" tide pools re-create Washington's rocky coast and sandy beaches. Huge glass windows provide underwater views of seals and sea otters; go up top to watch them play in their pools. Kids love the Discovery Lab, where they can touch starfish, sea urchins, and sponges, then examine baby barnacles and jellyfish. Nearby, cylindrical tanks hold a fascinating octopus. ⊠ *1483 Alaskan Way, at Pier 59, Downtown* ☎ *206/386–4300* ⊕ *www.seattleaquarium.org* ✆ *$16; $28 with a one-hour, narrated harbor cruise* ☉ *Daily 9:30–6 (last entry at 5).*

> SEATTLE CITYPASS
>
> If you're in Seattle for several days (rather than just one) before or after your cruise, look into the CityPass, which give admission to six different attractions for just $54—nearly half off what admission for all six would have been without a discount. The pass gives admission to the Space Needle, the Seattle Aquarium, a Seattle harbor tour, the Pacific Science Center, Woodland Park Zoo, and either the Museum of Flight or Experience Music Project/Science Fiction Museum.

❺ **Seattle Art Museum (Downtown).** Postmodern architect Robert Venturi designed this five-story museum to be a work of art in itself: large-scale vertical fluting adorns the building's limestone exterior, accented by terra-cotta, cut granite, and marble. Sculptor Jonathan Borofsky's several-stories-high *Hammering Man* pounds away outside the front door. The extensive collection surveys Asian, Native American, African, Oceanic, and pre-Columbian art. Among the highlights are the anonymous 14th-century Buddhist masterwork *Monk at the Moment of Enlightenment* and Jackson Pollock's *Sea Change*. A ticket includes a free visit to the Seattle Asian Art Museum if used within a week. A ticket to the latter is good for $3 off admission here within the same period. ⊠ *1300 1st Ave., Downtown* ☎ *206/654–3100* ⊕ *www.seattleartmuseum.org* ✆ *$15, free first Thurs. of month* ☉ *Tues.–Sun. 10–5 (Thurs. and Fri. until 9).*

Fodor'sChoice ★

Fodor'sChoice ★

Olympic Sculpture Park. A large tract (9 acres) of industrial land north of the Pike Place Market has been transformed into one of the most breathtaking and cutting-edge attractions in Seattle: the Olympic Sculpture Park, part of the Seattle Art Museum. The gently sloping park is planted with native shrubs and plants and crisscrossed with walking paths; it overlooks Puget Sound, and sunny days bring the astounding panorama of the Olympic Mountain Range into view. Sit, picnic, or stroll the grounds, which are dotted with works by such artists as Richard Serra, Anthony Caro, Louise Bourgeois, Mark di Suvero, and Alexander Calder, whose bright-red steel "Eagle" sculpture is a local favorite. You may even see a real bald eagle passing by overhead. ⊠ *2901 Western Ave., Downtown* ☎ *206/654–3100* ⊕ *www.seattleartmuseum.org* ✆ *Free* ☉ *Open daily; park opens 30 min before sunrise and closes 30 min after sunset.*

SEATTLE CENTER

A few blocks north of downtown at the base of Queen Anne Hill, Seattle Center is a legacy of the 1962 World's Fair. Today the 74-acre site is home to a multitude of attractions that encompass a children's museum, an opera hall, a science museum, a monorail, a basketball arena, and

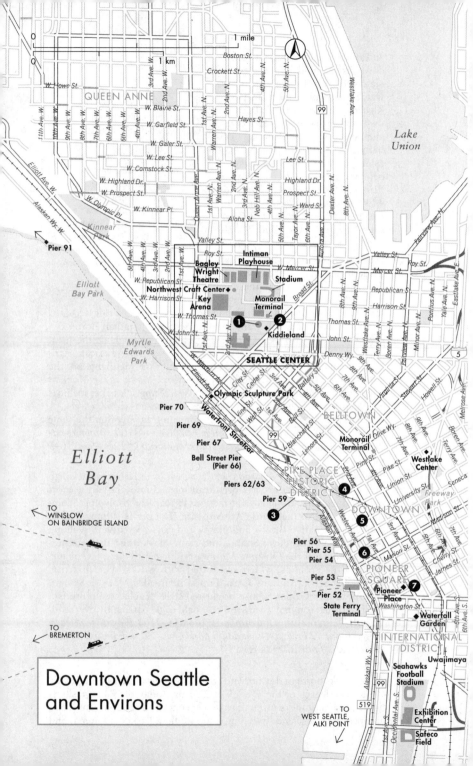

Downtown Seattle and Environs

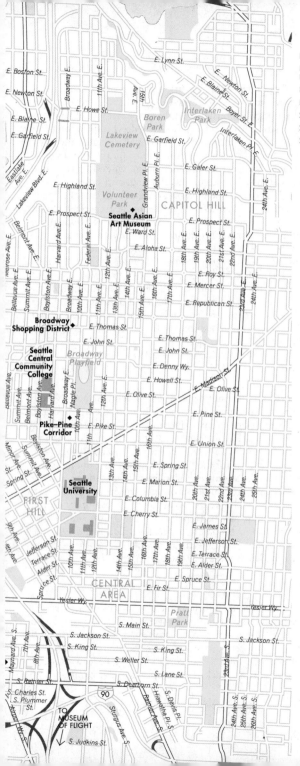

2

much more. For more information, call ☎206/684–7200 or check out ⊕*www.seattlecenter.com.*

❷ **Experience Music Project (EMP/SFM).** Seattle's most controversial archi-
❋ tectural statement is a 140,000-square-foot interactive museum celebrating American popular music—and the city's many contributions
to rock-and-roll history. Architect Frank Gehry drew inspiration from
electric guitars to achieve the building's "swoopy" design. Funded by
Microsoft cofounder Paul Allen, it's a fitting home for the world's largest collection of Jimi Hendrix memorabilia; the guitar god was a native
Seattleite. Other exhibits house guitars, clothing, and other artifacts
once owned by Bob Dylan, Hank Williams, Kurt Cobain, and the bands
Pearl Jam, Soundgarden, Heart, and the Kingsmen. Experiment with
instruments and recording equipment in the interactive Sound Lab,
or attend music performances, workshops, and private events in the
Sky Church concert hall, JBL Theater, or Revolution Cafe. ⊠*325 5th
Ave. at Harrison St., Lower Queen Anne* ☎*206/367–5483* ⊕*www.
emplive.org* ☜*$15* ◷*May 22–Sept. 7, daily 10–7, free first Thurs. of
month; rest of year, daily 10–5.* The same building also houses the **Science Fiction Museum.** This interactive multimedia museum truly takes
you "out there" with spaceship rooms and a science-fiction heroes hall
of fame. The Fantastic Voyages exhibit focuses on time travel, and the
Out of this World exhibit explores the future. ⊠*325 5th Ave. N, at
Harrison, Lower Queen Anne* ☎*206/724–3284* ⊕*www.empsfm.org*
☜*Free (with admission to SAM)* ◷*May 22–Sept. 7, daily 10–7; rest
of year, daily 10–5.*

❶ **Space Needle.** The distinctive exterior of the 605-foot-high Space Needle
❋ is visible throughout downtown—but the view from the inside out is
Fodor'sChoice even better. A less-than-one-minute ride up to the observation deck
★ yields 360-degree vistas of Downtown Seattle, the Olympic Mountains,
Elliott Bay, Queen Anne Hill, Lake Union, and the Cascade Range. The
Needle was built just in time for the World's Fair in 1962, but has since
been refurbished with educational exhibits, interactive stations, and the
glass-enclosed SpaceBase store and Pavilion spiraling around the tower's
base. If you dine at the exclusive, revolving SkyCity restaurant on the
top floor, admission to the observation deck is free. Or just enjoy views
from the coffee bar. ⊠*400 Broad St., at 5th Ave., Lower Queen Anne*
☎*206/905–2100* ⊕*www.spaceneedle.com* ☜*$16* ◷*Mon.–Thurs.
9:30 AM–11 PM; Fri.–Sat. 9 AM–11:30 PM; Sun. 9 AM–11 PM.*

WHERE TO EAT

Downtown is a good area for lunch; come evening, its action centers
around hotel restaurants and a handful of watering holes. Pioneer Square
and Belltown, on the other hand, come alive nightly with music and
other entertainment. Pioneer Square features bars and restaurants that
cater to baseball fans en route to Safeco Field, while Belltown's many
chic restaurants and bars are packed with hipsters and urbanites.·

2

DOWNTOWN

$$$ FRENCH ★ ✕**Campagne.** The white walls, picture windows, snowy linens, fresh flowers, and candles at this charming eatery overlooking Pike Place Market and Elliott Bay evoke Provence. So does the robust French country fare, with starters such as anchovy-chickpea crostini and roasted marrow bone served with baguette. Main plates include roasted guinea hen with sauteed escargots, Berkshire pork short rib served with vegetables, and Wagyu beef shoulder tenderloin with red-wine jus. The outstanding wine list compliments the food beautifully. The adjacent Café Campagne serves weekend brunch, weekday lunch, and dinner daily. ⊠*Inn at the Market, 86 Pine St., Downtown* ☎*206/728–2800* ⊕*www.campagnerestaurant.com* ⌒*Reservations essential* ⊟*AE, DC, MC, V* ⊗*No lunch; closed Mon.*

$ LATIN AMERICAN ✕**Copacabana Restaurant.** Much of the strategy that preserved Pike Place Market in the 1960s was hatched at this small Bolivian café. The food served here includes such tasty fare as spicy shrimp soup, *saltenas* (savory meat-and-vegetable pies), paella (the house specialty), and *pescado à la Español* (halibut in a saffron-tomato-onion sauce). Tasty food, cold beer, and great views are good reasons to linger. ⊠*1520½ Pike Pl., Downtown* ☎*206/622–6359* ⌒*Reservations not accepted* ⊟*AE, D, MC, V* ⊗*Dinner ends at 9 on weekdays and Sun.*

$$$–$$$$ CONTEMPORARY ★ ✕**Dahlia Lounge.** Romantic Dahlia Lounge started the valentine-red-walls trend, and it's still working its magic on Seattle couples. It's cozy and then some, but the food plays its part, too. Crab cakes, served as an entrée, lead a daily-changing regionally oriented menu. Other standouts are the grilled-bread salad with pesto, seared scallops, grilled lamb with smashed English peas, and such desserts as triple coconut-cream pie and doughnuts. Seattle's most energetic restaurateur, chef-owner Tom Douglas also owns Etta's Seafood in Pike Place Market, Lola on 4th Avenue, and the excellent Palace Kitchen on 5th Avenue. But Dahlia is the one that makes your heart go pitter-pat. Try the weekend brunch here after you hit the Pike Place Market. ⊠*2001 4th Ave., Downtown* ☎*206/682–4142* ⊕*www.tomdouglas.com* ⌒*Reservations essential* ⊟*AE, D, DC, MC, V* ⊗*No lunch weekends.*

$ SEAFOOD ✕**Emmett Watson's Oyster Bar.** This unpretentious spot can be hard to find—it's in the back of Pike Place Market's Soames-Dunn Building, facing a small flower-bedecked courtyard. But for those who know their oysters, finding this place is worth the effort. Not only are the oysters very fresh and the beer icy cold, but both are affordable and available in any number of varieties. If you don't like oysters, try the salmon soup or the fish-and-chips—flaky pieces of fish with very little grease. ⊠*1916 Pike Pl., Downtown* ☎*206/448–7721* ⌒*Reservations not accepted* ⊟*AE, MC, V* ⊗*No dinner Sun.*

$$$ ECLECTIC ✕**FareStart Restaurant.** This restaurant, a project of the FareStart job-training program, gives job training to homeless men and women. They prepare an American-style lunch of sandwiches, burgers, and fries during the week from 11 to 2. Reservations are essential for the $25 Thursday dinner, prepared by a guest chef from a top restaurant around Seattle. The cuisine changes with the chef. Whenever you go, you're assured a great meal for a great cause, and a real taste of Seattle's

community spirit. Reservations available online or by phone. ✉*2004 Westlake Ave., on the corner of 7th, Downtown* ☎*206/267–7601* ⊕*www.farestart.org* ▤*AE, MC, V* ⊘*No lunch weekends. No dinner Fri.–Wed.*

$$
ITALIAN
✕**Il Fornaio.** This Italian restaurant is the cornerstone of the Pacific Place mall that houses it. When shopping, there seems to be an opportunity to stop for a bite at Il Fornaio at every turn. There's a casual café on the street level, then an even more casual espresso counter on the mall's first level, and finally the elegant full-service dining room upstairs. Though the fresh breads and wood-fired pizzas are widely acclaimed, the entire menu has much to offer, most notably the seasonal antipasti, vegetarian minestrone, handmade ravioli, and the rosemary-scented rotisserie chicken. ✉*600 Pine St., Downtown* ☎*206/264–0994* ⊕*www.ilfornaio.com* ▤*AE, DC, MC, V.*

$$
ITALIAN
✕**The Pink Door.** With its Post Alley entrance and meager signage, many enjoy the Pink Door's speakeasiness almost as much as the savory Italian food. In warm months patrons partake on the deck shaded by a grape arbor while enjoying the stunning view of Elliott Bay. The antipasto—which includes fresh cheese, bean salad, prosciutto, salami, and grilled peppers—is a deliciously sharable appetizer; squid-ink spaghetti (with prawns, mussels, and clams) and cioppino are standout entrées, though nothing stands too far out—people come here mostly for the atmosphere. The whimsical bar is often crowded, the staff is saucy and irreverent, and cabaret acts regularly perform on a small corner stage. There's no place in town quite like it. ✉*1919 Post Alley, Downtown* ☎*206/443–3241* ⊕*www.thepinkdoor.net* ⌫*Reservations recommended* ▤*AE, MC, V* ⊘*No lunch Sun.*

$$$
CONTEMPORARY
✕**Place Pigalle.** Large windows look out on Elliott Bay in this cozy spot tucked behind a meat vendor in Pike Place Market's main arcade. In nice weather open windows let in the fresh salt breeze. Flowers brighten each table, and the staff is warm and welcoming. Despite its name, this restaurant has only a few French flourishes on an otherwise American/Pacific Northwest menu that changes seasonally. Go for the rich oyster stew or the onion soup gratinée, the Dungeness crab (in season), or the fish of the day. Local microbrews are usually on tap, and the wine list is well edited. ✉*81 Pike St., Downtown* ☎*206/624–1756* ▤*AE, MC, V* ⊕*www.placepigalle-seattle.com* ▤*AE, MC, V* ⊘*Brunch only on Sun.*

BELLTOWN

$$
ECLECTIC
✕**Brasa.** This has long been a Seattle favorite. The outstanding menu is prone to change, but the paella and roasted suckling pig seem to be getting all the praise these days. More traditional, but equally toothsome and carefully prepared, are the roasted chicken with wilted bitter greens and truffle oil and steak frites. Tip: If you don't want to shell out the big bucks for dinner, join in on one of the city's most popular happy hours (5 to 7). The lounge serves tapas, small plates, pizzas, and sandwiches. The dimly lighted space is a good place to sample the Belltown scene in an established restaurant that isn't just style over substance. ✉*2107 3rd Ave., Belltown* ☎*206/728–4220* ⊕*www.brasa.com* ⌫*Reservations essential* ▤*AE, DC, MC, V* ⊘*No lunch.*

2

$$–$$$
SEAFOOD

✕**Etta's Seafood.** Tom Douglas's seafood restaurant near Pike Place Market has a sleek and slightly whimsical design and views of Victor Steinbrueck Park. Brunch, served on weekends, always includes zesty seafood omelets, but the chef also does justice to French toast, eggs and bacon, and Mexican-influenced breakfast dishes such as huevos rancheros. For dinner, start with a cold glass of white wine and oysters on the half shell, then sample the fresh Dungeness crab cakes in season or coho salmon in Douglas's signature "Rub With Love" seasoning. Leave room for a slice of banana cream pie. ✉*2020 Western Ave., Belltown* ☎*206/443–6000* ⊕*www.tomdouglas.com* ▤*AE, D, DC, MC, V.*

$$–$$$
ECLECTIC
★

✕**Palace Kitchen.** The star of this chic yet convivial Tom Douglas eatery (he's also responsible for Dahlia Lounge, Etta's, Lola, and Serious Pie) may be the 45-foot bar, but the real show takes place in the giant open kitchen at the back. Sausages, wood-grilled chicken wings, olive poppers, Penn Cove mussels, roast pork ravioli, and a nightly selection of exotic cheeses vie for your attention on the ever-changing menu of small plates. There are always a few entrées, mouthwatering desserts, and a rotisserie special from the apple-wood grill. ✉*2030 5th Ave., Belltown* ☎*206/448–2001* ▤*AE, D, DC, MC, V* ☻*No lunch.*

$$–$$$
AMERICAN
★

✕**Restaurant Zoë.** Reservations are recommended at this chic eatery on a high-trafficked Belltown corner. Its tall windows, lively bar scene, and charming waitstaff add to the popularity, which comes mainly from its inspired kitchen. The talents of chef-owner Scott Staples can be seen in his Painted Hills beef short rib served with roasted potatoes and blue cheese, and his roasted halibut served with English pea puree and artichoke-butter sauce. Zoë is a great representative of the kind of fine dining experience that Seattle excels at, wherein a sleek, urban space, upscale cooking, and a hip crowd that enjoys people-watching come together to create not a pretentious, overblown, and overpriced spectacle but a place that is unfailingly laid-back, comfortable, and satisfying. ✉*2137 2nd Ave., Belltown* ☎*206/256–2060* ⊕*www.restaurantzoe. com* ▤*AE, D, MC, V* ⚷*Reservations essential* ☻*No lunch.*

$$–$$$
JAPANESE

✕**Shiro's Sushi Restaurant.** Willfully unconcerned with atmosphere, this simple spot is a real curiosity amid Belltown's chic establishments. The focus is entirely on the exceptional menu of authentic Japanese eats. Seaweed becomes a haute-cuisine dish at this formal but friendly café, and a sure hand guides the sushi bar, where Shiro himself often holds court. Be sure to try the sour plum handroll. ✉*2401 2nd Ave., Belltown* ☎*206/443–9844* ⊕*www.shiros.com* ▤*AE, MC, V.*

$$–$$$
★
ITALIAN

✕**Tavolata.** An airy Belltown space with light-wood booths, soaring ceilings, and modern finishes is a standout for soul-satisfying Italian food. Crispy breads, fresh cheese and olives, handmade pastas, grilled octopus, beet salad, Swiss-chard ravioli, roasted black sea bass . . . Shall we go on? Superb wines are on hand to wash it all down. The place is open quite late, and the hip customers seem to love that—come prepared for a noisy but festive atmosphere. As one diner put it: "Tavolata: Oooooh my yumminess." ✉*2323 2nd Ave., Belltown* ☎*206/838– 8008* ⊕*www.tavolata.com* ▤*AE, MC, V.*

WHERE TO STAY

$$$$ ⊡ **Alexis Hotel.** The Alexis, a Kimpton hotel, occupies two historic buildings near the waterfront. It's a fine place to stay, with a focus on art (including a rotating collection of paintings in the corridor between wings); subdued colors, imported Italian and French fabrics, and antiques can be found in the standard rooms and public spaces. It's really the specialty-theme suites that set this property apart. For instance, the Author's Suite offers a selection of good books, some even signed by the authors, and a beautiful wood-burning fireplace to read beside. A few rooms have water views; book early to secure one of those. Downstairs, the Library Bistro & Bookstore Bar is one of the city's favorite hideaways. **Pros:** $10 million 2007 restoration still shows. **Cons:** standard guest rooms are small for the price, the breakfast served downstairs doesn't quite match what's charged, neighborhood noise can be a problem. ⊠ *1007 1st Ave., Downtown* ☎ *206/624–4844 or 888/850–1155* ⊕ *www.alexishotel.com* ⋽ *89 rooms, 32 suites* ⊡ *In-room: safe, refrigerator (some), Wi-Fi. In-hotel: restaurant, room service, bar, gym, spa, concierge, laundry service, public Wi-Fi, parking (fee), some pets allowed, no-smoking rooms* ☐ *AE, D, DC, MC, V.*

$$$–$$$$ ⊡ **The Edgewater.** Raised high on stilts above Elliott Bay—with the
★ waves lapping right underneath it—Seattle's premier waterside hotel affords spectacular west-facing views of ferries and sailboats, seals and sea birds, and the distant Olympic Mountains. The whole hotel has a rustic-chic, elegant-hunting-lodge look, with plaid rugs and fabrics and peeled-log furnishings (though rooms tend to be small). Note that there is a significant price jump between the Waterfront rooms and the Waterfront Premium rooms—and the upgrade is not necessarily worth it unless you want a little more space. There's also an enormous, party-style Beatles Suite, where the famous Brits stayed in 1964. The elegant Six Seven restaurant is set to an indoor-outdoor bay vista. **Pros:** rooms on the non-bay side still offer a fantastic view of the city, hotel is within walking distance of downtown. **Cons:** thin walls, small rooms, some rooms look out over parking lot. ⊠ *2411 Alaskan Way, Pier 67, Waterfront* ☎ *206/728–7000 or 800/624–0670* ⊕ *www. edgewaterhotel.com* ⋽ *213 rooms, 10 suites* ⊡ *In-room: refrigerator, Wi-Fi. In-hotel: restaurant, room service, bar, gym, bicycles, concierge, laundry service, public Wi-Fi, parking (fee), no-smoking rooms* ☐ *AE, D, DC, MC, V.*

$$$$ ⊡ **The Fairmont Olympic Hotel.** The grande dame of Seattle hotels seems
Fodor'sChoice to occupy its own corner of the universe, one that feels more like Old
★ New York or Europe than the Pacific Northwest. The lobby of this 1924 Italian Renaissance Revival–style historic property has intricately carved wood paneling, graceful staircases that lead to mezzanine lounge areas, and plush couches occupied by men in suits and well-dressed older ladies—not a fleece jacket or pair of Birkenstocks in sight. Though it's hard to imagine kids being truly comfortable here, the hotel does its best to accommodate families. **Pros:** historic elegance now extends to rooms due to 2008 renovation, fitness center includes full-service health club, spa, and indoor swimming pool. **Cons:** executive suites nearly the same size as the deluxe rooms, hotel may be too formal for some.

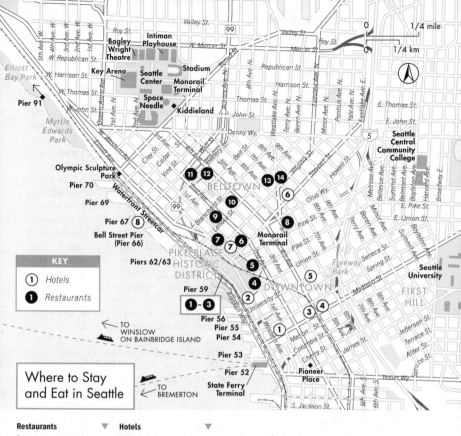

Where to Stay and Eat in Seattle

✉ *411 University St., Downtown* ☎ *206/621–1700 or 888/363–5022* ⊕ *www.fairmont.com/seattle* ⇨ *241 rooms, 209 suites* ⇘ *In-room: safe, refrigerator, DVD (some), Wi-Fi. In-hotel: 3 restaurants, room service, bar, pool, gym, concierge, laundry service, public Wi-Fi, parking (fee)* ⊟ *AE, D, DC, MC, V.*

$$$$ ⊡ **The Four Seasons Hotel Seattle.** The newest hotel jewel in downtown
★ Seattle gazes out over Elliott Bay and the Olympic Mountains from Union Street and 1st Avenue, just south of the Pike Place Market. Steps from Benaroya Hall and the Seattle Art Museum, the hotel is a polished and elegant, with Eastern accents and plush furnishings set against a definite modern Northwest backdrop, in which materials, such as stone and fine hardwoods, take center stage, as seen in the sleek reception area. A day spa and an infinity-pool terrace will help you relax after a long day of exploring Seattle's hilly terrain. Floor-to-ceiling windows in the guest rooms are unforgettable; lovely linens, comfortable living spaces, and sleek marble bathrooms with deep soaking tubs are an added bonus. The vibe here isn't pretentious, but it's certainly not laid-back Northwest either: Guests seem to know that they are in for a real treat. ART Restaurant and Lounge, headed up by Kerry Sear, offers up fabulous cocktails and fairly good Northwest cuisine, with stunning views. A trip to the bar is a must if you're in the area—try the Alpine martini (Absolut Citron with Douglas Fir sorbet) during happy hour, 5 to 7 Sunday through Thursday. **Pros:** dynamite service, amazing views. **Cons:** excessively neutral palate, somewhat predictable room decor. ✉ *99 Union St., Downtown* ☎ *206/749–7000* ⊕ *www. fourseasons.com* ⇨ *129 rooms, 19 suites* ⇘ *In-room: safe, refrigerator (some), DVD, Wi-Fi. In-hotel: restaurants, room service, bar, pool, gym, concierge, laundry service, public Wi-Fi, parking (fee)* ⊟ *AE, D, DC, MC, V.*

$$–$$$ ⊡ **Hotel Max.** Fans of minimalism, travelers interested in cutting-edge
★ local artists, and anyone who wants to feel like a rock star will be very happy with the Max, a super stylish hotel that swears it's created a new design aesthetic, "Maximalism." The hallway of each floor is dedicated to a different local photographer or artist, and giant black-and-white photos cover each door; scenes range from Americana to live concert shots from Seattle's grunge heyday (5th floor). The beds are huge and heavenly—a surprising bit of substance from a hotel that prides itself on appearance. The restaurant downstairs, Red Fin, is super hip and offers great Asian cuisine. **Pros:** stylish decor, local art, quiet rooms. **Cons:** rooms can be small, bathrooms have cramped showers and no counter space. ✉ *620 Stewart St., Downtown* ☎ *206/728–6299 or 866/833–6299* ⊕ *www.hotelmaxseattle.com* ⇨ *163 rooms* ⇘ *In-room: safe, refrigerator (some), Wi-Fi (fee). In-hotel: restaurant, room service, gym, laundry service, concierge, public Wi-Fi, parking (fee), no-smoking rooms* ⊟ *AE, D, DC, MC, V.*

$$$$ ⊡ **Hotel Monaco.** The Hotel Monaco, a Kimpton hotel, is the pet-friend-
★ liest hotel in town: not only are pets catered to with special events like doggie fashion shows, but guests who had to leave the pets at home can opt to have a goldfish (who comes with an adorable "hello my name is" introduction card) to keep them company. The hotel is full of bright

raspberry-and-cream striped wallpaper, gold sunburst decorations, and animal prints. For a more low-key experience, opt for a room with blue and white walls. **Pros:** special menu just for pets, no discernable animal smell, must work very hard to spot stray fur, Aveda bath products. **Cons:** decor might be too dark or too much for some, rooms a little small, some street noise. ✉ *1101 4th Ave., Downtown* ☎ *206/621–1770 or 800/945–2240* ⊕ *www.monaco-seattle.com* 📞 *144 rooms, 45 suites* ♿ *In-room: refrigerator, DVD, Wi-Fi. In-hotel: restaurant, room service, bar, gym, spa, concierge, laundry service, public Wi-Fi, airport shuttle, parking (fee), no-smoking rooms, some pets allowed* ▭ *AE, D, DC, MC, V.*

$ ▦ **Pensione Nichols.** One of the few affordable options downtown is also a unique and endearing place. Proprietor Lindsey Nichols attends to her guests with great enthusiasm and humor. It could be called a hostel for grown-ups, or one for young people who want more privacy and style than a hostel can provide. The bed-and-breakfast is in a historic building, so the rooms are a mixed bag of sizes and layouts, but most have wrought-iron furnishings and all have new beds. Breakfast is served in the light-filled common area overlooking Elliott Bay. **Pros:** guests get an astonishing amount for the price, common area great for meeting other travelers, great location in the heart of Pike Place, very pet friendly. **Cons:** must climb three flights of stairs to get here, only suites have windows (guest rooms have skylights). ✉ *1923 1st Ave., Downtown* ☎ *206/441–7125* ⊕ *www.pensionenichols.com* 📞 *8 rooms with three shared baths, 2 suites with bath* ♿ *In-room: no phone, no TV, Wi-Fi. In-hotel: no elevator, public Wi-Fi, some pets allowed* ▭ *AE, D, DC, MC, V* ⏐◎⏐ *CP.*

$$$$ ▦ **W Seattle.** The W set the bar for Seattle's trendy hotels, and it's still
★ a great choice for hip yet reliable luxury. Candlelight and a fireplace encourage lingering around the lobby on deep couches strewn with throw pillows, and the hotel's bar is popular with guests and locals alike. Decorated in black, brown, and French blue, guest rooms would almost be austere if they didn't have the occasional geometric print to lighten things up a bit. Floor-to-ceiling windows maximize striking views of the sound and the city. **Pros:** bar downstairs attracts locals and guests alike, great way to watch and mingle with Seattle life. **Cons:** not the best choice for families, bar downstairs makes for interesting noises at night, hallways are quite dark. ✉ *1112 4th Ave., Downtown* ☎ *206/264–6000 or 877/946–8357* ⊕ *www.whotels.com* 📞 *436 rooms, 8 suites* ♿ *In-room: safe, refrigerator (some), DVD, Wi-Fi (fee). In-hotel: restaurant, room service, bar, gym, concierge, laundry service, public Wi-Fi, parking (fee), some pets allowed, no-smoking rooms* ▭ *AE, D, DC, MC, V.*

NIGHTLIFE

The grunge-rock legacy of Nirvana, Soundgarden, and Pearl Jam still reverberates in local music venues, which showcase up-and-coming pop, punk, heavy metal, and alternative bands, along with healthy doses of other genres.

Two free papers, the *Stranger* and *Seattle Weekly* (distributed on Thursday; see ⊕*www.thestranger.com* or ⊕*www.seattleweekly.com*), provide detailed music, art, and nightlife listings. Friday editions of the *Seattle Times* have pullout sections detailing weekend events.

Bars and clubs stay open until 2 AM. Cabs are easy to find, and some buses run until the early morning hours (see ⊕*www.transit.metrokc. gov*). After the witching hour, cabs are the best option for those not willing to hoof it. Pioneer Square—home to a plethora of rock, jazz, and electronic music clubs—features a joint cover charge of $10 that covers admission to six bars; simply pay the cover at the first club you visit, get a hand stamp, and roam at will.

BARS AND CLUBS

Barca (✉*1510 11th Ave., Capitol Hill* ☎*206/325–8236* ⊕*www.barcaseattle.com*) is the place one can start an evening out with drinks and tasty bar food. It has a trés chic decor of large tables and velvet-lined booths, dark lighting, and lots of mood. There is plenty of bar space early on in the evening and a mezzanine with ample seating, too. Because they can tout the largest vodka selection in the state at their Vodka Bar, as well as a renowned menu of mixed drinks, the bar fills up rather early. As the evening unfolds, the bar becomes a frenzy of drinking, merrymaking, and fantastic people watching.

★ **The Crocodile** (✉*200 2nd Ave., Downtown* ☎*206/441–5611* ⊕*www. thecrocodile.com*) is one of the few places that can call itself "the heart and soul of Seattle" without raising many eyebrows. Indeed, it is, and has been since 1991, the heart and soul of Seattle's music scene. Nirvana, Pearl Jam, Mudhoney, and REM have all taken the stage here. Seattleites mourned the abrupt closing of this Belltown club in 2007, and rejoiced even harder when it reopened, all beautiful and renovated, in 2009. Nightly shows are complemented by cheap beer on tap and awesome pizza right next door at Via Tribunali. All hail the Crocodile!

Dimitriou's Jazz Alley (✉*2033 6th Ave., Downtown* ☎*206/441–9729* ⊕*www.jazzalley.com*) is where Seattleites go to see nationally known jazz artists. The cabaret-style theater, where intimate tables for two surround the stage, runs smoke-free shows nightly except Monday. Those with reservations for dinner, served during the first set, receive priority seating.

Elysian (✉*1221 E. Pike St., Captiol Hill* ☎*206/860–1920* ⊕*www. elysianbrewing.com*) is a Capitol Hill brewpub with worn booths and tables scattered across a bi-level warehouse space and so-so food. The standouts here are the beers, which are a good representation of the thriving brewing scene in the Northwest. Seasonal brews are sometimes outstanding, with IPAs, lagers, and ales showcasing hops, spices, and even pumpkin flourishes. Always on tap are the hop-heavy Immortal IPA, the rich Perseus Porter, and the crisp Elysian Fields Pale Ale.

Umi Sake House (✉*2230 1st Ave., Belltown* ☎*206/374–8717* ⊕*www. umisakehouse.com*) offers a great selection of sake and sake-based cocktails in a space designed to look like someone shoehorned a real *izakaya* (a sake house that also serves substantial snacks, like a tapas bar or gastropub) into a Belltown building—there's even an enclosed patio, which they refer to as the "porch." Despite its chic interior, Umi is less of a meat market than some Belltown spots—unless you're here late on a Friday or Saturday night.

★ **Zig Zag Café** (✉*1501 Western Ave., on the Pike Hill climb, Pike Place Market* ☎*206/625–1146* ⊕*www.zigzagcafe.net*) is hands-down the most innovative bar in Seattle. The Pike Place Market hideout expertly serves up its many award-winning cocktails nightly until 2 AM in a laid-back and usually friendly atmosphere (though some visitors complain that the table service is only so-so). Several memorable cocktails include the Don't Give Up the Ship (gin, Dubonnet, Grand Marnier, and Fernet Branca); the One Legged Duck (rye whiskey, Dubonnet, Mandarine Napoleon, and Fernet Branca); and Satan's Soulpatch (bourbon, sweet and dry vermouth, Grand Marnier, orange, and orange bitters). A simple food menu includes cheese and meat plates, bruschetta, and soup, salad, olives, and nuts. A small patio is the place to be.

SHOPPING

Seattle's retail core might feel business-crisp by day, but it's casual and arts-centered by night, and the shopping scene reflects both these moods. Within a few square blocks—between 1st Avenue on the west and Boren Avenue on the east, and from University Street to Olive Way—you can find department-store flagships, several high-gloss vertical malls, dozens of upper-echelon boutiques, and elite retail chains. One block closer to Elliott Bay, on Western Avenue, several high-end home-furnishings showrooms make up an informal "Furniture Row." The Waterfront, with its small, kitschy stores and open-air restaurants, is a great place to dawdle. ■TIP→ Seattle's best shopping is found in the small neighborhood made up of 4th, 5th, and 6th avenues between Pine and Spring streets, and 1st Avenue between Virginia and Madison streets.

ART GALLERIES

★ **Foster/White Gallery.** One of the Seattle art scene's heaviest hitters, Foster/White, has digs as impressive as the works it shows: a century-old building with high ceilings and 7,000 square feet of exhibition space. Internationally acclaimed glass artist Dale Chihuly, and paintings, sculpture, and drawings by Northwest masters Kenneth Callahan, Mark Tobey, and George Tsutakawa are on permanent exhibit. ✉*220 3rd Ave. S, Pioneer Square* ☎*206/622–2833* ⊕*www.fosterwhite.com* ✎*Free* ☉*Tues.–Sat. 10–6.*

William Traver Gallery. A classic gallery space with white walls and creaky, uneven wood floors, William Traver is like a little slice of Soho in Seattle—without the attitude. Light pours in from large picture windows; until the new Four Seasons is completed, the second-story space has glimpses of Elliott Bay. The focus is on Northwest artists. Pieces are exquisite—never too whimsical or gaudy—and the staff is extremely courteous to those of us who can only enjoy this place as a museum and not a shop. After you're done tiptoeing around the gallery, head back downstairs and around the corner to **Vetri**, which sells glass art and objects from emerging artists at steep but much more reasonable prices. ⊠*110 Union St. #200, Downtown* ☎*206/587–6501* ⊕*www.travergallery.com* ✉*Free* ⊙*Tues.–Fri. 10–6, Sat. 10–5, Sun. noon–5.*

GIFT SHOPS

Made in Washington (⊠*1530 Post Alley, Downtown* ☎*206/467–0788 or 800/338–9903* ⊕*www.madeinwashington.com*), in Pike Place Market, features hundreds of quality products from local artists and small businesses. Honey, jams, delicious smoked salmon, artwork, and tchotchkes galore fill up the shelves here. There's also a branch in downtown's Westlake Center.

Pike & Western Wine Shop (⊠*1934 Pike Pl., Downtown* ☎*206/441–1307* ⊕*www.pikeandwestern.com*) is one of the best wine shops in the city (another, north of the market, is McCarthy & Schiering— ⊕*www.mccarthyandschiering.com*—in Queen Anne). It has a comprehensive stock of wines from the Pacific Northwest, California, Italy, and France—and expert advice from friendly salespeople to guide your choice.

MALLS

★ **Pacific Place** (⊠*600 Pine St., at 6th Ave., Downtown* ☎*206/405–2655* ⊕*www.pacificplaceseattle.com*) wraps shopping, dining, and an excellent movie multiplex around a four-story, light-filled atrium, making this a cheerful destination even on a stormy day. The mostly high-end shops include Cartier, Tiffany & Co., MaxMara, Coach, and Brookstone, though you can find some old standards here like Victoria's Secret, Aveda, and Eddie Bauer. A third-floor skybridge provides a rainproof route to the fantastic Nordstrom next door. One of the best things about the mall is its parking garage, which is surprisingly affordable given its location and has valet parking for just a few bucks more.

VANCOUVER, BRITISH COLUMBIA

Updated by Sue Kernaghan

Cosmopolitan Vancouver has a spectacular setting. Tall fir trees stand practically downtown, the Coast Mountains tower close by, the ocean laps at the doorstep, and people from every corner of the earth create a youthful and vibrant atmosphere.

Vancouver is a young city, even by North American standards. It was not yet a town in 1871, when British Columbia became part of the Canadian confederation. The city's history, such as it is, remains visible to the naked eye: eras are stacked east to west along the waterfront like some century-old archaeological dig—from cobblestone, late-Victorian Gastown to shiny postmodern glass cathedrals of commerce grazing the sunset.

Long a port city in a resource-based province, Vancouver is relatively new to tourism and, for that matter, to its famous laid-back West Coast lifestyle. Most locals mark Expo '86, when the city cleaned up old industrial sites and generated new tourism infrastructure, as the turning point. Another makeover is in the works now, as Vancouver, with Whistler, prepares to host the 2010 Winter Olympics. The mild climate, exquisite natural scenery, and relaxed outdoor lifestyle continually attract new residents, and the number of visitors is increasing for the same reasons.

There is much to see and do in Vancouver, but when time is limited (as it usually is for cruise-ship passengers), the most popular options are a stroll through Gastown and Chinatown, a visit to Granville Island, or a driving or biking tour of Stanley Park. If you have more time, head to the Museum of Anthropology, on the University of British Columbia campus; it's worth a trip.

VISITOR INFORMATION

For maps and information, stop at the **Vancouver Visitor Centre** (✉ *200 Burrard St.* ☎ *604/683–2000*). It's across the street from Canada Place and next door to the Fairmont Waterfront Hotel.

ON THE MOVE

GETTING TO THE PORT

Arriving in Vancouver makes a scenic finish to an Alaska cruise. Entering Burrard Inlet, ships pass the forested shores of Stanley Park and sail beneath the graceful sweep of the Lions Gate Bridge. Most ships calling at Vancouver dock at the Canada Place cruise-ship terminal on the downtown waterfront, a few minutes' walk from the city center. Its rooftop of dramatic white sails makes it instantly recognizable.

A few vessels depart from the Ballantyne cruise-ship terminal, which is a 10- to 15-minute, C$15 cab ride from downtown. Your hotel or cruise line may provide shuttle service to Ballantyne.

Contacts Ballantyne cruise ship terminal (✉ *655 Centennial Rd.* ☎ *604/665–9000 or 888/767–8826* ⊕ *www.portvancouver.com*). **Canada Place cruise ship terminal** (✉ *999 Canada Place Way* ☎ *604/665–9000 or 888/767–8826* ⊕ *www.portvancouver.com*).

ARRIVING BY AIR

Vancouver International Airport is 16 km (10 mi) south of downtown in the suburb of Richmond. It takes 30 to 45 minutes to get downtown from the airport.

Contacts Vancouver International Airport (☎ *604/207–7077* ⊕ *www.yvr.ca*).

AIRPORT TRANSFERS

The Vancouver Airporter Service bus leaves the domestic and international terminals approximately every 30 minutes, stopping at major downtown hotels and at the Canada Place cruise-ship terminal. It's C$14 one-way and C$22 round-trip. Taxi stands are in front of the terminal building; the fare downtown is about C$35 (about C$40 to Ballantyne Pier). Local cab companies include the reliable Black Top Cabs and Yellow Cabs, both of which serve the whole Vancouver area. Limousine service from LimoJet Gold costs about C$41 one-way for a 3-passenger sedan; $47 one-way for a 6-passenger stretch limo.

The Canada Line, the newest addition to Vancouver's rapid transit system, was, at this writing, due to open by September 2009. Once available, the line will run passengers directly from the Vancouver International Airport to the Canada Place cruise-ship terminal (and stops en route) in just 25 minutes. The station is inside the airport, on Level 4 between the domestic and international terminals. The trains, which are fully wheelchair accessible and allow plenty of room for luggage, will leave every six minutes from the airport and every three minutes from downtown Vancouver. Fares are $3.75 each way.

Contacts Black Top Cabs (☎604/681–2181). **LimoJet Gold** (☎604/273–1331 or 800/278–8742 ⊕ www.limojetgold.com). **TransLink** (☎604/953-3333 ⊕ www.translink.ca). **Vancouver Airporter Service** (☎604/946–8866 or 800/668–3141 ⊕ www.yvrairporter.com). **Yellow Cab** (☎604/681–1111).

ARRIVING BY CAR

From the south, I–5 from Seattle becomes Highway 99 at the U.S.–Canada border. Vancouver is a three-hour drive (226 km [140 mi]) from Seattle. It's best to avoid border crossings during peak times such as holidays and weekends. Highway 1, the Trans-Canada Highway, enters Vancouver from the east. To avoid traffic, arrive after rush hour (8:30 AM).

Vancouver's evening rush-hour traffic starts early—about 3 PM on week-days. The worst bottlenecks outside the city center are the North Shore bridges, the George Massey Tunnel on Highway 99 south of Vancouver, and Highway 1 through Coquitlam and Surrey. The BC Ministry of Transportation (☎800/550–4997 ⊕ www.drivebc.ca) has updates.

Vincipark offers secure underground parking in a two-level garage at Canada Place. Rates are C$27 per day for cruise-ship passengers (C$20 per day if reserved in advance); reservations, by phone or Web, are recommended. The entrance is at the foot of Howe Street. Cruisepark has a secured uncovered lot five minutes away from Canada Place, and offers a free shuttle service to and from Canada Place and Ballantyne cruise-ship terminals. Reservations via Web or phone are recommended. Rates start at C$19.20 per day or C$134 per week.

Contacts Vincipark (✉ 999 Canada Place Way ☎604/684–2251 or 866/856–8080 ⊕ www.vinciparkcanadaplace.ca). **Cruisepark** (✉ 455 Waterfront Rd. ☎800/665–0050 ⊕ www.cruisepark.com).

EXPLORING VANCOUVER

Vancouver is easy to navigate. The heart of the city—which includes the downtown area, the Canada Place cruise-ship terminal, Gastown, Chinatown, Stanley Park, and the West End high-rise residential neigh-borhood—sits on a peninsula hemmed in by English Bay and the Pacific Ocean to the west; by False Creek, the inlet home to Granville Island, to the south; and by Burrard Inlet, the working port of the city, to the north, past which loom the North Shore mountains.

DOWNTOWN AND GASTOWN

Many sights of interest are steps from the Canada Place cruise-ship terminal, in Vancouver's downtown core, and a few blocks east in the historic district of Gastown. Gastown is where Vancouver originated after "Gassy" Jack Deighton canoed into Burrard Inlet in 1867 and built a saloon. In 1885, when the Canadian Pacific Railway announced that Burrard Inlet would be the terminus for the new transcontinental railway, the little town—called Granville Townsite at the time—saw

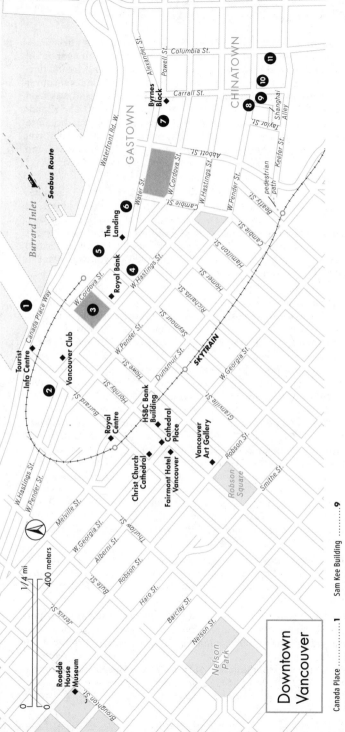

Downtown Vancouver

Canada Place **1**
Chinese Cultural Centre Museum and Archives **11**
Dr. Sun Yat-Sen Classical Chinese Garden **10**
Gaoler's Mews **7**
Marine Building **2**

Sam Kee Building **9**
Sinclair Centre **3**
Steam clock **6**
Vancouver Chinatown Millennium Gate **8**
Vancouver Lookout! **4**
Waterfront Station **5**

its population boom. But on June 13, 1886, two months after Granville's incorporation as the City of Vancouver, a clearing fire got out of control and burned down the entire town. It was rebuilt by the time the first transcontinental train arrived, in May 1887, and Vancouver then became a transfer point for trade with the Far East and was soon crowded with hotels, warehouses, brothels, and saloons. The Klondike gold rush encouraged further development, but the area began to decline after about 1912. In 1971 Gastown, along with Chinatown, was declared a historic district; the area has since been revitalized, and is home to boutiques, cafés, loft apartments, and souvenir shops.

GETTING THERE

A stroll from Canada Place into Gastown will take less than 15 minutes each way; allow an additional 30 minutes for the Vancouver Lookout at Harbour Centre. Note that the area just to the south of Gastown (roughly east of Cambie and south of Cordova) is one of Vancouver's roughest neighborhoods. Although Gastown itself (along Water Street) is busy with tourists and quite safe during the day, you may want to avoid walking through the area after dark.

WHAT TO SEE

① **Canada Place.** When Vancouver hosted the Expo '86 world's fair, this former cargo pier was transformed into the Canadian pavilion. Extending four city blocks (about half a mile) north into Burrard Inlet, the complex mimics the style and size of a luxury ocean liner, with exterior promenades and open deck space. The Teflon-coated fiberglass roof, shaped like five sails (the material was invented by NASA and once used in astronaut space suits!), has become a Vancouver skyline landmark. Home to Vancouver's main cruise-ship terminal, Canada Place can accommodate up to four luxury liners at once. It's also home to the luxurious **Pan Pacific Hotel** and the **Vancouver Convention Centre East**(☎604/647–7390). The new Vancouver Convention Centre West opened next door in 2009. At the north end of the complex, at the **Port Authority Interpretive Centre** (☎604/665–9179 ☑Free ☺ Weekdays 8–5), you can catch a video about the workings of the port, see some historic images of Vancouver's waterfront, or try your hand at a virtual container-loading game. Also at the north end, the **CN IMAX Theatre** (☎604/682–4629 ☑C$12, higher prices for some films) shows films on a screen five stories tall. ✉999 Canada Place Way, Downtown ☎604/775-7200 ⊕www.canadaplace.ca.

❼ **Gaoler's Mews.** Once the site of the city's first civic buildings—the constable's cabin and customs house, and a two-cell log jail—this atmospheric brick-paved courtyard today is home to cafés, an Irish pub, and architectural offices. ✉Behind 12 Water St., Gastown.

❷ **Marine Building.** Terra-cotta bas-reliefs depicting the history of transportation—airships, steamships, locomotives, and submarines—as well as Maya and Egyptian motifs and images of marine life, adorn this 1930 art deco structure. Step inside for a look at the beautifully restored interior, then walk to the corner of Hastings and Hornby streets for the best view of the building. ✉355 Burrard St., Downtown.

❸ Sinclair Centre. Vancouver architect Richard Henriquez knitted four buildings into Sinclair Centre, an office-retail complex that takes up an entire city block between Cordova and Hastings and Howe and Granville streets. Inside are high-end designer-clothing shops, federal government offices, and a number of fast-food outlets. The two Hastings Street buildings—the 1910 **Post Office,** which has an elegant clock tower, and the 1911 **Winch Building**—are linked with the 1937 **Post Office Extension** and the 1913 **Customs Examining Warehouse** to the north. As part of a meticulous restoration in the mid-1980s, the post-office facade was moved to the Granville Street side of the complex. The original clockwork from the old clock tower is on display inside, on the upper level of the arcade. ⊠*757 W. Hastings St., Downtown.*

❻ Steam Clock. An underground steam system, which also heats many local buildings, supplies the world's first steam clock—possibly Vancouver's most-photographed attraction. On the quarter hour a steam whistle rings out the Westminster chimes, and on the hour a huge cloud of steam spews from the apparatus. The ingenious design, based on an 1875 mechanism, was built in 1977 by Ray Saunders of Landmark Clocks (at 123 Cambie Street) to commemorate the community effort that saved Gastown from demolition. ⊠*Water and Cambie Sts., Gastown.*

❹ Vancouver Lookout! The lookout looks like a flying saucer stuck atop a high-rise, and at 553 feet high it affords one of the best views of Vancouver. A glass elevator whizzes you up 50 stories to the circular observation deck, where knowledgeable guides point out the sights and give a tour every hour on the hour. On a clear day you can see Vancouver Island and Mt. Baker in Washington State. The top-floor restaurant makes one complete revolution per hour; the elevator ride up is free for diners. ■TIP→ Tickets are good all day, so you can visit in daytime and return for another look after dark. ⊠*555 W. Hastings St., Downtown* ☎*604/689–0421* ⊕*www.vancouverlookout.com* ⊠*C$13* ☉*May–mid-Oct., daily 8:30 AM–10:30 PM; mid-Oct.–Apr., daily 9–9.*

❺ Waterfront Station. This former Canadian Pacific Railway passenger terminal was built between 1912 and 1914 as the western terminus for Canada's transcontinental railway. After Canada's two major railways shifted their focus away from passenger service, the station became obsolete, but a 1978 renovation turned it into an office-retail complex and depot for SkyTrain, SeaBus, and West Coast Express passengers. This is where you catch the SeaBus for the 13-minute trip across the harbor to the waterfront public market at Lonsdale Quay in North Vancouver. ⊠*601 W. Cordova St., Downtown* ☎*604/953–3333 SeaBus and SkyTrain, 604/488–8906 or 800/570–7245 West Coast Express.*

CHINATOWN

Vancouver's Chinatown, declared a historic district in 1971, is one of the oldest and largest such areas in North America. Many Chinese immigrants came to British Columbia during the 1850s seeking their fortunes in the Cariboo gold rush. Thousands more arrived in the 1880s, recruited as laborers to build the Canadian Pacific Railway. Though much of Vancouver's Chinese community has now moved to suburban Richmond, Chinatown is still a vital neighborhood. The style of architecture in Vancouver's Chinatown is patterned on that of Guangzhou (Canton).

GETTING THERE

Although Chinatown is less than a mile from the Canada Place cruise-ship terminal, it's best to get there by cab or bus to avoid walking through the city's rough skid-row neighborhood. You can get a taxi at the stand in front of Canada Place or take the SkyTrain to Stadium Station and walk east a few blocks along Keefer or Pender streets.

WHAT TO SEE

⑪ **Chinese Cultural Centre Museum and Archives.** This Ming Dynasty–style facility is dedicated to promoting an understanding of Chinese-Canadian history and culture. A compelling permanent exhibit on the first floor traces the history of Chinese Canadians in British Columbia. The art gallery upstairs hosts traveling exhibits by Chinese and Canadian artists. A Chinese-Canadian military museum is also on-site. A monument across Columbia Street commemorates the community's contribution to the city, province, and country. ⊠ *555 Columbia St., Chinatown* ☎ *604/658–8880* ⊕ *www.cccvan.com* ☺ *C$4.50, Tues. by donation* ☺ *Tues.–Sun. 11–5.*

⑩ **Dr. Sun Yat-Sen Classical Chinese Garden.** The first authentic Ming Dynasty–
★ style garden outside China, this small garden was built in 1986 by 52 artisans from Suzhou, China. It incorporates design elements and traditional materials from several of Suzhou's centuries-old private gardens. No power tools, screws, or nails were used in the construction. Guided tours (45 minutes long), included in the ticket price, are conducted on the hour between mid-June and the end of August (call ahead for off-season tour times); they are valuable for understanding the philosophy and symbolism that are central to the garden's design. ■TIP→ **Covered walkways make this a good rainy-day choice.** ⊠ *578 Carrall St., Chinatown* ☎ *604/662–3207* ⊕ *www.vancouverchinesegarden.com* ☺ *C$10* ☺ *May–mid-June and Sept., daily 10–6; mid-June–Aug., daily 9:30–7; Oct., daily 10–4:30; Nov.–Apr., Tues.–Sun. 10–4:30.*

⑨ **Sam Kee Building.** *Ripley's Believe It or Not!* recognizes this structure, dating from about 1913, as the narrowest office building in the world. In 1913, when the city confiscated most of merchant Chang Toy's land to widen Pender Street, he built in protest on what he had left—just 6 feet. These days the building houses an insurance agency whose employees make do with the 4-foot-10-inch-wide interior. ⊠ *8 W. Pender St., Chinatown.*

⑧ **Vancouver Chinatown Millennium Gate.** This brightly painted, three-story-high arch spanning Pender Street was erected in 2002 to commemorate the Chinese community's role in Vancouver's history. The gate incorporates both Eastern and Western symbols, and both traditional and modern Chinese themes. Just east of the gate is the entrance to **Chinatown Heritage Alley,** the site of Vancouver's first Chinese settlement. At the end of the alley is a replica of the West Han Dynasty Bell, a gift to Vancouver from the city of Guangzhou, China. Surrounding the bell is a series of panels relating some of the area's early history. ⊠ *Pender at Taylor St., Chinatown* ☎ *No phone* ☺ *Free.*

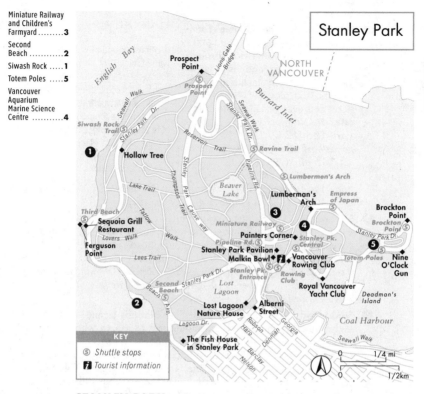

STANLEY PARK

Fodor'sChoice ★ A morning or afternoon in Stanley Park gives you a capsule tour of Vancouver that includes beaches, the ocean, Douglas fir and cedar forests, and a view of the North Shore mountains. One of the most popular ways to see the park is to walk, rollerblade, or cycle along Vancouver's famous Seawall Walk, a 9-km (5½-mi) seaside pathway around the park's circumference. The seawall extends an additional mile east past the marinas, cafés, and waterfront condominiums of Coal Harbour to Canada Place downtown, so you could start your walk or ride from there.

GETTING THERE

To get to the park by public transit, take Stanley Park Bus 19 from the corner of Pender and Howe, downtown. It's possible to see the park by car, entering at the foot of Georgia Street and driving counterclockwise around the one-way Stanley Park Drive. An even better option is to take the free **Stanley Park Shuttle** (☎604/257–8400 ⊕*www.vancouver.ca/parks/*), which provides frequent transportation between the park entrance and all the major sights daily from mid-June to mid-September. However, at the time of writing the service had been suspended indefinitely.

WHAT TO SEE

❸ Miniature Railway and Children's Farm-
☕ yard. A child-size steam train takes kids and adults on a ride through the woods. Next door is a farmyard full of critters, including goats, rabbits, and pigs. ■ TIP➔ **A family ticket gets everyone in for the child's rate.** ✉ *Off Pipeline Rd., Stanley Park* ☎ *604/257–8531* ⊕ *vancouver.ca/parks/parks/stanley/fun.htm* 🎫 *Each site C$6, C$3 for adults accompanying children* ⊙ *Feb.–mid-May, weekends 11–4, weather permitting; late June–Labor Day, daily 10:30–5; call for holiday and off-season hours.*

TOURING TIP

A whimsical option is a ride with Stanley Park Horse-Drawn Tours (☎ *604/681–5115* ⊕ *www.stanleypark.com*); the C$26.99 fare usually includes a free bus ride (though it was temporarily unavailable at this writing; call ahead) from the Canada Place cruise-ship terminal to Stanley Park.

❷ Second Beach. The 50-meter pool, which has lifeguards and waterslides,
☕ is a popular spot in summer. The sandy beach has a playground and covered picnic areas. If you like romantic beachside sunsets, this is one for the books. ☎ *604/257–8371 summer only* ⊕ *www.vancouver.ca/parks/* 🎫 *Beach free, pool C$5.15* ⊙ *Pool mid-May–mid-June, weekdays noon–8:45, weekends 10–8:45; mid-June–late July, daily 10–8:45; Aug.–Labor Day, daily 10–8:30.*

❶ Siwash Rock. According to a local First Nations legend, this 50-foot-high offshore promontory is a monument to a man who was turned into stone as a reward for his unselfishness. The rock is visible from the seawall; if you're driving, you need to park and take a short path through the woods. Watch for the Hollow Tree nearby. This 56-foot-wide burnt cedar stump has shrunk over the years but still gives an idea of how large some of the old-growth trees can be.

❺ Totem poles. Totem poles are an important art form among native peoples along British Columbia's coast. These eight poles, all carved in the latter half of the 20th century, include replicas of poles originally brought to the park from the north coast in the 1920s, as well as poles carved specifically for the park by First Nations artists. The several styles of poles represent a cross section of B.C. native groups, including the Kwakwaka'wakw, Haida, and Nisga'a. An information center near the site has a snack bar, a gift shop, and information about B.C.'s First Nations.

❹ Vancouver Aquarium Marine Science Centre. Massive pools with windows
☕ below water level let you come face to face with beluga whales, sea
★ lions, dolphins, and harbor seals at this research and educational facility. In the Amazon rain-forest gallery you can walk through a jungle populated with piranhas, caimans, and tropical birds, and in summer you'll be surrounded by hundreds of free-flying butterflies. Other displays, many with hands-on features for kids, show the underwater life of coastal British Columbia and the Canadian Arctic. Beluga whale and dolphin shows, as well as dive shows (where divers swim with aquatic life, including sharks), are held daily. For an extra fee you can join an Animal Encounter and help the trainers feed and train otters, sea turtles, and sea lions. There's also a café and a gift shop. Be prepared

for lines on weekends and school holidays. ■ TIP→ **The quietest times to visit are before 11 AM or after 3 PM**. ☎604/659–3474 ⊕www.vanaqua. org ☑C$19.95 ⊙July–Labor Day, daily 9:30–7; Labor Day–June, daily 9:30–5.

★ **GRANVILLE ISLAND**

This 35-acre peninsula in False Creek, just south of downtown Vancouver, is home to one of North America's most successful urban-redevelopment schemes. Once a derelict industrial site, Granville Island is now a vibrant urban park, with a bustling public market, several theaters, galleries, crafts shops, and artisans' studios.

GETTING THERE

The favorite way to get to Granville Island is via the mini AquaBus ferries (it's about a 2-minute ride) that depart from the south end of Hornby Street. It's a 15-minute walk from downtown Vancouver to where the ferries depart. The Aquabus delivers passengers across False Creek to the **Granville Island Public Market**, which has a slew of food and other stalls. False Creek ferries leave every five minutes for Granville Island from a dock behind the Vancouver Aquatic Centre, on Beach Avenue. Still another option is to take a 20-minute ride on a Trans-Link bus: from Waterfront Station or stops on Granville Street, take False Creek South Bus 50 to the edge of the island. Buses 4 UBC and 7 Dunbar will also take you within a few minutes' walk of the island. The market is a short walk from the bus or ferry stop. If you drive, parking is free for up to three hours, and paid parking is available in four garages on the island.

Another way to travel is to hop on the **Downtown Historic Railway** (☎604/665–3903 ⊕www.trams.bc.ca), two early-20th-century electric trams that on summer weekends and holiday afternoons run from Science World to Granville Island. At this writing, Olympics-related construction has forced the railway to cease operations, but it's expected to be back online soon and new trams are planned for 2010.

WHAT TO SEE

Fodor'sChoice **Granville Island Public Market.** Because no chain stores are allowed in
★ this 50,000-square-foot building, each shop here is unique. Dozens of stalls sell locally grown produce direct from the farm; others sell crafts, chocolates, cheese, fish, meat, flowers, and exotic foods. On Thursday in summer market gardeners sell fruit and vegetables from trucks outside. At the north end of the market you can pick up a snack, lunch, or coffee at one of the many food stalls. The Market Courtyard, on the water side, is a good place to catch street entertainers. Weekends can get madly busy. ⊠1689 Johnston St., Granville Island ☎604/666–6477 ⊕www.granvilleisland.com ⊙Daily 9–7.

OUTSIDE DOWNTOWN

Fodor'sChoice **Museum of Anthropology.** On a cliff top overlooking the Pacific, the MOA
★ houses one of the world's leading collections of Northwest Coast First Nations art. The Great Hall displays dramatic cedar poles, bentwood boxes, and canoes adorned with traditional Northwest Coast painted designs; exquisite carvings of gold, silver, and argillite (black shale) are also on display. The museum's collection also includes tools, textiles,

masks, and other artifacts from around the world, as well as a gallery of European ceramics. Behind the museum are two Haida houses set on the cliff over the water. Free guided tours—given twice daily in summer, usually at 11 and 2 (call to confirm times)—are very informative. The museum is about 30 minutes, or a C$25 taxi ride, from Canada Place. To reach the museum by transit, take UBC Bus 4 from Granville Street or Bus 44 from Burrard Street downtown to the university loop, a 10-minute walk from the museum. ⊠ *University of British Columbia, 6393 N.W. Marine Dr., Point Grey* ☎ *604/822–5087* ⊕ *www.moa.ubc.ca* ⊠ *C$14; $C7 Tues. 5–9* ⊙ *Memorial Day–mid-Oct., Tues. 10–9, Wed.–Mon. 10–5; mid-Oct.–Memorial Day, Tues. 10–9, Wed.–Sun. 10–5.*

WHERE TO EAT

A diverse gastronomic experience awaits you in cosmopolitan Vancouver. A wave of Asian immigration and tourism has brought a proliferation of upscale Asian eateries. Cutting-edge restaurants currently perfecting and defining Pacific Northwest fare—including such homegrown regional favorites as salmon and oysters, accompanied by British Columbia wines—have become some of the city's leading attractions.

You're also spoiled for choice when it comes to casual and budget dining. Good choices include Asian cafés or any of the pubs listed in the Nightlife section; many have both an adults-only pub and a separate restaurant section where kids are welcome. A bylaw bans smoking indoors in all Vancouver restaurants, bars, and pubs.

Vancouver dining is fairly informal. Casual but neat dress is appropriate everywhere. A 15% tip is expected. A 5% Goods and Services Tax (GST) is added to the food portion of the bill and a 10% liquor tax is charged on wine, beer, and spirits. Some restaurants build the liquor tax into the price of the beverage, but others add it to the bill.

$$–$$$
CONTEMPORARY

✕ **Aqua Riva.** This lofty modern room, replete with dramatic art deco murals and an open kitchen, is yards from the Canada Place cruise-ship terminal. A wall of windows affords striking views over the harbor and the North Shore mountains. Food from the wood-fired oven, rotisserie, and grill includes thin-crust pizzas with innovative toppings, roasted wild salmon, and spit-roasted chicken. Lunch brings a good selection of salads, pizzas, sandwiches, and salmon dishes. A microbrew and martini list rounds out the menu. ⊠ *200 Granville St., Downtown* ☎ *604/683–5599* ⊟ *AE, DC, MC, V* ⊙ *No lunch weekends.*

$$$$
SEAFOOD
Fodor'sChoice
★

✕ **C Restaurant.** Save your pennies, fish fans—dishes such as twice-cooked sablefish served with oyama chorizo ravioli or bacon-glazed scallops have established this spot as Vancouver's most innovative seafood restaurant. Start with shucked oysters from the raw bar or perhaps the candied salmon belly. The six- or ten-course tasting menus with optional wine pairings highlight regional seafood. Both the ultramodern interior and the waterside patio overlook False Creek, but dine before dark to enjoy the view. ⊠ *2–1600 Howe St., Downtown* ☎ *604/681–1164* ⊟ *AE, DC, MC, V* ⊙ *No lunch weekends*

$$$–$$$$
SEAFOOD

✕ **The Fish House in Stanley Park.** This 1930s former sports pavilion with two verandas and a fireplace is surrounded by gardens, tucked between

Stanley Park's tennis courts and putting green. Chef Karen Barnaby's food, including fresh oysters, grilled ahi tuna steak with a green-peppercorn sauce, and corn-husk-wrapped salmon with a maple glaze, is flavorful and unpretentious. Check the fresh sheet for the current day's catch. Traditional English afternoon tea is served between 2 and 4 daily. ✉*8901 Stanley Park Dr., Stanley Park* ☎*604/681–7275 or 877/681–7275* ⊟*AE, DC, MC, V.*

$ ✕**Go Fish.** If the weather's fine, head for this seafood stand on the docks
SEAFOOD near Granville Island. It's owned by Gord Martin, of Bin 941/942 fame,
★ so it's not your ordinary chippie. The menu is short—highlights include fish-and-chips, grilled salmon or tuna sandwiches, and oyster po'boys—but the quality is first-rate, and the accompanying Asian-flavored slaw leaves ordinary cole slaw in the dust. There are just a few (outdoor) tables, so go early or be prepared to wait. To get here, walk along the waterfront path from Granville Island; by car, drive east from Burrard on 1st Avenue until it ends at the docks. ✉*1505 W. 1st Ave., Fisherman's Wharf, Kitsilano* ☎*604/730–5040* ⊟*MC, V* ☉*Mon.–Fri. 11:30–6:30, weekends 12–6:30.*

$–$$ ✕**Hon's Wun-Tun House.** This Vancouver minichain has been keeping
CHINESE residents and tourists in Chinese comfort food since the 1970s. You can find better Chinese food elsewhere, but Hon's locations are convenient and the prices are reasonable. The best bets on the 300-item menu are the dumplings and noodle dishes, any of the Chinese vegetables, and anything with barbecued meat. The Robson Street outlet has a separate kitchen for vegetarians and an army of fast-moving waitresses. The original Keefer Street location is in the heart of Chinatown. ✉*1339 Robson St., West End* ☎*604/685–0871* ⊟*MC, V* ✉*268 Keefer St., Chinatown* ☎*604/688–0871* ⊟*MC, V.*

$–$$ ✕**Salt Tasting Room.** If your idea of a perfect lunch or light supper revolves
IRISH around fine cured meats, artisanal cheeses, and a glass of wine from a wide-ranging list, find your way to this sleek, spare space in a decidedly unsleek Gastown lane. The restaurant has no kitchen and simply assembles its first-quality provisions, perhaps meaty *bundnerfleisch* (cured beef), local pork-liver paté, or B.C.–made Camembert, with accompanying condiments, into artfully composed grazers' delights—more like an upscale picnic than a full meal. There's no sign out front, so look for the saltshaker flag in Blood Alley, which is off Abbott Street, half a block south of Water Street. ✉*45 Blood Alley, Gastown* ☎*604/633–1912* ⊟*AE, MC, V.*

$$$ ✕**The Teahouse in Stanley Park.** The former officers' mess in Stanley Park
CONTEMPORARY is perfectly poised for watching sunsets over the water. The Pacific Northwest menu is not especially innovative, but it includes such specialties as red-wine-poached pear salad, and mushrooms stuffed with crab and mascarpone cheese, as well as seasonally changing treatments of lamb and B.C. salmon, In summer you can dine on the patio. ✉*7501 Stanley Park Dr., Ferguson Point, Stanley Park* ☎*604/669–3281 or 800/280–9893* ⊟*AE, MC, V.*

WHERE TO STAY

Accommodations in Vancouver range from luxurious waterfront hotels to neighborhood B&Bs and basic European-style pensions. Many of the best choices are in the downtown core, either in the central business district or in the West End near Stanley Park. The chart in the Port Essentials section shows high-season prices, but from mid-October through May rates throughout the city can drop as much as 50 percent. Most Vancouver hotels are completely no-smoking in both rooms and public areas.

$$–$$$ ⊞**Days Inn.** Two blocks from the Canada Place cruise-ship terminal, this moderately priced, well-secured boutique hotel operates a free shuttle to the two cruise-ship terminals as well as Vancouver's train and bus station. Rooms in this 1918 eight-story building (with an elevator) are small and lack views, but are freshly renovated with checked duvets, pine furniture, and crown moldings. The two-bedroom, one-bathroom corner units are a good value for groups and families. This hotel is entirely no-smoking. **Pros:** good value for downtown location. **Cons:** noisy on weekends. ⊠*921 W. Pender St., Downtown* ☎*604/681–4335 or 877/681–4335* ⊕*www.daysinnvancouver.com* ↘*80 rooms, 5 suites* ☼*In-room: safe, refrigerator (some), Wi-Fi. In-hotel: restaurant, laundry facilities, laundry service, public Internet, public Wi-Fi, parking (fee), no-smoking rooms* ▤*AE, D, DC, MC, V.*

$$$$ ⊞**Fairmont Waterfront.** This luxuriously modern 23-story hotel is across the street from the Convention Centre and the Canada Place cruise-ship terminal, but it's the floor-to-ceiling windows with ocean and mountain views in most of the guest rooms that really make this hotel special. Adorned with blond-wood furniture and contemporary Canadian artwork, each room also has a window that opens. Elevator waits can be frustrating, so consider asking for a room on a lower floor, though you'll be sacrificing view for this minor convenience. Next to the mountain-view pool is a rooftop herb garden—an aromatic retreat open to guests. The hotel's canine ambassador, Holly, is available for petting, pampering, and taking for strolls. **Pros:** harbor views, proximity to cruise-ship terminal, the lovely rooftop pool near the patio herb garden. **Cons:** occasional elevator line-ups; the lobby lounge can get busy. ⊠*900 Canada Pl. Way, Downtown* ☎*604/691–1991* 🖷*604/691–1999* ⊕*www.fairmont.com/waterfront* ↘*489 rooms, 29 suites* ☼*In-room: safe (some), refrigerator, Internet. In-hotel: restaurant, room service, bar, pool, gym, concierge, laundry service, executive floor, public Wi-Fi, parking (fee), some pets allowed, no-smoking rooms* ▤*AE, D, DC, MC, V.*

$$$–$$$$ ⊞**O Canada House B&B.** This beautifully restored 1897 Victorian within walking distance of downtown is where the first version of "O Canada," the national anthem, was written, in 1909. Each bedroom has late-Victorian antiques, and modern comforts such as bathrobes help make things homey. The top-floor room is enormous, with two king beds and a private sitting/dining area. A separate one-room cottage suite in the garden is a romantic option, though it faces onto the back alley and is a bit cramped. Breakfast, served in the dining room, is a lavish affair. **Pros:** gracious service, fantastic breakfast, residential location. **Cons:** rooms on the small side (except the top floor). ⊠*1114 Barclay*

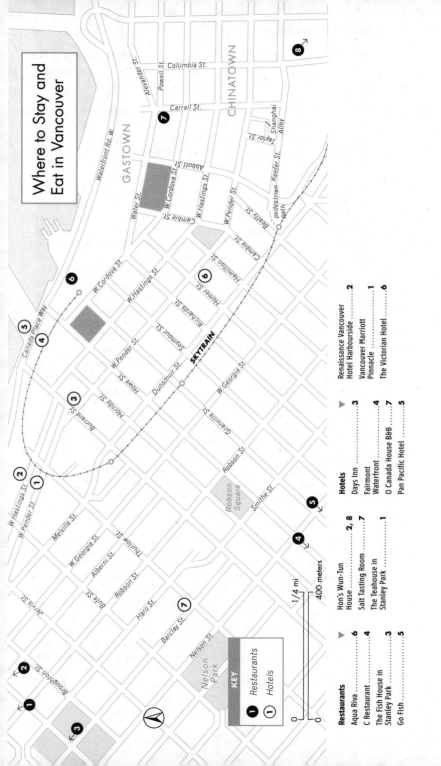

Where to Stay and Eat in Vancouver

GASTOWN

CHINATOWN

SKYTRAIN

Robson
Square

Nelson
Park

Streets

W. Hastings St.
W. Pender St.
Broughton St.
Jervis St.
Melville St.
W. Georgia St.
Thurlow St.
Alberni St.
Bute St.
Robson St.
Haro St.
Barclay St.
Nelson St.
Burrard St.
Hornby St.
Howe St.
Dunsmuir St.
Seymour St.
Richards St.
Hamilton St.
Homer St.
Cambie St.
Beatty St.
Smithe St.
Robson St.
W. Georgia St.
Granville St.
Canada Place Way
W. Cordova St.
W. Hastings St.
W. Pender St.
Water St.
W. Cordova St.
Cambie St.
Abbott St.
W. Hastings St.
W. Pender St.
Carrall St.
Alexander St.
Powell St.
Columbia St.
Taylor St.
Keefer St.
Shanghai Alley
Waterfront Rd. W.

pedestrian path

KEY

1 Restaurants
1 Hotels

1/4 mi
400 meters

Restaurants

▶ Aqua Riva 6
C Restaurant 4
The Fish House in
Stanley Park 3
Go Fish 5

Hon's Wun-Tun
House 2, 8
Salt Tasting Room 7
The Teahouse in
Stanley Park 1

Hotels

Days Inn 3
Fairmont
Waterfront 4
O Canada House B&B 7
Pan Pacific Hotel 5

Renaissance Vancouver
Hotel Harbourside 2
Vancouver Marriott
Pinnacle 1
The Victorian Hotel 6

St., West End ☎604/688–0555 or 877/688–1114 🖷604/488–0556 ⊕*www.ocanadahouse.com* ➲*7 rooms* ☀*In-room: no a/c, refrigerator, Wi-Fi. In-hotel: parking (no fee), public Wi-Fi, no kids under 12, no-smoking rooms* ☰*MC, V* ⊗*BP.*

$$$$ **Pan Pacific Hotel.** A centerpiece of waterfront Canada Place, the luxu-
★   rious Pan Pacific shares a complex with part of the Vancouver Convention Centre and Vancouver's main cruise-ship terminal. Rooms are large
and modern, with maple wood throughout, Italian linens, and stunning
harbor, mountain, or skyline views, all of which have been enjoyed by
a host of royals, celebs, and well-heeled newsmakers. The 26-room
Roman bath–theme Spa Utopia and Salon is sumptuous, and the health
and fitness center is state-of-the-art. **Pros:** harbor views; it's only an
elevator ride to the cruise-ship terminal; the "go the extra mile" service
attitude. **Cons:** the atrium is open to the convention center's main lobby,
so the hotel foyer, lounge, and entrance fill with delegates bearing conference badges and talking shop, nabbing the best seats in the house,
and vying for taxis. ✉*999 Canada Pl., Downtown* ☎604/662–8111,
800/663–1515 in Canada, 800/937–1515 in U.S. 🖷604/685–8690
⊕*www.panpacific.com* ➲*464 rooms, 39 suites* ☀*In-room: refrigerator, safe, kitchen (some), Internet. In-hotel: 2 restaurants, room service,
bar, pool, gym, spa, concierge, laundry service, parking (fee), Wi-Fi,
some pets allowed, no-smoking rooms* ☰*AE, D, DC, MC, V.*

$$$–$$$$ **Renaissance Vancouver Hotel Harbourside.** Like the Vancouver water-
front, this business-district hotel is constantly transforming as the Olym-
pics approaches, but rooms are larger than average and have either
step-out or full-size glassed-in balconies with city or (in the more expen-
sive rooms) full or partial water and mountain views. There's direct
access to a water park and indoor pool, making this a good choice for
families. The hotel is also handy to a waterfront path leading to Stanley
Park and Canada Place. **Pros:** at the outer edge of the financial district,
waterfront views, a five-minute walk from Canada Place cruise-ship ter-
minal. **Cons:** a 5-block walk from major shopping. ✉*1133 W. Hastings
St., Downtown* ☎604/689–9211 or 800/905–8582 🖷604/689–4358
⊕*www.renaissancevancouver.com* ➲*442 rooms, 6 suites* ☀*In-room:
safe (some), Internet, Wi-Fi. In-hotel: restaurant, room service, bar, pool,
gym, concierge, laundry service, executive floor, public Wi-Fi, parking
(fee), some pets allowed, no-smoking rooms* ☰*AE, D, DC, MC, V.*

¢–$ **The Victorian Hotel.** Budget hotels can be beautiful, too, as proven
by the hardwood floors, high ceilings, and chandeliers at this prettily
restored 1898 European-style pension. Offering some of Vancouver's
best-value accommodations, guest rooms in the two connecting three-
story buildings have down duvets and oriental rugs; a few have bay
windows or mountain views. **Pros:** great location for the price, helpful
staff, clean, comfortable. **Cons:** location near the "rummy part of town"
a few blocks east. It's relatively safe (honest), but common sense says
you would probably take a cab to the door after midnight rather than
walk. ✉*514 Homer St., Downtown* ☎877/681–6369 or 604/681–
6369 🖷604/681–8776 ⊕*www.victorianhotel.ca* ➲*39 rooms, 18 with
bath* ☀*In-room: no a/c, refrigerator (some), Wi-Fi (some). In-hotel:
public Wi-Fi, parking (fee), no-smoking rooms* ☰*AE, MC, V* ⊗*CP
(in winter only).*

NIGHTLIFE

For information on events, pick up a free copy of the *Georgia Straight,* available at cafés and bookstores around town, or look in the entertainment section of the *Vancouver Sun* (Thursday's paper has listings). For tickets, book through **Ticketmaster** (☎*604/280–4444* ⊕*www.ticketmaster.ca*). You can pick up half-price tickets on the day of the event, as well as full-price advance tickets, at **Tickets Tonight** (⊠*200 Burrard St., Downtown* ☎*604/684–2787* ⊕*www.ticketstonight.ca*), at the Vancouver Tourist Info Centre.

BARS, PUBS, AND LOUNGES

A massive deck with expansive False Creek views is the big draw at **Bridges** (⊠*1696 Duranleau St., Granville Island* ☎*604/687–4400*), near the public market. There's a cozy pub and a restaurant at the same site. A seaside patio, casual Pacific Northwest restaurant, and house-brewed beer make the **Dockside Brewing Company** (⊠*Granville Island Hotel, 1253 Johnston St., Granville Island* ☎*604/685–7070*) a popular hangout. For a pint of properly poured Guinness and live traditional Irish music every Tuesday and Thursday night, try the **Irish Heather** (⊠*212 Carrall St., Gastown* ☎*604/688–9779*). Harbor views, pub food, and traditionally brewed beer are the draws at **Steamworks** (⊠*375 Water St., Gastown* ☎*604/689–2739*), brewpub on the edge of Gastown; a coffee bar and a restaurant open to all ages are also on-site.

COMEDY

The **Vancouver TheatreSports League** (☎*604/738–7013* ⊕*www.vtsl. com*), a hilarious improv troupe, performs four nights a week at the **New Revue Stage** (⊠*1601 Johnston St.*) on Granville Island. Stand-up comedians perform Tuesday to Saturday evenings at **Yuk Yuk's** (⊠*1015 Burrard St., Downtown* ☎*604/696–9857* ⊕*www.yukyuks.com*) in the Century Plaza Hotel.

SHOPPING

Unlike many cities where suburban malls have taken over, Vancouver is full of individual boutiques and specialty shops. Antiques stores, ethnic markets, art galleries, gourmet-food shops, and high-fashion outlets abound, and you can find strong Asian and First Nations influences in crafts, home furnishings, and foods. Store hours are generally 10–6 Monday, Tuesday, Wednesday, and Saturday; 10–9 Thursday and Friday; and 11–6 Sunday.

You'll pay both 7% Provincial Sales Tax (PST) and 5% Goods and Services Tax (GST) on most purchases.

SHOPPING DISTRICTS

Robson Street, stretching from Burrard to Bute, is the city's main fashion-shopping and people-watching artery. Gap and Banana Republic have their flagship stores here, as do Canadian fashion outlets Club Monaco and Roots. Souvenir shops and cafés line the way; west of Bute, Asian food shops, video outlets, and cheap noodle bars abound. Shops in and near **Sinclair Centre** (⊠*757 W. Hastings St., Downtown*) cater to sophisticated and pricey tastes. Bustling **Chinatown**—centered on Pender and

Main streets—is at its liveliest on weekend evenings in summer, when the Chinatown Night Market, an Asian-style outdoor street market, sets up along Keefer Street. There's an even bigger Asian-style nighttime market, also on summer weekends, south of Vancouver at the **Richmond Night Market** (⊠*12631 Vulcan Way, off Bridgeport Rd. at Sweden Way, Richmond* ☎*604/244–8448*). **Granville Island** has a lively public market and a wealth of galleries, crafts shops, and artisans' studios. **South Granville,** along Granville Street between Broadway and 16th Avenue, is lined with high-end fashion, home decor, art galleries, and specialty food shops. Treasure hunters should check out the 300 block of **West Cordova Street,** near Gastown, where offbeat shops sell curios, vintage clothing, and locally designed fashions. **Yaletown,** a gentrified former warehouse district centered on Davie and Hamilton streets, is home to chic fashion and housewares shops.

ART GALLERIES

Gallery Row along Granville Street between 5th and 15th avenues has about a dozen high-end contemporary art galleries. Gastown has the city's best selection of First Nations and Inuit galleries.

Buschlen Mowatt (⊠*1445 W. Georgia St., West End* ☎*604/682–1234*) exhibits the works of contemporary Canadian and international artists. **Hill's Native Art** (⊠*165 Water St., Gastown* ☎*604/685–4249*) has Vancouver's largest selection of First Nations art. The **Inuit Gallery of Vancouver** (⊠*206 Cambie St., Gastown* ☎*604/688–7323 or 888/615–8399*) exhibits Northwest Coast and Inuit art.

CLOTHES

Dream (⊠*311 W. Cordova St., Gastown* ☎*604/683–7326*) is where up-and-coming local designers sell their wares. You'll find affordable North American fashions—and an Italian café—at **L2** on Leone's lower floor. For outdoorsy clothes that double as souvenirs (many sport maple-leaf logos), check out the sweatshirts, leather jackets, and other cozy casuals at **Roots** (⊠*1001 Robson St., West End* ☎*604/683–4305*).

Ports of Call

WORD OF MOUTH

"We booked our own tours when we cruised to Alaska . . . we booked a helicopter to see the glacier (and land on it) in Juneau. We booked a kayak trip in Sitka and spent time in the town. I loved kayaking in Sitka. It was lightly raining part of the time, but it didn't matter. The views were dramatic and the experience was very "whole body."

—Orcas

Updated by
Jessy Bow-
man, Sue
Kernaghan,
Edward
Readicker-Hen-
derson, Tom
Reale, and
Sarah Wyatt

THERE'S NEVER A DULL DAY on an Alaskan cruise, and whether your ship is scheduled to make a port call, cruise by glaciers, or glide through majestic fjords, you'll have constant opportunities to explore the culture, wildlife, history, and amazing scenery that make Alaska so unique. Most port cities are small and easily explored on foot, but if you prefer to be shown the sights, your ship will offer organized shore excursions at each stop along the way. Popular activities include city tours, flight-seeing, charter fishing, river rafting, and visits to native communities. You can also, for the sake of shorter trips and/or more active excursions, readily organize your own tour through a local vendor.

The ports visited and the amount of time spent in each vary depending on the cruise line and itinerary, but most ships stop in Ketchikan, Juneau, and Skagway—the three big draws in Southeast Alaska. Some ports, such as Homer and Metlakatla, are visited by only a couple of the small-ship cruise lines, while other adventure ships head out to explore the wild places in the Bering Sea. Each town has its highlights. For example, Ketchikan has a wealth of native artifacts, Skagway has lots of gold-rush history, Sitka has a rich Russian and native heritage, and Juneau has glacier trips. There are also ample shopping opportunities in most ports (fewer in Wrangell), but beware of tacky tourist traps. All Southeast towns, but especially Haines, Sitka, and Ketchikan, have great art galleries.

PORT ESSENTIALS

RESTAURANTS AND CUISINE

Not surprisingly, seafood dominates most menus. In summer, salmon, halibut, crab, cod, and prawns are usually fresh. Restaurants are informal and casual clothes are the norm; you'll never be sent away for wearing jeans in an Alaskan restaurant.

WHAT IT COSTS					
	¢	$	$$	$$$	$$$$
Alaskan Ports	under $9	under $9	$9–$15	$16–$25	over $25
Canadian Ports	under C$15	under C$15	C$15–C$27	C$28–C$40	over C$40

*Prices are per person for a main course at dinner.

OUTDOOR ACTIVITIES

There are hikes and walks in or near every Alaska port town. Well-maintained trails are easily accessible from even the largest cities; lush forests and wilderness areas, port and glacier views, and mountaintop panoramas are often within a few hours' walk of downtown areas. More adventurous travelers will enjoy paddling sea kayaks in the protected waters of Southeast and South Central Alaska; companies in most ports rent kayaks and give lessons and tours. Fishing enthusiasts from all over the world come to Alaska for a chance to land a trophy salmon or halibut. Cycling, glacier hikes, flightseeing, or bear-viewing shore excursions in some ports also offer cruise passengers an opportunity

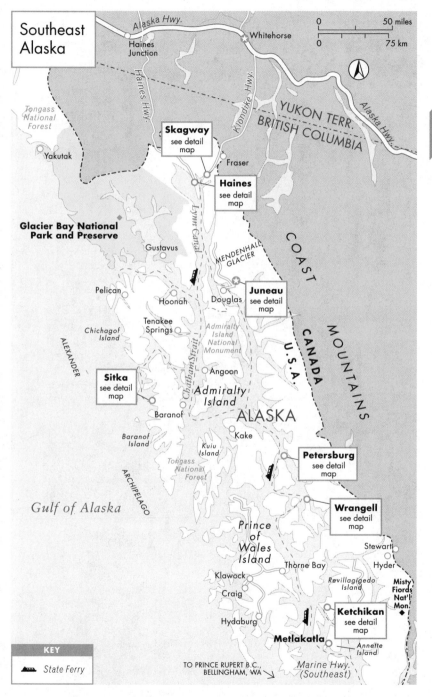

Southeast Alaska

Alaska Hwy.

Whitehorse

Haines
Junction

0   50 miles
0   75 km

3

*Tongass
National
Forest*

Yakutat

Skagway
see detail
map

Fraser

YUKON TERR.
BRITISH COLUMBIA

Haines
see detail
map

Haines Hwy.

Klondike Hwy.

Alaska Hwy.

**Glacier Bay National
Park and Preserve**

Gustavus

MENDENHALL
GLACIER

C
O
A
S
T

Pelican

Hoonah   Douglas

Juneau
see detail
map

*Chichagof
Island*

Tenakee
Springs

*Admiralty
Island
National
Monument*

CANADA

U.S.A.

M
O
U
N
T
A
I
N
S

ALEXANDER

Lynn Canal

Chatham Strait

Angoon

Sitka
see detail
map

Baranof

*Admiralty
Island*

ALASKA

*Baranof
Island*

Kake

*Kuiu
Island*

*Tongass
National
Forest*

Petersburg
see detail
map

Gulf of Alaska

ARCHIPELAGO

*Prince
of
Wales
Island*

Wrangell
see detail
map

Stewart

Thorne Bay

*Revillagigedo
Island*

Hyder

**Misty
Fiords
Nat'l
Mon.**

Klawock

Craig

Hydaburg

Ketchikan
see detail
map

Metlakatla

*Annette
Island*

KEY

State Ferry

TO PRINCE RUPERT B.C.,
BELLINGHAM, WA

*Marine Hwy.
(Southeast)*

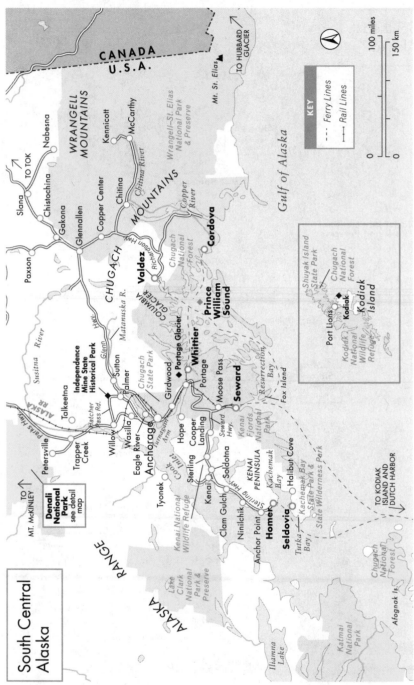

South Central Alaska

to engage with Alaska's endless landscape.

BARS AND SALOONS

Shooting the breeze at a bar or saloon can be a delightfully colorful contrast to barstool-surfing the cruise-ship lounge areas. There isn't really a difference between saloons and bars; some saloons offer a setting that lets travelers pretend they've stepped back in time to the gold rush, but other places that call themselves bars can be equally historic and interesting. High-volume watering holes in the busiest ports (such as the Red Dog in Juneau and the Red Onion in Skagway) serve food in addition to drinks. Pubs in Canadian ports often have an Irish or British rather than gold-rush theme; all serve food, and many even brew their own beer.

NAVIGATING THIS CHAPTER

To help you plan your trip, we've compiled a list of the most worthwhile excursions available in each port of call (keep in mind that these lists aren't comprehensive; your cruise line may offer other options). Also look out for "Best Bets" boxes; these highlight a port's top experiences so you don't shell out for a flightseeing trip in one place, for example, when the experience would be better elsewhere. ⇨ *For in-depth information on outdoor activities all around Alaska, see Chapter 4, Sports and Wilderness Adventures.*

SHOPPING

Alaskan native handicrafts range from Tlingit totem poles—a few inches high to more than 30 feet tall—to Athabascan beaded slippers and fur garments. Traditional pieces of art (or imitations thereof) are found in gift shops up and down the coast: Inupiat spirit masks, Yupik dolls and dance fans, Tlingit button blankets and silver jewelry, and Aleut grass baskets and carved wooden items. Salmon, halibut, crab, and other frozen fish are very popular souvenirs (shipped home to meet you, of course) and make great gifts. Most towns have at least one local company that packs and ships fresh, smoked, or frozen seafood.

To ensure authenticity, buy items tagged with the state-approved AUTHENTIC NATIVE HANDCRAFT FROM ALASKA "Silverhand" label, or look for the polar-bear symbol indicating products made in Alaska. Although these symbols are designed to ensure authentic Alaskan and native-made products, not all items lacking them are inauthentic. This applies in particular to native artists who may or may not go through the necessary paperwork to obtain the Silverhand label. Before buying something, ask questions to ensure its authenticity. Better prices are found in the more remote villages, in museum shops, or in crafts fairs such as Anchorage's downtown Saturday Market.

SHORE EXCURSIONS

Shore excursions arranged by the cruise line are a convenient way to see the sights, but you'll pay extra for this convenience. Before your cruise, you'll receive a booklet describing the shore excursions your cruise line offers. Most cruise lines let you book excursions in advance online, where you'll find descriptions and sometimes pricing; all sell them on board during the cruise. If you cancel your excursion, you may incur penalties, the amount varying with the number of days remaining until the tour. Because these trips are specialized, many have limited capacity and are sold on a first-come, first-served basis.

CORDOVA

Cordova, decidedly and delightfully off the beaten Alaska path, is a peaceful, coastal Alaskan town with no roads to the outside and some marvelous sights. Against a backdrop of snowy Mt. Eccles, Cordova is the gateway to the Copper River delta—one of the great birding areas of North America. Perched on Orca Inlet in eastern Prince William Sound, Cordova began life early in the 20th century as the port city for the Copper River–Northwestern Railway, which was built to serve the Kennicott copper mines 191 mi away in the Wrangell Mountains. The mines and the railroad shut down in 1938, and Cordova's economy now depends heavily on fishing. Attempts to develop a road along the abandoned railroad line connecting to the state highway system were dashed by the 1964 earthquake, so Cordova remains isolated. Access to the community is limited to airplane or ferry.

COMING ASHORE

SHORE EXCURSIONS

Ilanka Cultural Center. Visit the Ilanka Cultural Center, where you will meet members of the Eyak Native Corporation, who will share their culture and the history of their people and present-day life experiences. ✉ *110 Nicholoff Way* ☎ *907/424–7903* ⊕ *www.ilankacenter. org* ✉ *This tour is offered to Cruise West passengers at no charge.*

Sea Kayaking in Orca Inlet. Don the gear provided by your naturalist guide and, after a beachside lesson, board two-person sea kayaks to paddle the shoreline while you watch for sea otters, harbor seals, and seabirds. A hearty snack of famous Copper River salmon is served. ☾ *4–7 hrs* ✉ *$75–$115.*

TRANSPORTATION AND TOURS

FROM THE PIER

Cruise ships dock at the boat harbor, and Cordova is a short walk uphill from here.

Tour buses meet ships, or you can catch a cab. A cab ride within the downtown area will run about $3.50.

CITY TOURS

Cordova Taxi Cab (☎ *907/424–5151*) provides half-hour tours of town for $15 per person, with a maximum of four people per cab.

VISITOR INFORMATION

Pick up maps and tour brochures from the **Cordova Chamber of Commerce Visitor Center** (✉ *404 1st St.* ☎ *907/424–7260* ⊕ *www.cordovachamber. com*). The Center can also suggest short self-led walking tours through this small, easily navigated town.

Check your e-mail at the **Cordova Public Library** (✉ *622 1st St.* ☎ *907/424–6667* ⊕ *www.cordovalirary.org*). Or try the **Orca Book &**

CORDOVA BEST BETS

Copper River delta sightseeing. Rent a car and drive the 50-mi road across the delta. Stop to watch birds and scan for wildlife at the roadside viewing areas, and end the trip at the Million Dollar Bridge and the Childs Glacier Recreation Area.

Take in a festival. Cordova has several noteworthy activities that are well worth looking into if you're nearby at the right time. The

Shorebird Festival is in May, the Copper River Wild! Salmon Festival takes place in July. There's also the Iceworm Festival (yes, there really is such a creature) in early February, accessible via the Alaska Marine Highway, a ferry system that runs year-round along Alaska's coast. For more information, go to www.dot. state.ak.us and clock on "ferries".

Sound Co. (✉507 1st St. ☎907/424–5305), with rates at $9 an hour (but you're only charged for the minutes used).

EXPLORING CORDOVA

Drive out of town along the Copper River Highway and visit the **Copper River delta.** This 700,000-acre wetland is one of North America's most spectacular vistas. The two-lane highway crosses marshes, forests, streams, lakes, and ponds that are home to countless shorebirds, waterfowl, and other bird species. Numerous terrestrial mammals including moose, wolves, lynx, mink, and beavers live here, too, and the Copper River salmon runs are world famous. When the red and king salmon hit the river in spring there's a frantic rush to net the tasty fish and rush them off to waiting markets and restaurants all over the country.

Exhibits at the **Cordova Museum** tell of early explorers to the area, native culture, the Copper River–Northwestern Railway/Kennicott Mine era, and the growth of the commercial fishing industry. An informative brochure outlines a self-guided walking tour of the town's historic buildings. Evening programs and regional art exhibits such as "Fish Follies" and "Bird Flew" are sponsored by the Historical Society. The gift shop features a selection of local postcards, Cordova and Alaskan gifts, and local history books. ✉622 1st St. ☎907/424–6665 ⊕www.cordova-museum.org ⌨$1 ⊙Memorial Day–Labor Day, Mon.–Sat. 10–6, Sun. 2–4; Labor Day–Memorial Day, Tues.–Fri. 10–5, Sat. 1–5.

SHOPPING

Orca Book & Sound Co. (✉507 1st St. ☎907/424–5305 ⊙Closed Sun.) is much more than a bookstore. In addition to books, it sells music, art supplies, children's toys, and locally produced art. The walls often double as a gallery for local works or traveling exhibits, and the store specializes in old, rare, out-of-print, and first-edition books, especially Alaskana. ■TIP➔ **In the back is an espresso-smoothie bar; the upstairs area has wireless Internet access for a small fee.**

WHERE TO EAT

¢–$ ✕ **Killer Whale Café.** Have a breakfast of espresso and baked goods or
CAFÉ   an omelet at this café. For lunch you can choose from a deli menu of
soups, salads, and sandwiches, followed by a fresh, homemade dessert.
✉ *507 1st St.* ☎ *907/424–7733* ▭ *MC, V* ⊘ *No dinner.*

DENALI NATIONAL PARK AND PRESERVE

Although it isn't technically a port of call, Denali National Park and
Preserve is one of the most popular land extensions to an Alaska cruise.
Anchorage, 240 mi south of the park, serves as a point of departure. It's
a fine place to see wildlife, including bears, caribou, moose, and wolves.
Nowhere in the world is there more stunning background scenery to
these wildlife riches, with 20,320-foot Mt. McKinley looming above
forested valleys, tundra-topped hills, and the glacier-covered peaks of
the Alaska Range.

GEOLOGY AND TERRAIN

The park's most prominent geological feature is the Alaska Range, a
600-mi-long crescent of summits that separates South Central Alaska
from the interior. These peaks are all immense, but the truly towering
ones are Mt. Hunter (14,573 feet), Mt. Foraker (17,400 feet), and Mt.
McKinley (20,320 feet). Mt. McKinley's granite heart is covered with
glacial ice, which is hundreds of feet thick in places. Glaciers are abundant along the entire Alaska Range, in fact, and a few are visible from the
park road. Muldrow Glacier is only 5 mi from the road, near Mile 67.

WILDLIFE

Nearly every wild creature that walks or flies in South Central and interior Alaska inhabits the park. Thirty-eight species of mammals reside
here, from wolves and bears to little brown bats and pygmy shrews
that weigh a fraction of an ounce. The park also has a surprisingly
large avian population in summer, when some 160 species have been
identified. Most of the birds migrate in fall, leaving only two-dozen
year-round resident species, including ravens, boreal chickadees, and
hawk owls. Some of the summer birds travel thousands of miles to nest
and breed in subarctic valleys, hills, and ponds. The northern wheatear
comes here from southern Asia, warblers fly here from Central and
South America, and the arctic tern annually travels 24,000 mi while
seasonally commuting between Denali and Antarctica.

The most sought-after species among visitors are the large mammals:
grizzlies, wolves, Dall sheep, moose, and caribou. All inhabit the forest
or tundra landscape that surrounds Denali Park Road. While traveling
the park road you can expect to see Dall sheep finding their way across
high meadows, grizzlies and caribou frequenting stream bottoms and
tundra, moose in the forested areas both near the park entrance and deep
in the park, and the occasional wolf or fox that may dart across the road.
Keep in mind that, as one park lover put it, "this ain't no zoo." You
might hit an off day and have few viewings, but you can enjoy the surroundings anyway. Under no circumstances should you feed the animals
or birds (a mew gull or ground squirrel may try to share your lunch).

EXPLORING DENALI

Denali National Park and Preserve. You can take a tour bus or the Alaska Railroad from Anchorage to the Denali National Park entrance. Princess, Holland America, and Royal Caribbean attach their own railcars behind these trains for a more luxurious experience. Most cruise passengers stay one or two nights in hotels at a riverside settlement called Denali Park, just outside the park entrance. Shuttle buses provide transportation from your hotel to the park's busy visitor center, where you can watch slide shows on the park, purchase maps and books, or check the schedule for naturalist presentations and sled-dog demonstrations. Access to the park itself is by bus on day tours. If you aren't visiting Denali as part of your cruise package, make reservations for a bus tour (including a snack or box lunch and hot drinks, prices are usually between $72.10 and $165.00 per adult and half that for children 14 and under). All the major hotels in the Denali Park area have good restaurants on the premises, and most travelers choose to dine there.

> ## MT. MCKINLEY
>
> Also commonly known by its Athabascan Indian name, Denali—"The High One"—North America's highest mountain is the world's tallest when measured from base to top: the great mountain rises more than 18,000 feet above surrounding lowlands. Unfortunately for visitors with little time to spend in the area, McKinley is wreathed in clouds on average two days of every three in summer, so cross your fingers and hope for a clear day when you visit.

The 90-mi Denali Park Road winds from the park entrance to Wonder Lake and Kantishna, the historic mining community in the heart of the park. Public access along this road is limited to tour and shuttle buses that depart from the Wilderness Access Center. The Park Road is paved for the first 14 mi and gravel the rest of the way. Bus drivers aren't in a hurry (the speed limit is 35 MPH) and make frequent stops to view wildlife or to explain Denali's natural history.

Your narrated park tour will probably last around six hours round-trip and will include Polychrome Pass and the visitor center at Eielson (at Mile 66 on the Park Road), which has been completely rebuilt and reopened to the public in June 2008. Long trips to Wonder Lake (11 grueling hours round-trip) provide a better chance to see Mt. McKinley and more of the park, but may not be available unless you spend an additional night in the Denali area. Check with your cruise line to see if these more expensive options are available. The Eielson–to–Wonder Lake stretch is particularly beautiful from mid-August to early September, when the tundra is ablaze with autumn's yellows, reds, and oranges.

The Wilderness Access Center near the park's entrance (at Mile 237 of the Parks Highway, or Mile 1 of the Park Road) is the transportation hub, with bus and campsite reservations, along with a fine film about Denali called Across Time and Tundra. The adjacent Backcountry Information building has hiking details for those heading into the wilderness,

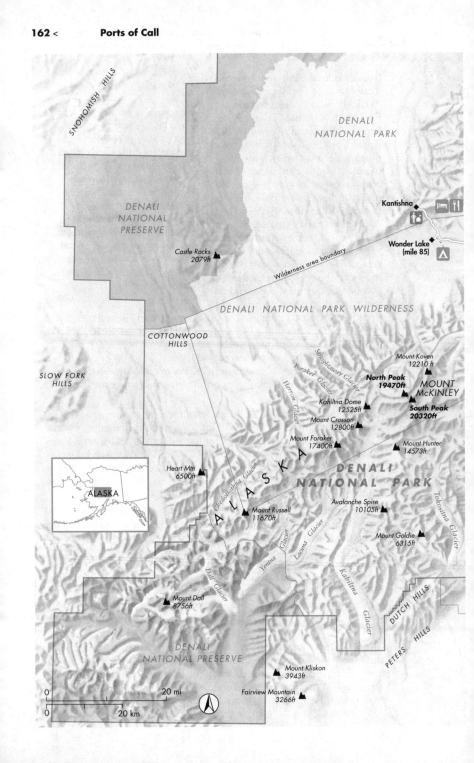

3

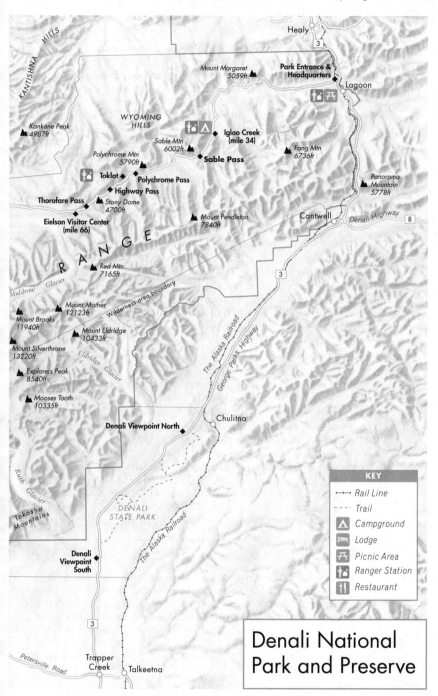

Healy

Park Entrance & Headquarters

Lagoon

Mount Margaret 5059ft

KANTISHNA HILLS

WYOMING HILLS

Kankone Peak 4987ft

Sable Mtn 6002ft

Igloo Creek (mile 34)

Sable Pass

Fang Mtn 6736ft

Polychrome Mtn 5790ft

Toklat

Polychrome Pass

Highway Pass

Panorama Mountain 5778ft

Thorofare Pass

Stony Dome 4700ft

Mount Pendleton 7840ft

Cantwell

Denali Highway 8

Eielson Visitor Center (mile 66)

R A N G E

Red Mtn 7165ft

3

Muldrow Glacier

Wilderness area boundary

Mount Mather 12123ft

Mount Brooks 11940ft

Mount Eldridge 10433ft

Mount Silverthrone 13220ft

Eldridge Glacier

The Alaska Railroad

George Parks Highway

Explorers Peak 8540ft

Mooses Tooth 10335ft

Denali Viewpoint North

Chulitna

Ruth Glacier

Tokosha Mountains

DENALI STATE PARK

The Alaska Railroad

Denali Viewpoint South

KEY	
⊢•⊣	Rail Line
- - -	Trail
🔺	Campground
🏨	Lodge
🔀	Picnic Area
👫	Ranger Station
🍴	Restaurant

3

Denali National Park and Preserve

Petersville Road

Trapper Creek

Talkeetna

including current data on animal sightings, river-crossing conditions, weather, and closed areas.

At Mile 1.5 of the park road (directly across from the train station), the Denali Visitor Center contains exhibits on the park's natural and cultural history. Two short hiking trails are nearby, and you can check out the naturalist presentations and sled-dog demonstrations by park rangers. An adjacent bookstore stocks titles on Denali's animals, wildflowers, and geology, and a food court is also here. *Box 9, Denali National Park 99755 ⊠Mi 1.5, Park Rd. 99755 ☎907/683–2294 year-round, 907/683–1266 in summer, 800/622–7275 or 907/272–7275 shuttle bus (in Alaska), 907/272–7275 or 800/622–7275 bus tour reservations ⊕www.nps.gov/dena for park info or www.reservedenali.com for bus tour info ☑Park: $10 per person or $20 per vehicle. Shuttle bus: round-trip fares $22.75 to Toklat River at Mile 53; $43.75 to Kantishna at Mile 91, the end of the road ⊙May 15–Sept. 18, 8 AM–6 PM.*

OUTDOOR ACTIVITIES

HIKING

Day hiking can be amazing in Denali. A system of forest and tundra trails starts at the park entrance. These trails range from easy to challenging, and are suitable for visitors of all ages and hiking abilities. Get hiking information and trail maps—along with bear and moose safety tips—from the Wilderness Access Center. Rangers lead hikes daily in summer.

RAFTING

Several rafting companies operate along the Parks Highway near the entrance to Denali and offer daily trips in the fairly placid stretches of the Nenana River and through the white water of Nenana River canyon. Gear and a courtesy pickup from your hotel are included.

Denali Outdoor Center (⊠Mi 0.5 Otto Lake Rd. for main office, Mi 240, Parks Hwy. for rafting check-ins; or Mi 238.9 for bookings and mountain-bike rentals ☎907/683–1925 or 888/303–1925 ⊕www. denalioutdoorcenter.com) takes adventuresome people on guided trips down the Nenana River rapids in inflatable rafts and kayaks. **Denali Raft Adventures** (☎907/683–2234 or 888/683–2234 ⊕www.denaliraft.com) launches its rafts several times daily on a variety of scenic and white-water Nenana River raft trips.

DUTCH HARBOR

Sometimes called "the Crossroads of the Aleutians," the twin cities of Unalaska and Dutch Harbor are among Alaska's most remote communities, some 800 air miles southwest of Anchorage. The combined communities are usually referred to simply as Unalaska/Dutch Harbor; they're connected by a bridge that spans a narrow channel between Unalaska and Amaknak Island. (Locals playfully call the span "The Bridge to the Other Side.") Unalaska/Dutch Harbor is hardly your typical tourist town, but since the mid-1990s the Aleutian Chain's economic hub has become something of a destination, served year-round by Anchorage-based airlines and visited seasonally by the state's Marine Highway System ferries and the occasional cruise ship, as well as adventurous independent travelers.

COMING ASHORE

TRANSPORTATION AND TOURS
FROM THE PIER
Dutch Harbor is connected to the town of Unalaska by bridge to Amaknak Island, and the port where most cruise ships dock. Access to Dutch Harbor is also gained by ferry ride from Homer; there is ferry service twice a month from April through October (☎*800/642–0066* ⊕*www.ferryalaska.com*). Once there, some cruise ships arrange shuttles into town, and it's possible to head across the bridge on foot. In fact, several town sites are within 2 mi of the pier. Cabs and car-rental services can also provide transportation from the pier, and individualized tours of the area can be arranged with the cab dispatcher. You can catch a cab ride from **Mr. Kab Taxi, Tours & Shuttle** (☎*907/581–5640*).

AREA TOURS
Extra Mile Tours (☎*907/581–6171* ⊕*www.unalaskadutchharbortour. com* ⊘*2- to 4-hr tour* ⊠*$50–$90*) explore the local community and find out more about the area's history.

VISITOR INFORMATION
Unalaska-Dutch Harbor Convention and Visitors Bureau (⊠*Box 545, Unalaska* ☎*907/581–2612 or 877/581–2612* ⊕*www.unalaska.info*).

Check your e-mail at the **Unalaska City Library** (⊠*64 Elanore Dr.* ☎*907/581–5060*), which is open and free to the public with a library card (also free, and relatively easy to acquire). For a fee, visitors can also access wireless at various places in town such as the Grand Aleutian Hotel and the airport.

EXPLORING DUTCH HARBOR

Church of the Holy Ascension. Under the guidance of Father Veniaminov, Unalaska/Dutch Harbor's first church was built in 1826. Now a National Historic Landmark, Holy Ascension is one of the oldest cruciform-style Russian churches in the nation, and it houses one of Alaska's richest collections of Russian artifacts, religious icons, and artwork. Both the church and neighboring Bishop's House have been restored, along with many of the church's Russian Orthodox icons. Tours of the church can be arranged through the Unalaska/Dutch Harbor Convention and Visitors Bureau. ⊠*Broadway Avenue, in downtown Unalaska* ☎*907/581–6565 (Parish)*.

Museum of the Aleutians. ($) Opened in 1999, this museum highlights the cultural, military, and natural history of the Aleutian and Pribilof Islands (the latter are located to the north, in the Bering Sea). Exhibits relate the story of the human presence here, from prehistoric to contemporary times; many of the native artifacts were once scattered around the

Continued on page 170

ALASKA'S GLACIERS
NOTORIOUS LANDSCAPE ARCHITECTS

(opposite) Facing the Taku Glacier challenge outside of Juneau. (top) River of ice

Glaciers—those massive, blue-hued tongues of ice that issue forth from Alaska's mountain ranges—perfectly embody the harsh climate, unforgiving terrain, and haunting beauty that make this state one of the world's wildest places. Alaska is home to roughly 100,000 glaciers, which cover almost 5% of the state's land.

FROZEN GIANTS

A glacier occurs where annual snowfall exceeds annual snowmelt. Snow accumulates over thousands of years, forming massive sheets of compacted ice. (Southeast Alaska's **Taku Glacier**, popular with flightseeing devotees, is one of Earth's meatiest: some sections measure over 4,500 feet thick.) Under the pressure of its own weight, the glacier succumbs to gravity and begins to flow downhill. This movement results in sprawling masses of rippled ice (Alaska's **Bering Glacier,** at 127 miles, is North America's longest). When glaciers reach the tidewaters of the coast, icebergs calve, or break off from the glacier's face, plunging dramatically into the sea.

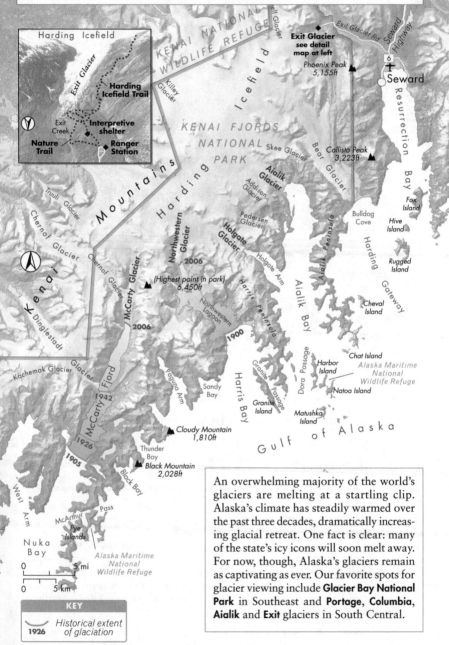

THE RAPIDLY RETREATING GLACIERS IN KENAI FJORDS NATIONAL PARK

Harding Icefield

Exit Glacier

Harding Icefield Trail

Exit Creek

Nature Trail

Interpretive shelter

Ranger Station

KENAI NATIONAL WILDLIFE REFUGE

Exit Glacier see detail map at left

Exit Glacier Rd

Seward Highway

Phoenix Peak 5,155ft

6

✝ **Seward**

Harding Icefield

KENAI FJORDS NATIONAL PARK

Skee Glacier

Callisto Peak 3,223ft

Bear Glacier

Resurrection Bay

Killey Glacier

Aialik Glacier

Addison Glacier

Pedersen Glacier

Holgate Glacier

Fox Island

Bulldog Cove

Hive Island

Rugged Island

Cheval Island

Truuli Glacier

Chernof Glacier

Harding Mountains

Chernof Glacier

Northwestern Glacier

2006

(Highest point in park) 6,450ft

Holgate Arm

Harris Peninsula

Aialik Peninsula

Aialik Bay

Harding Gateway

Kenai Mountains

Dinglestadt Glacier

McCarty Glacier

2006

Northwestern Lagoon

1900

Paguna Arm

Granite Passage

Dora Passage

Harbor Island

Chat Island

Alaska Maritime National Wildlife Refuge

Kachemak Glacier

Kachemak Glacier

McCarty Fjord

1942

Sandy Bay

Harris Bay

Granite Island

Natoa Island

Cloudy Mountain 1,810ft

Matushka Island

Gulf of Alaska

1926

West Arm

1905

Thunder Bay

Black Mountain 2,028ft

Black Bay

McArthur Pass

Pye Islands

Nuka Bay

Alaska Maritime National Wildlife Refuge

| 0 | | 5 mi |
| 0 | | 5 km |

An overwhelming majority of the world's glaciers are melting at a startling clip. Alaska's climate has steadily warmed over the past three decades, dramatically increasing glacial retreat. One fact is clear: many of the state's icy icons will soon melt away. For now, though, Alaska's glaciers remain as captivating as ever. Our favorite spots for glacier viewing include **Glacier Bay National Park** in Southeast and **Portage, Columbia, Aialik** and **Exit** glaciers in South Central.

KEY

⌣
1926 — *Historical extent of glaciation*

ICY BLUE HIKES & THUNDEROUS BOATING EXCURSIONS

Glaciers enchant us with their size and astonishing power to shape the landscape. But let's face it: nothing rivals the sheer excitement of watching a bus-size block of ice burst from a glacier's face, creating an unholy thunderclap that resounds across an isolated Alaskan bay.

Most frequently undertaken with a seasoned guide, **glacier trekking** is becoming increasingly popular. Many guides transport visitors to and from glaciers (in some cases by helicopter or small plane), and provide ski excursions, dogsled tours, or guided hikes on the glacier's surface. Striding through the surreal landscape of a glacier, ice crunching underfoot, can be an otherworldly experience. Whether you're whooping it up on a dogsled tour, learning the fundamentals of glacier travel, or simply poking about on a massive field of ice, you're sure to gain an acute appreciation for the massive scale of the state's natural environment.

You can also experience glaciers **via boat,** such as the Alaska Marine Highway, a cruise ship, a small chartered boat, or even your own bobbing kayak. Our favorite out of Seward is the ride with Kenai Fjords Tours. Don't be discouraged by rainy weather. Glaciers often appear even bluer on overcast days. When piloting your own vessel, be sure to keep your distance from the glacier's face.

■TIP➔ **For more information about viewing Alaska's glaciers, see Chapter 1: Sports & Wilderness Adventures.**

Taking in the sights at Mendenhall Glacier

DID YOU KNOW?

What do glaciers and cows have in common? They both *calve*. While bovine calving refers to actual calf-birth, the word is also used to describe a tidewater glacier's stunning habit of rupturing icebergs from its terminus. When glacier ice meets the sea, steady tidal movement and warmer temperatures cause these frequent, booming deposits.

GLACIER-VIEWING TIPS

■ The most important rule of thumb is never to venture onto a glacier without proper training or the help of a guide.

■ Not surprisingly, glaciers have a cooling effect on their surroundings, so wear layers and bring gloves and rain gear.

■ Glaciers can powerfully reflect sunlight, even on cloudy days. Sunscreen, sunglasses, and a brimmed hat are essential.

■ Warm, thick-soled waterproof footwear is a must.

■ Don't forget to bring a camera and binoculars (preferably waterproof).

world, but have been repatriated to the Aleuts' homeland. Exhibits on the Aleuts' centuries-long habitation of this place are complemented by others that feature the Russian occupation, the gold rush, World War II, and Unalaska/Dutch Harbor's importance as a fishing port. In summer the museum sponsors archaeological digs, which participants may join for a few hours, a day, a week, or a month. ✉ *314 Salmon Way* ☎ *907/581–5150* ⊕ *www.aleutians.org.*

World War II Military Installations. Unalaska/Dutch Harbor's importance in the fight against Japan is clearly evident. The Aleutian World War II National Historic Area has been established near the airport to honor those killed in the Aleutian Chain during the war and to preserve and celebrate the military's legacy here. Remnants of bunkers, tunnels, Quonset huts, pillboxes, and other military relics are scattered throughout the local landscape, at places like Bunker Hill, Memorial Park, and Unalaska Lake. ✉ *Amaknak Island, Airport Beach Rd.*

> ### DUTCH BEST BETS
>
> ■ **Climb Mount Ballyhoo.** Enjoy a short hike and ascend a 1,589-foot peak.
>
> ■ **Catch a Halibut.** Do what the locals do and hook one of the big ones on a day trip.
>
> ■ **Celebrate History.** Discovery the Aleutian World War II National Historic Area and view remnants of WWII artifacts, foundations, and more.

SHOPPING

There aren't many souvenir shops in Unalaska/Dutch Harbor. The best place to find paintings, photographs, carvings, and other artwork and crafts done by local artists is **Nicky's Place** (✉ *E. Front Beach Rd.* ☎ *907/581–1570*), which also features a bookstore and an espresso bar. Books, crafts, and artwork can also be found at the store at the **Museum of the Aleutians** (✉ *Salmon Way, near the Grand Aleutian Hotel*).

SPORTS AND ACTIVITIES

Fishing. The really, really big attraction here is halibut. It's not unusual to hook into female members of this flatfish species weighing 100 pounds or more. The International Game Fish Association's world-record halibut of 459 pounds was hooked in nearby waters. Local streams also host large runs of Pacific salmon; the best known is the one in the **Iliuliuk River,** which flows out of **Unalaska Lake.** You'll have to buy a one-day fishing license.

Hiking, Bird-Watching, Wildlife-Viewing. Visitors can explore this treeless landscape without fear of encountering bears, which don't inhabit the island. And the near-constant breezes tend to keep mosquitoes and other biting bugs at bay. Most of the tundra-covered terrain is flat to gently rolling, which makes for easy exploring. In midsummer the tundra is brightened by abundant wildflowers. Also abundant here are bald eagles and foxes, and myriad species of songbirds, seabirds, shorebirds, and waterfowl make this a birder's delight. In late summer the island is also a berry-picker's delight, with rich crops of salmonberries and blueberries.

More ambitious adventurers can ascend the volcanic cone of 6,680-foot **Mount Makushin,** Unalaska Island's tallest mountain. Easier summits to reach are those of 2,136-foot **Pyramid Peak** and 1,589-foot **Mount Ballyhoo.**

Every July, locals and visitors compete in a scramble up to Mount Ballyhoo's top in the aptly named **Ballyhoo Run.** Much of the land surrounding Unalaska/Dutch Harbor is privately owned, and visitors are asked to obtain a permit from the **Ounalashka Corporation** (⊠ *Salmon Way, near the Grand Aleutian Hotel*).

GLACIER BAY NATIONAL PARK AND PRESERVE

Fodor'sChoice ★ **Glacier Bay National Park and Preserve.** Cruising Glacier Bay is like revisiting the Little Ice Age—it's one of the few places in the world where you can approach such a variety of massive tidewater glaciers. You can witness a spectacular process called "calving," foreshadowed by a cannon-blast-like sound, in which bergs the size of 10-story office buildings come crashing down from the side of a glacier. Each cannonblast signifies another step in the glacier's steady retreat. The calving iceberg sends tons of water and spray skyward, propelling mini–tidal waves outward from the point of impact. Johns Hopkins Glacier calves so often and with such volume that large cruise ships can seldom come within 2 mi of its face.

GETTING TO GLACIER BAY

Competition for entry permits into Glacier Bay is fierce. To protect the humpback whale, which feeds here in summer, the Park Service limits the number of ships that can call. Check your cruise brochure to make sure Glacier Bay is included in your sailing. Most ships that do visit spend at least one full day exploring the park. There are no shore excursions or landings in the bay—the steep-sided and heavily forested fjords aren't conducive to pedestrian exploration—but a Park Service naturalist boards every cruise ship.

Although the Tlingit have lived in the area for 10,000 years, the bay was first popularized by naturalist John Muir, who visited in 1879. Just 100 years before, the bay had been completely choked with ice. By 1916, though, the ice had retreated 65 mi—the most rapid glacial retreat ever recorded. To preserve its clues to the world's geological history, Glacier Bay was declared a national monument in 1925, and became a national park in 1980. Today Muir's namesake glacier, like others in the park, continues to retreat dramatically. Its terminus is now scores of miles farther up the bay from the small cabin he built at its face during his time there.

Your experience in Glacier Bay will depend partly on the size of your ship. Large cruise ships tend to stay mid-channel, while small yachtlike ships spend more time closer to shore. Smaller ships give you a better view of the calving ice and wildlife, but on a big ship you can get a loftier perspective. Both come within ¼ mi of the glaciers themselves.

For more info, check out: ⊕ *www.nps.gov/glba.*

Glacier Bay
National Park
and Preserve

BRITISH
COLUMBIA

ALASKA

KEY

1794 Historical extent
of glaciation

ALASKA

CANADA
UNITED STATES

Muir Glacier

Riggs Glacier

1907

Reindeer Glacier

Carroll Glacier

1966

1976
1972
1948

1960

Tarr Inlet

1892

1966
1892

1929

Caseme Glacier

Queen Inlet

1966 Wachusett

1907

1929

RUSSELL
ISLAND

1907
1892

1949

1880

Adams Inlet

West Arm

Lamplugh Glacier

Reid Glacier

1907

1892

Tidal Inlet

1892

East Muir Arm Inlet

1907

1879

1907
1892

1860

1907
1919

1860

Glacier Bay

1857

1845

Brady Icefield

1966

Geikie Inlet

DRAKE
ISLAND

Beartrack Cove

1892

WILLOUGHBY
ISLAND

Beartrack River

Wood Lake

Berg Bay

BEARDSLEE ISLANDS

Visitor Center/
Glacier Bay Lodge

Brady Glacier

Dundas River

Bartlett Cove

1794

Bartlett Cove

Airport

1794

1961

Palma Bay

Dixon Harbor

Dundas Bay

1750-80

Gustavus

PLEASANT
ISLAND

Graves Bay

Taylor Bay

North Passage

Icy Strait

LEMESURIER
ISLAND

INIAN
ISLANDS

South Passage

0   10 miles

0   15 km

ELFIN
COVE

Cross Sound

GLACIER RUNDOWN

The most frequently viewed glaciers are in the west arm of Glacier Bay. Ships linger in front of five glaciers, giving you ample time to admire their stunning and ever-changing faces. First, most ships stop briefly at Reid Glacier, which flows down from the Brady Icefield, before continuing on to Lamplugh Glacier—one of the bluest in the park—at the mouth of Johns Hopkins Inlet. Next, at the end of the inlet, is the massive Johns Hopkins Glacier, where you're likely to see a continuous shower of calving ice. (Sometimes there are so many icebergs in the inlet that ships must avoid the area.) Farther north, near the end of the western arm, is Margerie Glacier, which is also quite active. Adjacent is Grand Pacific Glacier, the largest glacier in the park.

HAINES

It's hard to imagine a more beautiful setting—a heavily wooded peninsula with magnificent views of Portage Cove and the snowy Coast Range—or a more perfectly charming coastal Alaskan town. Haines's popularity as a stop for cruise ships both large and small is growing, especially as travelers look for an alternative to the crowds in Skagway.

Nestled on the collar of the Chilkat Peninsula—a narrow strip of land that divides the Chilkat and Chilkoot Inlets—Haines encompasses an area that has been occupied by Tlingit peoples for centuries. Missionary S. Hall Young and famed naturalist John Muir were intent on establishing a Presbyterian mission in the area, and with the blessing of local chiefs they chose the site that later became Haines.

Haines has always been a well-balanced community; its history contains equal parts enterprising gold-rush boomtown and regimented military outpost. The former is evidenced by Jack Dalton, who in the 1890s maintained a toll route from the settlement of Haines into the Yukon, charging $1 for foot passengers and $2.50 per horse. His Dalton Trail later provided access for miners during the 1897 gold rush to the Klondike.

The town's military roots are visible at Fort William Henry Seward, at Portage Cove just south of town. For 17 years (1923–39) prior to World War II, the post, renamed Chilkoot Barracks in commemoration of the gold-rush route, was the territory's only military base. The fort's buildings and grounds are now a National Historic Landmark.

Today the community is recognized for the native dance and art center at Fort Seward, the Haines Public Library (named Best Small Library in the United States in 2005), and the superb fishing, camping, and outdoor recreation to be found at Chilkoot Lake, Portage Cove, Mosquito Lake, and Chilkat State Park. Northwest of the city is the Alaska Chilkat Bald Eagle Preserve.

COMING ASHORE

SHORE EXCURSIONS

Chilkat Bald Eagle Preserve Float Trip. A raft trip through the Chilkat Bald Eagle Preserve introduces you to some eagles and—if you're lucky—a moose or a bear. The trip starts with a 30-minute guided van tour through Chilkat Valley to the heart of the preserve. Then you board rafts for a gentle, scenic float trip down the Chilkat River (no children under age 7). In October the trees are filled with some 3,000 bald eagles. ⊙ *4 hrs* ▭*$119.*

Chilkoot Bicycle Adventure. This easy half-day drive-and-bike tour starts with a van ride to Lutak Inlet. From there you can hop on a mountain bike for a 7- to 8-mi jaunt along this picturesque bay, which boasts a backdrop of mountains and glaciers. Eagles are a common sight, and brown bears an occasional one. ⊙ *3 hrs* ▭*$89.*

Chilkat Rain Forest Nature Hike. Explore a lush Alaskan rain forest on this 3-mi guided hike along Chilkoot Inlet, which focuses on the area's plant, animal, and bird life. The path is easy and well maintained, and spotting scopes are provided to watch for bald eagles, mountain goats, and other wildlife along the way. ⊙ *3½–4 hrs* ▭*$69–$80.*

Deluxe Haines Highlights. This bus tour includes a visit to Fort Seward and the Sheldon Museum or American Bald Eagle Foundation wildlife educational center before venturing out to Letnikof Cove (on the Chilkat Peninsula) for a view across the mighty Chilkat River to Rainbow Glacier and a tour of a working fish processing facility and smokery. ⊙ *3 hrs* ▭*$64.*

Offbeat Haines. Embark on a small group adventure to visit three of Haines's most unusual and out-of-the-way attractions. The trip includes time at the delightfully eclectic Hammer Museum (the only museum in the world devoted to hammers), Extreme Dreams Art Studio, downtown Haines, Fort Seward, and Dalton City. The last of these was created for the Walt Disney film *White Fang*, and is now home to the Haines Brewing Company and other local businesses. ⊙ *2–2½ hrs* ▭*$44–$55*

Sub-Alpine Mountain Explorer. Hold on to your seat as you take the wheel of a four-wheel drive Kawasaki "Mule" on the Takshanuk Mountain Trail for a scenic off-road adventure through Alaska's pristine wilderness. Spectacular views include a panoramic look at the Lynn Canal and Chilkoot Lake. On the way down the mountain you'll gather around a warm fire and enjoy lunch of halibut or chicken. After descending the rest of the trail, a motorcoach awaits for a tour through historic Fort Seward. ⊙ *4 hrs* ▭*$129.*

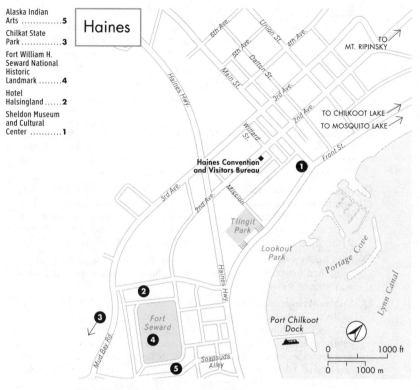

TRANSPORTATION AND TOURS

FROM THE PIER

Cruise ships and catamaran ferries dock in front of Fort Seward, and downtown Haines is just a short walk away (about ½ mi). Complimentary shuttle service is provided to downtown and the Fort Seward area. Tours are available through **Haines Shuttle and Tours** (☎907/766–3138). The Haines ferry terminal is 4½ mi northwest of downtown, and the airport is 4 mi west.

GETTING HERE ON YOUR OWN

If your cruise ship only stops in Skagway, you can catch a fast catamaran to Haines for a delightful day away from the crowds. **Haines-Skagway Fast Ferry** (☎907/766–2100 or 888/766–2103) provides a passenger catamaran ferry between Skagway and Haines ($68 round-trip, and 45 minutes each way), with several runs a day in summer. **Alaska Fjordlines** (☎907/766–3395 or 800/320–0146 ⊕www.alaskafjordlines.com) operates a high-speed catamaran from Skagway and Haines to Juneau and back, stopping along the way to watch whales and other marine mammals in Lynn Canal. The morning catamaran leaves Haines at 8:45 AM, and the connecting bus from Auke Bay arrives in Juneau at noon. Passengers are back in Haines by 7:30 PM. Check your itinerary carefully to make sure you'll return before your ship's scheduled departure.

VISITOR INFORMATION

You can pick up walking-tour maps at the **Haines Convention and Visitors Bureau** (⊠*122 2nd Ave., near Willard St* ☎*907/766–2234 or 800/458–3579* ⊕*www.haines.ak.us*).

Check your e-mail for free at **Haines Library** (⊠*111 3rd Ave. S* ☎*907/766–2545* ⊕*www.haineslibrary.org*).

EXPLORING HAINES

④ ★ **Ft. William H. Seward National Historic Landmark.** Circle the sloping parade ground of Alaska's first U.S. Army post, where stately clapboard homes stand against a mountain backdrop. The Haines Convention and Visitors Bureau provides a walking-tour brochure.

⑤ ☾ **Alaska Indian Arts.** Dedicated to the revival of Tlingit art, this nonprofit organization is housed in the former fort hospital on the south side of the Ft. Seward parade ground. You can watch artists carving totem poles and metalsmiths working in silver. ⊠*Fort Seward* ☎*907/766–2160* ⊕*www.alaskaindianarts.com* ⊡*Free* ☉*Weekdays 9–5.*

② **Hotel Halsingland.** In Fort Seward, wander past the huge, gallant, white-columned former commanding officer's home, now a part of the hotel on Officers' Row.

① **Sheldon Museum and Cultural Center.** Steve Sheldon began assembling native artifacts, items from historic Ft. Seward, and gold-rush memorabilia, such as Jack Dalton's sawed-off shotgun, in the 1880s, and started an exhibit of his finds in 1925. Today the Alaska family's personal collection anchors an impressive array of artifacts, including an 18th-century carved ceremonial hat belonging to the Brown Bear Clan, Chilkat blankets, and a model of a Tlingit tribal house. ⊠*11 Main St.* ☎*907/766–2366* ⊕*www.sheldonmuseum.org* ⊡*$3* ☉*Mid-May–mid-Sept., weekdays 10–4, weekends 1–4; mid-Sept.–mid-May, Mon.–Sat. 1–4.*

③ **Chilkat State Park.** This park on the Chilkat Inlet has beautiful and accessible viewing of both the Davidson and Rainbow glaciers as well as public campgrounds. The Seduction Point Trail, about 7 mi one way, takes hikers to the very tip of the peninsula upon which Haines sits. ☎*907/766–2292* ⊕*www.dnr.state.ak.us/parks.*

OUTDOOR ACTIVITIES

Battery Point Trail is a fairly level path that hugs the shoreline for 2 mi, providing fine views across Lynn Canal. The trail begins a mile east of town, and a campsite can be found at Kelgaya Point near the end. For other hikes, pick up a copy of "Haines Is for Hikers" at the Haines Convention and Visitors Bureau. **Alaska Nature Tours** (☎*907/766–2876* ⊕*www.alaskanaturetours.net*) conducts bird-watching and natural-history tours through the Alaska Chilkat Bald Eagle Preserve, and leads hiking treks in summer and ski tours in winter.

SHOPPING

Tresham Gregg's **Sea Wolf Gallery** (⊠*Fort Seward* ☎*907/766–2540* ⊕*www.tresham.com*) sells wood carvings, silver jewelry, prints, and T-shirts with his native-inspired designs. Haines's most charming gallery, the **Wild Iris Gallery** (⊠*Portage St.* ☎*907/766–2300*) displays attractive jewelry, prints, and fashion wear created by owners Madeleine and Fred Shields. It's just up from the cruise-ship dock, and its summer gardens are to die for.

Birch Boy Products (☎*907/767–5660 or 877/769–5660* ⊕*www.birchboy.com*) produces tart and tasty birch syrup; it's sold in local gift shops.

WHERE TO EAT

$–$$ ✕**Bamboo Room.** Pop culture meets greasy spoon in this unassuming
AMERICAN coffee shop with red-vinyl booths, which has been in the same family for more than 50 years. The menu doesn't cater to light appetites—it includes sandwiches, burgers, fried chicken, chili, and halibut fish-and-chips, but the place really is at its best for an all-American breakfast (available until 3 PM). The adjacent bar has pool, darts, a big-screen TV, and a jukebox. ⊠*2nd Ave. near Main St.* ☎*907/766–2800* ☰*AE, D, DC, MC, V.*

¢–$ ✕**Mountain Market.** Meet the locals over espresso and a fresh-baked pas-
AMERICAN try at this busy corner natural-foods store, deli, café, wine-and-spirits shop, de facto meeting hall, and hitching post—the only thing missing is Wi-Fi connectivity. But Mountain Market is great for lunchtime sandwiches, wraps, soups, and salads. Friday is pizza day, but come early, since it's often gone by early afternoon. ⊠*3rd Ave. and Haines Hwy.* ☎*907/766–3340* ☰*AE, D, MC, V.*

WHERE TO DRINK

Locals might rule the pool tables at **Fogcutter Bar** (⊠*122 Main St.* ☎*907/766–2555*), but they always appreciate a little friendly competition. Like many bars in Southeast Alaska, the Fogcutter sells drink tokens that patrons often purchase for their friends; you'll notice folks sitting at the bar with a small stack of these tokens next to their beverage. Purchase one for a keepsake—or for later use. **Haines Brewing Company** (⊠*108 Whitefang Way* ☎*907/766–3823*), a microbrewery among the Dalton City buildings at the fairgrounds, sells sample trays for $5.

HOMER

It's a shame that of the hundreds of thousands of cruise passengers who visit Alaska each year only a very few get to see Homer. Its scenic setting on Kachemak Bay, surrounded by mountains, spruce forest, and glaciers, makes Homer unique even in Alaska. Homer lies at the base of a 4-mi-long sandy spit that juts into Kachemak Bay and provides beautiful bay views. Founded just before the turn of the 20th century as a gold-prospecting camp, this community was later used as a coal-mining headquarters. Today Homer is a funky fishing port famous for its halibut and salmon fishing, and serves as a base for bear-viewing flights. It's also one of the top arts communities in Alaska, with several first-rate galleries, a theater company, and an active music-and-dance scene.

COMING ASHORE

SHORE EXCURSIONS

Gull Island, Seldovia, or Halibut Fishing. Since Homer isn't a common port and the town itself offers so much to explore, shore excursion offerings aren't as predictable here as in other ports of call. Your ship may offer boat charters to Gull Island (a nearby island chock-full of cacophonous seagulls and other seabirds) or Seldovia (a small, scenic town with quality art galleries across Katchemak Bay). Halibut fishing is also huge here, and if you take one fishing charter excursion during your trip this would be the place to do it. ⊙ *Durations vary* ✉ *Prices vary.*

TRANSPORTATION AND TOURS

FROM THE PIER
Ships and Alaska Marine Highway ferries dock at the end of the Homer Spit, where you can find charters, restaurants, and shops. The routine for cruise lines calling in Homer is to provide a shuttle from the Spit to downtown.

VISITOR INFORMATION

In the Homer Chamber of Commerce's **Visitor Information Center,** brochures from local businesses and attractions fill racks. ✉ *201 Sterling Hwy.* ☎ *907/235–7740* ⊕ *www.homeralaska.org* ⊙ *Memorial Day–Labor Day, weekdays 9–7, weekends 10–6.*

Check your e-mail for free at the **Homer Public Library** (✉ *500 Hazel Ave.* ☎ *907/235–3180* ⊕ *library.ci.homer.ak.us*), or check out a list of additional Internet spots at the Visitor Information Center.

EXPLORING HOMER

⟲ Protruding into Kachemak Bay, the **Homer Spit** provides a sandy focal
Fodor'sChoice point. A paved path stretches most of the 4 mi, providing a delightful
★ biking or walking option, and at the end are restaurants and hotels, a harbor filled with commercial-fishing boats, charter-fishing businesses, sea-kayaking outfitters, art galleries, and on-the-beach camping spots. Fly a kite, walk the beaches, drop a line in the fishing hole, or just wander through the shops looking for something interesting.

★ **Islands and Ocean Center** provides a wonderful introduction to the Alaska Maritime National Wildlife Refuge. The refuge covers some 3.5 million acres spread across some 2,500 Alaskan islands, from Prince of Wales Island in the south to Barrow in the north. Opened in

> **HOMER BEST BETS**
>
> ■ **Charter a fishing boat.** Nothing beats wrestling a monster halibut out of the icy depths.
>
> ■ **People-watch on the Spit.** Homer is home to a thriving arts community, and makes for an interesting cultural mix.
>
> ■ **Cruise to a waterfront restaurant.** Crossing the bay to the Saltry Restaurant for a meal is another favorite experience.

2003, this 37,000-square-foot facility with towering windows facing Kachemak Bay is a must-see for anyone interested in wild places—and it's free! A film takes visitors along on a voyage of the Fish and Wildlife Service's research ship, the MV *Tiglax*. Interactive exhibits detail the birds and marine mammals of the refuge (the largest seabird refuge in America), and one room even re-creates the noisy sounds and pungent smells of a bird rookery. In summer guided bird-watching treks and beach walks are offered. ✉ *95 Sterling Hwy.* ☎ *907/235–6961* ⊕ *www.islandsandocean.org* 🎟 *Free* ⊘ *Memorial Day–Labor Day, daily 9–6; Labor Day–Memorial Day, Tues.–Sat. noon–5.*

BIRD-WATCHING

Bird lovers love Homer. Sandpipers, Aleutian terns, and murrelets nest here throughout the year. For extensive information about bird-watching in the area, visit ⊕ *www. birdinghomeralaska.org.*

Kachemak Bay abounds in wildlife. Shore excursions or local tour operators take you to bird rookeries in the bay or to gravel beaches for clam digging. Most charter-fishing trips include an opportunity to view whales, seals, sea otters, porpoises, and seabirds close up. The bay supports a large population of bald eagles, gulls, murres, puffins, and other birds.

Directly across Kachemak Bay from the end of the Homer Spit, **Halibut Cove** is a small community of people who make their living on the bay or by selling handicrafts. There are several art galleries and a restaurant that serves local seafood. The cove itself is lovely, especially during salmon runs, when fish leap and splash in the clear water.

Central Charter Booking Agency (☎ *907/235–7847 or 800/478–7847* ⊕ *www. centralcharter.com*) runs frequent boats to the cove from Homer.

☾ ★ For an outstanding introduction to Homer's history—both human and natural—visit the **Pratt Museum,** where you can see a saltwater aquarium and exhibits on pioneers, flora and fauna, Native Alaskans, and the 1989 *Exxon Valdez* oil spill. Spy on wildlife with robotic video cameras set up on a seabird rookery and at the McNeil River Bear Sanctuary. In 2005 the Pratt was presented with the National Award for Museum Service, the highest national honor for museums. Outside are a wildflower garden and a short nature trail. The museum also leads 1½-hour walking tours of the harbor for $5 per person several times a week. ✉ *Bartlett St. off Pioneer Ave.* ☎ *907/235–8635* ⊕ *www. prattmuseum.org* 🎟 *$6* ⊘ *Mid-May–mid-Sept., daily 10–6.*

Seldovia, isolated across the bay from Homer, retains the charm of an earlier Alaska. The town's Russian heritage is evident in its onion-dome church and its name, derived from a Russian place-name meaning "herring bay." You can find excellent fishing, whether you drop

GETTING TO SELDOVIA

Seldovia can be reached from Homer by tour boat; contact **Central Charter Booking Agency** (☎ *907/235–7847 or 800/478–7847* ⊕ *www.centralcharter.com*). They run a daily six-hour trip that leaves at 11 AM and charges $50 for adults, round-trip. The dock of the small-boat harbor is in the center of town—allowing for easy exploration.

your line into the deep waters of Kachemak Bay or cast into the surf for silver salmon on the shore of Outside Beach, near town. Self-guided hiking and berry picking in late July are other options.

OUTDOOR ACTIVITIES

BIKING

The **Seldovia Boardwalk Hotel** (☎907/234–7816) rents bikes, an ideal way to see Seldovia.

BEAR-WATCHING

Homer is a favorite departure point for viewing Alaska's famous brown bears in Katmai National Park. **Emerald Air Service** (☎907/235–6993 ⊕www.emeraldairservice.com) is one of several companies offering all-day and custom photography trips starting around $595 per person. **Hallo Bay Wilderness** (☎907/235–2237 or 888/535–2237 ⊕www.hallobay.com) offers guided close-range viewing without the crowds. Day trips are offered, but it's the two- to seven-day stays at this comfortable coastal location that provide the ultimate in world-class bear- and wildlife-viewing.

FISHING

Homer is both a major commercial fishing port (especially for halibut) and a very popular destination for sport anglers in search of giant halibut or feisty king and silver salmon. Quite a few companies offer charter fishing in summer for around $190 per person per day (including bait and tackle). Several booking agencies set up fishing charters, including **Central Charter Booking Agency** (☎907/235–7847 or 800/478–7847
★   ⊕www.centralcharter.com) and **Homer Ocean Charters** (☎800/426–6212 ⊕www.homerocean.com) . Also try **Inlet Charters** (☎907/235–6126 or 800/770–6126 ⊕www.halibutcharters.com).

SEA KAYAKING

Several local companies offer guided sea-kayaking trips to protected coves within Kachemak Bay State Park and nearby islands. **True North Kayak Adventures** (☎907/235–0708 ⊕www.truenorthkayak.com) has a range of such adventures, including a six-hour paddle to Elephant Rock for $130 and an all-day boat and kayak trip to Yukon Island for $150 (both trips include round-trip water taxi to the island base camp, guide, all kayak equipment, and bakery lunch). For something more unusual, book an overnight trip to Kasitsna Bay through the beautiful **Across the Bay Tent & Breakfast** (☎907/235–3633, 907/345–2571 Sept.–May ⊕www.tentandbreakfastalaska.com). Grounds are gorgeous, facilities are basic, and guests can take kayak tours, rent a mountain bike, or just hang out on the shore.

> **COMPETE!**
>
> Anyone heading out on a halibut charter is advised to buy a $10 ticket for the **Homer Jackpot Halibut Derby** (☎907/235–7740 ⊕www.homerhalibutderby.com) ; first prize for the largest halibut is more than $40,000. Every year, local papers publish sob stories about people who decided to save the 10 bucks and wound up catching a fish that would have won them thousands—don't be that guy!

SHOPPING

A variety of art by the town's residents can be found in the galleries on and around Pioneer Avenue. The **Bunnell Street Gallery** (⊠ *106 W. Bunnell St., at Main St.* ☎ *907/235–2662* ⊕ *www.bunnellstreetgallery. org*) displays innovative contemporary art, all of it produced in Alaska. The gallery, which occupies the first floor of a historic trading post, also hosts workshops, lectures, musical performances, and other community events.

Ptarmigan Arts (⊠ *471 E. Pioneer Ave.* ☎ *907/235–5345*) is a cooperative gallery with photographs, paintings, pottery, jewelry, woodworking, and other works by local artisans.

WHERE TO EAT

$$$–$$$$
SEAFOOD
Fodor'sChoice
★

✕ **Saltry Restaurant.** On a hill overlooking Halibut Cove, this is a wonderful place to soak up a summer afternoon. Local seafood is the main attraction, prepared in everything from curries and pastas to sushi. The restaurant is small, and although the tables aren't exactly crowded together, it's definitely intimate. When weather permits, get a table on the deck. Dinner seatings are at 6 and 7:30; before or after dinner you can stroll around the boardwalks at Halibut Cove and visit the art galleries or just relax on the dock. Sea otters often play just offshore. Reservations are essential for the ferry ($28 round-trip), which leaves Homer Spit at 5 PM. A noon ferry ($48) will take you to the Saltry for lunch (¢–$), stopping along the way for wildlife-viewing. ⊠ *9 W. Ismilof Rd.* ⬧ *Box 6410, Halibut Cove 99603* ☎ *907/235–7847, 800/478–7847 Central Charters* ⟳ *Reservations essential* ⊕ *www.halibut-cove-alaska. com/saltry.htm* ⊟ *D, MC, V* ☉ *Closed Labor Day–Memorial Day.*

¢
CAFÉ

✕ **Two Sisters Bakery.** This very popular café is just a short walk from both Bishops Beach and the Islands and Ocean Center. In addition to fresh breads and pastries, Two Sisters specializes in deliciously healthful lunches, such as vegetarian focaccia sandwiches, homemade soups, quiche, and salads. Sit on the wraparound porch on a summer afternoon, or take your espresso and scone down to the beach to watch the waves roll in. ■TIP➔**Upstairs are three comfortable guest rooms ($), all with private baths.** Your latte and Danish pastry breakfast is served in the café. ⊠ *233 E. Bunnell Ave.* ☎ *907/235–2280* ⊕ *www.twosisters-bakery.net* ⊟ *MC, V.*

WHERE TO DRINK

The spit's infamous **Salty Dawg Saloon** (⊠ *4380 Homer Spit Rd.* ☎ *907/235–6718*) is a tumbledown lighthouse of sorts, sure to be frequented by a carousing fisherman or two, along with half the tourists in town.

HUBBARD GLACIER

The 24-million-acre international wilderness that embraces Hubbard can only be described with superlatives. For example, the massive St. Elias and Fairweather ranges form the largest nonpolar glaciated mountain system in the world. British Columbia's only winter range for Dall sheep is here, and the region supports a population of both grizzlies and rare, silver-blue "glacier" bears.

This glacier is famous for "surging"—moving forward quickly. Most glaciers slide an inch or two a day. However, in 1986, the Hubbard Glacier made headlines around the world by advancing to the mouth of Russell Fjiord, damming it, and creating a huge lake that lasted five months. By September it was advancing 30 meters a day. This was an event without precedent in recent geologic history, and it was mapped by the Landsat 5 satellite from 6 mi above Earth. Seals, sea lions, and porpoises were trapped behind the dam, and efforts were mounted to relocate them. "Russell Lake" eventually reached a level almost 90 feet higher than the level of Disenchantment Bay. When the dam broke on October 8, it produced an enormous rush of fresh water—something like a tidal wave in reverse.

The glacier surged again in summer 2002, creating another dam in the space of a month—by coincidence, just about the time glaciologists convened in Yakutat for an international symposium on fast glacier flow. Nervous Yakutat residents continue to lobby the government to build a channel to make sure the glacier cannot form "Russell Lake" again. They fear this would change river courses, endanger important fisheries, and inundate the Yakutat Airport, the chief transportation link with the rest of Alaska.

EXPLORING HUBBARD GLACIER

The Hubbard Glacier is an icy tongue with its root on Mt. Logan in Yukon Territory. The vast Hubbard icefield originates near 15,300-foot Mt. Hubbard and flows 76 mi to lick the sea at Yakutat and Disenchantment bays. With its 400-foot snout, Hubbard Glacier is also a prime pausing point for cruise ships. Hubbard calves great numbers of icebergs, making it difficult to get close. There are no roads to the glacier. Unless you are a seasoned mountaineer with ice experience, Hubbard Glacier is no shore excursion.

JUNEAU

Juneau, Alaska's capital and third-largest city, is on the North American mainland but can't be reached by road. The city owes its origins to two colorful sourdoughs (Alaskan pioneers)—Joe Juneau and Richard Harris—and to a Tlingit chief named Kowee, who led the two men to rich reserves of gold at Snow Slide Gulch, the drainage of Gold Creek around which the town was eventually built. That was in 1880, and shortly thereafter a modest stampede resulted in the formation of a mining camp, which quickly grew to become the Alaska district government capital in 1906. The city may well have continued under its original appellation—Harrisburg, after Richard Harris—were it not for Joe Juneau's political jockeying at a miner's meeting in 1881.

For some 60 years after Juneau's founding gold was the mainstay of the economy. In its heyday the AJ (for Alaska Juneau) Gold Mine was the biggest low-grade ore mine in the world. It was not until World War

II, when the government decided it needed Juneau's manpower for the war effort, that the AJ and other mines in the area ceased operations. After the war, mining failed to start up again, and government became the city's principal employer. Juneau's mines leave a rich legacy, though; the AJ Gold Mine alone produced more than $80 million in gold.

Perhaps because of its colorful history, Juneau is full of contrasts. Its dramatic hillside location and historic downtown buildings provide a frontier feeling, but the city's cosmopolitan nature comes through in fine museums, noteworthy restaurants, and a literate and outdoorsy populace. Here you can enjoy the Mt. Roberts Tramway, plenty of densely forested wilderness areas, quiet bays for sea kayaking, and even the famous drive-up Mendenhall Glacier.

JUNEAU BEST BETS

■ **Walk South Franklin Street.** Juneau's historic downtown still retains much of its hardscrabble mining feel. While away hours in the saloons and shops of this charming district.

■ **Ride the Mt. Roberts Tram.** On Juneau's favorite attraction, enjoy panoramic views of the area's stunning scenery from 1,800 feet above town.

■ **Marvel at the Mendenhall Glacier.** With an otherworldly blue hue and a visitor center that answers all your glacier questions, Alaska's most accessible—and most popular—glacier is a must-see.

COMING ASHORE

SHORE EXCURSIONS
ADVENTURE
Exploring Glaciers by Helicopter and Dog Sled. Fly deep into the Juneau Icefield by helicopter on this high-adventure excursion. A guide greets you when you land, explains dogsledding, then takes you on a sled ride across the snow-covered glacier. Return to Juneau by helicopter, with additional flightseeing en route. ☾3 hrs ⊠$495–$540.

Mendenhall River Rafting. Suit up in rubber rain boots, protective clothing, and life jackets at Mendenhall Lake before your professional guide takes you down the Mendenhall River through alternating stretches of calm water and gentle rapids. Children love this one (the minimum age is 6). ☾3½ hrs ⊠$120.

Photo Safari by Land and Sea. A professional photographer guides you to Juneau "photo hot spots," while sharing picture-taking tips and techniques. The first part of the tour takes place on land, and includes Mendenhall Glacier and the colorful downtown area. Next you board a covered exploration vessel for a journey through the waterways of Stephen's Passage to photograph marine wildlife. Your photographer guide will help you take full advantage of the conditions and opportunities of the day. ☾4½–5 hrs ⊠$195.

Pilot's Choice Helicopter Flightseeing. One of Alaska's most popular helicopter tours includes a landing on the Juneau Icefield for a walk on a glacier. Boots and rain gear are provided. ☾3–4 hrs ⊠$349–$399.

Tram and Guided Alpine Walk. You start with a short tour of downtown Juneau, then ride up the Mt. Roberts Tramway on this very popular trip. Once you reach the top— 1,800 feet over the city—a guide takes you through pristine rain forest and alpine meadows. The hike is ½ mi over gravel and boardwalk trails, and is conducted in all weather conditions. Sturdy, comfortable walking shoes and warm, waterproof clothing are advised. If you'd rather relax than hike, the tram complex has lots of shops and a restaurant called the Timberline Bar & Grill. You can return via the tram at any time. ⏱2½ hrs ⌂$74.

Alpine Zipline & Rain-forest Eco-Tour. Get set to fly through the trees of a scenic alpine rain forest on this "Certified Green" eco-adventure. Guides lead you from tree to tree until you reach a platform where you are greeted with spruce tea and a local snack. On the final zip, your landing spot is a uniquely designed tree house. Your guides will point out interesting sights in the rain forest during the walk back to the lodge. ⏱3½ hrs ⌂$140.

SCENIC

Gold Mine Tour and Gold Panning. Don a hard hat and follow a former miner underground for a three-hour tour of the historic A.J. Gold Mine south of Juneau. You're guaranteed to "strike it rich" during the gold-panning demonstration. Approximately 45 minutes of the tour is spent inside the old tunnels. Tours depart from downtown by bus. This trip is highly recommended for an authentic look into Juneau's rich mining history. ⏱1½ hrs ⌂$55.

Grand Tour of Juneau. Take this bus excursion to see Mendenhall Glacier, spawning salmon at the Macaulay Salmon Hatchery, and the Glacier Gardens rain forest. ⏱5 hrs ⌂$99.

TASTES OF ALASKA

Floatplane Ride and Taku Glacier Lodge Salmon Bake. Fly over the Juneau Icefield to rustic Taku Glacier Lodge, where you can dine on outstanding barbecued salmon. Hole-in-the-Wall Glacier is directly across the inlet from the lodge. Nature trails wind through the surrounding country, where black bears and bald eagles are frequently sighted. Afterward, explore the virgin rain forest or relax in the lodge. This tour consistently gets rave reviews. ⏱3½ hrs ⌂$279–$284.

Gold Creek Salmon Bake. Alaska wild salmon barbecued over an open fire is included at this all-you-can-eat outdoor meal. After dining you can walk in the woods, explore the abandoned Wagner mine, and return to your ship at your leisure. ⏱1½–2 hrs ⌂$39.

TRANSPORTATION AND TOURS

FROM THE PIER

Most cruise ships dock on the south edge of town between the **Marine Park** and the **A.J. Dock**. Several ships can tie up at once; others occasionally anchor in the harbor. Juneau's downtown shops are a pleasant walk from the docks. A shuttle bus ($2 all day) runs from the A.J. Dock to town whenever ships are in port.

CITY TOURS

Juneau Trolley Car Company (☎ *907/586–7433 or 877/774–8687* ⊕ *www. juneautrolley.com*) conducts narrated tours, stopping at 13 of Juneau's historic and shopping attractions. An all-day pass is $19. **Mighty Great Trips** (☎ *907/789–5460* ⊕ *www.mightygreattrips.com*) leads bus tours that include a visit to Mendenhall Glacier. The **Juneau Steamboat Company** (☎ *907/723–0372* ⊕ *www.juneausteamboat.com*) offers one-hour scenic tours of Gastineau Channel aboard an authentic wood-fired steam launch, similar to those used around Juneau in the late 1800s and early 1900s. Tours come with entertaining narration that focuses on the historic mines of the Juneau area.

VISITOR INFORMATION

Pick up maps, bus schedules, charter-fishing information, and tour brochures at the small kiosks on the pier at Marine Park and in the cruise-ship terminal on South Franklin Street. Both are staffed when ships are in port.

The **Centennial Hall Visitor Center** has details on local attractions and nature trails. ⊠ *101 Egan Dr.* ☎ *907/586–2201 or 888/581–2201* ⊕ *www.traveljuneau.com* ⊘ *May–Sept., weekdays 8:30–5, weekends 9–5.*

Check your e-mail at **Universe Cyber Lounge** (⊠ *109 S. Franklin St.* ☎ *907/463–4330*).

EXPLORING JUNEAU

Downtown Juneau is compact enough that most of its main attractions are within walking distance of one another. Note, however, that the city is very hilly, so your legs will get a real workout. Look for the 20 signs around downtown that detail Juneau's fascinating history.

❺ **Alaska State Capitol.** Completed in 1931 and remodeled in 2006, this rather unassuming building houses the governor's office and hosts state legislature meetings in winter, placing it at the epicenter of Alaska's increasingly animated political discourse. Historical photos line the upstairs walls. Feel free to stroll right in. ■ TIP→ **You can pick up a self-guided tour brochure as you enter.** ⊠ *Corner of Seward and 4th Sts.* ☎ *907/465–4648* ⊘ *Weekdays 8–5.*

❷ **Alaska State Museum.** This is one of Alaska's finest museums. Visitors
★ interested in native cultures will enjoy examining the 38-foot walrus-hide *umiak* (an open, skin-covered Eskimo boat). Natural-history exhibits include preserved brown bears and a two-story-high eagle-nesting tree. Russian-American and gold-rush displays and contemporary art complete the collection. ■ TIP→ **Be sure to visit the cramped gift shop with its extraordinary selection of native art, including baskets, carvings,**

and masks. ✉ *395 Whittier St.* ☎*907/465–2901* ⊕*www.museums. state.ak.us* 🎫*$5* ⊙ *Mid-May–mid-Sept., daily 8:30–5:30; mid-Sept.– mid-May, Tues.–Sat. 10–4.*

⑩ **Evergreen Cemetery.** Many Juneau pioneers, including Joe Juneau and Richard Harris, are buried here. Juneau (1836–99), a Canadian by birth, died in Dawson City, Yukon, but his body was returned to the city that bears his name. Harris (1833–1907), whose name can be found on downtown's Harris Street, died here. A meandering gravel path leads through the graveyard, and at the end of it is the monument commemorating the spot where Chief Kowee was cremated.

⑦ **Glacier Gardens Rainforest Adventure.** Spread over 50 acres of rain forest, Glacier Gardens has ponds, waterfalls, hiking paths, a large atrium, and gardens. The roots of fallen trees, turned upside down and buried in the ground, act as bowls to hold planters that overflow with begonias, fuchsias, and petunias. Guided tours in covered golf carts lead you along the 4 mi of paved paths, and a 580-foot-high overlook provides dramatic views of the Mendenhall wetlands wildlife refuge, Chilkat mountains, and downtown Juneau. A café and gift shop are here, and the conservatory is a popular wedding spot. ■TIP➔ **The Juneau city bus, which departs from multiple locations in downtown Juneau, stops right in front of Glacier Gardens.** ✉*7600 Glacier Hwy.* ☎*907/790–3377* ⊕*www.*

glaciergardens.com 🖃*$22 including guided tour* 🕙*May–Sept., daily 9–6; closed in winter.*

 Governor's Mansion. Completed in 1912, this stately colonial-style home overlooks downtown Juneau. With 14,400 square feet, six bedrooms, and 10 bathrooms, it's no miner's cabin. Out front is a totem pole that tells three tales: the history of man, the cause of ocean

tides, and the origin of Alaska's ubiquitous mosquitoes. Alaska's first female and youngest governor, Sarah Palin, lived here with her husband ("First Dude" Todd Palin) and their children. Unfortunately, tours of the residence are not permitted. 🖃*716 Calhoun Ave.*

Junau-Douglas City Museum. Among the exhibits interpreting local mining and Tlingit history are old mining equipment, a reconstructed Tlingit fish trap, a three-dimensional model of the Treadwell Mine, historic photos, a diorama of an Assay Lab, and an interactive exhibit on Juneau as Alaska's capital city. 🖃*114 4th St.* 🕾*907/586–3572* ⊕*www.juneau. org/parksrec/museum* 🖃*$4* 🕙*May–Sept., weekdays 9–5, weekends 10–5; Oct.–Apr., Tues.–Sat. 10–4.*

Marine Park. On the dock where the cruise ships "tie up" is a little urban oasis with benches, shade trees, and shelter. It's a great place to enjoy an outdoor meal from one of Juneau's street vendors, and on Friday evenings in summer it features live performances by Juneau musicians. A visitor kiosk is staffed according to cruise-ship schedules.

Mt. Roberts Tramway. One of Southeast Alaska's most popular tourist ★ attractions, this tram whisks you from the cruise terminal 1,800 feet up the side of Mt. Roberts. After the six-minute ride you can take in a film on the history and legends of the Tlingits, visit the nature center, go for an alpine walk on hiking trails (including the 5-mi round-trip hike to Mt. Roberts's 3,819-foot summit), purchase native crafts, or enjoy a meal while savoring mountain views. A local company leads guided wilderness hikes from the summit, and the bar serves locally brewed beers. 🕾*907/463–3412 or 888/461–8726* ⊕*www.goldbelttours.com* 🖃*$25* 🕙*May–Sept., daily 9–9; closed in winter.*

South Franklin Street. The buildings on South Franklin Street (and neighboring Front Street), among the oldest and most inviting structures in the city, house curio and crafts shops, snack shops, and two salmon shops. Many reflect the architecture of the 1920s and 1930s. When the small **Alaskan Hotel** opened in 1913 Juneau was home to 30 saloons; the Alaskan gives today's visitors the most authentic glimpse of the town's whisky-rich history. The barroom's massive, mirrored, oak back bar is accented by Tiffany lights and panels. Topped by a wood-shingled turret, the 1901 **Alaska Steam Laundry Building** now houses a coffeehouse and other stores. The **Senate Building,** another of South Franklin's treasured landmarks, is across the street.

3 State Office Building. The building's sprawling eighth-floor patio, which faces the Gastineau Channel and Douglas Island, is a popular lunch destination for state workers and assorted residents. On most Fridays at noon, concerts inside the four-story atrium feature a grand old theater pipe organ, a veteran of the silent-movie era. Also here are the historic old witch totem pole; the Alaska State Library, with a fine collection of historical photos; and computers with public Internet access. If you're having trouble finding the building, just ask for directions to the "S.O.B."—the locals are fond of acronyms. ⊠ *4th and Calhoun Sts.*

> **GETTING THERE**
>
> **Mendenhall Glacier Tours** (☎ *907/789–5460* ⊕ *www.mightygreattrips.com*) provides direct bus transport between downtown and the glacier for $14 round-trip or tours that include time at the glacier for $27–35 per person.

OUTSIDE TOWN

9 Macaulay Salmon Hatchery. Watch through an underwater window as salmon fight their way up a fish ladder from mid-June to mid-October. Inside the busy hatchery, which produces almost 125 million young salmon annually, you will learn about the environmental considerations of commercial fishermen and the lives of salmon. A retail shop sells gifts and salmon products. ⊠ *2697 Channel Dr.* ☎ *907/463–4810 or 877/463–2486* ⊕ *www.dipac.net* ⌂ *$3.25 including short tour* ⊙ *Mid-May–mid-Sept., weekdays 10–6, weekends 10–5; Oct.–mid-May by appointment.*

8 One of Juneau's most popular sights, **Mendenhall Glacier,** is 12 mi from downtown. Like many other Alaskan glaciers, it is retreating up the valley, losing more than 100 feet a year as massive chunks of ice calve off into a small lake. The visitor center has educational exhibits, videos, and natural-history walks. Nearby hiking trails offer magnificent views of the glacier itself. A visit to the glacier is included in most Juneau bus tours. ⊠ *End of Glacier Spur Rd. off Mendenhall Loop Rd.* ☎ *907/789–0097* ⊕ *www.fs.fed.us/r10/tongass/districts/mendenhall* ⌂ *Visitor center $3 in summer, free in winter* ⊙ *May–Sept., daily 8–7:30; Oct.–Apr., Thurs.–Sun. 10–4.*

Fodor's Choice ★

OUTDOOR ACTIVITIES

HIKING

Gastineau Guiding (☎ *907/586–8231* ⊕ *www.stepintoalaska.com*) leads a variety of hikes in the Juneau area. Especially popular are their walks from the top of the tram on Mt. Roberts.

MOUNTAIN BIKING

Driftwood Lodge (⊠ *435 Willoughby Ave.* ☎ *907/586–2280* ⊕ *www.driftwoodalaska.com*) has basic mountain bikes for rent.

ROCK CLIMBING

While it isn't technically an *outdoor* activity, Juneau's indoor climbing gym, the **Rock Dump** (⊠ *1310 Eastaugh Way* ☎ *907/586–4982* ⊕ *www.rockdump.com*), is one of the finest in Alaska, and it's near where most cruise ships dock. The Dump has climbing walls for all abilities from beginner to expert; day passes are $10, and rental equipment is available.

WHALE-WATCHING

Alaska Whale Watching (☎907/321–5859 or 888/432–6722 ⊕*www. akwhalewatching.com*) offers small-group excursions (up to 12 guests) aboard a luxury yacht with an onboard naturalist. The company also offers a whale-watching/fishing combination tour, which is popular with multigenerational groups. Several companies lead whale-watching trips from Juneau. **Juneau Sportfishing & Sightseeing** (☎907/586–1887 ⊕*www. juneausportfishing.com*) has been around for many years, and its boats carry a maximum of six passengers, providing a personalized trip.

SHOPPING

Across from the tram, the **Raven's Journey** (✉*435 S. Franklin St.* ☎907/463–4686) specializes in high-quality native Alaskan masks, grass baskets, carvings, dolls, ivory and silver jewelry, and more.

Rie Muñoz, of the **Rie Muñoz Gallery** (✉*2101 N. Jordan Ave.* ☎907/789–7449 or 800/247–3151 ⊕*www.riemunoz.com*), is one of Alaska's best-known artists. She's the creator of a stylized, simple, and colorful design technique that is much copied but rarely equaled. The gallery is located in Mendenhall Valley, a 10-minute walk from the airport. In downtown Juneau, see Rie Muñoz's paintings and tapestries at **Decker Gallery** (✉*233 S. Franklin St.* ☎907/463–5536 or 800/463–5536). Next door to Heritage Coffee, climb the stairs to **Wm. Spear Design** (✉*172 S. Franklin St.* ☎907/586–2209 ⊕*www.wmspear.com*), where this lawyer-turned-artist produces a fun and colorful collection of enameled pins and zipper pulls.

WHERE TO EAT

$$$$ ✕**Gold Creek Salmon Bake.** Trees, mountains, and the rushing water of
SEAFOOD Salmon Creek surround the comfortable, canopy-covered benches and tables at this authentic salmon bake. Fresh-caught salmon is cooked over an alder fire and served with a succulent sauce. For $35 there are all-you-can-eat salmon, pork spareribs, and chicken along with baked beans, rice pilaf, salad bar, corn bread, and blueberry cake. Wine and beer are extra. After dinner you can pan for gold in the stream, wander up the hill to explore the remains of the Wagner gold mine, or roast marshmallows over the fire. A round-trip bus ride from downtown is included. ✉*1061 Salmon Lane Rd.* ☎907/789–0052 or 800/323–5757 ▤*AE, MC, V* ⊗*Closed Oct.–Apr.*

$$–$$$ ✕**Hangar on the Wharf.** Crowded with locals and travelers, the Hangar
ECLECTIC occupies the building where Alaska Airlines started business. Flight-theme puns dominate the menu (i.e., "Pre-flight Snacks" and the "Plane Caesar"), but the comfortably worn wood and vintage airplane photos create a casual dining experience that outweighs the kitsch. Every seat has views of the Gastineau Channel and Douglas Island. On warm days, outdoor seating is offered. This Juneau hot spot makes a wide

selection of entrées, including locally caught halibut and salmon, filet mignon, great burgers, and daily specials. Two dozen beers are on tap. On Friday and Saturday nights jazz or rock bands take the stage, and prime rib arrives on the menu. ⊠*2 Marine Way, Merchants Wharf Mall* ☎*907/586–5018* ⊕*www.hangaronthewharf.com* ▤*AE, D, MC, V.*

¢   ✕**Heritage Coffee Company.** Juneau's favorite coffee shop is a down-
CAFÉ   town institution, with locally roasted coffees, gelato, fresh pastries, and all sorts of specialty drinks. ■**TIP→ The window-front bar is good for people-watching while you sip a chai latte.** The same folks also operate several other coffee outposts, including the **Glacier Cafe** in Mendenhall Valley, which boasts a bigger menu that includes breakfast burritos and omelets, along with lunchtime paninis, wraps, soups, salads, and burgers, plus various vegetarian dishes. ⊠*174 S. Franklin St.* ☎*907/586–1087* ⊠*216 2nd St.* ☎*907/586–1752* ⊠*Mendenhall Mall Rd.* ☎*907/789–0692* ⊕*www.heritagecoffee.com* ▤*AE, D, MC, V* ⊗*No dinner.*

$$–$$$ ✕**Twisted Fish.** Juneau's liveliest downtown eatery serves up creative pan-
SEAFOOD   Asian seafood and Alaska classics. Housed in a log-frame waterfront building adjacent to the Taku Store and the base of the Mt. Roberts Tramway, Twisted serves fish as fresh as you'll find. Grab a seat on the deck for prime-time Gastineau Channel gazing and a bowl of Captain Ron's chowder. Inside, you'll find a dining room with a roaring river-rock hearth and flame-painted salmon, porpoises, marlin, and tuna decorating the walls. ⊠*550 S. Franklin St.* ☎*907/463–5033* ▤*AE, D, MC, V* ⊗*Closed Oct.–Mar.*

WHERE TO DRINK

Juneau is one of the best saloon towns in all of Alaska. If you're a beer fan, look for **Alaskan Brewing Company** (⊠*5429 Shaune Dr.* ☎*907/780–5866* ⊕*www.alaskanbeer.com*). These tasty brews, including Alaskan Amber, Pale Ale, IPA, Stout, Alaskan Summer Ale, and Smoked Porter, are brewed and bottled in Juneau. You can visit the brewery (and get free samples of the goods) 11 to 6 daily May through September, with 20-minute tours every half hour. Between October and April tours take place Thursday through Sunday 11 to 4. ■**TIP→ This is no designer brewery—it's in Juneau's industrial area, and there is no upscale café/bar attached—but the gift shop sells T-shirts and beer paraphernalia.** he frontier quarters of the **Red Dog Saloon** (⊠*278 S. Franklin St.* ☎*907/463–3658*), Alaska's best-known saloon, have housed the once infamous, but now rather touristy Juneau watering hole since 1890. Every conceivable surface in this two-story bar is cluttered with life preservers, business cards, and memorabilia.

KETCHIKAN

Famous for its colorful totem poles, rainy skies, steep–as–San Francisco streets, and lush island setting, Ketchikan is a favorite stop. Some 14,000 people call it home, and in summer cruise ships crowd the shoreline, floatplanes depart for Misty Fiords National Monument, and salmon-laden commercial fishing boats head home to Tongass Narrows. Ketchikan has a rowdy, blue-collar heritage of logging and fishing, somewhat softened by the loss of many timber-industry jobs and the gradual rise of cruise-ship tourism. With a little effort, though, visitors can still glimpse the rugged frontier spirit that once permeated this hardscrabble cannery town.

Ketchikan is at the foot of 3,000-foot Deer Mountain, near the southeast corner of Revillagigedo (locals shorten it to Revilla) Island. Prior to the arrival of white miners and fishermen in 1885, the Tlingit used the site, at the mouth of Ketchikan Creek, as a summer fish camp. Gold discoveries just before the turn of the 20th century brought more immigrants, and valuable timber and commercial fishing resources spurred new industries. By the 1930s the town bragged it was the "salmon-canning capital of the world." You'll still find some of the Southeast's best salmon fishing here.

KETCHIKAN BEST BETS

■ **Exploring Creek Street.** No visit to Ketchikan would be complete without a stroll along this elevated wooden boulevard, once the site of the town's rip-roaring bordellos.

■ **Totem gazing at Saxman Totem Pole Park.** View one of the best totem collections in all of Southeast Alaska at this must-see stop.

■ **Rain-forest Canopy Tours.** Zip through the towering trees of Ketchikan's coastal rain forest, experiencing the majesty of this unique ecosystem from a bird's-eye view.

COMING ASHORE

SHORE EXCURSIONS
ADVENTURE

Alaska Canopy Adventures. Featuring a series of zip lines, nature trails, and suspension bridges, canopy tours provide an up-close view of the coastal forests. A course at the Alaska Rainforest Sanctuary, 16 mi south of town (⊕ *www.alaskacanopy.com*), has the longest of the tour's eight zip lines, stretching 850 feet and whisking you along some 135 feet off the ground. (Book online or with your cruise line.) ☉*3¼ hrs* ✉*$179.*

Misty Fiords by Floatplane. Aerial views of granite cliffs that rise 4,000 feet from the sea, waterfalls, rain forests, and wildlife are topped off with a landing on a high wilderness lake. ☉*2 hrs* ✉*$ 259.*

Misty Fiords Wilderness Cruise and Flight. See this beautiful area from the air and sea on a 20-minute floatplane trip and a 2¾-hour cruise. The plane lands in the heart of the wilderness, where you climb onboard a small boat for the narrated voyage back to Ketchikan. ☉*4 hrs* ✉*$319.*

Sportfishing. Cast your line for Alaska king and silver salmon or halibut along the Inside Passage. All equipment is provided, and you can buy your license on board. Group size is limited. Fish will be cleaned, and arrangements can be made to have your catch frozen or smoked and shipped home. ☉*5 hrs* ✉*$190–$199.*

Tatoosh Islands Sea Kayaking. A scenic drive to Knudson Cove is followed by a boat ride to Tatoosh Islands, where you board an easy-to-paddle sea kayak for a whale's-eye view of a remote part of Tongass National Forest. The minimum age is 7. ⊙4½ *hrs* ☞*$144–$149.*

Mountain Point Snorkeling Adventure. Stay warm as you immerse yourself in Mountain Point's waters in a state-of-the-art 7-mm wetsuit complete with hood, boots, and gloves. Water temperatures reach a surprising 65 degrees. Observe and handle a variety of multicolored invertebrates and fish while snorkeling over the kelp forest. After PADI certified professional guides lead you on the marine-life tour, hot beverages are provided before you return to your ship. ⊙3 *hrs* ☞*$99.*

CULTURAL

Saxman Totem Pole Park. Learn about Tlingit culture in this native village with more than 20 totem poles. You can watch totem-pole carvers and a theatrical production in the Beaver Clan House. ⊙2½ *hrs* ☞*$59–$65.*

Totem Bight and Ketchikan City Tour. Visit the bustling center of Ketchikan and Totem Bight State Park to the north, where totem poles and a native clan house face the saltwater. ⊙2½ *hrs* ☞*$40–$45.*

TRANSPORTATION AND TOURS

FROM THE PIER

Most ships dock or tender passengers ashore directly across from the Ketchikan Visitors Bureau on Front and Mission streets, in the center of downtown. A new dock, several blocks north on the other side of the tunnel, is still within easy walking distance of most of the town's sights. Walking-tour signs lead you around the city. For panoramic vistas of the surrounding area—and a wee bit of exercise—climb the stairs leading up several steep hillsides.

To reach sights farther from downtown, rent a car, hire a cab, or ride the local buses. Metered taxis meet the ships right on the docks and also wait across the street. Rates are $3.70 for pick-up and $3.50 per mi. Up to six passengers can hire a taxi to tour for $75 per hour. Local buses run along the main route through town and south to Saxman. The fare is $1.

VISITOR INFORMATION

Ketchikan Visitors Bureau. The helpful visitors bureau is right next to the cruise-ship docks. Half the space is occupied by day-tour, flightseeing, and boat-tour operators. ⊠*131 Front St.* ☎*907/225–6166 or 800/770–3300* ⊕*www.visit-ketchikan.com* ⊙*May–Sept., daily 8–5, 6–6 when cruise ships are docked.*

Check your e-mail ($6/hour) right near the dock at **SeaPort Cyber** (⊠*5 Salmon Landing, Suite 216* ☎*907/247–4615* ⊕*www.seaportel.com*).

EXPLORING KETCHIKAN

 ★ **Creek Street.** This was once Ketchikan's infamous red-light district. During Prohibition, Creek Street was home to numerous speakeasies, and, in the early 1900s more than 30 houses of prostitution operated here. Today the small, colorful houses, built on stilts over the creek waters,

3

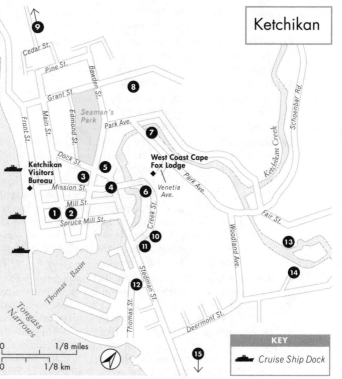

have been restored as trendy shops. Sea kayakers often paddle up the creek at high tide.

❻ Creek Street Footbridge. Stand over Ketchikan Creek for good salmon-viewing when the fish are running. In summer you can see impressive runs of coho, king, pink, and chum salmon, along with smaller numbers of steelhead and rainbow trout heading upstream to spawn. ■TIP➜**Keep your eyes peeled for sea lions snacking on the incoming fish.**

❸ Deer Mountain Hatchery and Eagle Center. Owned by the Ketchikan Indian Corporation, tens of thousands of king and coho salmon are raised at this hatchery on Ketchikan Creek. Midsummer visitors can view natural spawning in the creek by pink, chum, and coho salmon and steelhead trout as well as workers collecting and fertilizing the salmon eggs for the hatchery. Also here is a nesting pair of injured bald eagles. Other resident birds are used in educational programs in the interpretive theaters. ⊠*1158 Salmon Rd.* ☎*907/228–4941 or 800/252–5158* ⊕*www.kictribe.org* ☞*$9 for hatchery admission, additional $4 for bird program* ⊙*Early May–Sept., daily 8–4:30.*

❿ Dolly's House. Formerly owned by the inimitable Dolly Arthur, this steep-roofed home once housed Creek Street's most famous brothel. The house has been preserved as a museum, complete with furnishings, beds, and a short history of the life and times of Ketchikan's best-known madam. ✉*Creek St.* ☎*907/225–6329 (summer only)* 💲*$5* ⊙*Daily 8–4, when cruise ships are in port; closed in winter.*

❽ Grant Street Trestle. At one time virtually all of Ketchikan's walkways and streets were made from wooden trestles, but now only one of these handsome wooden streets remains, constructed in 1908.

❸ St. John's Church. Built in 1903, this church is the oldest remaining house of worship in Ketchikan. Its interior is formed from red cedar cut in the native-operated sawmill in nearby Saxman. ✉*Mission St.* ☎*907/225–3680* ⊕*www.stjohnsketchikan.com.*

❼ Salmon Falls. Get out your camera and set it for high speed at the fish ladder, a series of pools arranged like steps that allow fish to travel upstream around a dam or falls. When the salmon start running from June onward, thousands of fish leap the falls (or take the easier fish-ladder route). They spawn in Ketchikan Creek's waters farther upstream. Many can also be seen in the creek's eddies above and below the falls. The falls, fish ladder, and a large carving of a jumping salmon are just off Park Avenue on Married Man's Trail. The trail was once used by married men for discreet access to the red-light district on Creek Street. ✉*Married Man's Trail off Park Ave.*

❷ Southeast Alaska Discovery Center. This impressive information center
ᙅ features exhibits—including one on the rain forest—that focus on the
★ resources, native cultures, and ecosystems of Southeast Alaska. The U.S. Forest Service and other federal agencies provide information on Alaska's public lands, and a large gift shop sells natural-history books, maps, and videos about the sights in Ketchikan and the Southeast. America the Beautiful–National Park and Federal Recreational Land Passes are accepted and sold. ✉*50 Main St.* ☎*907/228–6220* ⊕ *www.fs.fed.us/r10/tongass/districs/discoverycenter* 💲*$5 May–Sept., free Oct.–Apr.* ⊙*May–Sept., weekdays 8–5, weekends 8–4; Oct.–Apr., Thurs.–Sun. 10–4.*

⓬ Thomas Street and Marina. From this street you can see Thomas Basin, the most accessible of Ketchikan's four harbors and home port to pleasure and commercial fishing boats. Old buildings, including the maroon-fronted Potlatch Bar, sit atop pilings, and you can walk out to the breakwater for a better view of busy Tongass Narrows.

❺ Tongass Historical Museum. Native artifacts and pioneer relics revisit the mining and fishing eras at this somewhat ho-hum museum in the same building as the library. Exhibits include a big, brilliantly polished lens from Tree Point Lighthouse, well-presented native tools and artwork, and photography collections. Other exhibits rotate, but always include Tlingit items. ✉*629 Dock St.* ☎*907/225–5600* 💲*$2* ⊙*May–Sept., daily 8–5; Oct.–Apr., Wed.–Fri. 1–5, Sat. 10–4, Sun. 1–4.*

⓮ Totem Heritage Center. Gathered from uninhabited Tlingit and Haida vil-
★ lage sites, many of the authentic native totems in this rare collection are well over a century old—a rare age for cedar carvings, which are frequently lost to decay in the Southeast's exceedingly wet climate. The center also features guided tours and displays crafts of the Tlingit, Haida, and Tsimshian cultures. Outside are several more poles carved in the three decades since this center opened. ✉*601 Deermount St.*

☎*907/225–5900* 🖊*$5* 🕐*May–Sept., daily 8–5; Oct.–Apr., week-days 1–5.*

❹ Whale Park. This small park on a traffic island across from St. John's Church is the site of the Chief Kyan Totem Pole, now in its third incarnation. The original was carved in the 1890s, but over the decades it deteriorated and was replaced in the 1960s. The current replica was erected in 1993, and the 1960s version is now housed in the Totem Heritage Center.

OUTSIDE TOWN

⑮ Saxman Totem Pole Park. A 2.5-mi paved walking path–bike trail parallels the road from Ketchikan to Saxman Totem Pole Park, named for a missionary who helped native Alaskans settle here before 1900. A totem park dominates the center of Saxman, with poles that represent a wide range of human and animal-inspired figures, including bears, ravens, whales, and eagles. There is a $3 charge to enter.Don't miss the adjacent carver's shed (free and open whenever the carvers are working). You can get to the park on foot, by taxi, or by city bus, and you can visit the totem park on your own, but to visit the tribal house and theater you must take a tour. Tickets are sold at the gift shop across from the totems. Call ahead for tour schedules. ✉*S. Tongass Hwy.* ✛ *2 mi south of town* ☎*907/225–4846* ⊕*www.capefoxtours.com.*

❾ Totem Bight. Totem Bight has many totem poles and a hand-hewn native tribal house; it sits on a scenic spit of land facing the waters of Tongass Narrows. The clan house is open daily in summer. About a quarter of the Ketchikan bus tours include Totem Bight. ✉*N. Tongass Hwy.* ✛*Approx. 10 mi north of town* ☎*907/247–8574* 🖊*Free* 🕐*Dawn-dusk* ⊕*www.alaskastateparks.org.*

OUTDOOR ACTIVITIES

We don't recommend it if you're looking for authenticity, but the **Great Alaskan Lumberjack Show** is a 60-minute lumberjack contest providing a Disneyesque taste of old-time woodsman skills, including ax throwing, buck-sawing, springboard chopping, log-rolling duels, and a 50-foot tree climb that ends in a free fall. Shows take place in a covered grandstand directly behind the Spruce Mill Development and go on, rain or shine, all summer. ✉*50 Main St.* ☎*907/225–9050 or 888/320–9049* ⊕*www.lumberjackshows.com* 🖊*$34* 🕐*May–Sept., 2–5 times daily; hrs vary.*

FISHING

Salmon are so plentiful in these waters that the town has earned the nickname "Salmon Capital of the World." The **Ketchikan Visitors Bureau** (✉*131 Front St.* ☎*907/225–6166 or 800/770–3300* ⊕*www.visit-ket-chikan.com*) has a full list of fishing charter companies, or sign up for a sportfishing adventure at your shore excursion desk.

FLIGHTSEEING

The dramatic fjords and isolated alpine lakes of the 2.3 million acre Misty Fiords National Monument don't exactly lend themselves to pedestrian exploration. But thanks to flightseeing services like **Island Wings Air Service** (☎*907/225–2444 or 888/854–2444* ⊕*www.islandwings.com*)

the sublime splendor of this region doesn't go unseen. Island Wings offers a popular two-hour tour that includes a 35-minute stopover at one of the monument's many lakes or fjords.

SEA KAYAKING

Southeast Exposure (☎*907/225–8829* ⊕*www.southeastexposure.com*) rents kayaks and mountain bikes and guides kayaking trips. **Southeast Sea Kayaks** (☎*907/225–1258 or 800/287–1607* ⊕*www.kayak-ketchikan.com*) leads tours of Ketchikan's historic waterfront and provides kayak rentals, along with guided trips to Misty Fiords.

SHOPPING

■ **TIP→** Because artists are local, prices for Native Alaskan crafts are sometimes lower in Ketchikan than at other ports. The Saxman Village gift shop has some Tlingit wares.

Design, art, clothing, and collectibles converge in the stylish **Soho Coho Contemporary Art and Craft Gallery** (⊠*5 Creek St.* ☎*907/225–5954 or 800/888–4070* ⊕*www.trollart.com*), where you'll find an eclectic collection of art and T-shirts featuring the work of owner Ray Troll—best known for his wacky fish art—and other Southeast Alaska artists.

For some of the Southeast's best canned, smoked, or frozen salmon and halibut, along with crab and clams, try **Salmon Etc.** on Mission St. **Simply Salmon,** its sister store, is on Creek Street. ⊠*322 Mission St.* ☎*907/225–6008 or 800/354–7256* ⊠*10 Creek St.* ☎*907/225–1616* ⊕*www.salmonetc.com.*

WHERE TO EAT

$$$–$$$$ ✕**Annabelle's Famous Keg and Chowder House.** Nestled into the ground
AMERICAN floor of the historic Gilmore Hotel, this unpretentious Victorian-style restaurant serves a hearty array of seafood and pastas, including several kinds of chowder and steamer clams. Prime rib on Friday and Saturday evenings is a favorite, and the lounge with a jukebox adds a friendly vibe. ⊠*326 Front St.* ☎*907/225–6009* ⊕*www.gilmorehotel. com* ▤*AE, D, MC, V.*

$–$$ ✕**Ocean View Restaurant.** This locals' favorite eatery has burgers, steaks,
MEXICAN pasta, pizzas, and seafood. They're all fine, but the main draws are authentic and very filling south-of-the-border dishes prepared under the direction of the Mexican-American owners. Three tables in the back have nice views of the Tongass Narrows. The kitchen is open until 11 PM nightly, after which, during the summer, the restaurant morphs into

a noisy nightclub until 2 AM. ✉*1831 Tongass Ave.* ☎*907/225–7566* ⊕*www.oceanviewmex.com* ⊟*MC, V.*

$$$–$$$$ ✕**Steamers.** Anchoring Ketchikan's Spruce Mill Mall, this lively, noisy,
AMERICAN and spacious restaurant is popular with cruise passengers, and features an extensive menu of fresh seafood (including king crab and steamer clams), pasta, and steaks. Vegetarian choices are available, and the servings fill you up. Tall windows face Ketchikan's busy waterfront, where cruise ships and floatplanes vie for your attention. ✉*76 Front St.* ☎*907/225–1600* ⊟*AE, D, MC, V* ⊘*Closed Oct.–Apr.*

WHERE TO DRINK

Ketchikan has quieted down in recent years as the economy shifted from logging to tourism, but it remains something of a party town, especially when crews stumble off fishing boats with cash in hand. You won't have any trouble finding something going on at several downtown bars. **First City Saloon** (✉*830 Water St.* ☎*907/225–1494*) is the main dance spot, with live music throughout the summer. The **Potlatch Bar** (✉*126 Thomas Basin* ☎*907/225–4855*) serves up music on weekends as well.

KODIAK ISLAND

On the second-largest island in the United States (Hawaii's Big Island is the largest), the town of Kodiak is the least touristy of all the Alaska port towns. It's an out-of-the-way destination for smaller cruise ships and Alaska state ferries, and despite its small population (just over 6,000 people), there's a lot of "big" stuff here: Kodiak is home to a very large commercial fishing fleet, and is almost always one of the top two or three in the country for tonnage of fish brought in. It's also home to the country's largest Coast Guard base, and the world-famous Kodiak brown bear, billed as the largest land carnivore in the world.

Russian explorers discovered the island in 1763, and Kodiak served as Alaska's first capital (back when Alaska was colonized by Russians, that is) until 1804, when the Russian government was moved to Sitka. Situated as it is in the northwestern Gulf of Alaska, Kodiak has been subjected to several natural disasters. In 1912 a volcanic eruption on the nearby Alaska Peninsula covered the town site in knee-deep drifts of ash and pumice. A tidal wave resulting from the 1964 earthquake destroyed the island's large fishing fleet and smashed Kodiak's low-lying downtown area.

Today commercial fishing is king in Kodiak. A clearinghouse for fish caught by islanders throughout the Kodiak archipelago—about 15,000 people are scattered among the islands—the city is among the busiest fishing ports in the United States. The harbor is also an important supply point for small communities on the Aleutian Islands and the Alaska Peninsula.

COMING ASHORE

SHORE EXCURSIONS

ADVENTURE

Kodiak Bear Viewing by Floatplane. Weather permitting, you can fly over Kodiak's lush green hills and remote backcountry waterways, then spend at least two hours on the ground watching the world's largest carnivores in their natural habitat. During the flight out and back the pilot will also point out marine and terrestrial mammals and other points of interest. ☉*1½–4½ hrs* ⊠*$250–$490.*

Halibut fishing. From picturesque St. Paul Harbor you can thread your way through the commercial fishing fleet and into the icy waters of the Gulf of Alaska in pursuit of the wily and tasty Pacific halibut. Be prepared to work for your food, though— the state record halibut weighed 459 pounds, and 100- to 200-pound fish are common. Along the way you can spot marine mammals such as seals, sea lions, and sea otters, and numerous seabirds as well. All bait and tackle is supplied, and local fish processors can arrange to clean, package, and ship your catch for you. ☉*6 hrs* ⊠*$275–$325.*

> ### KODIAK BEST BETS
>
> ■ **Visit the world's largest bears.** Join one of the local flight operators and spend the day watching these animals devour amazing quantities of salmon.
>
> ■ **Relax, have a brew.** Stop by the local brewery for a tasting session and tour, and stock up on fresh local beer for your stay.
>
> ■ **Walk off those calories.** Pick up a map of the Kodiak hiking trails at the Visitors' Bureau and head for the hills. Chances are you won't be eaten by a bear.

SCENIC

Waterfront and Wildlife Cruise. Take a cruise along the waterfront and view the fishing fleet, canneries, the Russian Orthodox church and seminary, and the abandoned World War II defense installation. Chances of seeing seabirds and marine mammals such as sea lions and sea otters are excellent. ☉*1½–3 hrs* ⊠*$180.*

TRANSPORTATION AND TOURS

FROM THE PIER

Most cruise ships dock at Pier 2, ½ mi south of downtown Kodiak. Most ships offer shuttles into town, but if yours doesn't, it's a 15-minute walk. You can catch a cab ride from **A&B Taxi** (☏*907/486–4343*).

AREA TOURS

Kodiak Island Charters (☏*907/486–5380 or 800/575–5380* ⊕*www. ptialaska.net/~urascal*) operates boat tours for fishing, hunting, and sightseeing aboard the 43-foot *U-Rascal.* They'll take you on a combined halibut and salmon trip, with sightseeing and whale-watching thrown in as well.

VISITOR INFORMATION

Pick up maps, details on kayaking trips, bear-viewing flights, marine tours, and more from the **Kodiak Island Convention & Visitors' Bureau** (⊠*100 E. Marine Way, Suite 200* ☏*907/486–4782* ⊕*www.kodiak. org* ☉*June–Sept., weekdays 8–5*).

Visitors can check e-mail at various private businesses with wireless communication (check with the Visitors' Bureau); alternatively, head to the **A. Holmes Johnson Memorial Library** (⊠ *319 Lower Mill Bay Rd.* ☎*907/486–8680* ⊕*www.city.kodiak.ak.us/library*).

EXPLORING KODIAK

★ **Alutiiq Museum and Archaeological Repository.** This museum is home to one of the largest collections of Alaska Native materials in the world, and contains archaeological and ethnographic items dating back 7,500 years. The museum displays only a fraction of its more than 150,000 artifacts, including harpoons, masks, dolls, stone tools, seal-gut parkas, grass baskets, and pottery fragments. The museum store sells native arts and educational materials. ⊠*215 Mission Rd., Suite 101* ☎*907/486–7004* ⊕*www.alutiiqmuseum.org* ✉*$5 donation requested* ⊙*June–Aug., weekdays 9–5, Sat. 10–5, Sun. by appointment; Sept.–May, Tues.–Fri. 9–5, Sat. 10:30–4:30.*

Baranov Museum. The Baranov Museum presents artifacts from the area's Russian past. On the National Register of Historic Places, the building was built in 1808 by Alexander Baranov to warehouse precious sea-otter pelts. W.J. Erskine made it his home in 1911. On display are samovars, a collection of intricate native basketry, and other relics from the early native Koniags and the later Russian settlers. A collection of 40 albums of archival photography portrays various aspects of the island's history. Contact the museum for a calendar of events. ⊠*101 Marine Way* ☎*907/486–5920* ⊕*www.baranovmuseum.org* ✉*$3* ⊙*May–Sept., Mon.–Sat. 10–4, Sun. noon–4; Oct.–Jan., Mar., and Apr., Tues.–Sat. 10–3.*

Fort Abercrombie State Park. As part of America's North Pacific defense in World War II, Kodiak was the site of an important naval station, now occupied by the Coast Guard fleet that patrols the surrounding fishing grounds. Part of the old military installation has been incorporated into Fort Abercrombie State Park, 3½ mi north of Kodiak on Rezanof Drive. The land is carpeted with spruce trees, and trails lead past old concrete bunkers and gun emplacements to magnificent shores. You can even see nesting puffins on the cliffs here. ⊠*Mile 3.7, Rezanof Dr.* ⒹꞋ*Alaska State Parks, Kodiak District Office, 1400 Abercrombie Dr., Kodiak 99615* ☎*907/486–6339* ⊕*www.dnr.state.ak.us/parks.*

Kodiak National Wildlife Refuge. One of the chief attractions in the area is the 1.6-million-acre Kodiak National Wildlife Refuge, which lies partly on Kodiak Island and partly on Afognak Island to the north, where spotting the enormous Kodiak brown bears is the main goal of a trip. Seeing the Kodiak brown bears, which weigh a pound at birth but up to 1,500 pounds when fully grown, is worth the trip to this rugged country. ■ TIP→ **The bears are spotted easily in July and August, feeding along salmon-spawning streams.** Charter flightseeing trips are available to the area, and exaggerated tales of encounters with these impressive beasts are frequently heard. ⊠*1390 Buskin River Rd., Kodiak* ☎*907/487–2600* ⊕*www.r7.fws.gov/nwr/kodiak.*

OUTDOOR ACTIVITIES

BEAR-WATCHING

Access to Kodiak bears from the road system is almost nonexistent. To see them normally requires traveling by boat or plane to remote streams, where bears feed on the abundant salmon runs. Here are a few of the local outfits that offer the service. **Harvey Flying Service** (☎907/487–2621 ⊕*www.harveyflyingservice.com*); **Andrew Airways** (☎907/487–2566 ⊕*www.andrewairways.com*); **Kodiak Treks** (✉*11754 S. Russian Creek Rd., Kodiak* ☎907/487–2122 ⊕*www.kodiaktreks.com*).

SHOPPING

Shopping in Kodiak is limited, but the town does have a downtown gift shop–gallery called **Norman's Fine Alaskan Gifts and Jewelry** (✉*414 Marine Way, Kodiak* ☎907/486–3315). They have some works by local artisans. The Alutiiq Museum store also sells native arts and educational materials.

WHERE TO EAT

$$–$$$ ✕**Henry's Great Alaskan Restaurant.** Henry's is a big, boisterous, friendly
AMERICAN place at the mall near the small-boat harbor. The menu is equally big, ranging from fresh local seafood and barbecue to pastas and even some Cajun dishes. Dinner specials, a long list of appetizers, salads, rack of lamb, and a tasty dessert list round out the choices. ✉*512 Marine Way* ☎907/486–8844 ⊕*www.henryskodiak.com* ▤*AE, MC, V.*

¢–$ ✕**Mill Bay Coffee & Pastries.** Serving lunches and fabulous pastries, this
CAFÉ charming little shop is well worth the trip. The coffee is fresh roasted on-site every other day. Inside, elegant antique furnishings are complemented by local artwork and handicrafts. ✉*3833 Rezanof Dr. E* ☎907/486–4411 ⊕*www.millbaycoffee.com* ▤*MC, V* ◷*No dinner.*

$$–$$$ ✕**Old Powerhouse Restaurant.** This converted powerhouse facility allows
JAPANESE a close-up view of Near Island and the channel connecting the boat harbors with the Gulf of Alaska. Enjoy fresh sushi and sashimi while watching the procession of fishing boats gliding past on their way to catch or deliver your next meal. Keep your eyes peeled for sea otters, seals, sea lions, and eagles, too. The menu also features tempura, *yakisoba* (fried noodles), and rice specials; there's live music on occasion. ✉*516 E. Marine Way* ☎907/481–1088 ▤*MC, V.*

WHERE TO DRINK

The **Kodiak Island Brewing Co.** (✉*338 Shelikof Ave.* ☎907/486–2537 ⊕*www.kodiakbrewery.com*) sells fresh-brewed, unfiltered beer in a variety of styles and sizes of containers, from 20-ounce bottles up to full kegs. Brewer Ben Millstein will also give you a tour of the facility on request. It's open from noon to 7 daily in summer, and from noon to 6 Monday to Saturday in winter. Some on-premises sales and consumption are allowed.

METLAKATLA

The village of Metlakatla—whose name translates roughly to "saltwater passage"—is on Annette Island, just a dozen miles by sea from busy Ketchikan but a world away culturally. A visit to this quiet community offers visitors a chance to learn about life in a small Inside Passage native community. Local taxis can take you to other sights around the island, including Yellow Hill and the old Air Force base.

In most Southeast native villages the people are Tlingit or Haida in heritage. Metlakatla is the exception, as most folks are Tsimshian (*sim-shee-ann*). They moved to the island from British Columbia in 1887, led by William Duncan, an Anglican missionary from England. The town grew rapidly and soon contained dozens of buildings on a grid of streets, including a cannery, a sawmill, and a church that could seat 1,000 people. Congress declared Annette Island a federal Indian reservation in 1891, and it remains the only reservation in Alaska today. Father Duncan continued to control life in Metlakatla for decades, until the government finally stepped in shortly before his death in 1918.

During World War II the U.S. Army built a major air base 7 mi from Metlakatla that included observation towers for Japanese subs, airplane hangars, gun emplacements, and housing for 10,000 soldiers. After the war it served as Ketchikan's airport for many years, but today the long runways are virtually abandoned save for a few private flights.

COMING ASHORE

Cruise ships dock at the Metlakatla dock adjacent to town. Buses from **Metlakatla Tours** (☎907/886–8687 ⊕*www.metlakatlatours.net/*) meet all ships and provide a standard shore excursion that includes a bus tour of town taking in most of the beautifully carved totem poles and a dance performance at the longhouse.

If you can supply your own laptop or Wi-Fi–enabled handheld device, check your e-mail at **Metlakatla Artists' Village** (✉*Airport Rd.* ☎*907/886–4437*).

EXPLORING METLAKATLA

William Duncan Memorial Church. Metlakatla's religious heritage still shows today. This clapboard church, topped with two steeples, burned in 1948 but was rebuilt several years later. It is one of nine churches in tiny Metlakatla. Father Duncan's Cottage is maintained to appear exactly as it would have in 1891, and includes original furnishings, personal items, and a collection of turn-of-the-20th-century music boxes. ✉*Corner of 4th Ave. and Church St.* ☎907/886–8687 ⊕*www.metlakatlatours.com* 🎫*$2* ⏱*Weekdays 8:30–12:30, or when cruise ships are in port.*

Longhouse and Artist's Village. Father Duncan worked hard to eliminate traditional Tsimshian beliefs and dances, but today the people of Metlakatla have resurrected their past; they perform old dances in traditional regalia. The best place to catch these performances is at the traditional longhouse (known as Le Sha'as in the Tsimshian dialect), which faces Metlakatla's boat harbor. Three totem poles stand on the back side of the building, and the front is covered with a Tsimshian design. Inside are displays of native crafts and a model of the fish traps that were once common throughout the Inside Passage. Native dance groups perform here on Wednesday and Friday in summer. Just next to the longhouse is an Artists' Village, where booths display locally made arts and crafts. The village and longhouse open when groups and tours are present.

MISTY FIORDS NATIONAL MONUMENT

Fodor'sChoice
★
In the past, cruise ships bypassed Misty Fiords on their way up and down the Inside Passage. But today more and more cruise passengers are discovering its unspoiled beauty as ships big and small feature a day of scenic cruising through this protected wilderness. At the southern end of the Inside Passage, Misty Fiords is usually visited just before or after a call at Ketchikan. The attraction here is the wilderness—3,500 square mi of it—highlighted by waterfalls and cliffs that rise 3,000 feet. Small boats enable views of breathtaking vistas. Traveling on these waters can be an almost mystical experience, with the greens of the forest reflected in waters as still as black mirrors. You may find yourself in the company of a whale, see bears fishing along the shore, or even pull in your own salmon for an evening meal. Park rangers may kayak out to your cruise ship to help point out wildlife and explain the geology of the area. ■ TIP→ Keep in mind that the name Misty refers to the weather you're likely to encounter in this rainy part of Alaska.

GETTING HERE ON YOUR OWN
The dramatic fjords and isolated alpine lakes of the 2.3-million-acre Misty Fiords National Monument don't exactly lend themselves to pedestrian exploration. But thanks to flightseeing services like **Island Wings Air Service** (☎ *907/225–2444 or 888/854–2444* ⊕ *www.island-wings.com*), the sublime splendor of this region doesn't go unseen. Based in Ketchikan, Island Wings offers a popular two-hour tour that includes a 35-minute stopover at one of the Monument's many lakes or fjords.

NOME

Nome is visited by Cruise West as part of its Bering Sea voyages, which include Homer, Kodiak, Dutch Harbor, the Pribilofs, Russia's Chukotka Peninsula, and sailing into the upper reaches of the Bering Sea far enough to cross the Arctic Circle where it intersects with the International Date Line. More than a century has passed since a great stampede for gold put a speck of wilderness called Nome on the Alaska map, but gold mining and noisy saloons are still mainstays in this frontier community on the icy Bering Sea. Only 165 mi from the coast of Siberia, Nome is considerably closer to Russia than either Anchorage or Fairbanks. Mainly a collection of ramshackle houses and low-slung commercial buildings, Nome looks like a vintage gold-mining camp or the neglected set of a Western movie—raw-boned, rugged, and somewhat shabby. What the town lacks in appearance is made up for with a cheerful hospitality and colorful history.

Nome's golden years began in 1898, when three prospectors known as the Lucky Swedes struck rich deposits on Anvil Creek, about 4 mi from what became Nome. The news spread quickly. When the Bering Sea ice parted the next spring, ships from Puget Sound, down by Seattle, arrived in Nome with eager stampeders. An estimated 15,000 people landed in Nome between June and October of 1900. Among the gold-rush luminaries were Wyatt Earp, the old gunfighter from the O.K. Corral, who mined the gold of Nome by opening a posh saloon; Tex Rickard, the boxing promoter, who operated another Nome saloon; and Rex Beach, the novelist.

A network of 250 mi or so of gravel roads around the town leads to creeks and rivers for gold panning or fishing for trout, salmon, and arctic grayling. You may also see reindeer, bears, foxes, and moose on the back roads that once connected early mining camps and hamlets.

COMING ASHORE

TRANSPORTATION AND TOURS
FROM THE PIER
Cruise ships dock a mile south of Nome at the city dock. Taxis are available to downtown for $5.

AREA TOURS
Most travelers take a tour of the area through **Nome Discovery Tours** (*Box 2024, Nome 99762* 907/443–2814 *www.nomechamber. org/discoverytours*), in which former Broadway showman Richard Beneville emphasizes Nome's gold rush and the region's Inupiat history.

VISITOR INFORMATION
To explore downtown, stop at the **Nome Convention and Visitors Bureau** (*301 Front St.* 907/443–6624, 800/478–1901 *in Alaska* *www. nomealaska.org/vc*) for a historic-walking-tour map, a city map, and information on local activities from flightseeing to bird-watching.

Check your e-mail for free at the **Kegoayah Kozga Library** (*223 Front St.* 907/443–6628 *www.nomealaska.org/library*).If you have a laptop, you can also access free wireless at several hotels and the local restaurant, **Airport Pizza** (*406 Bering St.*).

EXPLORING NOME

Carrie M. McClain Memorial Museum. Head here for the history of the Nome gold rush, from the "Lucky Swedes" discovery in 1898 to Wyatt Earp's arrival in 1899 and the stampede of thousands of people into Nome in 1900. The museum also has exhibits about the Bering Strait Inupiat Eskimos, plus displays on the Nome Kennel Club and its All-Alaska Sweepstakes. However, the highlight of the museum is the historical photo collection: thousands of pictures from the early days make it a perfect place to lose yourself on a rainy day. *223 Front*

St. ☎*907/443–6630* ✉*Free* ۞*June–early Sept., daily 10–5:30; early Sept.–May, Tues.–Fri. noon–5:30.*

WHERE TO EAT

$$–$$$

STEAK

Fodor'sChoice

★

✕**Airport Pizza.** This family-friendly pizza joint isn't like any other. Not only does it make some of the best food in town with a menu boasting great pizza and toppings, but it also features Tex-Mex, sandwiches, and a full breakfast menu. What's given this restaurant national attention is its delivery service: not only in town, but also to the surrounding Bush villages. Call up, order a pizza, and for $30 it'll be put on the next plane out. There are 15 beers on tap (many of which are microbrews), an extensive wine selection, and nightly music and games year-round. It also has a drive-thru coffee shop. ✉*406 Bering St.* ☎*907/443–7992* ▭*D, MC, V.*

SHOPPING

Nome is one of the best places to buy ivory, because many of the Eskimo carvers from outlying villages come to Nome first to sell their wares to dealers. The **Arctic Trading Post** (✉*Bering and Front Sts.* ☎*907/443–2686*) has an extensive stock of authentic Eskimo ivory carvings and other Alaskan artwork, jewelry, and books. The **Maruskiyas of Nome** (☎*907/443–2955*) on Front Street specializes in authentic native Alaskan artwork and handicrafts, including ivory, baleen, and jade sculptures, jewelry, dolls, and masks.

PETERSBURG

Getting to Petersburg is a heart-quickening experience. Only ferries and the smallest cruise ships can squeak through Wrangell Narrows, with the aid of more than 50 buoys and markers along the 22-mi passage. The inaccessibility of Petersburg is part of its charm, for unlike several other Southeast communities, this one is never overwhelmed with hordes of visitors.

At first sight Petersburg invokes the spirit of Norway; tidy white homes and storefronts line the streets, bright-color swirls of leaf and flower designs (called rosemaling) decorate a few older homes, and row upon row of sturdy fishing vessels pack the harbor. The Scandinavian feel is no accident—this prosperous fishing community was founded by Norwegian Peter Buschmann in 1897.

COMING ASHORE

SHORE EXCURSIONS

LeConte Glacier Flightseeing. One of the best flightseeing tours in Alaska takes you to the southernmost calving glacier in North America, which is backed by one of the Southeast's most beautiful collections of mountain peaks, including the Devil's Thumb. ۞*50 mins* ✉*$215.*

The Town That Fish Built. Here's a chance to explore all the landmarks of this pretty fishing town by bus, and see the largest salmon ever landed at the Clausen Museum. You'll travel 3 mi from town to stop at Sandy Beach, where ancient natives built fish traps, before returning to your ship. ⊘ *2 hrs* ⌦ *$25.*

Waterfront Walking Tour. A guide will relate the history and fishing heritage of Petersburg as you explore the old part of town on foot. ⊘ *1½ hrs* ⌦ *$20.*

TRANSPORTATION AND TOURS

FROM THE PIER

Four cruise companies include stops at Petersburg: American Safari Cruises, Majestic America Line, Cruise West, and Lindblad Expeditions. All of these are smaller, adventure-oriented ships. The ships dock in the South Harbor, which is about a ½-mi walk from downtown.

CITY TOURS

If you want to learn about local history, the commercial fishing industry, and the Tongass National Forest, you can take a guided tour with Viking Travel (*see Outdoor Activities, below*).

VISITOR INFORMATION

The **Petersburg Visitor Information Center,** within walking distance of the harbor, is a good source for local information, including details on tours, charters, and nearby outdoor recreation opportunities. ✉ *1st and Fram Sts.* ☎ *907/772–4636, 866/484–4700* ⊕ *www.petersburg.org.*

Check your e-mail for free at **Petersburg Public Library** (✉ *12 Nordic Dr.* ☎ *907/772–3349* ⊕ *www.psglib.org*).

EXPLORING PETERSBURG

One of the most pleasant things to do in Petersburg is to roam among the fishing vessels tied up at dockside. This is one of Alaska's busiest, most prosperous fishing communities, and the variety of boats is enormous. You can see small trollers, big halibut vessels, and sleek pleasure craft. Wander, too, around the fish-processing structures (though beware of the pungent aroma). Just by watching shrimp, salmon, or halibut catches being brought ashore, you can get a real appreciation for this industry and the people who engage in it.

 Clausen Memorial Museum. The museum's exhibits explore commercial fishing and the cannery industry, the era of fish traps, the social life of Petersburg, and Tlingit culture. Don't miss the museum shop; the

126.5-pound king salmon—the largest ever caught commercially—as well as the Tlingit dugout canoe; the Cape Decision lighthouse station lens; and *Earth, Sea and Sky,* a 3-D wall mural outside. ✉*203 Fram St.* ☎*907/772–3598* ⊕*www. clausenmuseum.net* ✉*$3* ⊗*May–early Sept., Mon.–Sat. 10–5; mid-Sept.–Apr. by appointment.*

LITTLE NORWAY FESTIVAL

Petersburg's Nordic heritage is gradually being submerged by the larger American culture, but you may still occasionally hear Norwegian spoken, especially during the Little Norway Festival, held here each year during the third weekend in May. If you're in town during the festival, be sure to partake in one of the fish feeds that highlight the Norwegian Independence Day celebration. You won't find better folk dancing and beer-batter halibut outside Norway.

❶ **Hammer Slough.** Houses on high stilts and the historic Sons of Norway Hall border this creek that floods with each high tide, creating a photogenic reflecting pool.

❹ **Eagle's Roost Park.** Just north of the Petersburg Fisheries cannery, this small roadside park is a great place to spot eagles, especially at low tide. On a clear day you will also discover dramatic views of the sharp-edged Coast Range, including the 9,077-foot summit of Devil's Thumb.

❷ **Petersburg Marine Mammal Center.** Visitors to this nonprofit research and learning center can share and gather information on marine mammal sightings, pick up reference material, and have fun with the interactive educational kiosk. ✉*Gjoa St. and Sing Lee Alley, behind Viking Travel* ☎*907/772–4170 summer only* ⊕*www.psgmmc.org* ✉*Free* ⊗*Mid-June–Aug., Mon.–Sat. 9–5.*

LeConte Glacier. The peaks of the Coastal Range behind the town mark the border between Canada and the United States; the most striking is Devil's Thumb, at 9,077 feet. About 25 mi east of Petersburg lies spectacular LeConte Glacier, the continent's southernmost tidewater glacier and one of its most active ones. It often happens that so many icebergs have calved into the bay that the entrance is carpeted bank to bank with the floating bergs. LeConte Glacier is accessible only by water or air; contact **Kaleidoscope Cruises** (☎*907/772–3736 or 800/868–4373* ⊕*www.petersburglodgingandtours.com*) to schedule a five-hour trip.

OUTDOOR ACTIVITIES

Viking Travel (✉*101 Nordic Dr.* ☎*907/772–3818 or 800/327–2571* ⊕*www.alaskaferry.com*) is a full-service travel agency that specializes in custom Alaska tours, and can book whale-watching, glacier, sea-kayaking, and other charters with local and regional operators.

CYCLING

Renting a bicycle is an especially pleasant way to see the sights. Ride along the coast on Nordic Drive, past the lovely homes, to the boardwalk and the city dump, where you might spot some bears. Coming back to town, take the interior route and you'll pass the airport and some

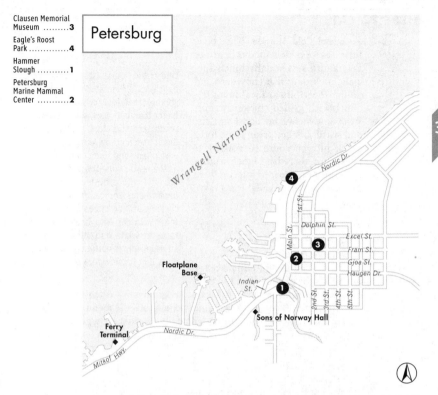

Petersburg

pretty churches before returning to the waterfront. Bikes are available from **Petersburg Cyclery** (⊠*1216 S. Nordic Dr.* ☎*907/772–3929*).

PICNICS

For a scenic hike, hop in a taxi for the 3-mi drive to Sandy Beach (on Nordic Drive, north of town), one of Petersburg's favorite spots for picnics, recreation, and eagle-viewing. There's even a petroglyph that's exposed at low tide.

SHOPPING

At **Tonka Seafoods,** across the street from the Sons of Norway Hall, you can tour the small custom seafood plant, check out the gift shop, and sample smoked or canned halibut and salmon. Be sure to taste the white king salmon—an especially flavorful type of Chinook that the locals swear by. Tonka will also ship. ⊠*22 Sing Lee Alley* ☎*907/772–3662 or 888/560–3662* ⊕*www.tonkaseafoods.com* ⊠*Free, tours $15* ⊗*June–Aug., daily 8–5; Sept.–May, Mon.–Sat. 8–5; tours at 1 PM (minimum 5 people).*

WHERE TO EAT

¢–$
SEAFOOD

×**Coastal Cold Storage.** This busy little seafood deli in the heart of Petersburg serves daily lunch specials, including fish chowders and halibut beer bits (a local favorite), along with grilled-chicken wraps, steak sandwiches, breakfast omelets, and waffles. It's a great place for a quick bite en route to your next adventure; there isn't much seating in the shop's cramped interior. Live or cooked crab is available for take-out, and the shop can process your sport-caught fish. ⊠ *306 N. Nordic Dr.* ☎*907/772–4177 or 877/257–4746* ▤*AE, D, DC, MC, V.*

¢
AMERICAN

×**Helse Restaurant.** Locals flock to this modest mom-and-pop place for lunch. It's the closest thing to home cooking Petersburg has to offer, and most days it's open from 8 to 5, even in winter. A couple dozen sandwiches grace the menu, as do rotating soups and homemade bread. The daily specials are a good bet, and the gyros are decent as well. Helse also doubles as an ice-cream and espresso stand. ⊠ *13 Sing Lee Alley* ☎*907/772–3444* ▤*MC, V.*

> ### LOCAL TREATS
>
> One of the Southeast's gourmet delicacies is Petersburg pink salad shrimp. Small (they're seldom larger than half your pinky finger), tender, and succulent, they're much treasured by Alaskans, who often send them "outside" as thank-you gifts. You can find the little critters fresh in meat departments and canned in gift sections at food stores throughout the Panhandle. Also, be sure to taste the white king salmon—it's an especially flavorful type of Chinook that locals swear by.

WHERE TO DRINK

The **Harbor Bar** (⊠ *310 N. Nordic Dr.* ☎*907/772–4526*), with ships' wheels, nautical pictures, and a mounted red snapper, is true to the town's seafaring spirit. A separate outside entrance leads to the bar's liquor store. Sample the brew and blasting music at the smoky **Kito's Kave** (⊠ *Sing Lee Alley* ☎*907/772–3207*), a popular hangout among rowdy local fishermen. La Fonda, a Mexican restaurant, leases space inside the bar.

PRINCE RUPERT, BRITISH COLUMBIA

Just 40 mi (66 km) south of the Alaskan border, Prince Rupert is the largest community on British Columbia's north coast. Set on Kaien Island at the mouth of the Skeena River and surrounded by deep green fjords and coastal rain forest, Prince Rupert is rich in the culture of the Tsimshian, people who have been in the area for thousands of years.

As the western terminus of Canada's second transcontinental railroad and blessed with a deep natural harbor, Prince Rupert was, at the time of its incorporation in 1910, poised to rival Vancouver as a center for trans-Pacific trade. This didn't happen, partly because the main visionary behind the scheme, Grand Trunk Pacific Railroad president Charles Hays, went down with the *Titanic* on his way back from a financing trip to England. Prince Rupert turned instead to fishing and forestry. A port of call for both BC and Alaska ferries, but relatively new to cruise ships, this community of 15,000 retains a laid-back, small-town air.

COMING ASHORE

SHORE EXCURSIONS

Khutzeymateen Grizzly Bear Viewing. Travel by boat to see one of North America's highest concentrations of grizzly bears, passing stunning scenery and two First Nations villages en route. Eagles, porpoises, and whales may also be spotted. Since boats are not permitted to land at the sanctuary, you'll watch the bears from a safe distance offshore. Viewing is best between mid-May and late July; trips may not be offered in August and September. ⊙ *5½ hrs* ⌧ *$235.*

Ancient Village, Petroglyphs & Rainforest Discovery. Join First Nations guides on a visit to traditional Tsimshian lands, follow trails through old-growth forest, see archaeological sites, and enjoy a traditional salmon barbecue. ⊙ *4 hrs* ⌧ *$96.*

Prince Rupert Deluxe Highlights. This three-in-one excursion includes a city tour, a trip to the North Pacific Cannery—a Canadian National Historic Site and the oldest salmon cannery on the coast—and a visit to the renowned Museum of Northern British Columbia. ⊙ *3½ hrs* ⌧ *$84.*

Traditions & Mysteries of the North Coast Native People. Learn about the life and history of the Tsimshian people at the Museum of Northern British Columbia, then enter a Tsimshian longhouse to join in a feast with mask dancing, stories, and songs. ⊙ *2½ hrs* ⌧ *$49.*

TRANSPORTATION

FROM THE PIER

Large cruise ships calling at Prince Rupert dock at the **Northland Cruise Terminal,** while smaller ships tie up at **Atlin Terminal** next door. Both terminals are in the city's historic Cow Bay district, steps from the Museum of Northern British Columbia and about five blocks from the central business district. The terminals for both British Columbia and Alaska ferries as well as the VIA Rail station are grouped together about 2 km (1 mi) from town.

Most points of interest are within walking distance of the cruise-ship terminals. **Far West Bus Lines** (☏ *250/624–6400*) offers service around town. For a taxi, contact **Skeena Taxi** (☏ *250/624–2185*).

VISITOR INFORMATION

Prince Rupert's **Visitor Information Centre** (☏ *250/624–5637 or 800/ 667–1994*) is at the Atlin Terminal. **Tourism Prince Rupert** (⊕ *www.tourismprincerupert.com*) has a useful Web site.

PRINCE RUPERT
BEST BETS

■ **Looking for wildlife?** The Khutzeymateen Grizzly Bear Sanctuary is home to North America's largest concentration of humpbacks and a strong population of orcas.

■ **Short on time?** Pay a visit to the excellent Museum of Northern British Columbia, followed by a stroll around the funky **Cow Bay** neighborhood.

■ **Want something different?** If you have a little extra time, hit the North Pacific Historic Fishing Village.

3

TIP

Public transport is limited, so an organized excursion is the best way to get to the Fishing Village.

TIME

■ TIP→ **If you're coming from Alaska, remember to adjust your watch.** British Columbia is on Pacific Time, one hour ahead of Alaska Time.

EXPLORING PRINCE RUPERT

Home to both of Prince Rupert's cruise-ship terminals, **Cow Bay** is a historic waterfront area of shops, galleries, seafood restaurants, yachts, canneries, and fishing boats. Cow Bay takes its name seriously; lampposts, benches, and anything else stationary is painted Holstein-style. While here, you can stop for a coffee or seafood lunch, shop for local crafts, or watch fishermen bring in their catch.

★ The **Museum of Northern British Columbia,** in a longhouse-style facility overlooking the waterfront, has one of the province's finest collections of coastal First Nations art, with artifacts portraying 10,000 years of Northwest Coast history. You may also have a chance to see artisans working in a nearby carving shed. Between June and August, museum staff also operate the **Kwinista Railway Museum,** a five-minute walk away on the waterfront. ✉*100 1st Ave. W* ☎*250/624–3207* ⊕*www.museumofnorthernbc.com* ✉*C$6* ⊘*June–Aug., daily 9–5; Sept.–May, Tues.–Sat. 9–5 (also whenever a ship is in port).*

SHOPPING

Prince Rupert has a great selection of locally made crafts and First Nations artwork. Look for items carved in argillite, a kind of slate unique to this region. The **Cow Bay Gift Galley** (✉*24 Cow Bay Rd.* ☎*250/627–1808*) has gifts, souvenirs, and local art. The **North Coast Artists' Cooperative Ice House Gallery** (✉*At the Atlin Cruise Ship Terminal* ☎*250/624–4546*) has paintings, jewelry, weaving, pottery and more, all by local artists.

WHERE TO EAT

$-$$ ✗ **Cow Bay Café.** Local seafood and creative vegetarian dishes shine at this
CONTEMPORARY   tiny waterfront café, where the friendly chef-owner makes almost everything (including breads and desserts) from scratch. What's on the chalkboard menu depends on what's fresh that day, but could include curries, Mexican dishes, or the popular crab cakes. The solariumlike room with floor-to-ceiling ocean-view windows only seats 35, so reservations are highly recommended. ✉*205 Cow Bay Rd., Cow Bay* ☎*250/627–1212* ▤*AE, MC, V* ⊘*Closed Sun. and Mon. No dinner Tues.*

$ ✗ **Cowpuccino's Coffee House.** When Rupertites want to while away a
CAFÉ   wet afternoon, they flock to this cozy meeting place in Cow Bay. You can curl up on the sofa with an espresso and a magazine or pull up a chair for homemade soup, sandwiches, panini, and luscious house-made desserts (try the cow patty: a chocolate-macaroon concoction). Hearty breakfasts are served here, too. Outdoor tables are a great place to watch eagles gathering across the street. ✉*25 Cow Bay Rd., Cow Bay* ☎*250/627–1395* ▤*MC, V.*

$$ **×OPA Sushi.** A historic net loft makes a suitably nautical setting for this
JAPANESE popular Cow Bay sushi spot, and the patio out back is a prime spot for
eagle-watching. Locals and visitors flock here for nigiri, sashimi, and
maki rolls made with wild, local British Columbian salmon, prawns,
octopus, and other treats from the sea. Donburi rice dishes, miso soup,
sake cocktails, and green-tea ice cream round out the menu. ⊠ *34
Cow Bay Rd., Cow Bay* ☎*250/627–4560* ⊟*MC, V* ⊘*Closed Sun.
and Mon.*

PRINCE WILLIAM SOUND

Every Gulf of Alaska cruise visits Prince William Sound. Along its shore-
line are quiet bays, trickling waterfalls, and hidden coves. In addition to
hosting brown and black bears, gray wolves, and Sitka blacktail deer,
the sound thrives with a variety of birds and all manner of marine life,
including salmon, halibut, humpback and killer whales, sea otters, sea
lions, and porpoises. Bald eagles often soar overhead or perch in tall
trees. The sound made worldwide headlines in 1989, when the *Exxon
Valdez* hit a reef and spilled 11 million gallons of North Slope crude.
Vast sections of the sound appear pristine today, with abundant wild-
life, but the oil has sunk into the beaches below the surface. The lasting
effects on the area of this lurking oil—sometimes uncovered after storms
and high tides—are still being studied.

EXPLORING PRINCE WILLIAM SOUND

The major attraction in Prince William Sound on most Gulf of Alaska
cruises is the day spent in **College Fjord.** This deep finger of water boasts
the largest colletion of tidewater glaciers in the world, and is ringed by
16 glaciers, each named after one of the colleges that sponsored early
exploration of the fjord.

A visit to **Columbia Glacier,** which flows from the surrounding Chugach
Mountains, is included on many Gulf of Alaska cruises (often via Val-
dez). Its deep aquamarine face is 5 mi across, and it calves new icebergs
with resounding cannonades. This glacier is one of the largest and most
readily accessible of Alaska's coastal glaciers.

The three largest Prince William Sound communities—Valdez, Whittier,
and Cordova—are all visited by cruise ships, but none is a major desti-
nation. Valdez (pronounced val-*deez*) and Cordova are visited only by
the smaller, expedition-style cruise ships. Whittier has replaced Seward
as a terminus for many sailings by Princess Cruises and Carnival Cruise
Lines, and some from Cruise West (although passengers actually fly
into Anchorage and take transportation provided by the cruise line to
Whittier). Cruise West has a special transfer tour from Anchorage to
their ships that passes through Whittier village and is included in the
fare. Unless you book a shore expedition such as sea kayaking, fishing,
or a sound cruise, you won't see much of Whittier (not that you'll be
missing anything).

SEWARD

Seward is one of Alaska's oldest and most scenic communities, set between high mountain ranges on one side and Resurrection Bay on the other, and you shouldn't miss it in your haste to get to Anchorage. One of the Kenai Peninsula's major communities, it lies at the south end of the Seward Highway, which connects with Anchorage and is the southern terminus of the Alaska Railroad. The city was named for U.S. Secretary of State William H. Seward, who was instrumental in arranging the purchase of Alaska from Russia in 1867. Resurrection Bay was named in 1791 by Russian fur trader and explorer Alexander Baranof. The town was established in 1903 by railroad surveyors as an ocean terminal and supply center. The biggest event in Seward's history was the 1964 Good Friday earthquake—the strongest ever recorded in North America. The tsunami that followed the quake devastated the town; fortunately, most residents saw the harbor drain almost entirely, knew the wave would follow, and ran to high ground. Since then the town has relied heavily on commercial fishing, and its harbor is important for shipping coal to Asia.

> ## SEWARD BEST BETS
>
> ■ **Get your sea legs.** Seward's main claims to fame and most notable draws are Resurrection Bay and Kenai Fjords National Park.
>
> ■ **Landlubber?** Visit the park at Exit Glacier north of town, any of the numerous trails in the area, or shop at one of the stores near the small boat harbor or in the downtown business district.
>
> ■ **Rainy day?** The Sealife Center is not to be missed. It's a combination aquarium, rescue facility for marine animals, and research center. If the seas are too rough or the rain too bothersome, there's interesting stuff here for all ages.

Historic downtown Seward retains its small-town atmosphere. Many of its early-20th-century buildings survived the 1964 earthquake or were rebuilt. Modern-day explorers can enjoy wildlife cruises, sportfishing, sailing, and kayaking in the bay or investigating the intricacies of marine biology at the Alaska SeaLife Center. If you're in Seward on July 4, you'll have the chance to see—and perhaps join—the second-oldest footrace in North America. Each year participants race straight up 3,022-foot Mt. Marathon from downtown. Seward also is the launching point for excursions into Kenai Fjords National Park, where you can spy calving glaciers, sea lions, whales, and otters.

COMING ASHORE

SHORE EXCURSIONS
ADVENTURE
Godwin Glacier Dog Sled Tour. These outstanding tours begin with a 15-minute helicopter flight to remote Godwin Glacier. Here you step onto the ice and learn about mushing from an Iditarod veteran, meet the dogs, and head out across the glacier by dog sled. ⏱ *2 hrs* 🚢 *$509.*

SCENIC

Portage Glacier. Passengers disembarking in Seward often take advantage of the chance to see Portage Glacier while en route to Anchorage. The drive along Turnagain Arm to Portage Glacier is one of Alaska's most beautiful. A boat transports you to the glacial face, which has receded dramatically in recent years. ⊙*1-hr boat tour* ⊡*$55.*

Resurrection Bay Cruise. Boats depart from the Seward harbor and cruise near Bear Glacier and past playful sea otters, a sea-lion rookery, and nesting seabirds (including puffins). Whales are commonly sighted, too. ⊙*3–5 hrs* ⊡*$69–$89.*

TRANSPORTATION AND TOURS

FROM THE PIER

Cruises officially start or end in Seward, but transportation from (or to) Anchorage is either included in your cruise fare or available as an add-on. Cruise ships dock approximately ½ mi from downtown.

AREA TOURS

Kenai Fjords Tours (☎*907/224–8068 or 877/777–4051* ⊕*www.kenaifjords.com*) has a very good half-day cruise of Resurrection Bay with a stop for a salmon bake on Fox Island ($89 including taxes for a five-hour cruise).

Major Marine Tours (☎*907/274–7300 or 800/764–7300* ⊕*www.majormarine.com*) conducts half-day and full-day cruises of Resurrection Bay and Kenai Fjords National Park. Park cruises are narrated by a national park ranger, and buffet meals featuring salmon and prime rib are an option.

Renown Charters and Tours (☎*907/224–3806 or 888/514–8687* ⊕*www.renowntours.com*) is the only outfit that operates tours into Resurrection Bay. Cruises include a four-hour whale-watching tour (March 31 through May 18) and a six-hour Kenai Fjords trip, which runs from May 19 through September 16. The latter trip is on a speedy and stable custom built catamaran.

VISITOR INFORMATION

The **Seward Chamber of Commerce** (☎*907/224–8051* ⊕*www.sewardak.org*) has a visitor information center at the cruise-ship dock that is staffed when ships are in port. The **Kenai Fjords National Park visitor center** (☎*907/224–7500* ⊕*www.nps.gov/kefj* ⊙*Daily 8:30–7*) is within walking distance: turn left as you leave the pier, then left again onto 4th Avenue; the center is two blocks ahead. Ask here about visiting scenic Exit Glacier, which is 13 mi northwest of Seward. The Alaska National Historical Society

> ### MARITIME EXPLORATIONS
>
> The protected waters of the bay provide the perfect environment for sailing, fishing, sea kayaking, and marine wildlife–watching. There are numerous tours to choose from—just check out the boardwalk area adjacent to the docks. Half-day tours include Resurrection Bay, while all-day tours also allow you to view parts of spectacular Kenai Fjords National Park. The more adventurous trips venture out of the bay and into the Gulf of Alaska when the notoriously fickle weather permits visits to the more distant glaciers and attractions.

operates a book and gift store in the Park Service center. The Chugach National Forest Ranger District office is at 334 4th Avenue. They have maps and information on local trails, cabins, and wildlife.

Check your e-mail at **The Sea Bean** (✉ *225 4th Ave.* ☎ *907/224–6623* ✉ *seabeancafe@gmail.com*), or **Rainy Days Internet Cafe** (✉ *1406 4th Ave., Suite D* ☎ *907/224–5774* ⊕ *www.rainydayscafe.com*). The **Seward Memorial Library** has free computer access as well (✉ *238 5th Ave.* ☎ *907/224–4082* ⊕ *www.cityofseward.net/library*).

EXPLORING SEWARD

Ⓒ **Alaska SeaLife Center.** If you have only a little time in Seward, make sure
Fodor'sChoice you try to spend some of it here. You'll find massive cold-water tanks
★ and outdoor viewing decks, as well as interactive displays of cold-water fish, seabirds, and marine mammals including harbor seals and a 2,000-pound sea lion. A research center as well as visitor center, it also rehabilitates injured marine wildlife and provides educational experiences for the general public. Appropriately, the center was partially funded with reparations money from the *Exxon Valdez* oil spill. Films, hands-on activities, a gift shop, and behind-the-scenes tours ($12 and up) complete the offerings. ✉ *301 Railway Ave.* ☎ *907/224–6300 or 888/378–2525* ⊕ *www.alaskasealife.org* 🎟 *$20* ⊙ *May–Sept. 15, daily 9–7; Sept. 16–Apr., daily 10–5.*

Iditarod Trail. The first mile of the historic original Iditarod Trail runs along the beach and makes for a nice, easy stroll, as does the city's printed walking tour—available at the visitors bureau, the converted railcar at the corner of 3rd Avenue and Jefferson Street, or the Seward Chamber of Commerce Visitor Center at Mile 2 on the Seward Highway.

Kenai Fjords National Park. Seward is the gateway to the 670,000-acre Kenai Fjords National Park. This is spectacular coastal parkland incised with sheer, dark slate cliffs, ribboned with white waterfalls, and tufted with deep-green spruce. Kenai Fjords presents a rare opportunity for an up-close view of blue tidewater glaciers as well as some remarkable ocean wildlife. If you take a day trip on a tour boat out of Seward, you can be pretty sure of seeing sea otters, crowds of Steller sea lions lazing on the rocky shelves along the shore, a porpoise or two, bald eagles soaring overhead, and tens of thousands of seabirds. Humpback whales and orcas are also sighted occasionally, and mountain goats frequent the seaside cliffs. Tours range in length from 4 to 10 hours.

One of the park's chief attractions is Exit Glacier, which can be reached only by the one road that passes into Kenai Fjords. Trails inside the park lead to the side and toe of the glacier, and a strenuous 6- to 8-hour hike brings you to an overlook of the vast Harding Icefield. ✉ *Box 1727, Seward 99664* ☎ *907/224–7500* ⊕ *www.nps.gov/kefj.*

Seward Museum. The Seward Museum displays photographs of the 1964 quake's damage, model rooms and artifacts from the early pioneers, and historical and current information on the Seward area. ✉ *336 3rd Ave., at Jefferson St.* ☎ *907/224–3902* 🎟 *$3* ⊙ *Mid-May–Sept., daily 9–5; Oct.–mid-May, weekends noon–4. Hrs may vary seasonally; call for recorded information.*

OUTDOOR ACTIVITIES

FISHING

For several weeks in August the **Seward Silver Salmon Derby** attracts hundreds of competitors for the $10,000 top prize. Get details from the **Fish House** (⌗*Small-boat harbor* ☎*907/224–3674 or 800/257–7760* ⊕*www.thefishhouse.net*), Seward's oldest booking agency for deep-sea fishing.

HIKING

The strenuous **Mt. Marathon** trail starts at the west end of Lowell Canyon Road and runs practically straight uphill. An easier and more convenient hike is the **Two Lakes Trail**, a loop of footpaths and bridges on the edge of town. A map is available from the **Seward Chamber of Commerce** (⌗*2001 Seward Hwy.* ☎*907/224–8051* ⊕*www.sewardak.org*).

> **EMBARKING IN SEWARD**
>
> Seward is an important embarkation or disembarkation port for cruise ship travelers. Many large cruise ships terminate (or start) their 7-day Alaskan voyages in Seward. Although many cruise ships stop in Seward, travelers are often shunted off to Anchorage on waiting buses or train cars with no time to explore this lovely town.

SHOPPING

⟳ The **Ranting Raven** (⌗*228 4th Ave.* ☎*907/224–2228*) is a combination gift shop, bakery, and lunch spot, adorned with raven murals on the side of the building. You can indulge in fresh-baked goods, espresso drinks, and daily lunch specials such as quiche, focaccia, and homemade soups while perusing the packed shelves of artwork, native crafts, and jewelry. **Resurrect Art Coffeehouse** (⌗*320 3rd Ave.* ☎*907/224–7161* ⊕*www.resurrectart.com*) is a darling coffeehouse and gallery-gift shop. It is housed in a 1932 church, and the ambience and views from the old choir loft are reason enough to stop by. Local art is showcased, and it's a good place to find Alaskan gifts that aren't mass-produced.

WHERE TO EAT

$$$$ ✕**Chinooks Waterfront Restaurant.** On the waterfront in the small-boat
SEAFOOD harbor, Chinooks has a dazzling selection of fresh seafood dishes, brews on tap, a great wine selection, and a stunning view from the upstairs window seats. Pasta dishes and a few beef specialties round out the menu. ⌗*1404 4th Ave.* ☎*907/224–2207* ▭*MC, V* ⊗*Closed mid-Oct.–May.*

$$$ ✕**Christo's Palace.** Serving Greek, Italian, Mexican, and seafood meals,
ECLECTIC this ornately furnished downtown restaurant is a surprisingly elegant hidden treasure. The nondescript facade belies the high, beamed ceilings, dark-wood accents, ornate chandeliers, and a large, gorgeous mahogany bar reputedly built in the mid-1800s and imported from San Francisco. Portions are generous, desserts are tempting, and there is a small selection of after-dinner cognacs. ⌗*133 4th Ave.* ☎*907/224–5255* ▭*AE, D, MC, V.*

¢–$ ✕**Railway Cantina.** This little hole-in-the-wall in the harbor area is a
MEXICAN   local favorite. A wide selection of burritos, quesadillas, and great fish
tacos incorporates local seafood and is supplemented by an array of hot
sauces, many contributed by customers who brought them from their
travels. ✉ *1401 4th Ave.* ☎ *907/224–8226* ▤ *MC, V.*

SITKA

Sitka was the home to the Kiksadi Clan of the Tlingit people for centuries prior to the 18th-century arrival of the Russians, who under the
direction of territorial governor Alexander Baranof coveted the Sitka
site for its beauty, mild climate, and economic potential. In 1799 Baranof established an outpost that he called Redoubt St. Michael, 6 mi
north of the present town, and moved a large number of his Russian
and Aleut sea-otter and seal hunters there from Kodiak Island.

The Tlingits attacked Baranof's people and burned his buildings in
1802, but Baranof returned in 1804 with formidable strength, including
shipboard cannons. He attacked the Tlingits at their fort near Indian
River (site of the present-day, 105-acre Sitka National Historical Park)
and drove them to Chichagof Island, 70 mi northwest of Sitka. The
Tlingits and Russians made peace in 1821, and eventually the capital
of Russian America was shifted from Kodiak to Sitka.

Today Sitka is known for its beautiful setting and some of Southeast
Alaska's most famous landmarks: the onion-dome Saint Michael's
church; the Alaska Raptor Center, where you can come up close to ail-
ing and recovering birds of prey; and Sitka National Historical Park,
where you can see some of the oldest and most skillfully carved totem
poles in the state.

COMING ASHORE

SHORE EXCURSIONS
ADVENTURE
***Sea Life Discovery* Semi-Submersible.** Large underwater windows on this
vessel let you see Sitka Sound's kelp forests, fish, and crab. Just outside
the boat, divers capture underwater camera images that are then displayed on the boat's video monitor. ⏱ *2 hrs* 🎫 *$84.*

Sitka Bike and Hike Tour. This guided, three-hour hike-and-bike excursion takes you out of town for a 5-mi ride over gently rolling terrain.
Stop at Thimbleberry Creek for a short hike that crosses a picturesque
waterfall and resume your bike ride to Whale Park. End at Theobroma
Chocolate Factory, where you can enjoy a locally made chocolate bar
before taking the bus back to town. ⏱ *3 hrs* 🎫 *$65–$79.*

Wilderness Sea Kayaking Adventure. Kayak Sitka's coves and tranquil
waterways against the backdrop of the Mt. Edgecumbe volcano. Warm
up with a hot beverage and snack at the base camp before returning to
your ship. ⏱ *3 hrs* 🎫 *$95–$109.*

Sportfishing. Try for the abundant salmon and halibut in these waters.
All equipment is provided; you buy your license on board. Your catch

can be frozen and shipped. ⊘*4 hrs* ⊠*$209*.

CULTURAL

History and Nature Walking Tour. A guided walk through Sitka details its political and natural history. This tour includes all the major sites plus a visit to the Sitka National Historic Park for a stroll through the rain forest, and time at the Alaska Raptor Center. Return downtown by van. ⊘*2½ hrs* ⊠*$54*.

Russian-America Tour. Stops at Castle Hill, the Russian Cemetery, St. Michael's Cathedral, and Sitka National Historic Park are included in this bus-and-walking tour of Sitka's rich Russian heritage. The finale is a Russian-style folk-dance performance by the New Archangel Dancers, local women who have mastered the timing and athletic feats required for this traditional style of dance. ⊘*2½ hrs* ⊠*$49*.

SCENIC

Sea Otter Quest. This search for the sea otter and other Sitka wildlife is a cruise passenger favorite. Creatures that you're likely to see from the boat include whales, eagles, puffins, and more. ⊘*3 hrs* ⊠*$119*.

Tongass Forest Nature Hike. This 4-mi hike provides an excellent introduction to the rain forests that surround Sitka. The hike covers a mix of boardwalk and gravel trails through tall spruce forests and open muskeg, and then loops back via the shore. Children under the age of 10 are not allowed to participate, and hikers need to be in good physical condition. ⊘*3 hrs* ⊠*$65*.

TRANSPORTATION AND TOURS

FROM THE PIER

Only the smallest excursion vessels can dock at Sitka. Medium to large cruise ships must drop anchor in the harbor and tender passengers ashore near **Harrigan Centennial Hall.** You can recognize the hall by the big Tlingit war canoe to the side of the building. Sitka is an extremely walkable town, and the waterfront attractions are all fairly close to the tender landing.

VISITOR INFORMATION

Also housed in Harrigan Centennial Hall is an information desk for the **Sitka Convention and Visitors Bureau** (☎*907/747–5940* ⊕*www.sitka.org*), where you can get a list of local charter-fishing operators.

Check your e-mail via Wi-Fi on your own device for free (with coffee purchase) at **Highliner Coffee** (⊠*327 Seward St.* ☎*907/747–4924*).

SITKA BEST BETS

■ **Take in the Totems.** Just east of downtown, Sitka National Historical Park features a workshop, interpretive center, and 15 top-notch totem poles spread along a meandering waterfront wooded trail.

■ **Visit the Alaska Raptor Center.** Alaska's only full-service avian hospital lets you get face-to-beak with more than 100 injured and rehabilitating bald eagles, hawks, owls, and other raptors.

■ **Stroll Around.** Sitka's ocean-front setting, picturesque streets, and rich, varied history make it one of the Southeast's best walking towns.

3

EXPLORING SITKA

It's hard not to like Sitka, with its eclectic blend of Native, Russian, and American history and its dramatic and beautiful setting. ■TIP→ **This is one of the best Inside Passage towns to explore on foot.**

❻ **Alaska Raptor Center.** The only full-service avian hospital in Alaska, the Raptor Center rehabilitates 100 to 200 birds each year. Situated just above Indian Creek, the center is a 20-minute walk from downtown. Well-versed guides provide an introduction to the rehabilitation center (including a short video), and guests are able to visit with one of these majestic birds. The Raptor Center's primary attraction is an enclosed 20,000-square-foot flight training center, built to replicate the rain forest, where injured eagles relearn survival skills, including flying and catching salmon. Visitors watch through one-way glass windows. A large deck out back faces an open-air enclosure for eagles and other raptors whose injuries prevent them from returning to the wild. Additional mews with hawks, owls, and other birds are along a rain-forest path. The gift shop sells all sorts of eagle paraphernalia, the proceeds from which fund the center's programs. ⊠ *1000 Raptor Way, off Sawmill Creek Rd.* ☎ *907/747–8662 or 800/643–9425* ⊕ *www.alaskaraptor. org* ☞ *$12* ⊗ *Mid-May–Sept., daily 8–4.*

> ### HISTORY & A VIEW
>
> For one of the best views in town, turn left on Harbor Drive and head for Castle Hill, where Alaska was handed over to the United States on October 18, 1867, and where the first 49-star U.S. flag was flown, on January 3, 1959, signifying the spirit of Alaska's statehood. Take the first right off Harbor Drive; then look for the entrance to Baranof Castle Hill State Historic Site. Make a left on the paved path (it's wheelchair accessible), which takes you to the top of the hill overlooking Crescent Harbor.

❷ **Harrigan Centennial Hall.** A Tlingit war canoe sits beside this brick building, which houses the **Sitka Historical Museum.** Check out its collection of Tlingit, Victorian-era, and Alaska-purchase historical artifacts; there's an auditorium for New Archangel Dancers performances, which take place when cruise ships are in port. ⊠ *330 Harbor Dr.* ☎ *907/747–6455 museum, 907/747–5940 Visitors Bureau* ⊕ *www.sitkahistory.org* ☞ *$1* ⊗ *Museum mid-May–mid-Sept., daily 8–5; mid-Sept.–mid-May, Tues.–Sat. 10–4. Information desk May–Sept., 8–3 when cruise ships are in port.*

❾ **Russian and Lutheran cemeteries.** Most of Sitka's Russian dignitaries are buried in these sites off Marine Street, which, thanks to their wooded locations, require a bit of exploring to locate. The most distinctive (and easily accessible) grave belongs to Princess Maksoutoff (died 1862), wife of the last Russian governor and one of the most illustrious members of the Russian royal family to be buried on Alaska soil.

❸ **Russian Bishop's House.** A registered historic landmark, this house facing the harbor was constructed by the Russian-American Company for Bishop Innocent Veniaminov in 1842 and completed in 1843. Inside the house, one of the few remaining Russian-built log structures in

Alaska, are exhibits on the history of Russian America, including several places where portions of the house's structure are peeled away to expose Russian building techniques. The ground level is a free museum, and Park Service rangers lead guided tours of the second floor, which houses the residential quarters and a chapel. ⊠ *501 Lincoln St.* ☎*907/747–6281* ⊕*www.nps.gov/sitk* ⊠*Tours* $5 ⊙*May–Sept., 9–5; Oct.–Apr. by appointment.*

❶ St. Michael's Cathedral. This cathedral, one of Southeast Alaska's best-
★ known national landmarks, is treasured by visitors and locals alike—so treasured that in 1966, as a fire engulfed the building, townspeople risked their lives and rushed inside to rescue the cathedral's precious Russian icons, religious objects, and vestments. Using original blueprints, an almost exact replica of onion-dome St. Michael's was completed in 1976. Today you can see what could possibly be the largest collection of Russian icons in the United States, among them the much-prized *Our Lady of Sitka* (also known as the *Sitka Madonna*) and the *Christ Pantocrator* (*Christ the World Judge*), displayed on the altar screen. ⊠*240 Lincoln St.* ☎*907/747–8120* ⊠*$2 requested donation* ⊙*May–Sept., daily 8:30–4; Oct.–Apr., hrs vary.*

❹ Sheldon Jackson Museum. Near the campus of **Sheldon Jackson College,**
★ this octagonal museum, which dates from 1895, contains priceless Aleut and Eskimo items collected by Dr. Sheldon Jackson (1834–1909), who traveled the remote regions of Alaska as an educator and missionary. This state-run museum features artifacts from every native Alaska culture; on display are carved masks, Chilkat blankets, dogsleds, kayaks, and even the impressive helmet worn by Chief Katlean during the 1804 battle against the Russians. The museum's gift shop, operated by the Friends of the Sheldon Jackson Museum, carries books, paper goods, and handicrafts created by Alaska native artists. ■TIP➔ **Native artisans are here all summer, creating baskets, carvings, or masks.** ⊠*104 College Dr.* ☎*907/747–8981* ⊕*www.museums.state.ak.us* ⊠*$4 mid-May–mid-Sept., $3 mid-Sept.–mid-May* ⊙*Mid-May–mid-Sept., daily 9–5; mid-Sept.–mid-May, Tues.–Sat. 10–4.*

❺ Sitka National Historical Park. The main building at this 113-acre park
FodorśChoice houses a small museum with fascinating historical exhibits and photos
★ of Tlingit native culture. Highlights include a brass peace hat given to the Sitka Kiksádi by Russian traders in the early 1800s and Chilkat robes. Head to the theater to watch a 12-minute video about Russian-Tlingit conflict in the 19th century. Also here is the **Southeast Alaska Indian Cultural Center,** where native artisans demonstrate silversmithing, weaving, wood carving, and basketry. Don't be afraid to strike up a conversation; the artisans are happy to talk about their work and Tlingit cultural traditions. At the far end of the building are seven totems (some more than a century old) that have been brought indoors to protect them from decay. Behind the center, a wide, 2-mi path takes you through the forest and along the shore of Sitka Sound. Scattered along the way are some of the most skillfully carved native totem poles in Alaska. Keep going on the trail to see spawning salmon from the footbridge over Indian River. Park Service rangers lead themed walks in summer, which focus on the Russian-Tlingit conflict, the area's natural history,

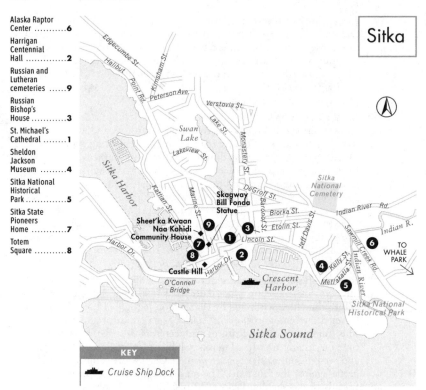

and the park's totem poles. ✉*106 Metlakatla St.* ☎*907/747–6281,*
907/747–8061 gift shop ⊕*www.nps.gov/sitk* ✉*$3* ⊘*Daily 8–5.*

❼ Sitka State Pioneers Home. This large, red-roof home for elder Alaskans
has an imposing 14-foot statue in front symbolizing Alaska's frontier
sourdough spirit ("sourdough" generally refers to Alaska's American
pioneers and prospectors); it was modeled by an authentic prospec-
tor, William "Skagway Bill" Fonda. Adjacent to the Pioneers Home is
Sheet'ka Kwaan Naa Kahidi community house, where you can watch
native dance performances throughout the summer. ✉*Lincoln and
Katlian Sts.* ☎*907/747–3213.*

❽ Totem Square. On this grassy square directly across the street from the
Pioneers Home are three anchors discovered in local waters and believed
to be of 19th-century British origin. Look for the double-headed eagle of
czarist Russia carved into the cedar of the totem pole in the park.

SHOPPING

Fairweather Gallery and Gifts (✉*209 Lincoln St.* ☎*907/747–8677*
⊕*www.fairweatherprints.com*) sells shirts, dresses, and other clothing
featuring hand-printed Alaska designs. The shop also has two back
rooms packed with works by local artisans. **Fishermen's Eye Fine Art**

Gallery (⊠*239 Lincoln St.* ☎*907/747–6080* ⊕*www.fishermenseye. com*) is a tasteful downtown gallery that prides itself on its vibrant collection of made-in-Sitka art including silver jewelry, native masks, and carved bowls.**Fresh Fish Company** (⊠*411 DeGroff St.* ☎*907/747–5565, 888/747–5565 outside Alaska* ⊕*www.akfreshfish.com*) sells and ships fresh locally caught salmon, halibut, and shrimp.

WHERE TO EAT

$$–$$$
JAPANESE

✕**Little Tokyo.** Sitka probably isn't the first place you expect to find Japanese food, but Little Tokyo delivers great rolls and *nigiri*. It's not fancy, but this small restaurant has a sushi bar where the chefs prepare all the standards, plus Alaska rolls (with smoked salmon and avocado). Udon noodle soups are popular on rainy afternoons, and bento-box dinners—complete with katsu entrées, California rolls, tempura, pot stickers, miso soup, and salad—are only $11. ⊠*315 Lincoln St.* ☎*907/747–5699* ▤*MC, V.*

$$$–$$$$
MEDITERRANEAN
Fodor'sChoice
★

✕**Ludvig's Bistro.** This remarkably creative eatery used to escape detection by most tourists (much to the pleasure of Sitkans). It's now almost always packed with food lovers from all corners of the globe, so be prepared for a wait—but rest assured that Ludvig's is worth it. The interior evokes an Italian bistro, with rich yellow walls and copper-topped tables. Seafood (particularly king salmon and scallops) is the specialty, and organic ingredients are used whenever possible. You'll also find Caesar salads, vegetarian specials, Angus filet mignon, and one of the state's best wine lists. From 2 to 5 the café serves Spanish-style tapas with house wine for $13–$17. ⊠*256 Katlian St.* ☎*907/966–3663* ▤*AE, MC, V* ⊙*Closed mid-Feb.–Apr.*

WHERE TO DRINK

As far as the locals are concerned, a spot in one of the limited green-and-white-vinyl booths at **Pioneer Bar** (⊠*212 Katlian St.* ☎*907/747–3456*), across from the harbor, is a fine destination. It's vintage Alaska, with hundreds of pictures of local fishing boats, rough-hewn locals clad in Carhartts and Xtra-Tuff boots, occasional live music, and pool tables.

SKAGWAY

Located at the northern terminus of the Inside Passage, Skagway is only a one-hour boat ride from Haines. You'll find the town to be an amazingly preserved artifact from North America's biggest, most storied gold rush. Most of the downtown district forms part of the Klondike Gold Rush National Historical Park, a unit of the national park system dedicated to commemorating and interpreting the frenzied stampede of 1897 that extended to Dawson City in Canada's Yukon.

Old false-front stores, saloons, and brothels—built to separate gold-rush prospectors from their grubstakes going north or their gold pokes heading south—have been restored, repainted, and refurbished by the federal government and Skagway's citizens. The town feels a little like a Disney theme park in spots, and it's made all the more surreal by the surrounding mountains. But the scene today is not appreciably different from what the prospectors saw in the days of 1898, except the street is now paved to make exploring easier.

COMING ASHORE

SHORE EXCURSIONS

ADVENTURE

Heli-Hike Glacier Trek. The helicopter flight that begins this popular trip is followed by a 4-mi hike to Laughton Glacier. Return to Skagway on the famous White Pass & Yukon Route Railway. Participants must be in strong physical condition. ⊙*5½ hrs* ⌨*$374.*

Hike and Float the Chilkoot Trail. This trip opens with a guided van tour to the historic gold-rush townsite of Dyea, start of the historic Chilkoot Trail. From here you hike 2 mi along the Taiya River, then board rafts for an easy 40-minute float back to Dyea. No children under 7 are allowed. ⊙*4¼ hrs* ⌨*$100–$105.*

Klondike Bicycle Tour. Ride a van to the top of the Klondike Pass and then bike 15 mi downhill, taking in the spectacular views of White Pass and Alaska's scenery along the way. Stops are made to take photographs of the area's glaciers, coastal mountains, and waterfalls. ⊙*2½ hrs* ⌨*$85.*

CULTURAL/SCENIC

Haines Highlights and Lynn Fjord Cruise. Escape the crowds in Skagway on a fast ferry that crosses Lynn Fjord to the scenic town of Haines. Tour historic Fort Seward and the Sheldon Museum; visit a restored fish canning line from the 1950s; and ride up the Chilkat River valley. Return by ferry to Skagway in time to catch your ship. ⊙*6 hrs* ⌨*$129.*

Skagway Streetcar. Ride in the Skagway Streetcar Company's vintage 1930s cars through town to the Gold Rush Cemetery and Reid Falls, accompanied by a knowledgeable tour guide dressed in Victorian-style costume. ⊙*2 hrs* ⌨*$42.*

White Pass & Yukon Railroad. The 20-mi trip in vintage railroad cars skims along the edge of granite cliffs, climbs to 2,865 feet at White Pass Summit, and zigzags through dramatic scenery—including the actual Trail of '98, worn into the mountainside a century ago. Alternate routes take you as far as Fraser, British Columbia (where bus connections are available for the trip back to Skagway), or Carcross, Yukon. ⊙*3½ hrs* ⌨*$112.*

TRANSPORTATION AND TOURS

FROM THE PIER

Skagway is a major stop for cruise ships in Alaska, and this little town sometimes has four large ships in port at once. Some dock a short stroll from downtown, others ½ mi away at the Railroad Dock, where city buses are waiting to provide transportation to the center of town. The charge is $2 one-way, or $5 for a day pass.

Virtually all the shops and gold-rush sights are along Broadway, the main strip that leads from the visitor center through the middle of town. It's a nice walk from the docks up through Broadway, but you can also take tours in horse-drawn surreys, antique limousines, and modern vans.

Continued on page 226

GOLD! GOLD! GOLD!

At the end of the 19th Century, scoundrels and starry-eyed gold seekers alike made their way from Alaska's Inside Passage to Canada's Yukon Territory, with high hopes for heavy returns.

"There are strange things done in the midnight sun By the men who moil for gold...."

—Robert Service, "The Cremation of Sam McGee"

Miners have moiled for gold in the Yukon for many centuries, but the Klondike Gold Rush was a particularly strange and intense period of history. Within a decade, the towns of Skagway, Dyea, and Dawson City appeared out of nowhere, mushroomed to accommodate tens of thousands of people, and just about disappeared again. At the peak of the rush, Dawson City was the largest metropolis north of San Francisco. Although only a few people found enough gold even to pay for their trip, the rush left an indelible mark on the nation's imagination.

An 1898 photograph shows bearded miners using a gold pan and sluice as they search for riches.

(above) Rush hour on Broadway, Skagway, 1898.

A GREAT STAMPEDE

Historians squabble over who first saw the glint of Yukon gold. All agree that it was a member of a family including "Skookum" Jim Mason (of the Tagish tribe), Kate and George Carmack, and Dawson Charlie, who were prospecting off the Klondike River in 1896. Over the following months, word spread and claims were quickly staked. When the first boatload of gold reached Seattle in July 1897, gold fever ignited with the *Seattle Post-Intelligencer's* headline: "GOLD! GOLD! GOLD! Sixty-Eight Rich Men On the Steamer Portland." Within six months, 100,000 people had arrived in Southeast Alaska, intent upon making their way to the untold riches.

Skagway had only a single cabin standing when the gold rush began. Three months after the first boat landed, 20,000 people swarmed its raucous hotels, saloons, gambling houses, and dance halls. By spring 1898, the town was labeled "little better than a hell on earth." When gold was discovered in Nome the next year and in Fairbanks in the early 1900s, Skagway's population dwindled to 700 souls.

A GRITTY REALITY

To reach the mining hub of Dawson City, prospectors had to choose between two risky routes from the Inside Passage. From Dyea, the Chilkoot Trail was steep and bitterly cold. The longer, bandit-ridden White Pass Trail from Skagway killed so many pack animals that it earned the nickname Dead Horse Trail. After the mountains, there were still over 500 mi to travel. For those who arrived, dreams were quickly washed away, as most promising claims had already been staked by the Klondike Kings. Many ended up working as labor. The disappointment was unbearable.

KLONDIKE KATE

The gold rush was profitable for clever entrepreneurs. Stragglers, outfitters, and outlaws took advantage of every opportunity to make a buck. Klondike Kate, a brothel keeper and dance-hall gal, had an elaborate song-and-dance routine that involved 200 yards of bright red chiffon.

TWO ENEMIES DIE IN A SKAGWAY SHOWDOWN

CON ARTIST "SOAPY" SMITH

Claim to Fame: Skagway's best-known gold-rush criminal, Soapy was the de facto leader of the town's loosely organized network of criminals and spies.

Cold-Hearted Snake: Euphemistically referred to as "colorful," he ruthlessly capitalized on the naïveté of prospectors.

Famous Scheme: Soapy charged homesick miners $5 to wire a message home in his counterfeit Telegraph Office (the wires ended in a tangled pile behind a shed).

Shot Through the Heart: In 1898, just days after he served as grand marshal of Skagway's 4th of July parade, Soapy barged in on a meeting set up by his rival, Frank Reid. There was a scuffle, and they shot each other.

Famous Last Words: When he saw Reid draw his gun, Soapy shouted, "My God, don't shoot!"

R.I.P.: Soapy's tombstone was continually stolen by vandals and souvenir seekers; today's grave marker is a simple wooden plank in Skagway's Gold Rush Cemetery.

GOOD GUY FRANK REID

Claim to Fame: Skagway surveyor and all-around good fellow, Frank Reid was known for defending the town against bad guys.

The Grid Man: A civil engineer, Reid helped to make Skagway's streets wide and gridlike.

Thorn in My Side: Reid set up a secret vigilante meeting to discuss one very thorny topic: Soapy Smith.

In Skagway's Honor: Reid killed Soapy during the shootout on the city docks, breaking up Soapy's gang and freeing the town from its grip.

Dyin' Tryin': Reid's heroics cost him his life—he died some days later from the injuries he sustained.

R.I.P.: The town built a substantial monument in Reid's memory in the Gold Rush Cemetery, which you can visit to this day; the inscription reads: HE GAVE HIS LIFE FOR THE HONOR OF SKAGWAY.

(above) Soapy Smith (front), so named for his first con, which involved selling "lucky soap," stands with five friends at his infamous saloon.

AREA TOURS

Fodor'sChoice ★ Visitors to Skagway can travel at least part of the way along the gold-rush route aboard the **White Pass & Yukon Route** (WP & YR) narrow-gauge railroad. The historic diesel locomotives tow vintage viewing cars up the route's steep inclines, hugging the walls of precipitous cliff sides and providing views of craggy peaks, plummeting waterfalls, lakes, and forests. Two or three times daily the WP & YR leaves Skagway for a three-hour, round-trip excursion to the White Pass summit. Sights along the way include Bridal Veil Falls, Inspiration Point, and Dead Horse Gulch. Longer trips into the Yukon, special steam excursions, and a Chilkoot Trail hikers' service are also offered. For dockside boarding, cruise passengers must purchase their train tickets aboard their ships. ⊠ *231 2nd Ave.* ☎ *800/343–7373* ⊕ *www.whitepassrailroad.com* ☉ *Mid-May–late Sept., daily.*

VISITOR INFORMATION

You can't help but notice the Arctic Brotherhood Hall—just up Broadway between 2nd and 3rd avenues—with its curious driftwood-mosaic facade. Inside is the **Skagway Convention and Visitors Bureau** (☎ *907/983–2854, 888/762–1898 message only* ⊕ *www.skagway.com*), along with public restrooms. From the pier you can see the large maroon-and-yellow building that houses the museum and visitor center of **Klondike Gold Rush National Historical Park** (☎ *907/983–2921* ⊕ *www.nps.gov/klgo*), which presents historical photographs, artifacts, and films. Rangers lead guided walks through town, and can provide details on nearby hiking trails (including the famous Chilkoot Trail). Next door to the visitor center is the White Pass & Yukon Route Depot, the departure point for Skagway's most popular shore excursion.

Check your e-mail at **Glacial Smoothies** (⊠ *336-B 3rd Ave.* ☎ *907/983–3223*).

EXPLORING SKAGWAY

Skagway is perhaps the easiest port in Alaska to explore on foot. The town is flat, and nearly all the historic sights are within a few blocks of the cruise-ship and ferry dock, so you can take all the time you want. Just walk up and down Broadway, detouring here and there into the side streets. Keep an eye out for the humorous architectural details and advertising irreverence that mark the Skagway spirit.

2 ★ **Arctic Brotherhood Hall.** The Arctic Brotherhood was a fraternal organization of Alaska and Yukon pioneers. Local members of the Brotherhood built the building's (now renovated) false front out of 8,833 pieces of driftwood and flotsam gathered from local beaches. The result: one of the most unusual buildings in all of Alaska. The AB Hall now houses the **Skagway Convention and Visitors Bureau,** along with public restrooms. ⊠ *Broadway between 2nd and 3rd Aves., Box 1029* ☎ *907/983–2854, 888/762–1898 message only* ⊕ *www.skagway.com* ⊙ *May–Sept., daily 8–6; Oct.–Apr., weekdays 8–noon and 1–5.*

④ Corrington's Museum of Alaskan History. Inside a gift shop, this impressive (and free) scrimshaw museum highlights more than 40 exquisitely carved walrus tusks and other exhibits that detail Alaska's history. A bright flower garden decorates the exterior. ⊠ *5th Ave. and Broadway* ☎ *907/983–2579* ⌨ *Free* ⊙ *Open when cruise ships are in port.*

⑤ Since 1927 locals have performed a show called *The Days of '98 with*
★ *Soapy Smith* at **Eagles Hall.** You'll see cancan dancers (including Molly Fewclothes, Belle Davenport, and Squirrel Tooth Alice), learn a little local history, and watch desperado Soapy Smith being sent to his reward. At the evening show you can enjoy a few warm-up rounds of mock gambling with Soapy's money. Performances of Robert Service poetry start a half-hour before showtime. ⊠ *Broadway and 6th Ave.* ☎ *907/983–2545 May–mid-Sept., 808/328–9132 mid-Sept.–Apr.* ⌨ *$16* ⊙ *Mid-May–mid-Sept., daily at 10:30, 2:30, and 8.*

③ Golden North Hotel. Built during the 1898 gold rush, the Golden North Hotel was—until closing in 2002—Alaska's oldest hotel. Despite the closure, the building has been lovingly maintained, and still retains its gold rush–era appearance; a golden dome tops the corner cupola. Today the downstairs houses shops. ⊠ *3rd Ave. and Broadway99840.*

① Klondike Gold Rush National Historical Park. Housed in the former White
★ Pass and Yukon Route Depot, this wonderful museum contains exhibits, photos, and artifacts from the White Pass and Chilkoot trails. It's a must-see for anyone planning on taking a White Pass train ride, driving the nearby Klondike Highway, or hiking the Chilkoot Trail. Films, ranger talks, and walking tours are offered. Special free Robert Service poetry performances by Buckwheat Donahue—a beloved local character and head of the Skagway Convention and Visitors Bureau—occasionally take place at the visitor center. ⊠ *2nd Ave. at Broadway* ☎ *907/983–2921 or 907/983–9224* ⊕ *www.nps.gov/klgo* ⌨ *Free* ⊙ *May–Sept., daily 8–6; Oct.–Apr., weekdays 8–5.*

⑥ Moore Cabin. Built in 1887 by Captain William Moore and his son Ben Moore, the tiny cabin was the first structure built in Skagway. An early homesteader, Captain Moore prospered from the flood of miners, constructing a dock, warehouse, and sawmill to supply them, and selling land for other ventures. Next door, the larger **Moore House** (1897–98) contains interesting exhibits on the Moore family. Both structures are maintained by the Park Service, and the main house is open daily in summer. ⊠ *5th Ave. between Broadway and Spring St.* ☎ *907/983–2921* ⊙ *Memorial Day–Labor Day, daily 10–5.*

 Skagway Museum. This nicely designed museum occupies the ground floor of the beautiful building that also houses Skagway City Hall. Inside, you'll find a 19th-century Tlingit canoe (one of only two like it

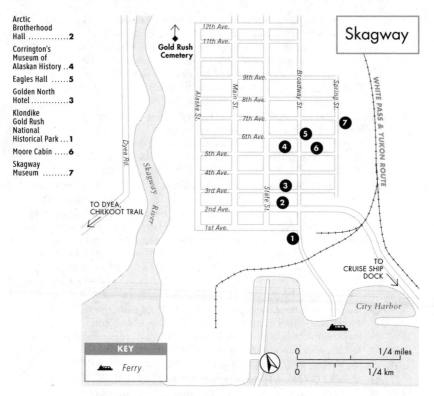

on the West Coast), historic photos, a red-and-black sleigh, and other gold rush–era artifacts, along with a healthy collection of contemporary local art and post–gold rush history exhibits. ⊠ *7th Ave. and Spring St.* ☎ *907/983–2420* 🖼 *$2* ⊙ *Mid-May–Sept., weekdays 9–5, weekends 10–4; Oct.–mid-May, hrs vary.*

OUTDOOR ACTIVITIES

Real wilderness is within a stone's throw of the docks, which makes this an excellent hiking port. Try the short jaunt to beautiful Lower Dewey Lake. Start at the corner of 4th Avenue and Spring Street, go toward the mountain, cross the footbridge over Pullen Creek, and follow the trail uphill. It's a 20-minute climb to the lake.

A less strenuous hike is the trip through Gold Rush Cemetery, where the epitaphs offer strange but lively bits of social commentary. Infamous villain Soapy Smith has a simple marker; hero Frank Reid has a much larger monument. To get to the cemetery, take the city bus to 23rd Avenue, where a dirt road leads to the graves; it's a 10-minute walk each way. To reach 300-foot-high Reid Falls, continue through the cemetery for ¼ mi. Trail maps are available at the Skagway Convention and Visitors Bureau.

SHOPPING

Corrington's Alaskan Ivory (⊠*525 Broadway* ☎*907/983–2579*) is the destination of choice for scrimshaw seekers; it has one the state's best collections of ivory art. For shoppers in search of locally produced silver jewelry, watercolor prints, and other handmade crafts, the artist-owned **Skagway Artworks** (⊠*555C Broadway* ☎*907/983–3443* ⊕*www.skagwayartworks.com*) can't be beat.

3

WHERE TO EAT

¢ ✕**Glacial Smoothies and Espresso.** This local hangout is the place to go
CAFÉ for a breakfast bagel or a lunchtime soup-and-sandwich combo. Prices are steeper than at some coffee shops—a 12-ounce mocha goes for $4—but the ingredients are fresh and local, and nearly everything on the menu is made on-site. Customers can cool down with a Mango Madness or Blueberry Blues smoothie, and soft-serve ice cream in summer. ⊠*3rd Ave. between Main and State Sts.* ☎*907/983–3223* ⊟*MC, V* ☻*No dinner.*

$–$$ ✕**Skagway Pizza Station.** Housed in a former gas station, this year-round
PIZZA restaurant is known for its comfort-food specials, such as meat loaf or stuffed pork chops with mashed potatoes and gravy. (Friday is prime-rib day.) The huge calzones are stuffed and served piping hot with sides of house marinara and ranch dressing—build your own or choose one of the chef's creations, like the Chicken Hawk Squawk with pineapple and jalapeños. Or do as the Skagwegians do and wash down one of the 14-inch pizzas with a pint or two of Alaskan Summer Ale. For dog-tired travelers who can't walk another block, the Pizza Station delivers for free. ⊠*4th Ave. between Main and State Sts.* ☎*907/983–2200* ⊟*MC, V.*

$$–$$$ ✕**Stowaway Cafe.** Always crowded, this noisy little harborside café is
CAFÉ just a few steps from the cruise-ship dock. Seafood is the attraction—including wasabi salmon and glacé de poisson—but you can also eat steaks, chicken, or smoked ribs. The café is open daily for dinner only. ⊠*205 Congress Way* ☎*907/983–3463* ⊟*AE, MC, V* ☻*Closed Oct.–Apr. No lunch.*

WHERE TO DRINK

Whereas Skagway was once host to dozens upon dozens of watering holes in its gold-rush days, the **Red Onion Saloon** (⊠*Broadway at 2nd Ave.* ☎*907/983–2222* ⊕*www.redonion1898.com*) is pretty much the sole survivor. The upstairs was once a brothel, and you'll find a convivial crowd of Skagway locals and visitors among the scantily clad mannequins who represent the building's former illustrious tenants. A ragtime pianist plays in the afternoon, and local musicians strut their stuff on Thursday nights. The saloon closes up shop for winter.

TRACY ARM

Tracy Arm and its sister fjord, Endicott Arm, have become staples on many Inside Passage cruises. Ships sail into the arm just before or after a visit to Juneau, 50 mi to the north. A day of scenic cruising in Tracy Arm is a lesson in geology and the forces that shape Alaska. The fjord was carved by a glacier aeons ago, leaving behind sheer granite cliffs. Waterfalls continue the process of erosion that the glaciers began. Very small ships may nudge their bows under the waterfalls so crew members can fill pitchers full of glacial runoff. It's a unique Alaska refreshment. Tracy Arm's glaciers haven't disappeared, though; they've just receded, and at the very end of Tracy Arm you'll come to two of them, known as the twin Sawyer Glaciers.

VALDEZ

Valdez is the largest of the Prince William Sound communities. This year-round ice-free port was originally the entry point for people and goods going to the interior during the gold rush. Today that flow has been reversed, Valdez harbor being the southern terminus of the trans-Alaska pipeline, which carries crude oil from Prudhoe Bay and surrounding oil fields nearly 800 mi to the north. This region, with its dependence on commercial fishing, is still feeling the aftereffects of 1989's massive oil spill. Much of Valdez looks modern, because the business area was relocated and rebuilt after its destruction by the 1964 Good Friday earthquake. Even though the town is younger than the rest of "civilized" Alaska, it's gradually acquiring a lived-in look.

COMING ASHORE

Fishing Charters. Step off the cruise boat for full or half-day fishing excursions for halibut, salmon, ling cod, and more. Various outfits can be found on the Convention center's Web site (*see below*). ☉ *Varies* 🕮 *Varies*.

TRANSPORTATION AND TOURS

FROM THE PIER
Ships tie up at the world's largest floating container dock. About 3 mi from the heart of town, the dock is used not only for cruise ships but also for cargo ships loading with timber and other products bound for markets "outside" (that's what Alaskans call the rest of the world). Ship-organized motor coaches meet you on the pier and provide

VALDEZ BEST BETS

■ **Tour the Sound.** Take a tour of Prince William Sound with Stan Stephens Tours, and get a seaside view of the Alyeska Pipeline terminal, where the 800-mi-long Trans-Alaska Pipeline loads oil into huge tanker ships.

■ **Visit a sea otter.** Several local companies offer sea-kayaking tours of varying lengths and degrees of difficulty.

■ **Hike on a glacier.** Worthington Glacier State Park at Thompson Pass is a roadside attraction. If you want to learn glacier travel or ice climbing, H2O Guides can hook you up.

transportation into town. Cabs and car-rental services will also provide transportation from the pier, and individualized tours of the area can be arranged with the cab dispatcher. Several local ground- and adventure-tour operators meet passengers as well.

VISITOR INFORMATION

Once in town, you find that Valdez is a very compact community. Almost everything is within easy walking distance of the **Valdez Convention and Visitors Bureau** (⊠*200 Chenega St.* ☏*907/835–2984* ⏛*www.valdezalaska.org*) in the heart of town. Motor coaches drop passengers at the Visitors Bureau.

COMPETE!

Many Alaskan communities have summer fishing derbies, but Valdez may hold the record for the number of such contests, stretching from late May into September. The Valdez Silver Salmon Derby begins in late July and runs the entire month of August. Fishing charters abound in this area of Prince William Sound for a good reason: the fertile waters provide some of the best saltwater sport fishing in all of Alaska.

If you bring a laptop or handheld device, ask at the VCVB for any of the free local wireless spots town, but if not, check your e-mail for free on a public computer at the **Consortium Library** (⊠*212 Fairbanks St.* ☏*907/835–4623* ⏛*www.ci.valdez.ak.us/library*).

EXPLORING VALDEZ

Valdez Museum. The Valdez Museum explores the lives, livelihoods, and events significant to Valdez and surrounding regions. Exhibits include a restored 1880s Gleason & Baily hand-pump fire engine, a 1907 Ahrens steam fire engine, a 19th-century saloon, information on the local native peoples, and an exhibit on the 1989 oil spill. Every summer the museum hosts an exhibit of quilts and fiber arts made by local and regional artisans. At a separate site a 35- by 40-foot model of **Historical Old Town Valdez** (⊠*436 S. Hazlet Ave.*) depicts the original town, which was devastated by the 1964 earthquake. There's also an operating seismograph and an exhibit on local seismic activity. A Valdez History Exhibits Pass includes admission to both the museum and the annex. ⊠*217 Egan Dr.* ☏*907/835–2764* ⏛*www.valdezmuseum.org* ⛾*$5* ☉*June–Aug., daily 9–5; Sept.–May, Mon.–Sat. 1–5.*

★ **Columbia Glacier** flows from the surrounding Chugach Mountains. Its deep aquamarine face is 5 mi across, and it calves icebergs with resounding cannonades. This glacier is one of the largest and most readily accessible of Alaska's coastal glaciers.

OUTDOOR ACTIVITIES

Anadyr Adventures (☏*907/835–2814 or 800/865–2925* ⏛*www. anadyradventures.com*) offers half-day sea-kayaking trips into Prince William Sound. Whether you're looking for a full-on winter backcountry heli-ski excursion or a shorter glacier experience, **H2O Guides** can hook you up. The guides can set up any level of icy adventure you desire, from a half-day walk on Worthington Glacier to full-day or multiday ice-climbing trips. They can also arrange fishing, flightseeing, multiday, and multisport trips. ☎907/835–8418 or 800/578–4354 ⊕www.h2oguides.com.

WHERE TO EAT

$$$ ✕**Edgewater Grill.** The view here overlooking the harbor is worth the
SEAFOOD price of the meal. Local seafood dominates the menu, and the halibut cheek is the specialty. Open for breakfast and dinner, this restaurant offers great food and friendly service. ⊠107 N. Harbor Dr. ☎907/835–3212 ▤ MC, V.

$ ✕**MacMurray's Alaska Halibut House.** At this very casual family-owned
SEAFOOD establishment you order at the counter, sit at the Formica-covered tables, and check out the photos of local fishing boats. The battered halibut is excellent—light and not greasy. Other menu items include homemade clam chowder, but if you're eating at the Halibut House, why try anything else? ⊠208 Meals Ave. ☎907/835–2788 ▤MC, V.

VICTORIA, BRITISH COLUMBIA

Although Victoria isn't in Alaska, it's a port of call for many ships cruising the Inside Passage. Victoria is the oldest city (founded 1843) on Canada's west coast and the first European settlement on Vancouver Island. It was chosen to be the westernmost trading outpost of the British-owned Hudson Bay Company in 1843, and became the capital of British Columbia in 1868. Just like the communities of Southeast Alaska, Victoria had its own gold-rush stampede in the 1800s, when 25,000 miners flocked to British Columbia's Cariboo country. Victoria has since evolved into a walkable, livable seaside town of gardens, waterfront pathways, and restored 19th-century architecture. Often described as the country's most British city, Victoria is these days—except for the odd red phone box, good beer, and well-mannered drivers—working to change that image, preferring to celebrate its combined native, Asian, and European heritage. Though it's quite touristy in summer, it's also at its prettiest then, with flowers hanging from 19th-century lampposts and strollers enjoying the beauty of its natural harbor. If you have the time, the beautiful Butchart Gardens, a short drive outside the city, are worth a trip.

COMING ASHORE

SHORE EXCURSIONS

Butchart Gardens. More than 700 varieties of flowers grow in these spectacular gardens north of town. If you're there in the evening you can witness the romantic nighttime illumination. Some excursions include a narrated tour of Victoria en route, while others offer such add-ons as a wine and chocolate tasting at a local winery. ⊙3½–4 hrs 🎫Gardens only: $70; with city tour: $109; with wine and chocolate tasting: $129.

Grand City Drive and Empress High Tea. Travel by bus through Victoria's downtown, past its historic residential neighborhoods, and along a scenic ocean drive. Some tours include a stop at a viewpoint atop Mount Tolmie. The tour finishes with an elaborate afternoon tea at the historic Fairmont Empress Hotel. ⊙*3 hrs* ⊠*$110.*

Whale-Watching. Orcas (killer whales), seals, sea lions, and porpoises are abundant in the waters off Victoria. Some of the covered jet boats are equipped with hydrophones so you can hear the whales communicate. ⊙*3½ hrs* ⊠*$120–$127.*

TRANSPORTATION AND TOURS
FROM THE PIER
Only the smallest excursion vessels dock downtown in Victoria's Inner Harbour. Cruise ships tie up at the Ogden Point cruise-ship terminal (⊕*www.victoriaharbour.org*), 2.4 km (1½ mi) from the Inner Harbour, and a few pocket cruise ships moor at Sidney, 29 km (18 mi) north of Victoria. When ships are in port a shuttle bus makes trips between Ogden Point and downtown Victoria at least every twenty minutes. The C$7 (US$6.50) fare allows you to make as many return trips as you like. The walk downtown is pleasant and will take 20 to 30 minutes.

Taxis also meet each ship, and fares run about C$1.00 per minute; the meter starts at $3. A cab from Ogden Point to the downtown core will cost about C$10–C$12. **Bluebird Taxi** (☎*250/384–1155, 800/665–7055*) serves the Victoria area.

GETTING AROUND
Most points of interest are within walking distance of the Inner Harbour. For those that aren't, public and private transportation is readily available. The public bus system is excellent; pick up route maps and schedules at the Tourism Victoria Visitor InfoCentre. City tours by horse-drawn carriage, pedi-cab, and double-decker bus, as well as limousine service, are available at the cruise-ship terminal.

■ TIP→ **If you're coming from Alaska, remember to adjust your watch.** British Columbia is on Pacific Time, one hour ahead of Alaska Time.

VISITOR INFORMATION
The **Tourism Victoria Visitor InfoCentre** (⊠*812 Wharf St.* ☎*250/953–2033 or 800/663–3883* ⊕*www.tourismvictoria.com*) is across the street from the Empress Hotel, on the Inner Harbour.

EXPLORING VICTORIA

❶ Victoria's heart is the **Inner Harbour,** always bustling with ferries, seaplanes, and yachts. In summer the waterfront comes alive with strollers and street entertainers.

❾ **Chinatown.** Chinese immigrants built much of the Canadian Pacific Railway in the 19th century, and their influence still marks the region. Victoria's Chinatown, founded in 1858, is the oldest and most intact such district in Canada. If you enter Chinatown from Government Street, you'll pass under the elaborate **Gate of Harmonious Interest.** Along Fisgard Street, merchants display paper lanterns, wicker baskets, and exotic produce. Mah-jongg, fan-tan, and dominoes were among the games of chance played along **Fan Tan Alley,** said to be the narrowest street in Canada. Once the gambling and opium center of Chinatown, it's now lined with offbeat shops, few of which sell authentic Chinese goods. ⊠*Fisgard St. between Government and Store Sts., Chinatown.*

❷ **Fairmont Empress.** Opened in 1908
♺ by the Canadian Pacific Railway, the Empress is one of the grand châ-teau-style railroad hotels that grace many Canadian cities. Designed by Francis Rattenbury, who also designed the Parliament Buildings across the way, the Empress, with its solid Edwardian grandeur, has become a symbol of the city. **Min-iature World** (☎*250/385–9731*), a display of more than 80 minia-ture dioramas, including one of the world's largest model railways, is on the Humboldt Street side of the

complex. ⊠*721 Government St., entrance at Belleville and Govern-ment, Downtown* ☎*250/384–8111, 250/389–2727 tea reservations* ⊕*www.fairmont.com/empress* ⊠*Free, afternoon tea C$55 May–Sept., C$39–C$49 Oct.–June.*

❼ **Maritime Museum of British Columbia.** The model ships, Royal Navy charts,
♺ photographs, uniforms, and ship bells at this museum in Victoria's original courthouse chronicle the province's seafaring history. Among the hand-built boats on display is the *Tilikum,* a dugout canoe that sailed from Victoria to England between 1901 and 1904. Kids can climb a crow's nest and learn some scary tales about the pirates of the coast. An 1899 hand-operated cage elevator, believed to be the oldest continuously operating lift in North America, ascends to the third floor, where the original 1888 vice-admiralty courtroom looks ready for a court-martial. ⊠*28 Bastion Sq., Downtown* ☎*250/385–4222* ⊕*www. mmbc.bc.ca* ⊠*C$10* ⊙*Daily 9:30–4:30.*

❽ **Market Square.** During Victoria's late-19th-century heyday, this three-level square, originally the courtyard of an old inn, provided everything a sailor, miner, or up-country lumberjack could want. Now beautifully restored to its original architectural, if not commercial, character, it's a traffic-free café- and boutique-lined hangout. ⊠*560 Johnson St., Old Town* ☎*250/386–2441.*

❸ **Parliament Buildings.** Officially the British Columbia Provincial Legis-lative Assembly Buildings, these massive stone structures are more popularly referred to as the Parliament Buildings. Designed by Francis Rattenbury (who also designed the Fairmont Empress Hotel) when he was just 25 years old and completed in 1898, they dominate the Inner

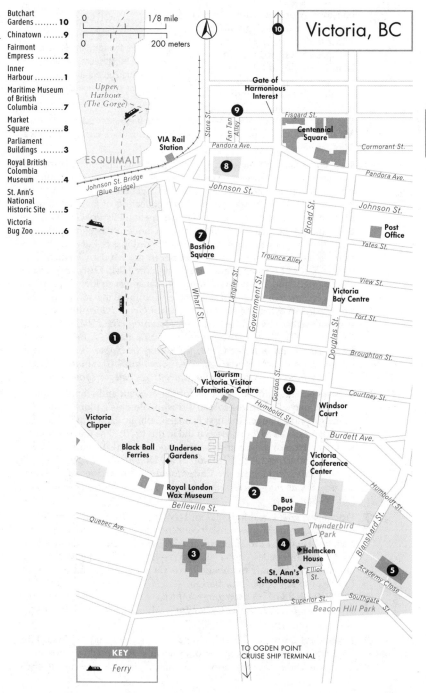

Victoria, BC

0 ___ 1/8 mile

0 ___ 200 meters

Upper Harbour (The Gorge)

ESQUIMALT

Johnson St. Bridge (Blue Bridge)

VIA Rail Station

Gate of Harmonious Interest

Store St.

Fan Tan Alley

❾

Fisgard St.

Centennial Square

Cormorant St.

Pandora Ave.

❽

Pandora Ave.

Johnson St.

Johnson St.

Broad St.

Post Office

❼

Bastion Square

Trounce Alley

Langley St.

Wharf St.

Government St.

Yates St.

View St.

Victoria Bay Centre

Fort St.

Douglas St.

Broughton St.

Tourism Victoria Visitor Information Centre

Humboldt St.

Gordon St.

❻

Windsor Court

Courtney St.

❶

Victoria Clipper

Black Ball Ferries

Undersea Gardens

Royal London Wax Museum

Belleville St.

❷

Bus Depot

Victoria Conference Center

Burdett Ave.

Humboldt St.

Quebec Ave.

❸

St. Ann's Schoolhouse

❹

Thunderbird Park

Helmcken House

Elliot St.

Blanshard St.

Academy Close

❺

Superior St.

Southgate St.

Beacon Hill Park

KEY

🚢 *Ferry*

TO OGDEN POINT CRUISE SHIP TERMINAL

3

Harbour. Atop the central dome is a gilded statue of Captain George Vancouver (1757–98), the first European to sail around Vancouver Island. Free 30- to 60-minute tours run several times an hour during the summer, and several times a day in the off-season. ⊠ *501 Belleville St., Downtown* ☎*250/387-3046* ⊕*www.leg.bc.ca* ✉*Free* ☉*Mid-May–early Sept., Mon.–Thurs. 9–5, Fri.–Sun. 9–7; early Sept.–mid-May, weekdays 9–4.*

> **GOT KIDS?**
>
> Chinatown, the Maritime Museum, the Royal BC Museum, and the Victoria Bug Zoo are all good choices for school-age children.

④ ☺ ★ Royal British Columbia Museum. This excellent museum, one of Victoria's leading attractions, traces several thousand years of British Columbian history. Its First Peoples Gallery, home to a genuine Kwakwaka'wakw big house and a dramatically displayed collection of masks and other artifacts, is especially strong. The Environmental History Gallery traces B.C.'s natural heritage, from prehistory to modern-day climate change, in realistic dioramas. An Ocean Station exhibit gets kids involved in running a Jules Verne–style submarine. In the Modern History Gallery a replica of Captain Vancouver's ship, the HMS *Discovery*, creaks convincingly, and a re-created frontier town comes to life with cobbled streets, silent movies, and the rumble of an arriving train. Also on-site is an IMAX theater showing *National Geographic* films on a six-story-tall screen. ⊠*675 Belleville St., Downtown* ☎*250/356-7226 or 888/447-7977* ⊕*www.royalbcmuseum.bc.ca* ✉*C$15, IMAX theater C$11, combination ticket C$23. Rates may be higher during special-exhibit periods* ☉*Museum: daily 9–5 (open until 10 PM most Fri. and Sat. early June–late Sept. Theater: daily 10–8; call for show times.*

⑤ St. Ann's National Historic Site. This former convent and school, founded in 1858, played a central role in British Columbia's pioneer life. The academy's little chapel, the first Roman Catholic cathedral in Victoria, has been restored to look just as it did in the 1920s. The 6-acre grounds, with fruit trees and herb and flower gardens, are also being restored as historic landscapes. ⊠*835 Humboldt St., Downtown* ☎*250/953-8829* ⊕*www.stannsacademy.com* ✉*By donation* ☉*Gardens daily dawn–dusk. Chapel mid-May–mid-Oct., daily 10–4; mid-Oct.–mid-May, Thurs.–Sun. 1–4.*

⑥ ☺ Victoria Bug Zoo. Local kids clamor to visit this offbeat mini-zoo, home to the largest live tropical insect collection in North America. You can even hold many of the 70 or so varieties, which include walking sticks, scorpions, millipedes, and a pharnacia—at 22 inches the world's longest insect. The staff members know their bug lore, and are happy to dispense scientific information. ⊠*631 Courtney St., Downtown* ☎*250/384-2847* ⊕*www.bugzoo.bc.ca* ✉*C$8* ☉*Mid-June–early Sept., daily 10–6; early Sept.–mid-June, Mon.–Sat. 10–5, Sun. 11–5.*

OUTSIDE TOWN

⑩ The Butchart Gardens. This stunning 55-acre garden and National Historic Site has been drawing visitors since it was planted in a limestone quarry in 1904. Seven hundred varieties of flowers grow in the site's

FodorśChoice ★

Japanese, Italian, rose, and sunken gardens. Highlights include the view over the ivy-draped and flower-filled former quarry, the dramatic 21-meter-high (70-foot-high) Ross Fountain, and the formal and intricate Italian garden, complete with a gelato stand. In July and August kids' entertainers perform Sunday through Friday afternoons, and jazz, blues, and classical musicians play at an outdoor stage each evening. The wheelchair- and stroller-accessible site is also home to a seed-and-gift shop, a plant identification center, two restaurants (one offering traditional afternoon tea), and a coffee shop; you can even call ahead for a picnic basket. Some transportation options to compare to your cruise line's shore excursion (which will most likely be well narrated): the Butchart Gardens Express Shuttle, run by Grey Line West, runs hourly service between downtown Victoria (leaving from the bus depot at 700 Douglas St., behind the Empress Hotel) and Butchart Gardens during peak season. The C$45 round-trip fare includes admission to the gardens. Alternatively, take Bus 75 from Douglas Street downtown. ✉ *800 Benvenuto Ave., Brentwood Bay* ☎ *250/652–5256 or 866/652–4422* ⊕ *www.butchartgardens.com* ✉ *Mid-June–late Sept. C$28, discounted rates rest of yr* ⊗ *Mid-June–Labor Day, daily 9* AM*–10* PM*; Sept.–mid-June, daily 9* AM*–dusk; call for exact times.*

SHOPPING

Victoria stores specializing in English imports are plentiful, though Canadian-made goods are usually a better buy. You'll pay both 7% Provincial Sales Tax (PST) and 6% Goods and Services Tax (GST) on most purchases.

Victoria's main shopping area is along Government Street north of the Fairmont Empress Hotel. At **Artina's** (✉ *1002 Government St., Downtown* ☎ *250/386–7000 or 877/386–7700*) you can find unusual Canadian art jewelry—all handmade, one-of-a-kind pieces. **Hill's Native Art** (✉ *1008 Government St.* ☎ *250/385–3911*) sells original West Coast native artwork. For imported linens and lace, have a look at the **Irish Linen Stores** (✉ *1019 Government St.* ☎ *250/383–6812*).

Munro's Books (✉ *1108 Government St.* ☎ *250/382–2464*), in a beautifully restored 1909 building, is one of Canada's prettiest bookstores. High-end fashion boutiques line **Trounce Alley,** a pedestrian-only lane north of View Street between Broad and Government streets. **Victoria Bay Centre** (✉ *1 Victoria Bay Centre, at Government and Fort Sts., Downtown* ☎ *250/952–5680*), a department store and mall, holds about 100 chain stores, boutiques, and restaurants. Just off Government Street, historic **Market Square** (✉ *560 Johnson St., Downtown* ☎ *250/386–2441*) offers everything from toys and music to jewelry, local arts, and New Age accoutrements.

From Government Street, turn right onto Fort Street and walk five blocks to **Antique Row,** between Blanshard and Cook streets, where dozens of antiques shops sell books, jewelry, china, furniture, artwork, and collectibles.

WHERE TO EAT

"Fresh, local, organic" has become a mantra for many Victoria chefs. Wild salmon, locally made cheeses, Pacific oysters, forest-foraged mushrooms, organic vegetables in season, local microbrews, and British Columbian wines can all be sampled here. Restaurants in the region are generally casual. A bylaw bans smoking in all Victoria restaurants, including indoor patios.

Casual but neat dress is appropriate everywhere. A 15% tip is expected. A 5% Goods and Services Tax (GST) is charged on food and a 10% liquor tax is charged on wine, beer, and spirits. Some restaurants build the liquor tax into the price of the beverage, but others add it to the bill.

$$$ ✕**Cafe Brio.** "Charming, comfortable, and hip with walls of art—all
CANADIAN backed by city's best chef and kitchen," is how one fodors.com user
★ describes this bustling Italian villa–style room. The frequently changing menu highlights regional, organic fare, and favorites include roast veal strip loin and crispy sweetbreads; butter-poached pheasant breast and confit leg; local sablefish, albacore tuna, Cowichan Bay duck breast, local lamb, and housemade charcuterie. Virtually everything, including the bread, pasta, and desserts is made in-house. ✉ *944 Fort St., Downtown* ☎*250/383–0009 or 866/270–5461* ⊟*AE, MC, V* ☉*No lunch.*

$–$$ ✕**The Noodle Box.** Noodles, whether Indonesian-style with peanut sauce,
ECLECTIC thick Japanese Udon in teriyaki, or Thai-style chow mein, are piled
★ straight from steaming woks in the open kitchen to bowls or cardboard take-out boxes at this local answer to fast food. Malaysian-, Singapore-, and Cambodian-style curries tempt those who like it hot. The brick, rose, and lime walls keep things modern and high-energy. ✉*818 Douglas St., Downtown* ☎*250/384–1314* ⌲*Reservations not accepted* ⊟*AE, MC, V* ✉*626 Fisgard St., Downtown* ☎*250/360–1312* ⌲*Reservations not accepted* ⊟*AE, MC, V.*

$–$$ ✕**Re-Bar Modern Food.** Bright and casual, this kid-friendly café in Bas-
VEGETARIAN tion Square is *the* place for vegetarians in Victoria, but don't worry, the almond burgers, enchiladas, decadent baked goodies, and big breakfasts keep omnivores happy, too. An extensive selection of teas and fresh juices shares space on the drinks list with espresso, microbrews, and B.C. wines. ✉*50 Bastion Sq., Downtown* ☎*250/361–9223* ⊟*AE, DC, MC, V* ☉*No dinner Sun.*

¢–$ ✕**Willie's Bakery & Cafe.** Housed in a handsome Victorian building near
CAFÉ Market Square, this bakery-café goes organic, free-range, and local in its omelets, brioches, French toast, and homemade granola breakfasts and its lunches of homemade soups, thick sandwiches made with house-baked bread, and tasty baked treats. A tiny brick patio with an outdoor fireplace is partially glassed in so you can lunch alfresco even on chilly days. ✉*537 Johnson St., Downtown* ☎*250/381–8414* ⌲*Reservations not accepted* ⊟*MC, V* ☉*No dinner.*

WHERE TO DRINK

Pub culture is an important part of life in Victoria, providing a casual, convivial atmosphere for lunch, a casual dinner, or an afternoon pint. The pubs listed here all serve food, and many brew their own beer. Patrons must be 19 or older to enter the pub itself, but many pubs have a restaurant section where kids are welcome, too. Smoking is banned indoors and on patios in all Victoria pubs.

Filling a two-story former bank building on Victoria's main shopping strip, **Irish Times Pub** (✉ *1200 Government St.* ☎*250/383–7775*) offers fish-and-chips, shepherd's pie, and Irish stew, as well as stout on tap and live Celtic music every night. Worth a cab ride over the Johnson Street Bridge, **Spinnakers Gastro Brewpub** (✉*308 Catherine St.* ☎*250/386–2739 or 877/838–2739*) has water views and some of the city's best food and beer. The restaurant welcomes all ages.

WRANGELL

Wrangell is on an island near the mouth of the fast-flowing Stikine River, and like much of the Southeast has suffered in recent years from a declining resource-based economy. The town is off the typical cruise-ship track, and is frequented by lines with an environmental or educational emphasis such as Cruise West, Majestic America Line, and Silversea Cruises. This small, unassuming timber-and-fishing community has lived under three flags since the arrival of the Russian traders. It was known as Redoubt St. Dionysius when it was part of Russian America; then it was called Fort Stikine after the British took it over. It became Wrangell when the Americans took over in 1867; the name came from Baron Ferdinand Petrovich von Wrangell, governor of the Russian-American Company.

COMING ASHORE

TRANSPORTATION AND TOURS

FROM THE PIER

Cruise ships calling in to Wrangell dock downtown, within walking distance of the museum and gift stores. Greeters welcome you and are available to answer questions. Wrangell's few attractions—the most notable being totem-filled Chief Shakes Island—are within walking distance of the pier. The Nolan Center houses an excellent museum, and Petroglyph Beach, where rocks are imprinted with mysterious prehistoric symbols, is 1 mi from the pier. Most cruise-ship visitors see it on guided shore excursions or by taxi. Call **Northern Lights Taxi** (☎*907/874–4646*) or **Star Cab** (☎*907/874–3622*).

AREA TOURS

Breakaway Adventures (☎*907/874–2488 or 888/385–2488* ⊕*www. breakawayadventures.com*) leads day trips up the majestic Stikine River by jet boat, including a visit to Chief Shakes Glacier, along with time to take a dip at Chief Shakes Hot Springs. **Sunrise Aviation** (☎*907/874–2319 or 800/874–2311* ⊕*www.sunriseflights.com*) is a charter-only air carrier that offers trips to the Anan Creek Wildlife Observatory, LeConte Glacier, or Forest Service cabins.

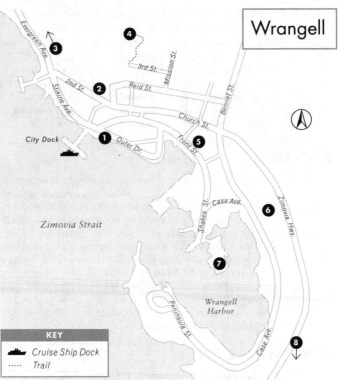

Wrangell

VISITOR INFORMATION

The **Wrangell Visitor Center** (☎ *907/874–2829 or 800/367–9745* ⊕ *www. wrangellalaska.org* ⊙ *During museum hrs*) is housed in the Nolan Center. Stop by for details on local adventure options and for free Internet access.

Check your e-mail for free at the **Irene Ingle Public Library** (⊠ *124 Second Ave.* ☎ *907/874–3535*).

EXPLORING WRANGELL

6 **Chief Shakes's Grave Site.** Buried here is Shakes V, who led the local Tlingit during the first half of the 19th century. A white picket fence surrounds the grave, and two killer-whale totem poles mark his resting spot overlooking the harbor. Find the grave on Case Avenue. ⊠ *Case Ave.*

7 ★ **Chief Shakes Island.** This small island sits in the center of Wrangell's protected harbor and is accessible by a footbridge from the bottom of Front Street. Seven totem poles surround a traditionally styled tribal house, built in the 1930s as a replica of one that was home to many of the various Shakes and their peoples. ⊠ *Off Shakes St.* ☎ *907/874–3481* 🖂 *$3.50* ⊙ *Daily when cruise ships are in port (ask at Wrangell Visitor Center) or by appointment.*

Shore Excursions for Kids

Skagway: Spend the day in real Alaskan wilderness. Get a map at the Convention and Visitors Bureau and take the entire family on the inexpensive city bus to 23rd Avenue, where a 10-minute walk on a dirt road leads to the Gold Rush Cemetery. Let the kids discover where the town's villain Soapy Smith and its hero Frank Reid are buried, and then continue along the trail a quarter mile to Reid Falls.

Ketchikan: One of the cheesiest, yet most kid-pleasing tastes of old-time woodsman skills is the Great Alaskan Lumberjack Show. All summer long this hour-long contest demonstrates such authentic "sports" as sawing, ax

throwing, chopping, and a log rolling duel. There's even a speed climb up a 50-foot tree. At 50 Main Street, all the fun's within walking distance of the cruise-ship pier.

Juneau: For a day of family togetherness, the Gold Creek Salmon Bake hits the spot. After an all-you-can-eat buffet lunch of barbecued fresh Alaska salmon (there's chicken and ribs for picky eaters), baked beans, corn bread, and blueberry cake, the kids can roast marshmallows over the open fire and explore the abandoned Wagner Mine. If you're lucky, you'll spot salmon spawning in the clear water beneath the Salmon Creek waterfall.

❷ Outside the **Irene Ingle Public Library** are a couple of ancient petroglyphs, which are worth seeing if you don't plan to make the trip to Petroglyph Beach. The library offers free Internet access and has a helpful staff. ✉*124 2nd Ave.* ☎*907/874–3535.*

❺ **Kiksetti Totem Park.** You'll find a couple of recently carved totem poles at this pocket-size park with Alaska greenery. ✉*Front St.*

❹ **Mt. Dewey.** Despite the name, this landmark is more a hill than a peak. Still, it's a steep 15-minute climb from town to the top through a second-growth forest. The trail begins from 3rd Street behind the high school, and an observation platform on top provides a viewpoint for protected waterways and quirkily named islands, including Zarembo, Vank, and Woronkofski.

❶ **Nolan Center.** Wrangell's museum moved into a building that acts as a
☾ centerpiece for cultural life in Wrangell. Exhibits provide a window on
★ the region's rich history. Featured pieces include decorative posts from Chief Shakes's clan house, petroglyphs, century-old spruce-root and cedar-bark baskets, masks, gold-rush memorabilia, and a fascinating photo collection. If you're spending any time in town, don't pass this up. Also in the building are the town's **Civic Center**, a 200-seat movie theater/performance space/convention center, and the **Wrangell Visitor Center** (☎*907/874–2829 or 800/367–9745* ⊕*www.wrangell.com*). The latter is staffed when the museum is open, and has details on local adventure options. ✉*296 Outer Dr.* ☎*907/874–3770* ☎*$5* ☾*May–Sept., Tues.–Sat. 10–5, and when ferry or cruise ships are in port; Oct.–Apr., Tues.–Sat. 1–5.*

❸ **Petroglyph Beach.** Scattered among other rocks at this public beach are three dozen or more large stones bearing designs and pictures chiseled by unknown, ancient artists. No one knows why the rocks at this curious site were etched the way they were, or even exactly how old these etchings are. You can access the beach via a boardwalk, where you'll find signs describing the site along with carved replicas of the petroglyphs. Most of the petroglyphs are to the right between the viewing deck and a large outcropping of rock in the tidal beach area. Because the original petroglyphs can be damaged by physical contact, only photographs are permitted. But you are welcome to use the replicas to make a rubbing from rice paper and charcoal or crayons (available in local stores). ⊠ *0.6 mi north of ferry terminal off Evergreen Ave.*

OUTSIDE TOWN

8 Anan Creek Wildlife Observatory. About 30 mi southeast of Wrangell in the Tongass National Forest, Anan is one of Alaska's premier black and brown bear–viewing areas. Each summer, from early July to mid-August, as many as 30 to 40 bears gather at this Southeast stream to feed on huge runs of pink salmon. On an average visit of about four hours you might spot up to 16 bears while strolling the 0.5-mi viewing boardwalk. There is a photo blind that affords the opportunity to view and photograph bears at eye level while they catch and eat salmon. Forest Service interpreters are on hand to answer questions. The site is accessible only by boat or floatplane. **Alaska Waters** (☎ *907/874–2378 or 800/347–4462 ⊕ www. alaskawaters.com*) is one of several local companies that offer day trips there. For additional details, contact the **Tongass National Forest Wrangell Ranger District** (☎ *907/874–2323 ⊕ www.fs.fed.us/r10/tongass*).

OUTDOOR ACTIVITIES

Rainwalker Expeditions (☎ *907/874–2549 or 888/276–2549 ⊕ www.rainwalkerexpeditions.com*) leads two-hour, half-day, and full-day guided natural-history, botany, wildlife, and bird-watching tours of wild places near Wrangell. The company also rents bikes, canoes, and sea kayaks if you want to head out on your own.

SHOPPING

Garnet Ledge, a rocky ledge near the Stikine River, is the source for garnets sold by local children for 25¢ to $50. Only children can collect these colorful but imperfect stones, the largest of which are an inch across. When cruise ships are in you can purchase garnets at a few covered shelters near the city dock. Local artist **Brenda Schwartz** (⊠ *7 Front St.* ☎ *907/874–3508 ⊕ www.marineartist.com*) creates watercolor scenes of the Alaskan coast on navigational charts of the region.

WHERE TO EAT

$$–$$$ ╳ **Zak's Cafe.** Despite its simple, no-nonsense atmosphere, Zak's is a stand-
AMERICAN out among Wrangell's limited dining choices, with good food and reasonable prices. Check out the day's specials or try the steaks, chicken, seafood, and salads. At lunch the menu includes burgers, sandwiches, fish-and-chips, and wraps. ⊠ *314 Front St.* ☎ *907/874–3355* ▭ *MC, V.*

Sports and Wilderness Adventures

4

WORD OF MOUTH

We traveled last week with ERA Alaska Flightsee-ing Tours. A 10 minute helicopter flight [into Denali Park] took us the equivalent distance of an 8-hour hike. Our guide, Jeffrey, knew everything about the plants and animals, carried a high-powered scope with him to point out far-away sheep and caribou, and customized the hike for our ability level. He took us along narrow sheep paths, through scree and soft tundra. After a 4-hour hike, when we were waiting for the helicopter back, my husband realized he had left his camera sometime when we stopped to rest earlier. Jeffrey promised to go back on his next hike to look for it. And he did. He's mailing it back to us.

—cp1776

Updated by
E. Readicker-
Henderson

ALASKA'S LANDSCAPE IS BIG ENOUGH to hold every traveler's dream: hidden in range after range of mountains are canyons and waterfalls, alpine valleys, salmon-rich rivers, clear lakes, blue glaciers, temperate rain forests, and sweeping, spongy tundra plains. Add in more than 5,000 mi of coast, and it's obvious: Alaska's the place for unforgettable outdoor adventuring!

Flip through this chapter to find planning tips; in-depth descriptions of sports, from kayaking to skiing to biking; our favorite regions and guides for each sport; and, finally, our best wildlife-viewing advice and experiences. In regional chapters we recommend more local outfitters and guides.

Alaska has more parks, wilderness areas, and wildlife refuges than all the other states combined. About one-third of Alaska's 375 million acres are set aside in protected public lands, and they are as varied as they are magnificent. Recreational activities include wildlife-viewing, hiking, mountain biking, kayaking, rafting, canoeing, fishing, hunting, mountaineering, skiing, and snowboarding. Limited road access (Alaska averages only 1 mi of road for every 42 square mi of land; the U.S. average ratio is 1 to 1) means that many destinations can only be reached via small airplane, boat, all-terrain vehicle, or what might be a really long walk. Dog sleds are frequently an option, too.

Even the most visited parks—Denali National Park and Preserve, Glacier Bay National Park and Preserve, and Kenai Fjords National Park—allow backpackers and kayakers abundant opportunities for remote wilderness experiences. Parks closer to roads and cities, like the massive Chugach State Park near Anchorage and Chena River State Recreation Area outside Fairbanks, draw more visitors, but it's still possible to be ten minutes outside a city and be all alone with the wilderness. Particularly remote and solitary experiences await in the state's least visited places, such as Wood-Tikchik State Park, where only two rangers patrol 1.6 million acres, or Aniakchak National Monument and Preserve, south of Katmai, where trekkers can go days or weeks without seeing another human.

PLANNING YOUR ADVENTURE

Trips to Alaska are best planned months, or even a year, in advance, particularly to the most popular destinations, such as Denali and Glacier Bay national parks. Prime time for summer backcountry sports is late May through early September. Winter sports are better enjoyed later in the season, in late February and March, when longer daylight hours return, temperatures start to rise a little, and snow conditions are unsurpassed for snowshoeing, skiing, and mushing.

Alaska's wilderness is enormous almost beyond comprehension. Visitors to the farther-flung reaches should come prepared for constantly changing and often harsh weather, difficult or impassable terrains, mosquitoes and gnats, bear or moose encounters, and other backcountry challenges. Never count on a schedule in the wilderness, and be ready for anything. A keen knowledge of the country, proper clothing, quality camping gear,

BEST WILDLIFE VIEWING		Bears	Birds	Caribou	Dall Sheep	Whales or Marine Animals
SOUTHEAST	Alaska Chilkat Bald Eagle Preserve & Chilkat River	◑	●	○	○	○
	Alaska Marine Highway	◑	●	○	○	●
	Glacier Bay National Park & Preserve	◑	●	○	○	●
	Mendenhall Wetlands State Game Refuge	◑	●	○	○	◑
	Pack Creek	●	●	○	○	●
SOUTH CENTRAL	Chugach State Park	●	●	○	●	●
	Kenai Fjords National Park	◑	●	○	○	●
INTERIOR	Creamer's Field Migratory Waterfowl Refuge	◑	●	○	○	○
	Denali National Park & Preserve	●	●	◑	●	○
BUSH	Arctic National Wildlife Refuge	◑	●	●	○	○
	Katmai National Park	●	●	◑	○	◑
	Kodiak National Wildlife Refuge	●	●	○	○	○
	Pribilof Islands	○	●	○	○	●
	Round Island (Walrus Islands State Game Sanctuary)	○	●	○	○	●

KEY: ● = likely ◑ = somewhat ○ = not likely

good physical condition, and excellent navigation skills are vital to successful and safe trips. Visitors without extensive wilderness experience can avoid logistical headaches and hazards by hiring local tour guides to provide equipment, direction, and necessary expertise.

CHOOSING A TRIP

Opportunities for outdoor adventures lie beyond the edge of every Alaskan village, port, and city. A day—or a week—of sea kayaking in Prince William Sound may begin a stone's throw from the streets of Whittier, which is only a scenic hour's drive south of Anchorage. A much more complex trip, such as a 10-day navigation of the North Fork Koyukuk River, may require a commuter flight from Fairbanks to the remote community of Bettles, and from there a prearranged flight into the headwaters high in the Brooks Range. So once you've figured out what you want to do, you need to carefully decide whether an organized tour or a do-it-yourself trip is most appropriate for you.

Your decision depends upon how much wilderness experience you have, what kind of physical condition you are in, how much time you have, and how much money you can afford to spend on gear and logistics. ■**TIP**➜ **The Alaska wilderness can be as difficult to navigate as it is beautiful; do not step into "the last frontier" poorly prepared. Plan ahead.** Alaska's backcountry is not a place to wing it. Know when to enlist the services of local guides or outfitters; allowing these professionals to provide vital gear, expertise, and direction can make your adventure safer, more comfortable, and more fulfilling.

RESOURCES With proper planning and the help of local professionals, there's an Alaska trip to be had—and likely many trips—just for you, no matter your age, physical ability, or level of wilderness savvy. When contacting outfitters, learn about the guides, the nature of the activities they offer, and the area you want to explore. Also be sure to determine how well the guides know the area and how long the company has been in operation. Make it a point to ask for references. Throughout this book you'll find in-depth information about all of Alaska's regions; contact information and insider tips are provided for parks, refuges, and wildlands that we think show the best of Alaska.

Here are some top organizations to help you get started:

A state-produced *Alaska Vacation Planner* (which also contains information on ecotourism) can be obtained from the **Alaska Travel Industry Association** (☎*907/929–2200, 800/862–5275 to order vacation planners* ⊕*www.travelalaska.com*).

The **Alaska Wilderness Recreation and Tourism Association** (☎*907/258–3171* ⊕*www.awrta.org*) can provide information on many businesses and activities across the state.

Recreational Equipment, Inc. (☎*907/272–4565* ⊕*www.rei.com*) is a great resource for equipment needs. The massive store in Anchorage has great gear-rental deals.

LARGE TOUR OPERATORS Larger tour companies will take care of everything if you want to just sit back and be guided through a specific part of the state doing a variety of activities. In some cases they offer shorter tours and activities for independent travelers. Ask about timing and pricing.

Gray Line of Alaska (☎*206/281–3535 or 888/452–1737* ⊕*www.graylinealaska.com*).

Princess Cruises and Tours (☎*800/426–0500* ⊕*www.princesslodges.com*).

SMALL TOUR OPERATORS Smaller, independent tour companies and agencies offer, you guessed it, smaller-scale tours and packages; they are good resources for tailormade Alaska journeys. See individual sports listed in this chapter for specialized Alaska-based companies.

Alaska Bound (☎*231/439–3000 or 888/252–7527* ⊕*www.alaskabound.com*).

Alaska Tour & Travel (☎*907/245–0200 or 800/208–0200* ⊕*www.alaskatravel.com*).

Alaska Tours (☎907/277–3000 or 866/317–3325 ⊕*www.alaskatours. com*).

Viking Travel, Inc. (☎907/772–3818 or 800/327–2571 ⊕*www.alaska-ferry.com*).

MONEY MATTERS

To reserve a spot, most tour operators require a deposit, with the balance due before your start date. In most cases, if you cancel your reservation you get at least a partial refund, but policies vary widely. ■TIP→ **Find out how far in advance you must cancel to get a full refund, and ask whether any allowances are made for cancellations due to medical emergencies.** If cancellation insurance is available, you may want to take it. You'll receive a full refund regardless of the reason for your cancellation.

Taxes are generally not included in the quoted price and can add substantially to the cost of your trip. Depending on the program, you should ask which members of the tour personnel customarily get tipped and what the going rate is.

SAFETY FIRST

In choosing a guide, a primary concern should be safety. A guide should be equipped with proper technical and first-aid gear and should know how to use it.

If you have no experience in the activity, ask what sort of training you'll receive. Honestly and carefully explain your own experience, goals, and abilities to your guide, and ask about the difficulty of the terrain. Fudging your own qualifications can lead to a miserable trip. One mile across hilly, trail-less tundra may demand the same energy as 2 or 3 mi on a flat, maintained trail. Most guides plan trips so that you'll have time to relax, enjoy the landscape, and look for wildlife, but it's a good idea to ask about the travel schedule and number of miles to be covered daily. As a general rule, hikers in good physical condition should be able to travel 2 mi an hour on maintained trails and about 1 mi per hour or less across trail-less terrain. Traveling 6 or 7 mi per day, even on trails, is likely to be tiring for a novice.

The amount of weight carried on your back will also influence your traveling ability, especially if you haven't carried a heavy pack before, so determine the amount of gear you'll be required to carry, particularly if you'll be hiking, backpacking, or glacier trekking. Figure out the weight you think you'll carry, walk around the block a few times, then start taking things out until you're comfortable. The wilderness is not the place to be surprised that you've overestimated your own abilities.

GEAR AND WEATHER

Ask what gear the company will provide. Guides normally provide group gear, such as tents and tarps, and expect you to provide your own personal equipment, such as boots, rain gear, a pack, and a sleeping bag. Some guides rent gear such as sleeping bags and packs.

Ask about the weather, but don't expect a firm answer. From the temperate rain forests of the Tongass National Forest in Alaska's Southeast to the inland deserts of the Northwest, climates vary greatly. No matter what region you visit, always come prepared for cool, wet weather, even in midsummer. Insect repellent (and sometimes head nets) may be required to ward off mosquitoes, flies, and no-see-ums during all snow-free months.

LODGING

From beautiful wilderness lodges to remote campsites to spongy tundra, your lodging options are immensely varied. Where will you be happiest settling in to sleep after a day of adventuring?

PUBLIC-USE CABINS

Not all Alaska wilderness trips require the expense of luxury lodges or the bare-bones lifestyle of tent camping. For between $25 and $75 per night backcountry travelers can have a million-dollar view and a roof over their heads at one of more than 250 public-use cabins available across the state. Cabin costs and locations depend upon which of five land-management agencies they fall under—the U.S. Forest Service, National Wildlife Refuges, National Park Service, Bureau of Land Management, or Alaska State Parks. Most cabins are remote or semiremote and must be reached by plane, boat, or trail. ■TIP→ **Almost all must be reserved in advance, either in person, by mail, or online; in some cases nominal service fees may be charged for cancellations.** However, if you haven't arranged a cabin before hitting town, check at the local Forest Service office; there's always a good chance of finding something, although it may not be in one of the most popular locations. Still, every view in Alaska is great.

Accommodations are rustic; most cabins have bunks or wooden sleeping platforms, tables, heating stoves, outdoor fire pits, outhouses, and, sometimes, rowboats or skiffs. Agency Web sites offer descriptions of individual cabins, including the number of bunks, types of stoves, and other amenities visitors can expect. You will need to bring in your own bedding and cooking fuel. Visitors who fly to cabins located on lakes or in coastal areas where skiffs are provided can usually rent outboards and gasoline tanks in the closest town and bring them along.

National Recreation Reservation Service. Contact this government organization to reserve any public-use cabin. ⊕*www.recreation.gov* ☎*877/ 444–6777, 518/885–3639 international.*

Alaska State Parks. More than 50 cabins are maintained over a huge area between Ketchikan and Fairbanks. Some are road accessible; reservations can be made up to six months in advance. Cabins vary in size, with sleeping capacity ranging from 3 to 10 people. For more information or to reserve a cabin online, contact the Department of Natural Resources Public Information Center in Anchorage. ☎*907/269–8400* ⊕*www.dnr.state.ak.us/parks/cabins/index.htm.*

Bureau of Land Management. Several public-use cabins are in the White Mountains National Recreation Area near Fairbanks. Cabins can be booked up to 30 days in advance by mail or phone or in person. Contact the Bureau of Land Management Land Information Center. ☎*1150*

University Ave., Fairbanks 99709-3844 ☎*907/474–2200 or 800/437–7021* ⊕*www.blm.gov/ak/st/en.html.*

National Park Service. Cabins are available in Kenai Fjords National Park, Wrangell–St. Elias National Park, and Yukon–Charley Rivers National Park. For the central information listing about the cabins, visit its Web site. ☎*907/224–2132 in Kenai Fjords, 907/822–5234 in Wrangell–St. Elias, 907/547–2233 in Yukon–Charley* ⊕*www.nps. gov/aplic/cabins.*

National Wildlife Refuges. Kodiak National Wildlife Refuge on Kodiak Island has eight public-use cabins. They can only be reached by float-plane or boat. Reservations are scheduled by a lottery. Applications, which may be mailed or delivered in person, are accepted until the last business day before the drawing date. ✇*1390 Buskin River Rd., Kodiak 99615* ☎*907/487–2600 or 888/408–3514* ⊕*kodiak.fws.gov.*

U.S. Forest Service. The agency maintains more than 150 cabins in the Southeast's Tongass National Forest, and more than 40 in the Chugach National Forest in South Central. Most cabins can be reached only by boat or plane; those accessible by trails are very popular and frequently booked months in advance. Maximum stays range from three to seven nights in summer. Cabin reservations may be made up to six months in advance. ☎*907/586–8806* ⊕*www.fs.fed.us/r10.*

WILDERNESS LODGES

If your goal is to really get away from it all, consider booking a remote Alaska wilderness lodge. Some of the most popular are in the river drainages of Bristol Bay, in the secluded bays of Southeast Alaska, along the western edge of Cook Inlet, around Katmai and Lake Clark national parks, and in the Susitna Valley north of Anchorage. Most of these lodges specialize in fishing and/or bear-viewing. Lodges in and near Denali emphasize opportunities to explore the wilderness as well as natural history programs. Activities can also include dog mushing, hiking, rafting, flightseeing, horseback riding, and gold panning.

Lodge stays generally include daily guided trips and all meals. Fees can be expensive (daily rates of $300–$900 or more per person), depending on location and services. Study the Web sites and list your favorites. E-mail or phone (many lodge operators provide toll-free numbers) with questions regarding activities offered, prices, gratuities, and what you should expect. ■TIP→ **Some of the more popular lodges need to be booked at least a year in advance, though last-minute cancellations can create openings even late in the season.**

For listings of wilderness lodges throughout Alaska, including individual Web sites, phone numbers, and general information, visit ⊕*www.travelalaska.com* or ⊕*www.alaska.com.* As you read through this book, you'll find plenty of recommendations for great wilderness lodges. Below we've listed three options.

Afognak Wilderness Lodge. This rustic log lodge is set in the heart of the coastal wilderness of Afognak State Park on Afognak Island, north of Kodiak. Featured activities include fishing, photography, and guided wildlife-viewing—including brown bear, deer, whales, and other marine wildlife. Guests stay in private, two-bedroom cabins with hot running water, Wi-Fi, and other creature comforts, and can relax in the sauna. ☎907/486–6442 or 866/978–4417 ⊕www.afognaklodge.com.

Denali Backcountry Lodge. Located in the very heart of Denali National Park and Preserve, lodge activities for overnight guests include naturalist programs; hiking; fishing; gold panning; mountain biking; and, for an extra fee, flightseeing when weather permits. Family-style meals emphasizing Alaska fare are included in the room rate. Deeper in the park than any other lodge, this is the real Alaska, which means endless views, no TV. ☎907/376–1992 or 877/233–6254 ⊕www.denalilodge.com.

> **STEP LIGHTLY**
>
> Ecotourists aim to travel responsibly. Typically, ecotourism is on a smaller scale and involves more education than traditional tourism; often you are led by guides who know the local natural history and cultures. Itineraries allow you a closer connection to the areas explored. As one Alaska guide says, "Slow down, take a deep breath, feel where you are." The **International Ecotourism Society** (⊕ www.ecotourism.org) is a great resource.

Tutka Bay Wilderness Lodge. Perched among spruces and coastal western hemlocks overlooking Kachemak Bay, the lodge is reached via plane or boat. You can spend your time sea kayaking, sportfishing, birding, bear- and marine wildlife–viewing, and relaxing in the open-air hot tub that's right on the beach. ☎907/235–3905 or 800/606–3909 ⊕www.tutkabaylodge.com.

CAMPING

Along Alaska's roads are hundreds of campgrounds, both public and private. They typically include sites for tent and RV camping, with fire pits, latrines, running potable water, and picnic benches. Most campsites are on a first-come, first-served basis.

BACKCOUNTRY AND PARKLAND CAMPING

If you wish to explore Alaska's vast wilderness, you will almost certainly have to establish your own campsites (though some parks do have remote tent sites). Before heading into the backcountry, contact the appropriate management agency, such as the state or national park that you'll be visiting for advice and/or restrictions.

Whenever camping in the wilderness, be on the lookout for water sources, effective drainage, protection from high winds, and game trails (which in bear country should be avoided—and nearly all of Alaska is bear country). Campers should practice low-impact camping techniques to minimize environmental damage. For example carry out *all* garbage; avoid camping on fragile vegetation; if possible, camp on already-established sites; never cut standing trees; wash yourself, your clothes, and your dishes at least 100 feet from water sources; bring a trowel and dig "cat-hole" latrines for human waste at least 100 feet from your camp, water sources, and trails; and burn or carry out toilet paper. When traveling in trail-less, particularly tundra, areas, fan out instead of walking single file to avoid trampling vegetation.

RESOURCES Information on roadside camping can be obtained at **Alaska Public Land Information Centers** (⊕ *www.nps.gov/aplic/center*) in Tok, Fairbanks, and Anchorage, and at park, refuge, and national-forest headquarters across the state.

CAR AND RV CAMPING

RV camping is popular along Alaska's road systems because it allows visitors the freedom to create their own itineraries while traveling in relative comfort. Although many drive their own vehicles up the Alaska Highway from Canada and the Lower 48, others choose to fly or cruise to Alaska and rent SUVs or motor homes once they arrive. Between June and August—peak summer season—motor-home rentals range from $125 to $200 per day, depending upon size and model. To save money, opt for weeklong packages and off-season prices offered by most rental companies.

Campgrounds and dump stations—including state, federal, and privately owned operations—as well as propane services, are in or near almost all communities along Alaska's highway system. State campgrounds provide overnight camping for $10 to $15 per night, depending upon the facility; dump-station use fees are $5. On public lands along remote stretches of highway, pleasant, free camping can sometimes be found in clearings, pulloffs, and old gravel pits. Sites in private campgrounds, which tend to be a bit more luxe, with showers and other facilities, usually run from $25 to $45.

RESOURCES **The Milepost** (⊕ *www.themilepost.com*) offers mile-by-mile information on all of Alaska's main highways.

The state of Alaska publishes a free informative guide called *RV Tips: Trip Information Planning Booklet: A practical guide to campgrounds, dump stations, and propane services along Alaska's highways.* It is available online (⊕ *www.dced.state.ak.us/oed/student_info/pub/rvtips.pdf*).

For more information about individual state campgrounds, locations, fees, and services, visit the Web site of the **Alaska Department of Natural Resources** (⊕ *www.dnr.state.ak.us/parks/asp/fees.htm*).

EQUIPMENT

Get the best equipment you can afford; it's an absolute must in Alaska. Quality gear is a good investment, and it can make your trip to Alaska safer and that much more comfortable and enjoyable. ■ TIP→ **Before you go on an organized trip, ask your guide what gear will be supplied, and what won't.**

THE ESSENTIAL ITEMS

When setting out for a day hike from base camp, it's wise to carry a first-aid kit, including bandages and moleskin; bear spray; a plastic bottle of drinking water; high-energy snacks; a warm sweater or jacket; windproof rain gear, in case the weather suddenly changes (avoid cotton clothing, as it does not retain body warmth when wet); a disposable lighter; fire starters, such as a candle or heat tab; a flare or flashlight; a knife (preferably a multifunctional pocketknife); a topographical map; toilet paper; sunglasses and sunblock; bug repellent; duct tape, for all kinds of emergencies; and a compass or a handheld global-positioning device. This list may seem long, but these items should combine to weigh less than 10 pounds and fit easily into a day pack. If you somehow get lost, hurt, or caught in a sudden weather event, carrying and knowing how to use these things could save your life.

BACKPACKS First decide whether to get a pack with an internal or external frame. If you choose the latter, pick one that balances the pack upright when you set it on the ground; this is a great help in the areas of Alaska that don't have trees. Internal frames are an advantage when going through brush, which is common in Alaska. A rainproof cover for your pack is a good idea, even if it's just a heavy plastic garbage bag.

TENTS Because winterlike storms can occur almost anytime, a freestanding four-season tent is recommended, one that can withstand strong winds and persistent rainfall (or even snow squalls). Tie-down ropes and tent flies are essential items, and mosquito netting is another must.

SLEEPING GEAR For sleeping comfort, bring a sleeping pad to add cushioning and insulation beneath your sleeping bag. Be sure your bag is warm enough for the changing conditions; even in midsummer, nighttime temperatures may fall to the freezing mark, especially in the mountains.

COOKING GEAR Bring a lightweight camping stove with fuel. Firewood may be scarce, and what there is may be wet. Burning wood is frowned upon or prohibited on many park lands in order to protect the surroundings.

Besides a stove, fuel, and matches or a butane lighter, necessary cooking items include light but sturdy utensils; a bowl and mug (drinking hot beverages is a great way to stay both warm and hydrated); a pot or two for heating water and cooking; a potholder; and a dependable—because everything can depend on it—pocketknife.

SPORTS, TOP REGIONS, AND TOURS

Alaska! It's a gigantic, vibrant state teeming with fish-packed rivers, snow-dusted mountaintops, and massive glaciers. Who has a travel wish list that *doesn't* include this enormous frontier? Thrill-seekers might check out helicopter skiing in the Chugach Mountains out of Girdwood, Valdez, or Cordova, or rafting in Denali National Park and Preserve. Sea kayakers will find solitude and abundant marine wildlife in the Southeast's Glacier Bay or South Central's Kenai Fjords.

Backcountry adventurers can escape civilization with a sled-dog team in Gates of the Arctic National Park far above the Arctic Circle, or in the Susitna Valley less than a two-hour drive north of Anchorage. The Aleutian and Pribilof islands are bird-watching meccas, while Katmai National Park and Kodiak National Wildlife Refuge are hot spots for bear viewing. An increasing number of trips and tours now make it possible to spend a week or two (or more) learning—and performing—feats from horse packing within sight of Mt. McKinley to hiking or mountain biking through some of the state's most challenging landscapes. Below you'll find some of our favorite sports, along with recommended trips and experiences, questions to consider, and suggestions to help you choose the right program. Check out the "Sports, the Outdoors, and

Guided Tours" sections in our regional chapters, from Anchorage to South Central to Southeast, for more details and additional rental and tour options.

BIKING

There's just nothing like pedaling through weaving stalks of fireweed and feeling a light breeze on your face as you take in the lush, intimidating, and all-encompassing landscape of Alaska. Biking is an excellent way to see the state, whether it's on a prearranged tour or an afternoon jaunt on some rented wheels. There are bike-rental shops in larger communities such as Anchorage and Fairbanks; they frequently offer street maps and can tell you their favorite routes. Alaska's dirt trails, including many within city parks, promise biking opportunities for cyclists of all abilities, while hundreds of miles of paved trails and highways provide choice touring routes. Whether you plan to grind your way up a dusty mountain path or cruise swiftly along a well-traveled highway, come prepared to handle emergencies. Always carry a basic bicycle repair kit including chain tool, Allen wrenches, spare inner tubes, and tube-repair materials, along with a compact bicycle-tire pump. Bring plenty of fluids (either in water bottles or camel packs), enough food to sustain your energy, and a light jacket or rain shell. And remember to take all proper animal-related precautions if you're peddling remote stretches of road.

TOP REGIONS AND EXPERIENCES

Biking is especially popular within the larger cities and along the road systems of South Central and the Interior. Favored touring routes include the unpaved Denali and Taylor highways and McCarthy Road. The Copper River Highway outside Cordova and some of the less traveled roads north of Fairbanks also beckon cyclists seeking several-speed adventures. Biking is a fantastic way to explore the Southeast's coastal towns via the Alaska Marine Highway System.

SOUTHEAST

Biking Southeast Alaska can be an exhilarating if sometimes wet experience. The **Alaska Marine Highway System** (☎ *800/642–0066* ⊕ *www. dot.state.ak.us/amhs*) charges a fee ($15–$50, depending on your route) if you bring your bike aboard. It's well worth it. While aboard the ferry, watch for breaching whales, then stop in small towns to check out gold-rush history, salmon bakes, and cute boardwalks and bed-and-breakfasts.

ANCHORAGE AND ENVIRONS

Alaska's largest city is laced with excellent biking opportunities—some challenging, others easy, all scenic—within and just outside the city limits. For a comprehensive guide to mountain biking in the Anchorage area, pick up a copy of *Mountain Bike Anchorage* by Rosemary Austin. The **Tony Knowles Coastal Trail** is 11 glorious mi of paved trail following the coastline from downtown past Westchester Lagoon. Check out the spectacular views of Mt. Susitna (locally called Sleeping Lady), Cook Inlet, and the Chugach Range. Ride the trail all the way to **Kincaid Park** to enjoy its 40 mi of dirt trails through acres of spruce and birch forest. Keep an eye out for moose! Our favorite trails include those along Anchorage's eastern edge in **Far North Bicentennial Park** and around **Eklutna Lake,** a short drive northeast of the city.

KENAI PENINSULA AND PRINCE WILLIAM SOUND

A relatively short drive from Anchorage, the Kenai Peninsula offers outstanding opportunities for mountain bikers seeking thigh-busting challenges amid extraordinary scenery. **Crescent Creek Trail** (at Mile 44.9 of Sterling Highway; drive 3 mi to the trailhead at end of gravel road), **Devil's Pass** (at Mile 39.5 of Seward Highway), **Johnson Pass** (at Miles 32.6 and 63.7 of Seward Highway), and the **Resurrection trail systems** offer miles of riding for a wide range of expertise. Cyclists here are subject to highly fickle mountain weather patterns. But remember that you're never really alone in wild Alaska: be sure to bring along bear spray and bug dope (repellent).

For maps and descriptions of trails, visit the state **Department of Natural Resources** Web site (⊕*www.dnr.state.ak.us/parks/aktrails/ats/ken-ats. htm*).

FAIRBANKS

Visitors to Alaska's Golden Heart City will find plenty of biking opportunities around town. People in these parts are becoming big biking fans—it's a trend that keeps lots of the trails well maintained. The **Back Door Trail** is part of the **Ester Dome Trails system,** which has miles of mountain-biking trails ranging from single tracks to fire roads. Back Door Trail stretches over 8 mi with an 800-foot elevation gain; it's rated by the Fairbanks Cycle Club as easy. To get started, drive west of Fairbanks on Parks Highway; turn right on Old Nenana Highway. Park at Ester Community Park near the firehouse just before the Ester turnoff.

One of our favorite rides, the paved multiuse **Farmers Loop Bike Path,** winds through suburbs and farmlands, passing by Creamer's Field Migratory Waterfowl Refuge. The path starts on the University of Alaska campus (at the corner of University and College) and takes you on a loop to the Steese Highway and back to town. The **University Ski Trails** on the University of Alaska Fairbanks campus (look for the well-marked trailhead and parking lot off Tanana Loop Road) are pretty good stuff, with 15 mi of dirt trails and a 1,500-foot elevation gain.

RESOURCES AND GUIDES

★ **Alaska Backcountry Bike Tours.** Based in Palmer, north of Anchorage, this company offers guided day and multiday trips; rental options include hard-tail and full-suspension bikes, as well as bob-trailers. ☎*866/354–2453* ⊕*www.mountainbikealaska.com.*

★ **Alaska Bicycle Tours/Sockeye Cycle Company.** Based in Haines, and in summertime in Skagway, these folks specialize in guided bike tours of the Southeast and remote sections of Canada's Northwest and Yukon. It recently celebrated 20 years of business in Alaska. ☎*907/766–2869 or 877/292–4154* ⊕*www.cyclealaska.com.*

Alaskabike. Starting in Anchorage, these multiday touring packages explore South Central and nearby scenic highways. ☎*907/245–2175* ⊕*www.alaskabike.com.*

Backroads. Offering challenging five- and six-day trips through South Central, this tried-and-true tour company is worth the investment. ☎510/527–1555 or 800/462–2848 ⊕www.backroads.com.

Denali Outdoor Center. This operator next to Denali National Park and Preserve offers bicycle rentals and guided tours along the edges of the park. ☎907/683–1925 or 888/303–1925 ⊕www.denalioutdoorcenter.com.

Downtown Bicycle Rental, Inc. Located in downtown Anchorage near the head of the popular Tony Knowles Coastal Trail, this rental shop has outstanding prices and a large selection of quality bikes and accessories. Shuttles to Flattop are also available. ☎907/279–5293 ⊕www.alaska-bike-rentals.com.

> ## BIKING TO CRESCENT
>
> The ascent is gradual, but the trek over Crescent Creek Trail, 100 highway mi south of Anchorage, can feel steeper and longer under a hot July sun. In places the trail goes almost vertical, and hairpin switchbacks broken by spruce roots require caution. None of that seems to matter, though, once Crescent Lake appears through the cottonwoods. On a windless afternoon the lake resembles an ice-blue gem surrounded by rocky ridgelines and an endless sky.

Fairbanks Cycle Club. Find information on touring and mountain-biking routes around Fairbanks. ☎907/459–8008 ⊕www.fairbankscycleclub.org.

Lifetime Adventures. Operating out of the state parks campground at Eklutna Lake, about 26 mi northeast of Anchorage, Lifetime rents bikes, trailers, and kayaks. You can take the popular Paddle & Pedal package in which you paddle in one direction and pedal your way back. ☎800/952–8624 ⊕www.lifetimeadventures.net.

CANOEING

The art of canoeing is peaceful, invigorating, and unsurpassed in Alaska, as the state boasts 3 million lakes and 3,000 rivers. Although it's possible to launch at any of hundreds of lakes and streams crossing Alaska's road system, the most easily accessed canoe trail systems with well-marked, maintained portages are found in South Central. Canoes, paddles, and life vests can be rented for $20 to $30 a day from area rental outfits.

Lakes and rivers around sea level in South Central are usually ice-free from mid-May through September, while those at higher elevations and in the Interior and northern regions are more likely ice-free from early June to mid-September. Many paddlers find the first couple of weeks after breakup and the final two weeks before freeze-up the most pleasant, for their cool temperatures and absence of mosquitoes and black flies.

TOP REGIONS AND EXPERIENCES

Three spectacular canoe trail systems are located in South Central, including the **Swan Lake Canoe Trail** and **Swanson River Canoe Trail,** both set in the 1.3-million-acre Kenai National Wildlife Refuge on the Kenai

Peninsula, and the **Nancy Lake Canoe Trail** in the Susitna Valley.

NORTH OF ANCHORAGE

The **Nancy Lake Canoe Trail** system is off the Parks Highway, about a 90-minute drive north of Anchorage. The system is managed by Alaska State Parks and features an 8-mi-long chain of lakes. Portages are well marked with orange, diamond-shaped signs marked with a "P." Wet sections are covered with boardwalk.

Experienced wilderness paddlers seeking some truly far-flung waters should explore systems like the Interior's Fortymile River Trail, Innoko River Trail, or Lower Beaver Creek Water Trails.

> ## PEACEFUL PADDLING
>
> From your canoe seat the world seems a simpler place. The air is still, the lake reflects autumn colors and blue sky. A trout rises for a midge, skims gracefully on the water's skin, and leaves behind a silver wake that brightens as it spreads. The full moon peeks over the mountains to the east—there will be frost in the morning—and you wonder as you paddle quietly back to camp if tonight you'll hear wolves howling.

KENAI PENINSULA

The **Swan Lake Canoe Trail** system includes a 60-mi-long series of lakes and small streams connected by overland portages ranging from a few hundred feet to more than a mile. The system can be entered through any of three trailhead entrances off Swanson River Road outside Sterling (head out of town on the Sterling Highway and turn off at Milepost 83.4). Trails are managed by the Kenai National Wildlife Refuge, which accurately describes the landscape as rolling hill country. There are plenty of spruce and birch forests here, plus amazing views of the Kenai Mountains to the east. Portages vary in condition.

The popular **Swanson River Canoe Trail** system, also set within the Kenai National Wildlife Refuge, is 50 mi long. The landscape is as wonderful as that of Swan Lake, with maintained portages ranging from a few hundred feet to more than a mile long. Follow the same driving directions as for Swan Lake out of Sterling.

RESOURCES AND GUIDES

Alaska Canoe & Campground. This outfit rents both gear and cabins within Kenai National Wildlife Refuge, as well as offering shuttles to both put-in and take-out points. ☎907/262–2331 ⊕www.alaskacanoetrips. com.

Alaska Department of Natural Resources. Check out the listings of canoe trails throughout the state, along with maps. ⊕www.dnr.state.ak.us/ parks/aktrails/atstrans.htm.

★ **Alaska Discovery.** One of the oldest outfits in the state and part of the Mountain Travel Sobek Company, these folks are based in Southeast and organize trips throughout the state, including a river trip on the Noatak River in the Brooks Range. ☎800/586–1911 ⊕www.akdiscovery. com.

Recreational Equipment, Inc. The Anchorage outpost rents canoes and accessories. ☎907/272–4565 ⊕www.rei.com.

DOGSLEDDING

Before snowmobiles and airplanes became mainstays of winter travel, dog teams provided transportation for rural Alaskans. Some of the finest dog teams in the state hailed from remote native villages. Today mushing is widely considered Alaska's state sport. That said, it's definitely not for everyone. For one thing, you have to like the cold. You also have to like roughing it. Even the nicest accommodations are only a step or two removed from camping. You also have to like dogs—a lot. Contrary to the romantic image you may have of sled dogs, they're not all cuddly, clean Siberian huskies. Most mushers, including the people who run dogsled tours, take very good care of their dogs, but the dogs are working animals, not show dogs; they're not, in the general sense of the word, pets.

> ## WOOF
>
> "Hike!" yells a musher as she releases the brake. On command, a team of surprisingly small but amazingly strong huskies charges off, howling with excitement. Of all the wild sporting adventures out there, dogsledding may be the wildest. There's usually enough snow for dogsled runs from late October or November through March or early April.

Here are some facts to consider: on some mushing trips participants travel by cross-country skiing or snowshoeing, rather than actually mushing, for at least part of the trip; some introduction to these sports is usually included in your orientation. ■ TIP→ **If you're not interested in skiing or snowshoeing, make sure you'll be given a sled. It's always a good idea to ask the outfitter how strenuous the pace is.** If you're expecting a relaxing vacation, don't pick an outfitter who will have you doing everything from hitching up the dogs to pitching tents.

TOP REGIONS AND EXPERIENCES

ANCHORAGE AND SOUTH CENTRAL

There are notable mushing communities in South Central, especially the Mat-Su Valley and Kenai Peninsula, and in the Interior around Fairbanks. Every year mushers traverse the wilderness between Anchorage and Nome in the famous **Iditarod Trail Sled Dog Race.** Other sprint and long-distance races in the area draw competitors and fans. Among the best are the **World Championship Sled Dog Race** held each February in Anchorage during the Fur Rendezvous celebration. On the Kenai Peninsula, Kasilof (off the Sterling Highway) is home to many notable mushers.

FAIRBANKS AND THE INTERIOR

The **Open North American Championships** are held every March in Fairbanks. The 1,000-mi-long **Yukon Quest,** considered even tougher than the Iditarod, runs between Fairbanks and Whitehorse, Yukon, and also lures mushers from around the globe. Local outfitters can set you up for a daylong sled ride, complete with a visit to the kennels.

RESOURCES AND GUIDES

Cotter Kennels. Operating outside Fairbanks, at the Chena Hot Springs Resort, these Yukon Quest winner and Iditarod top-three finishers offer dogsled rides in winter and dog-cart rides in summer. ☎ *907/451–8104* ⊕ *www.chenahotsprings.com.*

IdidaRide Sled Dog Tours. This family outfit out of Seward—including Mitch Seavey, winner of the 2004 Iditarod and the 2008 Alaska Sweepstakes—on the Kenai Peninsula runs wintertime tours out of Anchorage, Seward, and Sterling with their Iditarod dogs. ☎907/224–8607 or 800/478–3139 ⊕www.ididaride.com.

Plettner Sled Dog Kennels. Lynda Plettner, Iditarod veteran, offers mushing tours through the Mat-Su Valley, with prices starting at $100; reservations are required. Summer kennel tours are offered as well. The kennels are located a 90-minute drive north of Anchorage off the Parks Highway. ☎877/892–6944 ⊕www.plettner-kennels.com.

FLIGHTSEEING

Amelia Earhart said, "You haven't seen a tree until you've seen its shadow from the sky." Alaska is full of trees and, luckily, full of flightseeing opportunities as well. Air-taxi services in all major cities and many smaller communities offer flightseeing tours. Most offer a variety of packages, allowing clients to design their own tours if discussed in advance. The smaller companies are often more flexible, while the multiplane companies can better match plane size to your needs. Prices usually depend on the size of the plane, number of clients, and the route and length of the tour. As with taxicabs, passengers can often split costs for charters. Generally, a half-hour flightseeing trip runs each person around $75 per person, depending on the kind of plane and the destination; some areas, planes, and routes can be a lot more expensive. Hourly rates, depending on the plane's size and the competition, can run from $85 to more than $300 per person. If there's a drop-off and pick-up involved, you pay for all the time the plane is operating, in both directions. ■TIP→ Shop around before committing to any one service; some very good flightseeing bargains are available.

Flights in smaller planes and helicopters are particularly dependent upon weather. In some cases, clouds may simply obscure certain sites, while bad weather often grounds pilots altogether, forcing tours to be canceled. This is an especially important point to remember if you're waiting for a pick-up from a remote cabin or campsite. Be prepared for weather delays. Ask about cancellation policies if you've paid in advance. Alaska's pilots are the best in the world. Trust their knowledge and skill to get you where you're going in safety.

TOP REGIONS AND EXPERIENCES
SOUTHEAST
In the Southeast, flightseeing services based in communities surrounding **Misty Fiords National Monument, the Tongass National Forest, Mendenhall Glacier,** and **Glacier Bay National Park and Preserve** offer aerial views of coastal mountain ranges, remote shorelines, glaciers, ice fields, and wildlife. Some even include opportunities to land and fish or view local wildlife, such as brown bears, black bears, sea otters, seals, and whales. Visitors passing through the Southeast on cruise lines or via the Alaska Marine Highway System will find flightseeing options in all ports.

ANCHORAGE AND SOUTH CENTRAL

This area is the state's air-travel hub. Plenty of flightseeing services operating out of city airports and floatplane bases can take you on spectacular tours of **Mt. McKinley, the Chugach Range, Prince William Sound, Kenai Fjords National Park,** and the **Harding Icefield.** Flightseeing services are available in Seward, Homer, Talkeetna, and other South Central communities. Anchorage hosts the greatest number and variety of services, including companies operating fixed-wing aircraft, floatplanes, and helicopters.

THE BUSH   Why not head to the state's most remote parts in a small plane? Check out scenic **Katmai National Park and Preserve** and the **Valley of 10,000 Smokes,** a volcanic region of steaming calderas and hardened lava moonscapes. Most services are based in the communities of King Salmon or Naknek, which are served by a common airport with jet service from Anchorage.

RESOURCES AND GUIDES

★ **Emerald Air Service.** Emerald is based in Homer, and will take you to remote southwestern bear country. All-day trips run $625 per person, and include a great hike and natural history experience on the ground. ☎*907/235–6993* ⊕*www.emeraldairservice.com.*

Frontier Flying Service, Inc. This Fairbanks-based operation serves Interior Alaska's isolated towns and villages. ☎*907/450–7200 or 800/478–6779* ⊕*www.frontierflying.com/index.shtml.*

Katmailand. This outfit has concessions at Brooks Lodge in Katmai National Park and offers flights over the Valley of 10,000 Smokes. ☎*800/544–0551* ⊕*www.katmailand.com.*

★ **Rust's Flying Service.** An Anchorage company in business since 1963, Rust's will take you on narrated flightseeing tours of Mt. McKinley and Denali, Columbia Glacier, and Prince William Sound, as well as flights to the Peninsula for bear viewing. It's also the only outfit that can arrange stays at the Mountain House in Denali National Park, high atop Ruth Glacier. ☎*907/243–1595 or 800/544–2299* ⊕*www.flyrusts.com.*

Southeast Aviation. This Ketchikan-based operation offers floatplane tours of the glaciers and mountains of Misty Fiords National Monument. Wildlife sightings are quite common. ☎*907/225–2900 or 888/359–6478* ⊕*www.southeastaviation.com.*

Talkeetna Aero Services. These folks are located a two-hour drive north of Anchorage, in the shadow of McKinley; take a twin-engine aerial tour of the mountain. It's the only service that actually flies over the summit of McKinley (weather allowing). ☎*907/733–2899, 907/683–2899, or 888/733–2899* ⊕*www.talkeetna-aero.com.*

Talkeetna Air Taxi. Check out McKinley and environs, then swoop down to a glacier to test your boots. ☎*907/733–2218 or 800/533–2219* ⊕*www.talkeetnaair.com.*

★ **Wings Airways and Taku Glacier Lodge.** This Juneau-based company specializes in tours of the surrounding ice fields and the Taku Flight & Feast ride, on which a salmon feast awaits you at a classic Alaskan cabin, complete with glacier views—one of the best day trips out of the state capital. ☎*907/586–6275* ⊕*www.wingsairways.com.*

GLACIER TREKKING

Roughly 100,000 glaciers flow out of Alaska's mountains, covering 5% of the state. These slow-moving "rivers of ice" concentrate in the Alaska Range, Wrangell Mountains, and the state's major coastal mountain chains: the Chugach, St. Elias, Coast, and Kenai ranges. The Juneau Ice Fields are the biggest non-polar chunk of ice on the continent. Alaska's largest glacier, the Bering, covers 2,250 square mi. If you're an adventurous backcountry traveler, glaciers present icy avenues into the remote corners of premier mountain wilderness areas. And every traveler enjoys the opportunity to walk on water. ⇨ *For information about glaciers, flip to Glaciers: Notorious Landscape Architects in Chapter 3.*

Glacier terrain includes a mix of ice, rock debris, and often-deep surface snow; sometimes frigid pools of meltwater collect on the surface. Watch out for glacier crevasses. Sometimes hidden by snow, especially in spring and early summer (a popular time for glacier trekking), these cracks in the ice may present life-threatening traps. Though some are only inches wide, others may be several yards across and hundreds of feet deep. ■TIP➡ **Glacier travel should be attempted only after you've been properly trained. If you haven't been taught proper glacial travel and crevasse-rescue techniques, hire a backcountry guide to provide the necessary gear and expertise.** Some companies offer day or half-day hikes onto glaciers that don't have the same physical demands as longer treks but that still require proper equipment and training. For instance, St. Elias Alpine Guides takes hikers of all ages and abilities on one of its glacier walks.

TOP REGIONS AND EXPERIENCES
SOUTHEAST
In the Southeast, visitors to the capital city of Juneau can drive or take the bus to **Mendenhall Glacier,** on the outskirts of town. This 85-mi-long, 45-mi-wide sheet of ice, just the tiniest finger of the 1,500-square-mi Juneau Icefields, provides awesome glacier-trekking opportunities. Guided tour packages are a very good idea for beginners.

SOUTH CENTRAL AND THE INTERIOR
The mountains outside the state's largest city have their share of glaciers. Among the most popular for trekkers of all abilities is **Matanuska Glacier,** at Mile 103 off the Glenn Highway (about a 90-minute drive northeast of Anchorage). Anchorage-based guides often use the Matanuska as a training ground for those new to navigating glaciers.

Talkeetna, a two-hour drive north of Anchorage, is a small community famous as the jumping-off point to some of the world's greatest and most challenging glacier treks. The town rests a short bush-plane hop from the foot of the Alaska Range and the base of Mt. McKinley. Miles of ice await the most intrepid and experienced trekkers. Local and Anchorage-based guide services offer training and tours into the region.

Far to the east, off McCarthy Road between Valdez and Glennallen, are the great ice fields of the Wrangell Mountains. Experienced outfitters based in the town of McCarthy get newcomers in touch with awesome ice where few outsiders dare visit.

RESOURCES AND GUIDES

Above & Beyond Alaska, LLC. If you're in the Juneau area and want to get your glacier fix, these folks offer treks to the popular Mendenhall Glacier. ☎907/364–2333 ⊕ *www.beyondak.com.*

Alaska Mountaineering School. Whether it's on mountaineering expeditions to McKinley or less extreme treks into the Alaska Range, this Talkeetna company takes the time to train you before heading out to glacier trek or hit the pristine backcountry. ☎907/733–1016 ⊕*www. climbalaska.org.*

NorthStar Trekking. A Juneau-based operation specializing in helicopter glacier trekking on the Juneau Icefield, these folks accommodate a broad range of physical abilities and provide an excellent intro to glacier trekking. All trips are conducted in small groups, and gear is provided. Flightseeing tours are also offered. ☎907/790–4530 or 866/590–4530 ⊕*www.northstartrekking.com.*

Fodor'sChoice
★ **St. Elias Alpine Guides.** Based in the town of McCarthy, within Wrangell–St. Elias National Park, these über-experienced guides conduct day hikes to nearby glaciers and extended glacier treks well beyond. ☎907/345–9048 or 888/933–5427 ⊕*www.steliasguides.com.*

HIKING AND BACKPACKING

From the Southeast's coastal rain forests and the Interior's historic Yukon River country to the high Arctic tundra, Alaska presents some of the continent's finest landscape for wilderness hiking and backpacking. Or if remote backcountry is not your preference, it's possible to travel well-maintained and well-marked trails on the edges of Alaska's largest cities and still get a taste of the wild—in some places just a few steps take you into the heart of a forest or to the base of a mountain pass. Many of the trails in road-accessible parklands, refuges, and forests are well maintained, and cross terrain that is easy for novice hikers, seniors, and families.

TOP REGIONS AND EXPERIENCES

Most of Alaska is pristine wilderness, with few or no trails. In such areas it's best to be accompanied by an experienced backcountry traveler who understands the challenges of trail-less wilderness: how to behave in bear country, how to navigate using map and compass techniques, and how to cross glacial streams. Below we've listed some notable exceptions—trails where you can experience Alaska's wilderness on slightly beaten paths. *For information about hiking Southeast's Chilkoot Trail, flip to Gold! Gold! Gold! in Chapter 3.*

SOUTHEAST   Virtually all Southeast hiking is in the 17-million-acre Tongass National Forest, administered by the U.S. Forest Service. It can be wet and steep here, but you also will be walking through temperate rain forest—lush and gorgeous!

FROM
ANCHORAGE
TO DENALI   **Chugach State Park,** along Anchorage's eastern edge, has dozens of trails, many of them suited for day hikes or overnight camping. Across Turnagain Arm, near Hope, hikers can step onto the **Resurrection Pass Trail,** which traverses the forests, streams, and mountains of the Chugach National Forest. And though it is best known for its trail-less wilderness, **Denali National Park and Preserve** has some easy-to-hike trails near the park entrance, not to mention miles of taiga and tundra waiting to be explored. Nearby "Little Denali"—**Denali State Park**—has the 36-mi-long Kesugi Ridge Trail, within easy reach of the Parks Highway.

FAIRBANKS
AND THE
INTERIOR   If you're in the Interior's main hub, definitely check out **Creamer's Field Migratory Waterfowl Refuge** for easy trails and great birding—the main field sees hundreds of Sandhill cranes during migration. Some 100 mi east of Fairbanks, the **Pinnell Mountain National Recreation Trail** offers a great three-day hike above the tree line.

RESOURCES AND GUIDES

Alaska Mountaineering School. Best known for its McKinley expeditions, this Talkeetna-based company also leads custom-designed backcountry expeditions in the Alaska Range. ☎907/733–1016 ⊕*www.climbalaska.org.*

Fodor'sChoice
★   **Alaska Nature Tours.** This company in Southeast Alaska leads summer naturalist-guided hiking trips into the Alaska Chilkat Bald Eagle Preserve near Haines. Other trips include beach walks and rain-forest hikes. ☎907/766–2876 ⊕*www.alaskanaturetours.net.*

★   **Arctic Treks.** These wilderness hiking and backpacking trips, sometimes combined with river floats, explore areas throughout the Arctic region's Brooks Range, including Gates of the Arctic and the Arctic National Wildlife Refuge. ☎907/455–6502 ⊕*www.arctictreksadventures.com.*

Go North Alaska Adventure Travel Center. Since 1991, this Fairbanks business has been organizing Brooks Range tours. It rents vehicles for driving Alaska's gravel roads—something not many other places do. ☎907/479–7272 or 866/236–7272 ⊕*www.paratours.net.*

Fodor'sChoice
★   **St. Elias Alpine Guides.** For more than a quarter century, this outfitter has been leading mountain hikes, nature tours, and extended backpacking expeditions in the St. Elias and Wrangell mountain ranges. ☎888/345–9048 or 907/345–9048 ⊕*www.steliasguides.com.*

HORSE PACKING

Horseback riding can be a rustic, elemental experience. Horseback riding in Alaska can be the experience of a lifetime. To minimize a horse-packing group's impact on the environment, most are limited to 12 riders, and some to just 3 or 4. Most outfitters post at least two wranglers for 12 guests, and some bring along another person who serves as cook and/or assistant wrangler. Outfitters who operate on federal lands must have a permit.

HIKING TERRAINS

RIVERS

Crossing Alaska's rivers requires care. Many are hard-to-read, swift, silty streams. They often flow over impermeable bottoms (either rock or permafrost), which means a good rain can raise water levels a matter of feet, not inches, in a surprisingly short time. For this very reason, avoid pitching tents near streams, particularly on gravel or sandbars. Warm days can also dramatically increase the meltwater from glaciers. Be aware of weather changes that might affect river crossings. Look for the widest, shallowest place you can find, with many channels. This may entail traveling up- or downstream. A guide who knows the region is invaluable at such times.

A sturdy staff, your own or made from a handy branch, is useful to help you keep your balance and measure the depths of silty water. Make sure one foot is firmly planted before you lift the next. Do not hurry, no matter how cold the water feels. You should unbuckle your pack when crossing a swift stream. Avoid wearing a long rain poncho; it can catch the water and tip you over. For added stability it helps for two or more people to link arms when crossing.

Hikers debate the best footwear for crossing Alaska's rivers. Some take along sneakers and wear them through the water; others take off their socks so they will remain dry and can comfort cold feet on the opposite shore. But bear in mind that Alaska waters are generally frigid, and the bottom is often rocky and rough; bare feet are not advised.

TUNDRA

Tundra hiking, especially in higher alpine country, can be a great pleasure. In places the ground is so springy you feel like you're walking on a trampoline. In the Arctic, however, where the ground is underlaid with permafrost, you will probably find the going as wet as it is in the Southeast forests. Summer sunshine melts the top, leaving puddles and marshy spots behind. Comfortable waterproof footgear can help when traversing such landscapes. Tundra travel can require the skill and stamina of a ballet dancer if the ground is tufted with tussocks.

FORESTS

Forest trails are hard to maintain and often wet, especially in coastal lowlands, and they may be potholed or blocked with beaver dams. The ground stays soggy much of the time, and brush grows back quickly after it is cut. Especially nasty is devil's club, a large, broad-leaved plant with greenish flowers that eventually become clusters of bright red berries; it's also thickly armored with stinging, needle-sharp thorns.

■TIP➔ **It's a good idea to find out how difficult the riding is and how much time is spent in the saddle each day.** Six hours of riding is a long day, and although some outfitters schedule that much, most keep the riding time to about four hours. Most trips move at a walk, but some trot, lope, and even gallop. As with many other guided adventures, special expertise is not required for most horse-packing trips, and guides will train you in the basics before setting out.

On trips into the wilderness, expect the food to be straightforward cowboy fare, cooked over a campfire or cookstove. Guides often pull double duty in the kitchen, and often a little help from group members is appreciated. If you have dietary restrictions, make arrangements beforehand. For lodging, don't allow yourself to be surprised: find out what the rooms are like if you're going to be staying in motels or cabins, and if the trip involves camping, ask about the campsites and the shower and latrine arrangements.

TOP REGIONS AND EXPERIENCES

SOUTH CENTRAL Encompassing more than 13 million acres of mountains, glaciers, and remote river valleys, **Wrangell–St. Elias National Park and Preserve**, the largest roadless wilderness left on the continent, is wild and raw. There's no better way to absorb the enormity and natural beauty of this region than on horseback. Centuries-old game trails and networks blazed and maintained by contemporary outfitters wind through lowland spruce forests and into wide-open high-country tundra. From there, horses can take you almost anywhere, over treeless ridgelines and to sheltered campsites on the shores of scenic tarns.

Closer to the state's population center in South Central, yet no less magnificent for horse packing, is the Kenai Peninsula. Outfitters frequently travel the well-groomed mountain trails of the **Chugach National Forest** and **Kenai Mountains.** In both regions, wildlife is abundant: moose, bear, Dall sheep, mountain goats, and wolves are frequently seen. Although overnight cabins are occasionally available, guests should come prepared to camp outdoors.

RESOURCES AND GUIDES

Alaska Horsemen Trail Adventures. This Cooper Landing–based company offers multiday pack trips into the Kenai Mountains via Crescent Lake, Resurrection, and other area trail systems. ☎*907/595–1806 or 800/595–1806 ⊕www.alaskahorsemen.com.*

Castle Mountain Outfitters. Based in Chickaloon, north of Anchorage in Matanuska Valley, this outfitter conducts a variety of trips ranging from guided hour-long horseback rides to one-week expeditions. ☎*907/745–6427 ⊕www.mtaonline.net/~cmoride/index.html.*

Wrangell Outfitters. This husband-and-wife team from Fairbanks takes visitors on horse-packing trips into the heart of Wrangell–St. Elias National Park and Preserve. ☎*907/479–5343 ⊕www.wrangelloutfitters.com.*

RIVER RAFTING

So much of Alaska is roadless wilderness that rivers often serve as the best avenues for exploring the landscape. This is especially true in several of Alaska's premier parklands and refuges. Here, as elsewhere, rivers are ranked according to their degrees of difficulty. ■TIP→ **Class I rivers are considered easy floats with minimal rapids; at the other extreme, Class VI rivers are extremely dangerous and nearly impossible to navigate. Generally, only very experienced river runners should attempt anything above Class II on their own.** Also be aware that river conditions change considerably from season to season and sometimes from day to day, so always check on a river's current condition. The National Weather Service Alaska–Pacific River Forecast Center keeps tabs on Alaska's most popular streams. The center's Web site (⊕*aprfc.arh.noaa.gov/ ak_ahps2.php*) provides the latest data on water levels and flow rates, including important flood-stage alerts.

Do-it-yourselfers would be wise to consult two books on Alaska's rivers: *Fast & Cold: A Guide to Alaska Whitewater* (Skyhouse), by Andrew Embick (though intended primarily for white-water kayakers, it has good information for rafters as well), and *The Alaska River Guide: Canoeing, Kayaking, and Rafting in the Last Frontier* (Alaska Northwest Books), by Karen Jettmar.

Fortunately you don't have to be an expert river runner to explore many of Alaska's premier waterways. Experienced rafting companies operate throughout the state. Some outfits emphasize extended wilderness trips and natural-history observations, whereas others specialize in thrilling one-day (or shorter) runs down Class III and IV white-water rapids that will get your adrenaline—and possibly your arms—pumping. And some combine a little of both.

TOP REGIONS AND EXPERIENCES

Never has the term "it's all good" been truer than in the context of river rafting in Alaska. Which region and river you float depends largely upon the impetus of your trip. White-water thrill-seekers will find challenging streams tumbling from the mountainous areas of South Central, while rafters interested in sportfishing may choose extended float trips on the gentler salmon- and trout-rich rivers of the Southwest. Birders and campers may consider the pristine rivers draining the North Slope of the Brooks Range or Northwest Alaska, or the Stikine River, which ends near Wrangell, in Southeast. Beyond your agenda, though, which river you choose to float should depend upon your rafting and back-country skills. If there's any question at all, go with an experienced river guide.

SOUTH CENTRAL For those seeking the adrenaline surge of white-water rafting, South Central offers many accessible and affordable options. **Chugach National Forest's Six-Mile River,** about a 90-minute drive south of Anchorage on the Seward Highway, is relished for its Class V and VI white water and spectacular canyon scenery. The Six-Mile is only for rafters who have done this kind of river before and who aren't intimidated by getting flipped. But there are plenty of easier options available off the highway system north of Anchorage, including the glacial **Eagle** and **Matanuska** rivers, each known for varying degrees of white water.

THE INTERIOR AND THE BUSH North of Anchorage via the Parks Highway, the **Nenana River** flows along the eastern side of Denali National Park and Preserve, offering a variety of conditions ranging from calm to Class III and IV. More people experience Alaskan white water here than anywhere else in the state; numerous outfitters right at the park entrance offer half- and full-day trips.

Flowing north out of the eastern Brooks Range to the Arctic Ocean, the **Kongakut, Noatak,** and **Hulahula** rivers promise far-flung wilderness adventures. Trips here are as much about seeing the high Arctic tundra landscape and wildlife as they are about the water.

RESOURCES AND GUIDES

Be certain that the guide gives you a safety talk before going on the water. It's important to know what you should do if you do get flipped out of the raft or if the boat overturns. Also, when arranging your trip well in advance, find out what gear and clothing are required. Ask if you'll be paddling or simply riding as a passenger. Reputable rafting companies will discuss all of this, but it never hurts to ask.

> ### RIOTOUS RIVERS
>
> From the Southeast Panhandle to the far reaches of the Arctic, Alaska is blessed with an abundance of wild, pristine rivers. The federal government has officially designated more than two dozen Alaska streams as "Wild and Scenic Rivers," but hundreds more would easily qualify. Some meander gently through forests or tundra. Others, fed by glacier runoff, rush wildly through mountains and canyons.

★ **Alaska Discovery.** This Juneau-based outfitter leads 9- to 12-day trips down two of North America's wildest rivers, the Tatshenshini and Alsek. The trips begin in Canada and end in Glacier Bay. Also check out the rafting/hiking trips in the Arctic National Wildlife Refuge and Gates of the Arctic. ☎ *800/586–1911* ⊕ *www.akdiscovery.com.*

Alaska Wildland Adventures. Head down the Kenai River and learn about the surroundings and wildlife with these guides. One of the oldest and largest outfitters on the peninsula, it has trips to suit anyone. ☎ *800/478–4100* ⊕ *www.alaskarivertrips.com.*

Denali Outdoor Center. This operator next to Denali National Park and Preserve offers raft trips on the Nenana. ☎ *907/683–1925 or 888/303– 1925* ⊕ *www.denalioutdoorcenter.com.*

Denali Raft Adventures, Inc. River trips are conducted on the glacially fed, white-water Nenana River, which skirts the eastern boundary of Denali National Park and Preserve. Trips vary from two-hour scenic floats to all-day white-water canyon trips. This is the only outfitter to put clients into dry suits—perfect for those who really don't like cold water. ☎ *907/683–2234 or 888/683–2234* ⊕ *www.denaliraft.com.*

Fodor'sChoice ★ **Nova.** These superexperienced guides—the company has been around for more than 30 years—offer white-water trips down the Matanuska, Chickaloon, and Talkeetna rivers in South Central Alaska; multiday float trips through Wrangell–St. Elias; and part-day trips on the Kenai Peninsula's Six-Mile River, the wildest white water commercially run in Alaska. White-water ratings range from Class I to Class V. ☎ *800/746– 5753* ⊕ *www.novalaska.com.*

SEA KAYAKING

Sea kayaking can be as thrilling or as peaceful as you want. More stable than a white-water kayak and more comfortable than a canoe, a sea kayak, even one loaded with a week's worth of gear, is maneuverable enough to poke into hidden crevices, explore side bays, and beach on deserted spits of sand. Don't assume, though, that if you've kayaked 10 minutes without tipping over you'll be adequately prepared to circumnavigate Glacier Bay National Park and Preserve. There's a lot to learn, and until you know your way around tides, currents, and nautical charts, you should go with an experienced guide who also knows what and how to pack and where to pitch a tent.

It's important to honestly evaluate your tolerance for cold, dampness, and high winds. Nothing can ruin a trip faster than pervasive discomfort, and it's worse once you're out on the water with no choice but to keep going.

> ### THE STROKES
>
> Anyone who doesn't mind getting a little wet and has an average degree of fitness can be a sea kayaker. The basic stroke is performed in a circular motion with a double-bladed paddle: you pull one blade through the water while pushing forward with the other through the air. Most people pick it up with a minimal amount of instruction.

TOP REGIONS AND EXPERIENCES

SOUTHEAST This largely roadless coastal region is the setting of North America's last great temperate wilderness. Sometimes called Alaska's Panhandle, this appendage of islands, mainland, and fjords is a sparsely populated, scenic paradise for sea kayaking. In Southeast, Ketchikan is a popular starting point for many sea kayakers. Set in the heart of the **Tongass National Forest** and an easy boat or floatplane ride from **Misty Fiords National Monument,** this former logging town is home to several sea-kayaking guides and rental businesses. Ketchikan is also a stop on the Alaska Marine Highway, making it convenient for travelers to simply drive or walk off the state ferry and spend a couple of days exploring local bays and fjords before boarding another ferry.

An equally popular destination for Southeast saltwater paddlers is **Glacier Bay National Park and Preserve.** The hub for this region is Juneau, where kayakers can hop a plane or ferry to the small community of Gustavus, located next to the park.

SOUTH CENTRAL **Prince William Sound,** with its miles of bays, islands, forests, and glaciers, is a big draw for sea kayakers. Popular ports include Whittier, Cordova, and Valdez. Of the three, Whittier and Valdez are on the state highway system, making them most accessible (Whittier is a one-hour drive south from Anchorage). Guides catering to ocean paddlers are found in all three ports.

Two Kenai Peninsula venues also lure sea kayakers. About a two-hour drive south of Anchorage, at the terminus of the Seward Highway, **Resurrection Bay** serves up awesome scenery and marine wildlife. Homer, perched over **Kachemak Bay,** at the terminus of the Sterling Highway (a five-hour drive south of Anchorage), is also an excellent spot.

RESOURCES AND GUIDES

Fodor'sChoice ★ **Alaska Discovery.** These experienced guides know Southeast Alaska intimately, and they emphasize skills and safety. Destinations include Tracy Arm, Glacier Bay, Icy Bay, Point Adolphus (for whale-watching), and Admiralty Island (with bear viewing at Pack Creek). Also check out the inn-to-inn paddling trip through the Kenai Peninsula's Kachemak Bay. ☎800/586–1911 ⊕www.akdiscovery.com.

Anadyr Adventures. Prince William Sound comes alive from a sea kayak. In business since 1989, this Valdez company has just added a trip that includes a glacier hike and kayaking in a cave, as well as through the beautiful waters of the sound. ☎907/835–2814 or 800/865–2925 ⊕www.anadyradventures.com.

Prince William Sound Kayak Center. Operating out of Whittier since 1981, this center provides kayak rentals (including fiberglass kayaks, much lighter and easier to paddle than plastic ones), introductory classes, guided day tours, and escorted trips in Prince William Sound. ☎907/472–2452 in winter, 877/472–2452 in summer ⊕www.pwskayakcenter.com.

Southeast Exposure. More than 20 years in the business translates into great trips with this Ketchikan outfit. Its most popular paddle is through Misty Fiords National Monument. ☎907/225–8829 ⊕www.southeastexposure.com.

Spirit Walker Expeditions. This veteran Southeast company (based in Gustavus) gives guided wilderness sea-kayaking trips that combine scenery, wildlife, solitude, and paddling within the Inside Passage, from day trips to weeklong expeditions. Guides prepare meals, offer instruction, and provide all gear. Beginners are welcome. ☎907/697–2266 or 800/529–2537 ⊕www.seakayakalaska.com.

SKIING AND SNOWBOARDING

Yes, Alaska has a lot of snow. It's not surprising then, that the state is also a great destination for Nordic, downhill, and extreme downhill skiing. Three of the state's largest cities—Anchorage, Fairbanks, and Juneau—have nearby ski areas, complete with equipment rentals and ski schools. Many of Alaska's towns have maintained trails for cross-country skiers. Anchorage's trail system ranks among the nation's finest and hosts world-class races.

For those who are more ambitious, Alaska's wilderness areas present plenty of opportunities and a variety of challenges. Unless you are knowledgeable in winter backcountry travel, camping techniques, and avalanche dangers, the best strategy is to hire a guide when exploring Alaska's backcountry on skis. ■TIP➔ **Given the extremes of Alaska's winters, your primary concern should be safety: be sure your guide has had avalanche-awareness and winter-survival training.** Conditions can change quickly, especially in mountainous areas, and what begins as an easy cross-country ski trip can suddenly become a survival saga if you're not prepared for the challenges of an Alaska winter.

TOP REGIONS AND EXPERIENCES
SOUTHEAST

Eaglecrest gets high marks for excellent spring skiing. Set 12 mi outside Juneau, ski season runs December through mid-April. This hill is rarely crowded, and the views on a bright day are remarkable. ⊕www.skijuneau.com.

SOUTH CENTRAL AND THE INTERIOR

Alyeska Resort, located 40 mi south of Anchorage in Girdwood, is Alaska's largest and best-known downhill ski resort. A new high-speed quad lift gets you up the mountain faster. The resort encompasses 1,000 acres of terrain for all skill levels. Ski rentals are available at the resort. ⊕*www.alyeskaresort.com.*

Closer to Anchorage, two much smaller ski-hill operations, **Alpenglow** and **Hilltop,** offer great runs for beginners. Both are also good options when the weather occasionally rules out Alyeska. ⊕*www.skialpenglow. com* and ⊕*www.hilltopskiarea.org.*

Moose Mountain, outside Fairbanks, is the ski and snowboard draw for visitors to the Interior. More than 1,250 feet of terrain includes everything from bunny slopes to vertical. Best of all, while the city is known for frigid winters, the mountain enjoys warmer temperatures. ⊕*fairbanks-alaska.com/moose-mountain-ski-resort.htm.*

RESOURCES AND GUIDES

Alaska Mountaineering School. Custom cross-country ski trips of varying lengths and degrees of difficulty can be arranged, primarily through Denali National and state parks, with an emphasis on natural history. ☎907/733–1016 ⊕*www.climbalaska.org.*

Fodor'sChoice ★ **Alaska Nature Tours.** This company in Southeast rents ski and snowboard gear and conducts trips into the amazing Alaska Chilkat Bald Eagle Preserve near Haines. ☎907/766–2876 ⊕*www.alaskanaturetours.net.*

Chugach Powder Guides. Founded in 1997, this helicopter-ski and Sno-Cat operation focuses on backcountry skiing and snowboarding in the Chugach Range out of Girdwood and Seward; Alaska Range adventures are also featured. When you see films of extreme helicopter skiing in Alaska, it's usually these guys. ☎907/783–4354 ⊕*www. chugachpowderguides.com.*

SPORTFISHING

Alaska's biggest hobby in the warmer months is sportfishing; the Anchorage *Daily News* even has a "fishing dude" who posts inside tips and videos online for those seeking the perfect catch (⊕*www.adn.com/ outdoors/fishing*). Six species of Pacific salmon (king, silver, sockeye, pink, steelhead—most people don't know steelhead was taxonomically promoted from trout to salmon a few years back—and chum) spawn in Alaska's innumerable rivers and creeks, alongside rainbow trout, cutthroat trout, arctic char, sheefish, Dolly Varden char, arctic grayling, northern pike, and lake trout, among other freshwater species. Salmon are also caught in saltwater, along with halibut, lingcod, and many varieties of rockfish (locally called snapper or sea bass).

Even though the world-record king salmon, weighing 97¼ pounds, was caught in the Kenai River, and many halibut exceeding 300 pounds are caught annually, some anglers will tell you that bigger isn't necessarily better. Sockeyes, salmon averaging 6 to 8 pounds, are considered by many to be the best tasting and best fighting of any fish, and most locals won't bother to eat a halibut that weighs over 30 pounds or so.

And though the sail-finned arctic grayling commonly weighs a pound or less, its willingness to rise for dry flies makes it a favorite among fly fishermen.

■TIP➔ Sportfishing regulations vary widely from area to area. Licenses are required for both fresh- and saltwater fishing. To learn more about regulations, contact the **Alaska Department of Fish and Game** (☎*907/465–4180 sportfishing seasons and regulations, 907/465–2376 licenses* ⊕*www. adfg.state.ak.us*). To purchase a fishing license online, visit the State of Alaska Web site (⊕*www.admin.adfg.state.ak.us/license*).

TOP REGIONS AND EXPERIENCES

Roadside fishing for salmon, trout, char, pike, and grayling is best in **South Central** and **Interior Alaska.** In fact, Alaska's best-known salmon stream, the **Kenai River,** parallels the Sterling Highway. But in most of the state, prime fishing waters can be reached only by boat or by air. Not surprisingly, hundreds of fishing charters and dozens of sportfishing lodges operate statewide, attracting anglers from around the world. **Southwest Alaska,** in particular, is known for its fine salmon, trout, and char fishing; many of its best spots are remote and expensive to reach, but fishing opportunities here are unparalleled.

SOUTHEAST
This huge coastal region is renowned for its outstanding sportfishing for salmon, rockfish, and halibut. Charters operate out of all main ports, and the action is frequently so good that catching your limit is almost a given. Splendid scenery is guaranteed—even when shrouded in misty rains, which are common. Streams offer fine angling for steelhead, cutthroat, rainbow, and Dolly Varden trout. The waters of **Prince of Wales Island** are especially popular among steelhead, salmon, and trout anglers, with the Karta and Thorne rivers among the favorites.

SOUTH CENTRAL AND THE INTERIOR
Alaska lives up to its reputation for angling excellence in South Central. From the hub of Anchorage, the Seward and Sterling highways provide access to the world-famous spots on the Kenai Peninsula. Anglers seeking rainbow trout, Dolly Varden, and salmon will do no better than the **Kenai River.** This dream stream—tinted an opaque emerald from glacial runoff—serves up fine fishing from ice-out in spring to freeze-up in late fall. The **Russian River,** a tributary that joins the upper Kenai River near Cooper Landing, is a dashing mountain stream that runs crystal-clear—except when it's chock-full of red salmon from mid-June through August. Other fine Kenai Peninsula streams include **Quartz Creek, Deep Creek,** and **Anchor River.** When the salmon are running, most of the better-known streams can be shoulder-to-shoulder fishermen, angling for a spot to stand as much as for fish. Luckily, for those looking to avoid combat fishing, a few miles' drive can make a considerable difference in conditions. Many excellent trout and salmon guides are based in the Kenai River towns of Cooper Landing, Sterling, Soldotna, and Kenai, and their experience can get you to places you'd never find on your own.

Saltwater angling out of the ports of **Whittier, Seward,** and **Homer** is legendary for king, pink, and silver salmon as well as huge halibut. Charter operators are in all three ports, offering half-day and full-day fishing trips.

North of Anchorage, the Parks Highway courses through the **Mat-Su Valley,** a scenic piece of wilderness backed by Mt. McKinley and veined with fine streams. Six species of salmon, rainbow trout, Dolly Varden, grayling, northern pike, and lake trout are among the draws here. Some of the most popular Parks Highway streams include **Willow, Sheep, Montana,** and **Clear** creeks. Fishing guides based in Wasilla, Houston, Willow, and Talkeetna offer riverboat and fly-in trips. Remember that salmon runs are seasonal. Kings run late May through mid-July, and silvers run from mid-July through August. And don't forget the lakes; scores of them brim with trout, landlocked salmon, arctic char, and grayling. Cast for them from canoes or float tubes on calm summer afternoons.

THE BUSH The most popular bush sportfishing region is the roadless **Southwest,** home of the richest salmon runs in the world. Along with huge schools of red salmon, kings, silvers, chums, and pinks, anglers will find trophy rainbow trout, Dolly Varden, arctic grayling, and arctic char. Many anglers fish with guides based out of remote fishing lodges located on rivers and lakes. Others do it themselves, arranging for bush planes to drop them off in headwater streams, then floating the river in rafts, fishing along the way until reaching a prearranged pickup point.

RESOURCES, GUIDES, AND CHARTERS

When hiring a guide, ask about species likely to be caught when you'll be visiting, catch limits, and any special equipment or clothing needs. Normally, all necessary fishing gear is provided, and the guides will teach you the appropriate fishing techniques. In some cases, catch-and-release may be emphasized. Prime time for saltwater fishing is July through mid-August; for river trips, mid-June through September.

Alaskan Fishing Adventures, Inc. Anglers are guided in several areas of the Kenai Peninsula, including Resurrection Bay, Cook Inlet (with two beachfront lodges), and the Kenai River, home of the famous Kenai king salmon that may weigh 90 pounds. Among the other species they catch are halibut, sockeye and silver salmon, and rainbow trout. Most boats have a four-person limit on rivers, a six-person limit on saltwater, although the company also has a new 12-passenger catamaran. ☎800/548–3474 ⊕www.alaskanfishing.com.

Alaska River Adventures. These Cooper Landing–based guides take small groups fishing throughout the region, with self-professed "well-seasoned old pros." ☎907/595–2000 or 888/836–9027 ⊕www.alaskariveradventures.com.

Central Charter Booking Agency. In Homer, this company can arrange fishing trips in outer Kachemak Bay and Lower Cook Inlet—areas known for excellent halibut fishing. Boat sizes vary considerably; some have a six-person limit, whereas others can take up to 16 passengers. ☎907/235–7847 ⊕www.centralcharter.com, www.endofthespit.com.

The Fish House. Operating out of Seward since 1974, this booking agency represents dozens of Resurrection Bay and Kenai Peninsula fishing charters and can hook you up for half-day or full-day charters, specializing in silver salmon and halibut. ☎907/224–3674 or 800/257–7760 ⊕www.thefishhouse.net.

Great Alaska Adventure Lodge. Alaska's oldest fishing and wildlife-viewing lodge provides rafting, hiking, glacier viewing, bear watching, and fishing—both fresh- and saltwater. ☎ *800/544–2261* ⊕*www.greatalaska. com.*

ENJOYING ALASKA'S WILDLIFE

Here are a couple of facts you might learn, watching Alaska's animals: up close, bears smell like very large, very wet dogs. And try to avoid ever having a whale breathe on you; that smell makes bears seem like roses.

Yes, it is possible to get that close to Alaska's wildlife—actually, it gets that close to you. But even if it remains in the distance, the possibilities—brown bears, black bears, moose with racks of antlers six feet across, the slow rise of a humpback whale breaching into full sunshine—are Alaska's truest, greatest glory.

And it isn't just the big things. Alaska's 375 million acres support more than 800 species of mammals, birds, and fish. The 105 different mammals range from fin whales the size of yachts to shrews the size of bottle caps (Alaska's shrews are the smallest of North America's land mammals, weighing 1/10 ounce). Up in the skies are 485 species of birds, ranging from hummingbirds to bald eagles, which are so common it's hard not to see them. Migrant birds come to Alaska from every continent (clearly understanding the best place to take a vacation) to take advantage of Alaska's rich breeding and rearing grounds in its wetlands, rivers, shores, and tundra. Toss in the vagrants it's possible to hit the 500-species mark on the life list, just in the borders of Alaska.

And if that weren't enough, sharing the waters with whales, seals, sea lions, dolphins, and porpoises are at least 430 different kinds of fish—including six kinds of salmon. In late summer Alaska's rivers can seem so thick with spawning salmon that it looks like you could walk across them without getting wet—although the bears who come down to feed might object.

Both black and brown (grizzly) bears live in virtually every part of the state, and it's not all that unusual for them to walk into towns from time to time. Across the state, bear-viewing areas let visitors get up close (but not too close) and personal with the wonder that is a bear. Watching a grizzly swat a salmon out of a stream and rip it open (with winter coming on, they'll eat only the fattiest parts of the fish, leaving the rest for eagles, ravens, crows, and more) is reason enough to come to Alaska.

But bears aren't the only big things running around Alaska's forests and plains. Anchorage has a moose problem, and almost anywhere in South Central and the Interior you might come across one of these beauties. Moose look slow and ungainly, but they can run close to 30 MPH and kick both forwards and backwards. Still, they're happiest standing in a pond eating grasses. It's not at all uncommon to see moose from almost any road in the state.

ALASKA'S TOP FISH AND THEIR SOURCES

SPECIES	COMMON NAME	WHERE FOUND
Arctic Char (F, S)	Char	SC, SW, NW, I, A
Arctic Grayling (F)	Grayling	SE, SC, SW, NW, I, A
Brook Trout (F)	Brookie	SE
Burbot (F)	Lingcod	SC, I, SW, NW, A
Chinook Salmon (F, S)	King	SE, SC, SW, I
Chum Salmon (F, S)	Dog	SE, SC, SW, NW, I
Coho Salmon (F, S)	Silver	SE, SC, SW, NW, I
Cutthroat Trout (F, S)	Cutt	SE, SC
Dolly Varden (F, S)	Dolly	SE, SC, SW, NW, I, A
Lake Trout (F)	Laker	SC, SW, NW, I, A
Northern Pike (F)	Northern	SC, SW, NW, I
Pacific Halibut (S)	'But	SE, SC, SW, NW
Pink Salmon (F, S)	Humpy	SE, SC, SW, NW
Rainbow Trout (F)	'Bow	SE, SC, SW, I
Sheefish (F)	Shee, Inconnu	NW, I
Smelt (F, S)	Hooligan	SE, SC, SW, NW, I, A
Sockeye Salmon (F, S)	Red	SE, SC, SW, NW, I
Steelhead (F, S)	Steelie	SE, SC, SW

(F) = Freshwater, (S) = Saltwater, (F, S) = Freshwater and Saltwater,
A = Arctic, SC = South Central, I = Interior, SE = Southeast, NW = Northwest, SW = Southwest

Caribou can be a little harder to find, even though the state has more than 100,000 of them. The massive Porcupine herd travels in the subarctic, moving across the Arctic National Wildlife Refuge and into Vuntut National Park in Canada. Denali National Park has a good-sized caribou population as well.

The coastal mountains of the Southeast and South Central harbor mountain goats, and the mountains of the South Central, Interior, and Arctic regions are home to white Dall sheep. Wolves and lynx, though more rarely seen, live in many parts of the Southeast, South Central, Interior, and Arctic regions; if you're lucky, a wolf may dash across the road in front of you, or a smaller mammal, such as a red fox or snowshoe hare, may watch you when you're rafting or even when you're traveling on wheels.

STRATEGIES FOR SPOTTING WILDLIFE

Know what you're looking for. Season and time of day are critical. Many animals are nocturnal and best viewed during twilight, which in summer in Alaska's northern regions can last all night. In winter, large creatures such as moose and caribou can be spotted from far away, as their dark bodies stand out against the snow. It is also possible to track animals after a fresh snowfall. But the simple truth is, animals will be where they want, when they want. It's not at all unusual for travelers to have ticked off every item of the Alaskan safari—moose, black bear, grizzly bear, caribou, wolf—without ever leaving the state's roads.

Be careful. Keep a good distance, especially with animals that can be dangerous. Whether you're on foot or in a vehicle, don't get too close. A pair of good binoculars or a spotting scope is well worth the expense and extra weight. Don't get too close to or even think about trying to touch wildlife (and, if you're traveling with pets, keep them leashed— dogs get very stupid when they smell bears, and that never goes anywhere good). **Move slowly,** stop often, look, and listen. The exception is when you see a bear; let the animal know you're there by making noise. Avoid startling an animal and risking a dangerous confrontation, especially with a mama bear with cubs or a cow moose with a calf. Moose injure far more people in Alaska than bears do.

Keep your hat on if you are in territory where arctic terns, gulls, or pomarine jaegers nest, often around open alpine or tundra lakes and tarns. These species are highly protective of their nests and young and are skillful dive-bombers. Occasionally, they connect with human heads, and the results can be painful.

Be prepared to wait; patience often pays off. And if you're an enthusiastic birder or animal watcher, **be prepared to hike over some rough terrain** to reach the best viewing vantage. **Respect and protect** the animal you're watching and its habitat—you, after all, are a visitor in its territory. Don't chase or harass the animals. The willful act of harassing an animal is punishable in Alaska by a $1,000 fine. This includes flushing birds from their nests and purposely frightening animals with loud noises. The basic rule is never get closer than a hundred yards to any animal. If they want to come up to you—not uncommon at many of the bear observatories, or on whale-watching trips—that's their business. But you are to keep your distance.

Don't disturb or surprise the animals, which also applies to birds' eggs, the young, the nests, and such habitats as beaver dams. It's best to let the animal discover your presence quietly, if at all, by keeping still or moving slowly (except when viewing bears or moose). If you accidentally disturb an animal, limit your viewing time and leave as quietly as possible. Never watch a single animal for longer than a half hour, at the very most. Even if they are ignoring you, your presence is still a cause of stress, and the animals need every bit of energy they have for getting through the upcoming winter. **Don't use a tape recorder or any device** to call a bird or to attract other animals if you're in bear country, as you might call a hungry bear. And **don't feed animals,** as any creature that comes to depend on humans for food almost always comes to a sorry end. Both state and federal laws prohibit the feeding of wild animals. For campers and hikers, it's a bad idea to smell like food anyway.

The **Alaska Marine Highway,** the route plied by Alaska's state ferries, passes through waters rich with fish, sea mammals, and birds. Throughout the Southeast, a ticket on the ferry almost always comes with sightings of whales, porpoises, and sea otters. Bald eagles are about as common as sparrows back home. Other great water expeditions for animal-watching include boat trips in **Kenai Fjords National Park,** and **Glacier Bay National Park and Preserve**; both are especially good places to spot humpback whales, puffins, seals, shorebirds, and perhaps a black or brown bear, as well as the occasional orca. **Denali National Park and Preserve** is known worldwide for its wildlife; you are likely to see grizzlies, moose, Dall sheep, caribou, foxes, golden eagles, and maybe even some of the park's rare wolves. The **Alaska Chilkat Bald Eagle Preserve** hosts the world's largest gathering of bald eagles each fall and winter. And just a few miles down the highway south of Anchorage, on the fringes of **Chugach State Park**, are well-marked spots where Dall sheep like to hang out on the land side of the road, and beluga whales swim by in the waters of the inlet.

TOP REGIONS AND EXPERIENCES

BEARS You can't be absolutely sure you'll spot a grizzly bear in **Denali National Park and Preserve** (☎907/683–2294 ⊕*www.nps.gov/dena*), but chances are better than 50–50, especially in the early morning, that you'll see grizzlies digging in the tundra or eating berries. Sometimes females even nurse their cubs within sight of the park road. Denali's grizzlies are Toklats, a subspecies that's much smaller and usually more cinnamon-colored than their more famous relatives in Kodiak and other parts of Alaska. For the most recent sightings, talk with the staff at the visitor center near the park entrance when you arrive, and the bus drivers who will take you into the park are seriously skilled at spotting wildlife.

Katmai National Park (☎907/246–3305 ⊕*www.nps.gov/katm*), on the Alaska Peninsula, has an abundance of bears, on average more than one brown bear per square mile, among the highest densities of any region in North America. In July, when the salmon are running up Brooks River, bears concentrate around Brooks River falls, resulting in a great view of these animals as they fish, and the spectacle of hundreds of salmon leaping the falls. Many operators in Homer and Anchorage run day-trips to the edges of Katmai, where you can fly in, watch bears for a few hours, and return to your hotel in time for dinner. It's not cheap, but is unforgettable.

Kodiak National Wildlife Refuge (☎907/487–2600 or 888/408–3514 ⊕*kodiak.fws.gov*), on Kodiak Island, is an excellent place to see brown bears, particularly along salmon-spawning streams.

The **McNeil River State Game Sanctuary,** on the Alaska Peninsula, hosts the world's largest gathering of brown bears. As many as 70 have been counted at one time at McNeil Falls, affording unsurpassed photographic opportunities. Peak season, when the local salmon are running, is early June through mid-August. Much-sought-after reservations are by a lottery conducted in March by the **Alaska Department of Fish and Game** (☎907/267–2182 ⊕*www.wildlife.alaska.gov*).

At **Pack Creek**, on Admiralty Island in Southeast, brown bears fish for spawning salmon—pink, chum, and silver. To get here, you can fly by air charter or take a boat from Juneau. If you time your visit to coincide with the salmon runs in July and August, you will almost surely see bald eagles. Permits are required to visit during the peak

Wilderness Safety Tips

PREPARATION

You need to be in good physical shape to venture into the backcountry. Avoid traveling alone. If your outdoor experience is limited, travel with a guide. Bring a tide book when traveling by boat along the coast. If backpacking, know in advance whether you'll have to cross large glacial rivers.

MAPS

Use maps (preferably 1 inch: 1 mi maps published by the U.S. Geological Survey) and a compass at the minimum. Other options for emergency use are electronic locator devices, global positioning systems, and hand-held aviation radios. Know how to use all your navigation equipment before you leave home.

WEATHER

Always be prepared for storms and wintry conditions and for unexpected delays. One of the most common phrases used by Alaska's pilots is "weather permitting." Never "push" the weather; every year people die in aviation, boating, and overland accidents trying get home despite dangerously stormy conditions.

STAY FOUND

Leave a detailed itinerary and list of emergency contacts with family and park rangers. Be specific about your destination and return date. Do not expect to be able to make a cell-phone call for help—most of Alaska's wilderness is cell-free. If you do get lost, those you've notified in town will know when and where to start looking. It's also smart to carry a whistle.

HYPOTHERMIA

Hypothermia, the lowering of the body's core temperature, is an ever-present threat in Alaska's wilderness.

Wear layers of warm clothing when the weather is cool and/or wet; this includes a good wind- and water-proof parka or shell, warm head- and hand gear, and waterproof or water-resistant boots. Heed the advice of locals who will tell you, "cotton kills." It does nothing to move moisture away from your skin, and can speed the onset of hypothermia. Any time you're in the wilderness, eat regularly to maintain energy, and stay hydrated.

Early symptoms of hypothermia are shivering, accelerated heartbeat, and goose bumps; this may be followed by clumsiness, slurred speech, disorientation, and unconsciousness. In the extreme, hypothermia can result in death. If you notice any of these symptoms in yourself or your group, stop, add layers of clothing, light a fire or camp stove, and warm up; a cup of tea or any hot fluid also helps. Avoid alcohol, which speeds hypothermia and impairs judgment. If your clothes are wet, change immediately. Be sure to put on a warm hat (most of the body's heat is lost through the head) and gloves. If there are only two of you, stay together: a person with hypothermia should never be left alone. Keep an eye on your traveling companions; frequently people won't recognize the symptoms in themselves until it's too late.

WATER SAFETY

Alaska's waters often carry *Giardia*, locally called beaver fever, a parasite that can cause diarrhea and sap your strength. In the backcountry, boil water, treat it with iodine tablets, or use a filter (available at camping stores).

bear-viewing period; contact **Admiralty Island National Monument** (☎*907/586–8800* ⊕*www.fs.fed.us/r10/tongass/districts/admiralty/ packcreek/index.shtml*).

In Southeast, near the town of Wrangell, **Anan Bear Reserve** is at one of the few streams where black and brown bears share the waters, fishing at the same time (although the black bears usually hide when the browns show up). More than a quarter-million salmon run Anan in July and August, making it a feast for as many as a hundred bears that fish the stream at different times during high season. Book trips through permitted outfitters in Wrangell. ⊕*www.fs.fed.us/r10/ro/naturewatch/ southeast/anan/anan.htm*.

The **Silver Salmon Creek Lodge** (☎*888/872–5666* ⊕*www.silversalmoncreek.com*) conducts a bear-viewing program along the shores of western Cook Inlet, near Lake Clark National Park, with lodging, meals, and guide services for both bear-viewing and sportfishing. There are also photo tours.

BIRDS   If you come on your own, try the following sure and easily accessed bets for bird spotting. In **Anchorage,** walk around Potter Marsh or Westchester Lagoon or along the Tony Knowles Coastal Trail and keep your eye out for shorebirds, waterfowl, and the occasional bald eagle. Songbird enthusiasts are likely to see many species in town or neighboring Chugach State Park. The **Anchorage Audubon Society** (☎*907/338– 2473* ⊕*www.anchorageaudubon.org*) has a bird-report recording and offers various trips, such as the Owl Prowl and Hawk Watch.

In **Juneau,** visit the Mendenhall Wetlands State Game Refuge, next to the airport, for ducks, geese, and swans. There are trails and interpretive signs. In **Fairbanks,** head for the Creamer's Field Migratory Waterfowl Refuge on College Road. In summer the field is so full of sandhill cranes, ducks, and geese that almost no one can take off or land without bumping into other birds. The woods behind the main field are full of songbirds and smaller species.

Homer, at the end of the Kenai Peninsula, has an annual shorebird festival (⊕*www.homeralaska.org/events/kachemakBayShorebirdFestival/ index.htm*) and maintains one of the state's most active birding groups. Those interested in feathers should check the Birder's Guide to Kachemak Bay Web site (⊕*www.birdinghomeralaska.org*) to get an idea of what Kenai offers. On the eastern side of the peninsula, boat trips into Resurrection Bay are a great chance to see puffins, as well as murres, murrelets, and more.

As for the national bird, more bald eagles gather on the Chilkat River, near **Haines** in Southeast Alaska, each November and December than live in the continental United States. In summer, rafting on almost any Alaska river brings the near certainty of sighting nesting shorebirds, arctic terns, and merganser mothers trailed by chicks. Approximately 200 species of birds have been sighted on the **Pribilof Islands,** but you will almost certainly need to be part of a guided tour to get there. The Aleutians—particularly Dutch Harbor—are also spots for adding to the life list, since many vagrants appear.

The folks at **Alaska Birding & Wildlife** (☎*877/424–5637* ⊕*www.alaska-birding.com*) can take you to St. Paul Island in the Pribilofs to see the huge range of birds and get to know local Aleut culture and customs.

Alaska Discovery (☎*800/586–1911* ⊕*www.akdiscovery.com*) offers trips to Pack Creek, including a floatplane trip, sea kayaking, and bear viewing.

With **Mariah Tours** (☎*877/777–2805* ⊕*www.alaskaheritagetours.com*), the Kenai Fjords National Park comes to life on tailor-made birding and photography boat tours, as well as on daily tours that take in the best of the park: whale-watching, glacier-viewing, and more. This is one of the best-run trips in the Fjords, and is part of Alaska Heritage Tours, which also runs a beautiful lodge in Seward.

The Web site of the **University of Alaska Fairbanks** (⊕*www.uaf.edu/museum/bird/products/checklist.pdf*) has a checklist of Alaska's 485 bird species.

★ The owners of **Wilderness Birding Adventures** (☎*907/694–7442* ⊕*www.wildernessbirding.com*) are both experienced river runners and expert birders. Among their trips is a rafting, hiking, and birding expedition through one of the world's last great wilderness areas, the Arctic National Wildlife Refuge.

CARIBOU The migrations of caribou across Alaska's Arctic regions are wonderful to watch, but they are not always easy to time because of annual variations in weather and routes that the herds follow. The U.S. Fish and Wildlife Service and Alaska Department of Fish and Game will have the best guess as to where you should be and when, but the migrations move through very remote parts of the state that are difficult and expensive to get to. For caribou on a budget, Denali National Park and Preserve is the place to go.

MARINE Keep in mind that many of the tours listed as whale-watching—for
ANIMALS example, anything in Kenai Fjords—are also likely to turn up porpoises, dolphins, seals, sea lions, and more. But if you're after something specific, here are a few places to consider.

⇨ *Skip ahead to the next section in this chapter for in-depth information about whale-watching cruises. For more on whales, go to Keepers of the Deep.*

At **Round Island,** outside Dillingham in the Southwest, bull walruses by the thousands haul out in summer. Part of the Walrus Islands State Game Sanctuary, Round Island can be visited by permit only. For details, contact the **Alaska Department of Fish and Game** (☎*907/842–2334* ⊕*www.wildlife.alaska.gov/index.cfm?adfg=refuge.rnd_is*). Access is by floatplane or, more commonly, by boat. Expect rain, winds, and the possibility of being weathered in. Rubber boots are essential, as are a four-season tent, high-quality rain gear, and plenty of food.

It's easier, but expensive (more than $1,000 for travel and tour), to visit the remote **Pribilof Islands,** where about 80% of the world's northern fur seals and 200 species of birds can be seen, but you may also encounter fog and Bering Sea storms. Tours to the Pribilofs leave from Anchorage. Contact the **Alaska Maritime National Wildlife Refuge**

(☎907/235–6546 ⊕*www.r7.fws.gov/nwr/akmar/index.htm*) for information about wildlife viewing.

WHALE-WATCHING CRUISES

Whales migrate along much of Alaska's coast from March through September: from the Southeast region's Inside Passage to South Central's Prince William Sound, Kodiak Archipelago, and Kenai Fjords National Park, and then north through the Bering, Chukchi, and Beaufort seas in Arctic waters. Whale-watching is not the average spectator sport. It's more like a seagoing game of hide-and-seek. For this reason, even if you're coming to Alaska for a "regular" cruise, you may want to consider a whale-watching trip on your own before or after your cruise if there's no opportunity to get onto an excursion during your cruise with a smaller (under 200 people) whale-watching vessel.

Whales are unpredictable, so be prepared to wait patiently, scanning the water for signs. Sometimes the whales can seem elusive; other times they might rub up against the boat. Also unpredictable are the weather and sea conditions. Bring along a jacket or fleece outerwear and rain gear to keep from getting wet and chilled, and consider using Dramamine or scopolamine patches if you're prone to seasickness.

Most cruises travel in or through waters that attract several species, although some focus on a particular type of whale. You have to weigh the pros and cons of traveling on small versus large boats. A trip with 15 people will be quite different from one with 150. Larger boats can handle stormy seas much better than smaller boats and offer much better indoor accommodations when the weather turns nasty. Smaller boats will appeal to those who want to steer clear of crowds and those who like to feel closer to the surrounding seascape. More flexible itineraries are another benefit of small boats.

RESOURCES AND GUIDES

Hop aboard the **Alaska Marine Highway** (☎800/642–0066 ⊕ *www. ferryalaska.com*) and enjoy one of Alaska's greatest means of travel: its ferry system plies the waters of the Inside Passage and South Central all the way to the far reaches of the southwestern chain.

Fodor'sChoice Part of the native-owned Alaska Heritage Tours, **Kenai Fjords Tours**
★ (☎907/265–4501 or 877/777–2805 ⊕*www.kenaifjords.com*) will take you to explore Resurrection Bay and Kenai Fjords National Park. Trips range from three-hour natural-history tours to five-hour gray whale–watching tours out of Seward.

Mariah Tours (☎907/265–4501 or 877/777–2805 ⊕*www.alaskaheritagetours.com*), also part of Alaska Heritage Tours, offers small-boat trips out of Seward for summertime whale-watching and glacier tours in Kenai Fjords National Park. Besides orcas and humpback whales, you're likely to see bald eagles, sea otters, sea lions, seals, and birds.

Icy Strait Point (⊕*www.icystraitpoint.com*) runs tours that ply the strait of the same name. The ship runs from a converted cannery next to the small town of Hoonah. The town's proximity to Point Adolphus—a favorite whale spot—means that trips from here maximize whale-watching time by cutting out extra travel time. There are daily trips into the strait, and the company also offers bear-watching trips on Admiralty Island, home to Southeast's densest concentration of bears.

Juneau-based **Orca Enterprises (with Captain Larry)** (☎ *907/789–6801 or 888/733–6722* ⊕ *www.orcaenterprises.com*) offers whale-watching tours via jet boats designed for comfort and speed. The operator, one of the best and most knowledgeable in Alaska, boasts a whale-sighting success rate of 99.9% between May 1 and October 15. Humpbacks and orcas are most frequently seen.

Sailing out of Whittier into Prince William Sound since 1989, **Sound Eco Adventures** (☎ *888/471–2312* ⊕ *www.soundecoadventure.com*) takes only six guests at a time aboard 30-foot boats. It's a convenient hour-long drive south of Anchorage; expect to see everything from harbor seals to humpbacks.

KEEPERS OF THE DEEP:
A LOOK AT ALASKA'S WHALES

It's unforgettable: a massive, barnacle-encrusted humpback breaches skyward from the placid waters of an Alaskan inlet, shattering the silence with a thundering display of grace, power, and beauty. Welcome to Alaska's coastline.

Alaska's cold, nutrient-rich waters offer a bounty of marine life that's matched by few regions on earth. Eight species of whales frequent the state's near-shore waters, some migrating thousands of miles each year to partake of Alaska's marine buffet. The state's most famous cetaceans (the scientific classification of marine mammals that includes whales, dolphins, and porpoises) are the humpback whale, the gray whale, and the Orca (a.k.a. the killer whale).

(top) A breaching humpback (left) An Orca whale

BEST REGIONS TO VIEW WHALES

Whales can be viewed throughout the world; after all, they are migratory animals. But thanks to its pristine environment, diversity of cetacean species, and jaw-dropping beauty, Alaska is perhaps the planet's best whale-watching locale.

From April through October, humpbacks visit many of Alaska's coastal regions, including the Bering Sea, the Aleutian Islands, and Prince William Sound. The **Inside Passage,** though, is the best place to see them: it's home to a migratory population of up to 600 humpbacks. Good bets for whale-viewing include taking a trip on the **Alaska Marine Highway,** spending time in **Glacier Bay National Park,** or taking a day cruise out of any of Southeast's main towns. While most humpbacks return to

Mutually curious!

Hawaiian waters in the winter, some spend the whole year in Southeast Alaska.

Gray whales favor the coastal waters of the Pacific, which terminate in the Bering Sea. Their healthy population—some studies estimate that 30,000 gray whales populate the west coast of North America—make

THE HUMPBACK: Musical, Breaching Giant

Humpbacks' flukes allow them to breach so effectively that they can propel two-thirds of their massive bodies out of the water.

Known for their spectacular breaching and unique whale songs, humpbacks are captivating. Most spend their winters in the balmy waters off the Hawaiian Islands, where females, or sows, give birth. Come springtime, humpbacks set off on a 3,000-mile swim to their Alaskan feeding grounds.

Southeast Alaska is home to one of the world's only groups of bubble-net feeding humpbacks. Bubble-netting is a cooperative hunting technique in which one humpback circles below a school of baitfish while exhaling a "net" of bubbles, causing the fish to gather. Other humpbacks then feed at will from the deliciously dense group of fish.

The Song of the Humpback
All whale species communicate sonically, but the humpback is the most musical. During mating season, males emit haunting, songlike calls that can last for up to 30 minutes at a time. Most scientists attribute the songs to flirtatious, territorial, or competitive behaviors.

QUICK FACTS:

Scientific name: *Megaptera novaeangliae*

Length: Up to 50 ft.

Weight: Up to 90,000 pounds (45 tons)

Coloring: Dark blue to black, with barnacles and knobby, lighter-colored flippers

Life span: 30 to 40 years

Reproduction: One calf every 2 to 3 years; calves are generally 12 feet long at birth, weighing up to 2,000 pounds (1 ton)

them relatively easy to spot in the spring and early summer months, especially around **Sitka** and **Kodiak Island** and south of the **Kenai Peninsula,** where numerous whale-watching cruises depart from Seward into **Resurrection Bay.**

Orcas populate nearly all of Alaska's coastal regions. They're most commonly viewed in the **Inside Passage** and **Prince William Sound,** where they reside year-round. A jaunt on the Alaska Marine Highway is one option, but so is a kayaking or day-cruising trip out of **Whittier** to Prince William Sound.

When embarking on a whale-watching excursion, don't forget rain gear, a camera, and binoculars!

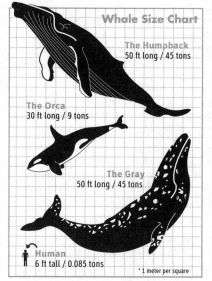

Whale Size Chart

The Humpback
50 ft long / 45 tons

The Orca
30 ft long / 9 tons

The Gray
50 ft long / 45 tons

Human
6 ft tall / 0.085 tons

* 1 meter per square

THE GRAY WHALE: Migrating Leviathan

Though the average lifespan of a gray whale is 50 years, one individual was reported to reach 77 years of age—a real old-timer.

While frequenting Alaska during the long days of summer, gray whales tend stay close to the coastline. They endure the longest migration of any mammal on earth—some travel 14,000 mi each way between Alaska's Bering Sea and their mating grounds in sunny Baja California.

Gray whales are bottom-feeders that stir up sediment on sea floor, then use their baleen—a comblike collection of long, stiff hairs inside their mouths—to filter out sediment and trap small crustaceans and tube worms.

Their predilection for near-shore regions, coupled with their easygoing demeanor—some "friendly" gray whales have even been known to approach small tour boats—cements their spot on the short list of Alaska's favorite cetacean celebrities. (Gray whales aren't always in such amicable spirits: whalers dubbed mother gray whales "devilfish" for the fierce manner in which they protected their young.)

QUICK FACTS:

Scientific name:
Eschrichtius robustus

Length: Up to 50 ft.

Weight: Up to 90,000 pounds (45 tons)

Coloring: Gray and white, usually splotched with lighter growths and barnacles

Life span: 50 years

Reproduction: One calf every 2 years; calves are generally 15 feet long at birth, weighing up to 1,500 pounds (3/4 ton)

AN AGE-OLD CONNECTION

Nearly every major native group in Alaska has relied on whales for some portion of its diet. The Inupiaq and Yup'ik counted on whales for blubber, oil, meat, and intestines to survive. Aleuts used whale bones to build their semisubterranean homes. Even the Tlingit, for whom food was perennially abundant, considered a beached whale a bounty.

Subsistence whaling lives on in Alaska: although gray-whale hunting was banned in 1996, the Eskimo Whaling Commission permits the state's native populations to harvest 50 bowhead whales every year.

Other Alaskan whale species:
Bowhead, northern right, minke, fin, and beluga whales also inhabit Alaskan waters.

barnacles

BARNACLES These ragged squatters of the sea live on several species of whales, including humpbacks and gray whales. They're conspicuously absent from smaller marine mammals, such as Orcas, dolphins, and porpoises. The reason? Speed. Scientists theorize that barnacles are only able to colonize the slowest-swimming cetacean species, leaving the faster swimmers free from their unwanted drag.

THE ORCA: Conspicuous, Curious Cetacean

Why the name killer whale? Perhaps for this animal's skilled and fearsome hunting techniques, which are sometimes used on other, often larger, cetaceans.

Perhaps the most recognizable of all the region's marine mammals, Orcas (also called killer whales) are playful, inquisitive, and intelligent whales that reside in Alaskan waters year-round. Orcas travel in multigenerational family groups known as pods, which practice cooperative hunting techniques.

Orcas are smaller than grays and humpbacks, and their 17-month gestation period is the longest of any cetacean. They are identified by their white-and-black markings, as well as by the knifelike shape of their dorsal fins, which, in the case of mature males, can reach 6 feet in height.

Pods generally adhere to one of three common classifications: **residents,** which occupy inshore waters and feed primarily on fish; **transients,** which occupy larger ranges and hunt sea lions, squid, sharks, fish, and whales; and **offshores,** about which little is known.

QUICK FACTS:

Scientific name: *Orcinus orca*

Length: Up to 30 ft.

Weight: Up to 18,000 pounds (9 tons)

Coloring: Smooth, shiny black skin with white eye patches and chin and white belly markings

Life span: 30 to 50 years

Reproduction: One calf every 3 to 5 years; calves are generally 6 feet long at birth, weighing up to 400 pounds (0.2 ton)

UNDERSTANDING ALASKA

Flora and Fauna of Alaska

FLORA AND FAUNA OF ALASKA

FAUNA

Arctic Ground Squirrel (C) (*Spermophilus parryii*): These yellowish-brown, gray-flecked rodents are among Alaska's most common and widespread mammals. Ground squirrels are known for their loud, persistent chatter. They may often be seen standing above their tundra den sites, watching for grizzlies, golden eagles, and weasels.

Arctic Tern (F) (*Sterna paradisaea*): These are the world's long-distance flying champs; some members of their species make annual migratory flights between the high Arctic and the Antarctic. Sleekly beautiful, the bird has a black cap and striking blood-red bill and feet. They often can be seen looking for small fish in ponds and coastal marshes.

Bald Eagle (A) (*Haliaeetus leucocephalus*): With a wingspan of 6 to 8 feet, these grand Alaska residents are primarily fish eaters, but they will also take birds or small mammals when the opportunity presents itself. The world's largest gathering of bald eagles occurs in Southeast Alaska each winter, along the Chilkat River near Haines.

Beluga Whale (B) (*Dephinapterus leucas*): Belugas are gray at birth, bluish gray as adolescents, and white as adults (*bye-lukha* is derived from the Russian word for "white"). Though they seem to favor fish, the belugas' diet includes more than 100 different species, from crabs to squid. They live along much of the coast, from the Beaufort Sea to the Gulf of Alaska.

Black-capped Chickadee (D) (*Parus atricapillus*): This songbird is one of Alaska's most common residents. As with two close relatives, the chestnut-backed and boreal chickadees, the black-cap gets through the winters by lowering its body temperature at night and shivering through the long hours of darkness.

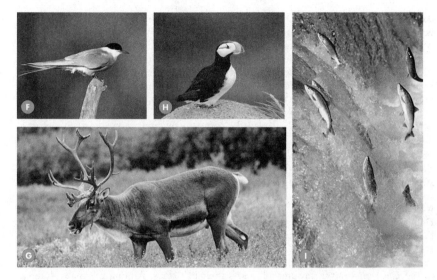

Caribou (G) (*Rangifer tarandus*): Sometimes called the "nomads of the north," caribou are long-distance wandering mammals. They are also the most abundant of the state's large mammals; in fact, there are more caribou in Alaska than people! The Western Arctic Caribou Herd numbers more than 400,000, while the Porcupine Caribou Herd has ranged between 120,000 and 180,000 over the past decades. Another bit of caribou trivia: they are the only members of the deer family in which both sexes grow antlers. Those of bulls may grow up to 5½ feet long with a span of up to 3 feet.

Common Loon (E) (*Gavia immer*): Some sounds seem to be the essence of wilderness: the howl of the wolf, the hooting of the owl, and the cry of the loon. The common loon is one of five *Gavia* species to inhabit Alaska (the others are the Arctic, Pacific, red-throated, and yellow-billed). Common loons are primarily fish eaters.

Excellent swimmers, they are able to stay submerged for up to three minutes.

Common Raven (*Corvus corax*): A popular character in Alaska native stories, the raven in indigenous culture is both creator and trickster. Entirely black, with a wedge-shaped tail and a heavy bill that helps distinguish it from crows, the raven is Alaska's most widespread avian resident.

Common Redpoll (*Carduelis flammea*): Even tinier than the chickadee, the common redpoll and its close cousin, the hoary redpoll (*Carduelis hornemanni*), are among the few birds to inhabit Alaska's Interior year-round. Though it looks a bit like a sparrow, this red-capped, black-bibbed songbird is a member of the finch family.

Dall Sheep (*Ovis dalli dalli*): One of four wild sheep to inhabit North America, the white Dall is the only one to reside within Alaska. Residents of high alpine areas, the sheep live in mountain chains from the St. Elias Range to the Brooks Range. Though both sexes grow horns, those of females are short spikes, while males grow grand curls that are "status symbols" displayed during mating season.

Dolly Varden (*Salvelinus malma*): This sleek, flashy fish inhabits lakes and streams throughout Alaska's coastal regions. A member of the char family, it was named after a character in Charles Dickens's novel *Barnaby Rudge,* because the brightly colored spots on its sides resemble Miss Dolly Varden's pink-spotted dress and hat. Some members of the species remain in freshwater all their life, while sea-run dollies may live in the ocean for two to five years before returning to spawn.

Golden Eagle (*Aquila chrysaetos*): With a wingspan of up to 7½ feet, this inland bird can often be spotted spiraling high in the sky, riding thermals. The bird usually nests on cliff faces and feeds upon small mammals and ptarmigan. The plumage of adult birds is entirely dark, except for a golden head. These migratory eagles spend their winters as far away as Kansas and New Mexico.

Great Horned Owl (*Bubo virginianus*): The best-known of Alaska's several species of owls, and one whose call is a familiar one here. It is a large owl with prominent ear tufts and a white throat with barred markings. Residing in forests from Southeast Alaska to the Interior, it preys on squirrels, hares, grouse, and other birds.

Harbor Seal (*Phoca vitulina*): Inhabiting shallow marine waters and estuaries along much of Alaska's southern coast, harbor seals may survive up to 30 years in the wild, on a diet of fish, squid, octopus, and shrimp. They, in turn, may be eaten or killed by orcas, sea lions, or humans. Solitary in the water, harbor seals love company on land, and will gather in large colonies. They weigh up to 250 pounds and range in color from black to white.

Hermit Thrush (*Catharus guttatus*): Some Alaskans argue that there is no northern song more beautiful than the flutelike warbling of the hermit thrush and its close relative, the Swainson's thrush (*Catharus ustulatus*). The two birds are difficult to tell apart, except for their songs, the hermit's reddish brown tail, and the color of their eye rings. Among the many songbird migrants to visit Alaska each spring, they begin singing in May while seeking mates and defending territories in forested regions of southern and central Alaska.

Horned Puffin (H) (*Fratercula corniculata*): Named for the black, fleshy projections above each eye, horned puffins are favorites among birders. Included in the group of diving seabirds known as alcids, puffins spend most of their life on water, coming to land only for nesting. They are expert swimmers, using their wings to "fly" underwater and their webbed feet as rudders. Horned puffins have large orange-red and yellow bills. A close relative, the tufted puffin (*Fratercula cirrhata*), is named for its yellow ear tufts.

Lynx (*Lynx canadensis*): The lynx is the only wild cat to inhabit Alaska. It's a secretive animal that depends on stealth and quickness. It may kill birds, squirrels, and mice, but the cat's primary

prey is the snowshoe hare (*Lepus americanus*), particularly in winter; its population numbers closely follow those of the hare's boom-bust cycles. Large feet and a light body help the lynx run through deep snowpack.

Moose (*Alces alces gigas*): The moose is the largest member of the deer family, the largest bulls standing 7 feet tall at the shoulders and weighing up to 1,600 pounds. The peak of breeding occurs in late September. Females give birth to calves in late May and early June; twins are the norm. Bulls enter the rut in September, the most dominant engaging in brutal fights. Though most commonly residents of woodlands, some moose live in or just outside Alaska's cities.

Mountain Goat (*Oreamnos americanus*): Sometimes confused with Dall sheep, mountain goats inhabit Alaska's coastal mountains. As adults, both males and females have sharp-pointed horns that are short and black (sheep have buff-colored horns). They also have massive chests and comparatively small hindquarters, plus bearded chins.

Musk Ox (*Ovibos moschatus*): The musk ox is considered an Ice Age relic that survived into the present at least partly because of a defensive tactic: they stand side by side and form rings to fend off predators such as grizzlies and wolves. Unfortunately for the species, that tactic didn't work very well against humans armed with guns. Alaska's last native musk oxen were killed in 1865. Musk oxen from Greenland were reintroduced here in 1930; they now reside on Nunivak Island, the North Slope of the Brooks Range, and in the Interior. The animal's most notable physical feature is its long guard hairs, which form "skirts"

that nearly reach the ground. Inupiats called the musk ox *oomingmak,* meaning "bearded one." Beneath those coarser hairs is fine underfur called qiviut, which can be woven into warm clothing.

Pacific Halibut (*Hippoglossus stenolepis*): The halibut is the largest of the flatfish to inhabit Alaska's coastal waters, with females weighing up to 500 pounds. Long-lived "grandmother" halibut may survive 40 years or more, producing millions of eggs each year. Bottom dwellers that feed on fish, crabs, clams, and squid, they range from the Panhandle to Norton Sound. Young halibut generally stay near shore, but older fish have been found at depths of 3,600 feet.

Pacific Salmon (*Oncorhynchus*): Five species of Pacific salmon spawn in Alaska's waters, including the king, silver, sockeye, pink, and chum. Hundreds of millions of salmon return to the state's streams and lakes each summer and fall, after spending much of their lives in saltwater. They form the backbone of Alaska's fishing industry and draw sportfishers from around the world.

Rainbow Trout (*Salmo gairdneri*): A favorite of anglers, the rainbow trout inhabits streams and lakes in Alaska's coastal regions. The Bristol Bay region is best known for large 'bows, perhaps because of its huge returns of salmon. Rainbows feed heavily on salmon eggs as well as the deteriorating flesh of spawned-out salmon. Sea-run rainbows, or steelhead, grow even larger after years spent feeding in ocean waters. The state record for steelhead/rainbow trout is 42 pounds, 3 ounces.

FLORA AND FAUNA OF ALASKA

Red Fox (*Vulpes vulpes*): Though it's called the red fox, this species actually has four color phases: red, silver, black, and cross (with a cross pattern on the back and shoulders). An able hunter, the red fox preys primarily on voles and mice, but will also eat hares, squirrels, birds, insects, and berries.

Sandhill Crane (*Grus canadensis*): The sandhill's call has been described as "something between a French horn and a squeaky barn door." Though others may dispute that description, few would disagree that the crane's calls have a prehistoric sound. And, in fact, scientists say the species has changed little in the 9 million years since its earliest recorded fossils. Sandhills are the tallest birds to inhabit Alaska; their wingspan reaches up to 7 feet. The gray plumage of adults is set off by a bright red crown. Like geese, they fly in Vs during migratory journeys.

Sea Otter (K) (*Enhydra lutris*): Sea otters don't depend on blubber to stay warm. Instead, hair trapped in their dense fur keeps their skin dry. Beneath their outer hairs, the underfur ranges in density from 170,000 to one million hairs per square inch. Not surprisingly, the otter takes good care of its coat, spending much of every day grooming. Otters also spend a lot of time eating. In one study, researchers found that adult otters consumed 14 crabs a day, equaling about one-fourth of their body weight.

Sitka Blacktailed Deer (*Odocoileus hemionus sitkensis*): The Panhandle's rain forest is the primary home of this deer, though it has been transplanted to Prince William Sound and Kodiak. Dark gray in winter and reddish brown in summer, it's stockier than the whitetails found in the Lower 48. The deer stay at lower elevations during the snowy months of winter, then move up to alpine meadows in summer.

Snowy Owl (L) (*Nyctea scandiaca*): Inhabiting the open coastal tundra, the snowy owl is found from the western Aleutian Islands to the Arctic. Adults are largely white (though females have scattered light brown spots) though immature birds are heavily marked with brown. Their numbers rise and fall with swings in the population of lemmings, their primary prey. Rather than hoots, the snowy emits loud croaks and whistles.

Steller's Sea Lion (Q) (*Eumetopias jubatus*): Its ability—and tendency—to roar is what gives the sea lion its name. Because they can rotate their rear flippers and lift their bellies off the ground, sea lions can get around on land much more easily than seals can. They are also much larger, the males reaching up to 9 feet and weighing up to 1,500 pounds. They feed primarily on fish, but will also eat sea otters and seals. They have been designated an endangered species because their populations north of the Panhandle have suffered huge declines.

Walrus (P) (*Odobenus rosmarus*): The walrus's ivory tusks can be dangerous weapons; there are stories of walruses killing polar bears when attacked. Weighing up to 2 tons, the walrus feeds mainly on clams, mussels, snails, crabs, and shrimp.

Willow Ptarmigan (O) (*Lagopus lagopus*): One of three species of ptarmigan (the others are the rock and the white-tailed), the willow is the most widespread. It is also Alaska's state bird. It tends to live in willow thickets, where it feeds and hides from predators. Aggressively protective parents, willow ptarmigan have been known to attack humans to defend their young.

Wolf (*Canis lupus*): The largest and most majestic of the Far North's wild canines, wolves roam throughout all of mainland Alaska. They form close-knit family packs, which may range from a few animals to more than 30. Packs hunt a variety of prey, from small mammals and birds to caribou, moose, and Dall sheep. They communicate with each other through body language, barks, and howls.

Wolverine (*Gulo gulo*): Consider yourself lucky if you see a wolverine, because they are among the most secretive animals of the north. They are also fierce predators, with enormous strength and endurance. Denali biologists once reported seeing a wolverine drag a Dall sheep carcass more than 2 mi; an impressive feat, since the sheep likely weighed four times what the wolverine did. They have been known to run 40 MPH through snow when chased by hunters. Though they look a lot like bears and have the ferocity of a grizzly, wolverines are in fact the largest members of the weasel family.

Wood Frog (*Rana sylvatica*): One of the few amphibians to inhabit Alaska, and the only one to live north of the Panhandle, these frogs range as far north as the Arctic, surviving winters through the help of a biochemical change that keeps them in a suspended state while frozen. Come spring, the bodies revive after thawing. Though they mate and lay eggs in water, wood frogs spend most of their lives on land.

FLORA

Balsam Poplar and Black Cottonwood (*Populus balsamifera* and *Populus trichocarpa*): These two closely related species sometimes interbreed and are difficult, if not impossible, to tell apart. Mature trees of both species have gray bark that is rough and deeply furrowed. In midsummer they produce cottony seedpods. They also have large, shiny, arrowhead-shaped leaves.

Birch (*Betula*): Ranging from Kodiak Island to the Brooks Range, birch trees are important members of Alaska's boreal forests. Deciduous trees that prefer well-drained soils, they have white bark and green heart-to-diamond-shaped leaves with sharp points and toothed edges. One species, the paper birch (*Betula papyrifera*), is easily distinguished by its peeling, paperlike bark.

Blueberry (J) (*Vaccinium*): A favorite of berry pickers, blueberries are found throughout Alaska, except for the farthest northern reaches of the Arctic. They come in a variety of forms, including head-high forest bushes and sprawling tundra mats. Pink, bell-shaped flowers bloom in spring, and dark blue to almost black fruits begin to ripen in July or August, depending on the locale.

Cow Parsnip (R) (*Heracleum lanatum*): Also known to some as Indian celery, cow parsnip resides in open forests and meadows. The plant may grow several feet high, with dull green leaves the size of dinner plates; thick, hairy, hollow stalks; and clusters of white flowers. Anyone who harvests—or walks among—this species must take great care. Oils on the stalks, in combination with sunlight, can produce severe skin blistering.

Devil's Club (N) (*Echinopanax horridum*): This is a prickly shrub that may grow 4 to 8 feet high and forms dense, spiny thickets in forests ranging from the Panhandle to South Central. Hikers need to be wary of this plant: its large, maple-like leaves (which can be a foot or more across) have spines, and needles cover its pale brown trunk. In late summer, black bears enjoy its bright red berries.

Salmonberry (M) (*Rubus spectabilis*): The salmonberry canes, on which the leaves and fruits grow, may reach 7 feet tall; they grow in dense thickets. The juicy raspberry-like fruits may be either orange or red at maturity; the time of ripening is late June through August.

Spruce (*Picea*): Three species of spruce grow in Alaska. Sitka spruce (*Picea sitchensis*) is an important member of coastal rain-forest communities; white spruce (*Picea glauca*) prefers dry, well-drained soils in boreal forests that stretch from South Central to the Arctic; black spruce (*Picea mariana*) thrives in wet, boggy areas.

Tall Fireweed (*Epilobium angustifolium*): The fireweed is among the first plants to reinhabit burn areas and, in the proper conditions, it grows well. Found throughout much of Alaska, it's a beautiful plant, with fuchsia flowers that bloom from the bottom to the top of stalks; it's said that the final opening of flowers is a sign that winter is only weeks away. Spring fireweed shoots can be eaten raw or steamed, and its blossoms can be added to salads. A related species is dwarf fireweed (*Epilobium latifolium*); also known as "river beauty," it is shorter and bushier.

Wild Prickly Rose (S) (*Rosa acicularis*): Serrated leaves grow on prickly spines, and fragrant five-petal flowers begin blooming in late spring. The flowers vary from light pink to dark red. Appearing in late summer and fall, bright red rose hips rich in vitamin C can be harvested for jellies, soups, or pie.

Willow (*Salix*): An estimated three dozen species of willow grow in Alaska. Some, like the felt-leaf willow (*Salix alaxensis*), may reach tree size; others form thickets; still others, like the Arctic willow (*Salix arctica*), hug the ground in alpine terrain. They often grow thickest in the subalpine zone between forest and tundra. Whatever the size, willows produce soft "catkins" (pussy willows), which are actually columns of densely packed flowers without petals.

—By Bill Sherwonit

INDEX

PHOTO CREDITS

NOTES

NOTES

NOTES

ABOUT OUR WRITERS

Jessica Bowman is an Anchorage writer who tackles a multitude of projects including blogging about beer, wine, and parties. Writing about wildlife, travel, and recreation is a pleasure only enjoyed in her spare time. She has an M.A. in writing from Middlesex University in London, UK. Jessica updated cruise-specific information for ports in South Central and the Bush.

Freelance writer Sue Kernaghan has written about British Columbia for dozens of publications throughout North America and the United Kingdom. A fourth-generation British Columbian, she has contributed to several editions of *Fodor's Vancouver and Victoria* as well as to *Fodor's Alaska, Great Canadian Vacations, Healthy Escapes,* and *Escape to Nature Without Roughing It.* Sue, who lives on Salt Spring Island, updated our coverage of Vancouver, Prince Rupert, and Victoria.

Linda Coffman, our resident Cruise Diva, updated Chapter 1, Choosing Your Cruise. She is a freelance travel writer who has been dishing out cruise-travel advice and information for more than a decade. Her articles have appeared online and in national magazines and newspapers, including *Porthole, Consumer's Digest,* the *Chicago Sun-Times,* and *USA Today.* An avid cruiser, she spends most of her time cruising in the Caribbean when she's not at home in Augusta, Georgia.

Heidi Johansen is a former Fodor's editor who now calls Seattle, Washington, home sweet home. She updated the Seattle section of Chapter 2.

Sarah Wyatt is a travel, cultural, and recreation writer with work appearing in the Associated Press, *Outdoors Northwest, Women's International Perspective, Nile Guide, Go For a Ride, Travel Muse, Hotels by City, Mensa Bulletin, Capitol Hill Times, West Seattle Herald, Winds of Change, Lighthouse Digest, Club Planet,* and *Recommend.* Sarah enjoys wildlife photography, outdoor recreation, and the performing arts. She updated our coverage of the Southeast ports.

Additional Alaska, Canada, and Pacific Northwest writers shared their expertise on the region. Teeka A. Ballas updated town information for each port in South Central Alaska. E. Readicker-Henderson updated the Sports and Wilderness Adventures chapter. Tom Reale updated Anchorage, and Laurel Schoenbohm covered Denali.